Florian Sarges

Elite Compatibility in Foreign Aid

An Institutional Approach for Increasing Aid Effectiveness

Nomos

The Deutsche Nationalbibliothek lists this publication in the Deutsche Nationalbibliografie; detailed bibliographic data are available on the Internet at http://dnb.d-nb.de

a.t.: Witten/Herdecke, Univ., Diss., 2015

Original title: Does 'Elite Compatibility' Improve Aid Effectiveness?
The influence factor of project design being incentive compatible with the interests of political and economical elites of the recipient country

ISBN 978-3-8487-3720-8 (Print)
978-3-8452-8015-8 (ePDF)

British Library Cataloguing-in-Publication Data
A catalogue record for this book is available from the British Library.

ISBN 978-3-8487-3720-8 (Print)
978-3-8452-8015-8 (ePDF)

Library of Congress Cataloging-in-Publication Data
Sarges, Florian
Elite Compatibility in Foreign Aid
An Institutional Approach for Increasing Aid Effectiveness
Florian Sarges
351 p.
Includes bibliographic references and index.

ISBN 978-3-8487-3720-8 (Print)
978-3-8452-8015-8 (ePDF)

1. Edition 2017

To my parents, naturally.

Acknowledgments

This work is based on my PhD thesis that was accepted at the the University of Witten/Herdecke, Germany, in August 2015. I would like to enunciate my earnest appreciation, gratefulness and respect to my first advisor Prof. Joachim Zweynert (University of Witten/Herdecke) and my second advisor Prof. Mansoob Murshed (ISS Den Haag/University of Rotterdam) for their sincere interest in supporting budding researchers, their extremely helpful advice and their efforts involved with the mentoring of my thesis.

For their decisive, meaningful and invaluable support in the making of this work, I express my deep gratidute to the following people (in alphabetical order):

Matthias Bellmann
Georg Birkhan
Daniel Clauss
Malte Fliedner
Sven Kirschlager
Herlind Megges
Hilmar Schäfer
Gianna Schulz

Berlin, March 2017 *Florian Sarges*

Contents

List of Acronyms

BCS	Background Conclusion Sheet (document type of the EuropeAid reports)
BoP	Bottom of the Pyramid
BOT	build-operate-transfer
CCT	conditional cash transfer
CPR	common-pool resource
DAC	Development Assistance Committee of the OECD
DFID	UK Department for International Development
EC	elite compatibility
HDI	Human Development Index
ITN	insecticide-treated bed net
IV	instrumental variable
LFA	Logical-framework Approach
MDGs	Millennium Development Goals
NORAD	Norwegian Agency for Development Cooperation
ODA	Official Development Assistance
OECD	Organisation for Economic Co-operation and Development
PPP	public-private partnership
ROM	Results-oriented Monitoring (component of evaluation at EuropeAid)
SIDA	Swedish International Development Cooperation Agency
UN	United Nations
UNDP	United Nations Development Programme

List of Figures

List of Tables

Chapter 1 Introduction

The effectiveness of aid: Nothing in the aid business is discussed and has been discussed more extensively. Anyone new to the field of aid is fascinated with the opportunity to 'help' and with apparently new methods do good for the 'deprived' – while the pejorative term of the "do-gooder" already suggests that the issue might be slightly more complicated and things are not always working out the way they are intended to.

The arguments usually cited in introductions like these are often the same: Opponents of the aid system will argue that, over 4.3 trillion spent dollars[1] and more than 50 years after the start of official development assistance (ODA)[2] in 1960, the situation has not changed substantially in the recipient countries, and that instead, ODA officially supports the world's worst authoritarian leaders. Proponents will argue that there is empirical proof that authoritarian leadership is advantageous for rapid development[3], and name China, the early Korea and Singapore as examples. Botswana will most likely be given as an example of a democratic African state with good development progress, or, more recently, the 'economic successes' of Ethiopia or Rwanda.

The UN's *Millennium Development Goals* (MDGs) ending in 2015 will once again (being the fifth UN development campaign of this sort) not have succeeded in halving poverty (which was one of their targets), and instead will give way for the next campaign, most likely arguing that "results are slowly kicking in, and now we need to continue with the follow-up", or using the rhetoric of "We've showed that we can achieve great results, but there's still a lot that remains to be done" (cf. *United Nations* 2014a: 4).

---

1 According to data from the *Organisation for Economic Co-operation and Development* (*OECD* 2014a), the cumulated value of net ODA disbursements between 1960 and 2013 (all donors excluding private flows) is at US$4,275,133.3 million (constant 2012 dollars).

2 In this study, the terms ODA, *development aid*, *development assistance* and *aid* will be used interchangeably. For a discussion on the financial positions eligible to be counted as ODA, see *Hynes and Scott* (2013).

3 Which is debated; cf. *Doucouliagos and Ulubaşoğlu* (2008) and *Masaki and van de Walle* (2014).

The ideological basis of the MDGs, the *big-push* idea, is older than official development assistance itself (*Rosenstein-Rodan* 1943), as is the quarreling between pro- and opponents of the technocratic development planning of ODA (*Frankel* 1952; *Lewis* 1953). In its lifetime, ODA has been accused of (cf. *Dunning* 2004: 410) and admitted to (*Christopher* 1993: 3) just serve political interests of the donor countries.

Monographs on 'recipes' for the solution of the poverty problem are world bestsellers, both from the hopeful side (*Sachs* 2005), as well as the critical side (*Easterly* 2006b). Ideas from the discourse of how to improve aid range from "clinical" analysis of each country's specific symptoms (*Sachs* 2005: 78) over "Just give money to the poor" (*Hanlon, Hulme & Barrientos* 2010; they are referring to conditional cash transfers, or CCTs) to the statement that aid is "an excellent method for transferring money from poor people in rich countries to rich people in poor countries" (attributed to *Péter Bauer*). In a setting like this, what is there to add?

1.1 Idea and Goal of This Survey

Within the vast amount of development theories of the past years, *Acemoğlu and Robinson* (2012b) deliver an interesting explanatory approach to the historical roots and causes of development, which centers around *inclusive* and *extractive* political and economical institutions. The 2012 book is a slightly more mass-compatible synthesis of earlier works in the same vein (2001; 2006; 2008), which have been coined the *historical-institutionalist* perspective in the development discourse. The logic of their arguments is very similar to *North, Wallis and Weingast* (2009), which is not very remarkable given the fact that the latter authors themselves also refer to earlier works of *Acemoğlu and Robinson* in their reasoning[4].

Acemoğlu and Robinson argue that one of the main differences between authoritarian and democratic political orders is the institutional setup: The elite that dominates authoritarian regimes pursues *extractive* institutions, whereas in a modern democratic system, the institutions are *inclusive*. Extractive institutions are geared towards selectively securing and perpetuating income and power of the elite, while inclusive institutions offer a 'level playing field' of unbiased exchange and contracting for the entire society.

4 Especially *Acemoğlu and Robinson* (2006); cf. *North et al.* (2009: 149).

In an extractive setup, the elite are not interested in change of these institutions, and any change is thus very unlikely to be initiated by the elites. However, if an option for development towards more inclusive institutions arises, it will only be effective with the support of the elites in power, and it will only receive support if there is a condition that makes it compatible with their interests[5].

The idea of this thesis is to transfer this concept to project design: A project design is only going to produce the desired results if it is compatible with the interests of political and/or economical elites of the recipient country who are involved in the project. This is what is termed "elite compatibility" in this study.

As such, the concept is:

- based on the idea of incentive compatibility from agency theory in new institutional economics,
- applied to ODA project design, and
- focused on the specific target group of elites.

It is important to note that the term 'elite', as applied in this research, does not carry any normative value component. It simply refers to those groups of key players who are involved in leadership roles of an ODA project in the recipient country. This explicitly includes local elites as well; a more in-depth discussion of the elite term is given in Chapter 3.

In the following, the role of *incentives* and *elites* for ODA is briefly outlined.

1.2 Incentives and ODA Effectiveness

A famous anecdotal illustration from colonial times is quoted by *Dobelli* (2010: 69)[6]: To fight a rat infestation in Vietnam, the authorities advertised a reward for every dead rat that would be delivered to them – the incentive quickly lead to a flourishing of rat breeding.

This is an example for an incentive gone wrong – a *perverse incentive*. Such effects are typical for ODA: In fact, the aid system "is haunted by perverse incentives at every turn", as *Gibson et al.* (2005: 234) phrase it. While some aid critics emphasize that aid itself is a perverse incentive and contend it should hence be discontinued as a whole (*Moyo* 2009), the ef-

5 The explanations have been substantially simplified for the purpose of this introduction. More apt summaries are provided in Chapter 2.

6 Other popular variants tell the same story, e.g., with snakes in medieval Italy.

fects are also present on many levels of the 'aid delivery chain'[7], both on the donor and the recipient side, and specifically visible on the project level.

Despite the fact that ODA projects are often referred to as "interventions" in the language of aid professionals, their nature as such often seems to be marginalized and it is forgotten that they actually do *intervene* with a previously existing system and its incentive structures. It might be for this reason that, for example, projects of *slum upgrading*, a project format 'invented' by *Turner and Fichter* (1972) often went wrong in their basic mechanisms (*Werlin* 1999) or simply lead to the same outcomes as they would in most other parts of the world: gentrification (e.g., *KFW* 2009: 2; *Fox* 2014).

A number of classical aid problems, such as missing maintenance and low life span of infrastructure, can be attributed to perverse incentives. The problematic feature of these outcomes is that project failure often introduces negative external effects; *GiveWell* (2009) highlight how infrastructure that suffers from deterioration due to neglected maintenance produces comparative cost disadvantages in the form of higher expenditures on vehicle repairs. As a *World Bank* study already noted in 1988, bad road conditions in practice rarely reduce traffic, but mainly increase transport cost (1988: v). Effects like these are also referred to as the *poverty penalty* (*Prahalad* 2001: 11).

Another phenomenon in the discussion of incentives in ODA is that positive outcomes are often not the result of those incentives that they are commonly attributed to. A prominent example are *microcredits*, world-famous also through mass media since *Grameen Bank* founder *Muhammad Yunus* was awarded the Nobel peace prize in 2006. The feature often cited as the decisive success factor for the bank's asserted low default rate is *group liability* (e.g., *Easterly* 2006b: 52): The incentive design of mutual liability was portrayed to diminish moral hazard and solve the adverse selection problem present in credit markets. This myth has persisted until today, most likely also due to the striking simplicity of the narrative. However, group liability has been proven not to have a major effect on the default rate of microcredit clients (e.g., *Giné & Karlan* 2014)[8].

---

7 To be accurate, the organization of aid delivery does not resemble a chain; see Section 4.3.2.

8 More in-depth studies attribute the success of the microcredit business not to the liability mechanism, but to process innovations that dramatically reduced the high cost induced by remoteness of area, informal market structures and small credit volume. Cf. *Banerjee and Duflo* (2011: 166ff.) for a good description.

Quite contrary to its importance, surprisingly little attention has been devoted to systematic treatment of 'incentives' in ODA-related research. The elite play a special role in in the incentive discussion: This group of actors faces a specific incentive dilemma that results from their position of limited access, as explained in the following section.

1.3 Elites and ODA Effectiveness

Are elites really relevant for the economic development of their country? Yes they are, say e.g., *Jones and Olken* (2005). No, they are not, say e.g., *Easterly and Pennings* (2014). While results of political leadership on the *macro* effects of a country are debated, the technical incentive dilemma of elites on the micro level is rather accessible. Two patterns of behavior result from the exclusive position: actions to *secure* the position (i.e., excluding competitors), and actions of *extracting rents* from the position. The problematic feature here is that both action patterns antagonize 'development'. This is the parallel of elite and agency theory, as these are the same phenomena to be found in a *principal-agent* relationship; the agent is in a position that is difficult to monitor for the principal, and he or she faces the moral hazard to extract rents from this position – thus counteracting the interests of the principal.

In contrast to this, a commonly perpetuated narrative in aid cooperation is that of the 'benevolent autocrat' (*Easterly* 2011). It is fueled by quotes such as those of *Yoweri Museveni*, president of Uganda, who eloquently managed to strike the right note of a rhetoric perfectly catering to the international ODA community:

> "I have made revenue collection a frontline institution because it is the one which can emancipate us from begging, from disturbing friends [...] instead of coming here to bother you, give me this, give me this, I shall come here to greet you, to trade with you."
>
> *Museveni* (2005), quoted in *Moss, Pettersson and van de Walle* (2006: 2)

Unfortunately, the political reality in most authoritarian-led recipient countries cannot hold up to the picture of such benevolence, and neither does *Museveni's* own record exactly attest him a correspondingly enlightened attitude towards human rights; during his rule of more than 29 years (as of 2015), his regime has been infamous also for manipulated elections accompanied by violent oppression and detention of political opponents (*Borzello* 2001; *Campbell* 2006; *McConnell* 2011). Uganda's recent entries in international headlines featured the archaic, legally supported persecution of homosexuals (*Mugerwa* 2014)[9].

Exclusion of Elites?

If elites are problematic for aid effectiveness, it is sometimes considered an obvious consequence to ask if this actor group should not just be bypassed to solve the issues. Naturally, on any national or other level involving official representatives, it would be a strongly questionable political venture to bypass those representatives[10]. But also in more lower-level contexts, the role of elites in ODA projects is important for two simple reasons: First of all, an organizational structure for aid delivery will always need local actors to assume leadership. Secondly, elites and non-elites are linked by local dependencies. This is one of the causes why excluding the (local) elites does in practice not eradicate elite compatibility effects but simply delays them, e.g., in forms of elite capture (*Wong* 2012) – the effects of the dependencies will eventually 'kick back in'. *Platteau* (2004: 239) attributes this effect also to the one-shot (vs. repeated) nature of the game[11]:

> "Imperfect knowledge of the game typically arises when aid agencies tend to underestimate the leverage of the local leader within the group, or to overestimate his or her degree of altruism as a result of the leader's cunning ability to deceive them or of their own naivety."

An approach to evade elite conflicts has been the method of *participatory* or *community-based designs*, which operate with a strong focus on the local level and are supposed to involve the beneficiaries directly. Ironically, these approaches can also deliver an example of the wrong way of elite integration, when projects of the 'participatory' label in reality integrate the elites of the target group, and not the beneficiaries themselves (*Rigon* 2014: 274). Thus, existing skewed hierarchies are reinforced by the project.

9 *Marriage* (2006) calls dealing with the disparity between ideals and reality in ODA "the comfort of denial".

10 On the local level, however, this 'bypassing' is classical practice for NGO-implemented projects which interact directly with target beneficiaries, and has been target to critique for this reason (*Kilby* 2000: 52).

11 'Game' in a game-theoretical sense.

But while it is easy to assume that such approaches might just be another example of ODA buzzwordism[12], i.e., concepts that appear sensible in theory but fail in the complex practice of ODA, evidence suggests that failures of participatory designs are often not due to a wrong institutional logic, but rather to uncritical implementation of the concepts (*Arnall et al.* 2013)[13], and that successful participatory designs do exist[14]. The clear strength of local-scope interventions appears to be their potential to address collective-action problems more directly – and as such also resolve (local-level) elite-compatibility problems more effectively.

What Is Elite Compatibility?

An elite-compatible project design does *not* mean a design attending to rent-seeking behavior of key players by making sure they receive maximum profit. In fact, this is precisely what is happening without the need for any further support: ODA projects are often extracted by involved elites (summarized under the notion of *elite capture*), and it is the problem of ODA is that these interests are not taken into account, but the involved actors are commonly assumed to be benevolent, i.e., act in the interest of 'development' and not their own interest (*Williamson* 2010: 19).

Elite compatibility instead refers to *aligning* those goals of the key player (profit maximization) with those that they previously conflicted with (i.e., maintenance), in other words: A design needs to ensure that the key player's profit is maximized if maintenance *is* provided. Such a more direct linkage of development incentives to the elite's interests should enhance effectiveness and sustainability of ODA projects (*DiCaprio* 2012: 4). While this 'alignment' may appear like a romantic endeavor to disenchanted practitioners, evidence both from research (e.g., *Pinhanez* 2012) as well as from the data used for this study provide examples that this may indeed be possible.

---

12 Cf. also the brilliant article by *Cornwall* (2007).

13 This argument is criticized by *Rist* (2007: 488) to be an old narrative: "[F]ailures, they would say, do not result from 'development' itself, but rather from erroneous interpretation or ill-considered implementation."

14 Further examples are discussed in Section 3.2.1.2.

1.4 Research Question and Design

The goal of this survey is to empirically test the relationship between an elite-compatible project design and the performance of ODA projects. Hence, the central research question is:

> "Is there a connection between project performance and features of elite-compatible project design in ODA projects?"

Further analysis is supposed to determine:

- whether issues of elite compatibility are characteristic for specific types of projects: high- and low- performers, specific sectors, high or low budgets, the type of implementing partner (i.e., governmental entities, NGOs, or private organizations), and participatory vs. non-participatory design approaches;
- whether patterns of elite compatibility problems can be identified depending on projects' characteristics;
- whether elite compatibility has an influence on specific project quality ratings, such as 'sustainability' or 'impact' ratings;
- most importantly, whether elite compatibility is an important category compared to 'other' problem or success factors, i.e., those not related to this complex.

Empirical Material

The empirical basis for this research are ex-post evaluation reports from *EuropeAid*, the aid program of the European Commission, and Europe's third-largest donor, with net ODA disbursements adding up to €9.262 billion in 2013 (*European Commission* 2014a: 156). The dataset comprises of quantitative data for 457 projects, for a subset of which (n = 137) qualitative ex-post evaluation reports are available. Projects' timeframe is the years 2005–2013; the reports cover all geographical zones and are filtered for all sectors of infrastructure.

Procedure & Design

The central research question focuses on the connection between the construct of elite compatibility and the measure of project performance. This is approached in three stages: (1) the definition of the 'project performance' criterion, (2) the measurement of the 'elite compatibility' construct, and finally, (3) the analysis of the interconnection between the two measures. Figure 1-1 depicts the overall procedure. In more detail:

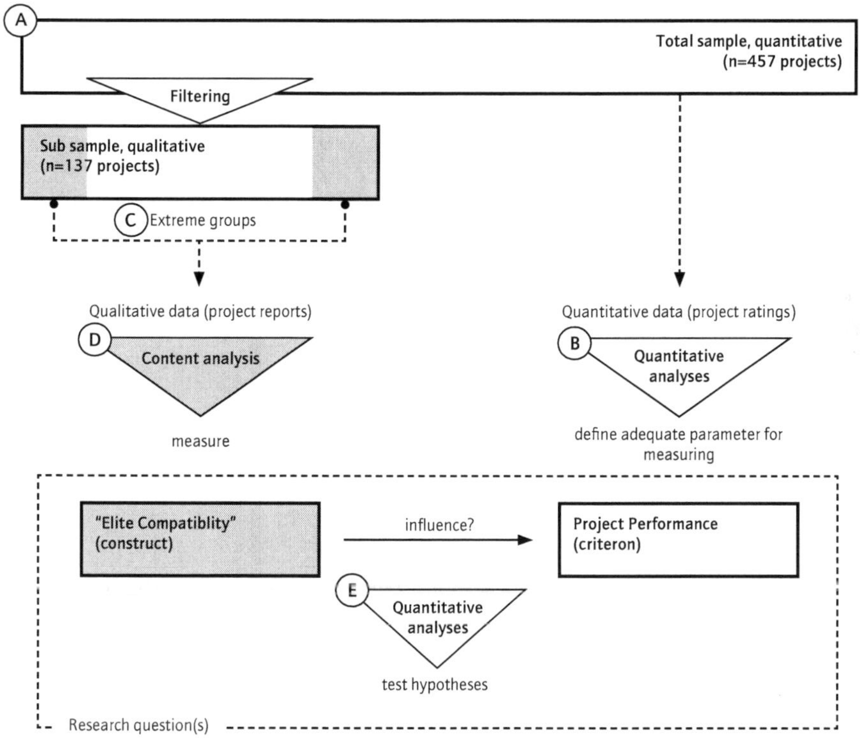

Figure 1-1: The dataset and procedure of this study

1. The large set of *quantitative* data (A) from the sample of n = 457 projects serves as a basis for defining an adequate parameter for measuring the dependent variable of project performance (B). The available data include ex-post *project ratings* in all five OECD categories (relevance, efficiency, effectiveness, impact, sustainability) and up to 16 sub-ratings.
2. The sub-set of *qualitative* ex-post *project reports* from n = 137 projects will serve to determine the occurrence of elite compatibility issues. In a first step, extreme groups are formed (C) based on the project performance criterion. The qualitative evaluation (D) is based on the method of manual *content analysis*: All problem descriptions are extracted from

the reports and classified whether or not the problem can be counted as an indicator of elite compatibility (and as what type).

The coding frame that is used for this evaluation of the extracted problem descriptions is based on the work of Gibson et al. (2005), one of the most complete documentations of incentive structures for the field of development cooperation: All incentive issues discussed in their survey are extracted and are then used to identify and categorize incentive issues that appear in the empirical material, the ex-post project reports.

3. Finally, quantitative methods will again be applied to test the central research hypothesis, the influence of elite compatibility on project performance (E), i.e., whether there are significant differences between the groups of high- and low-performing projects. To control for other factors such as budget, sector etc., test results from the total quantitative sample can be utilized.
4. Subsequently, the additional hypotheses mentioned above will be tested, involving *quantitative* data. The focus here is on the interconnection between elite compatibility and other project variables; available data include e.g., the disbursed budget, planned and actual time frame, sector and geographical zone of the project, as well as the type of implementing partner (e.g., governmental agency, NGO, private organization). Additionally, qualitative variables that have been collected in the evaluation process are used. Both the data as well as the respective procedures are described more in-depth in Chapter 6.

The rest of this study is structured as follows:

- After this introduction, Chapter 2 will provide an overview of the discussion of ODA effectiveness and the deficits, and outline the development theory of *Acemoğlu and Robinson* (2012b), which the elite-compatibility concept derives from. Then, their approach is transferred from the development-theory level to the project level – as the concept of *elite compatibility*. This concept is illustrated using typical challenges of ODA projects.
- Chapter 3 presents the historical roots of elite theory and the current elite-related research in the development context.
- Chapter 4 will discuss the theoretical background of elite compatibility, the model of *incentive compatibility,* and related concepts from new institutional economics (NIE), as well as the role of NIE in the development discourse. Then, the relevant incentive phenomena by which elite compatibility manifests itself in ODA projects are presented.

- Chapter 5 provides background information on the empirical material and on its source, EuropeAid. Challenges of aid evaluation are discussed both from a more general viewpoint, as well as specifically for the empirical material used in this study.
- Chapter 6 explains the operationalization of both the criterion "project performance" and the independent variable "elite compatibility". The development of the coding frame used for the content analysis of the reports is described. Finally, the results from the evaluation of the project reports are presented and discussed.
- Chapter 7 summarizes the main results and draws a conclusion.

1.5 What This Survey Will Not Provide

"In academic economics, a theory is never fully accepted until it can be put into a mathematical model" (*Easterly* 2014b: 289). This survey does not form a theory that could be put into a mathematical model. Its aim is to empirically test a hypothesis about a specific aspect of project design, and is of exploratory nature.

This study does neither intend nor claim to find *the* reason for success or failure; instead, the elite compatibility phenomenon is explored as a contribution to the performance of a project. Neither can a conceptual exploration capture the complexity of in-the-field reality. A concept like the one proposed in this survey *has to be* reductionist. But what it can (and is trying to) offer is a line of thought that may be used as an input for discussion and project design 'philosophy'.

1.6 The Developmentalist Paradox: A Disclaimer

Discussions on measures of 'development' of a country implicitly carry the notion of asymmetry, i.e., that the advisor knows something about the nation in question that its people do not (summarized as the *ignorance hypothesis* of development, see Chapter 2). This notion was cosmetically tackled by changing the name from 'development aid' to development cooperation' in the 1990s, suggesting that the venture would from now on happen on a par (see also *Dahl* 2008: 180) – which it does in the same way as conversations between a bank and a credit client do[15].

To those readers not entirely familiar with the details of the discourse, surveys on elites in ODA recipient countries, e.g., the discussions on *neo-patrimonialism* and *elite capture* as featured in Chapter 3, may leave the impression that the phenomena of self-interest maximization are alleged to be a distinct feature of developmental states and their inherent 'culture'. It is important to point out that this study does not affiliate with the notion of this paradox. On the contrary, I argue that it is exactly the allegation of 'irrational' or 'different' economic logic, e.g., in a slum district that must be the starting point for wrong conclusions.

As *van de Walle* (2012: 113) highlights, "[p]olitical clientelism exists in all modern states in one form or another, but just as clearly, its precise manifestations vary enormously." Indeed, phenomena of exploiting insider-outsider relationships are a global feature. E.g., *Gazibo* (2012: 3) points to repeated scandals of large-scale corruption in France and Italy, other reminders could include corruption in large-scale infrastructure projects such as the Frankfurt Airport extension (*Bergmann* 2003); for a political-economic discussion of corruption with a European focus, see, e.g., *Della Porta* (1997).

While the rationality assumption and self-interest maximizing behavior in economic theories are heavily debated (see also Section 4.1), the substantial problem array in ODA projects related to corruption, patronage and elite capture makes it safe to assume that self-interest is a motive of high practical relevance. A design that includes mechanisms to absorb the negative effects of potential exploitation is hence based on the same assumption that is used to tackle collective action and moral hazard problems worldwide[16]. As *DiCaprio* (2012: 10) comments:

> "[…] even when it's not costly, elites are rational actors and require incentives to act in a developmental way. When their actions positively impact national welfare, this comes from a confluence of self interest with national objectives."

---

15 To be precise, however, the bargaining power of the recipient is higher than that of a regular bank credit client. This is due to a number of specifics of the aid game, the most important of which being the *Samaritan's dilemma*; see Section 4.3.2.

16 This somewhat universalist view has to be differentiated from the "universalist claims" (*Nederveen Pieterse* 2010: 1) that were the foundation for neoliberal policy implementations of the *structural adjustment programs* of the 1980s (*Simon* 2013). Cf. also Section 6.5.2.

This is precisely what this study is about on project level: the alignment of project design with elite self-interest, aiming at positively impacting project performance.

Chapter 2 The 'Elite Compatibility' Concept

This chapter will devolve the concept of *elite compatibility* in three steps:

- First, an overview of the ODA effectiveness debate is provided and the deficits of the mainstream debate are discussed (Section 2.1).
- The idea for the elite compatibility concept derived from the development theory of *Acemoğlu and Robinson* (2012b). Their approach is presented in its aspects relevant for this study (Section 2.2).
- Finally, the transfer from the development-theory level to the project level in the form of elite compatibility is explained: The theoretical foundations used for operationalization are provided, and the concept is illustrated using examples of typical challenges of ODA projects (Section 2.3).

This chapter does not intend to engage into an in-depth discussion of either the effectiveness debate or development theories, but instead provides an overview of the context of this study, and the origin of its fundamental idea.

2.1 The Old Tradition of the ODA Effectiveness Debate

"What Works in Development?" is the eponymous question of a miscellany by *Cohen and Easterly* (2009); a frequently cited seminal publication by the *World Bank* (1998) was subtitled with the promise to explain "what works, what doesn't, and why". The effectiveness of development assistance[1] is easily one of the most extensively discussed questions of the field until today. This appears natural, since it serves as a criterion for the 'right to exist' of a very large political and business branch worldwide. Consequently, the measure of effectiveness is an integral component in the repertoire of success criteria of the large organizations of ODA[2], and as such,

---

1 As this study is focused on ODA, other fields of the development discourse, such as Public-Private Partnerships (PPP) or bottom-of-the-pyramid (BoP) market development are not discussed.

2 The five criteria *relevance, efficiency, effectiveness, impact* und *sustainability* have been defined by the Development Assistance Committee (DAC) of the OECD in 1991. In the same committee, the international organizations of ODA appointed them as the standard criteria for evaluation in 2000 (*OECD* 1991: 6;

a favored focus for popular-scientific publications as well as a frequent topic in mass media. Also in the scientific domain, it is the subject of an ever-growing plethora of journal publications and scientific surveys and constitutes its own genre of literature. A survey by *Christensen et al.* (2010) on the 'aid effectiveness' literature available in English lists over 152 articles as of March 2010 alone.

Naturally, the question "what works", i.e., whether something that is named "development aid" is effective or not, strongly depends on the definition of the term 'development'. This definition will be briefly discussed in the following section.

2.1.1 Effective for What? Concepts of 'Development'

A challenging feature of the concept of 'development' is that it encloses both theory and practice as well as positive and normative (both in the sense of moral as well as prescriptive/instrumental) ideas (*Potter* 2014: 83). Maybe this is why *Hettne* (1995: 15) stated that "to a large extent development is contextually defined, and should be an open-ended concept"[3]. Indeed, the term's definition is a highly contested field that is frequently discussed in introductory literature on development theory (*Meier* 2001; *Rist* 2007; *Hettne* 2008a; *Nederveen Pieterse* 2010; *McKay* 2012).

The notion of 'development' has the dubious honor of being one of the prominent examples in *Pörksen's* essay on what he refers to as *plastic words*[4] (1995: 16). These are words that are characterized by a history of semantic diffusion through a process of 're-import': At first, a plastic word had a clearly defined meaning and was part of ordinary language, was then picked up by scientific discourse with a shift in meaning, and after a while was adopted by wide (public) technocratic discourse that diffused back into ordinary language by 'emigrating back' (ibid.: 17). Due to its extensive and wide use after diffusion, it is then of "semantical pli-

---

2000: 6). The evaluation process is discussed in more detail in the context of this study's empirical material in Section 5.2.

3 At the same time, exactly this argument is an indicator for empty buzzwords (see *Cornwall & Brock* 2005: 1044).

4 *Poerksen* (1995: 7) credits the invention of the term to *Thomas Weck*.

ancy" (ibid.: 9), while at the same time subject to authority due to scientific 'coverage'.[5]

Pörksen describes how the term 'development' originated from an active and transitive meaning (e.g., someone develops a roll of film) before it was adopted most prominently by the works of *Marx* (1867)[6], shifting to intransitive usage, i.e., from now on, it was process that happens by itself without interaction. As such, it finally remigrated back to common language; it is this semantic stage of the term 'development' that *Pörksen* discusses and classifies as 'plastic' in contemporary common language, and not that as used in the context of ODA, which is again different. The curious detail is that the 'development' term took a second turn:

The starting point for foreign aid and development planning[7] is often seen in the inauguration speech of US president *Truman* in January 1949[8]. It was this occasion where the term was actually first used in dedication to a mass audience, by classifying countries as "underdeveloped"[9]. *Rist* (2014: 73) highlights how in this context, 'development' received its transitive meaning, as it was from that point on used in development economics (i.e., an actor could now 'develop' a region). Thus, it had now returned to its original grammatical construction, but in a new context, and has since been used in both the transitive (developing a country) and intransitive (a developing country) form.

Over time, with the changing ideologies and theories that dominated the development discourse, the meaning of the term 'development', or rather:

5 The term 'sustainability' has a similar historical pattern of meaning; see *Howarth* (2002) and *Scoones* (2007), as well as, for an excellent review in German, *Tremmel* (2003).

6 For instance, in *Das Kapital*, he used the term of "development phases of society" (*Marx* 1867: XI; original: "Entwicklungsphasen") and "development of the economic formation of society" (ibid., original: "Entwicklung der ökonomischen Gesellschaftsformation"), and "historical level of development" (37, original: "geschichtliche[] Entwicklungshöhe".

7 The application of the 'development' term in an economical context seems to have been introduced by *List* (1841: 17). For a more complete overview of the history of meaning, cf. *Esteva* (2010: 3).

8 According to *Easterly* (2014b: 53), the "first idea of technocratic development in its modern form" goes back even further, to a plan prepared by *Sun Yat-Sen* as a reaction to the Versailles treaty component of handing the German-controlled Shantung province over to Japan.

9 "[...] we must embark on a bold new program for making the benefits of our scientific advances and industrial progress available for the improvement and growth of underdeveloped areas" (*Truman* 1949).

its dominant aspect changed correspondingly. Table 2-1 gives a simplified overview of the past decades[10].

Table 2-1: Meanings of 'development' over time

Period	Perspectives	Meanings of 'development'
1800s	Classical political economy	Remedy for progress; catching up
1870>	Latecomers	Industrialization, catching-up
1850>	Colonial economics	Resource management, trusteeship
1940>	Development economics	Economic growth – industrialization
1950>	Modernization theory	Growth, political and social modernization
1960>	Dependency theory	Accumulation – national, autocentric
1970>	Alternative development	Human flourishing
1980>	Human development	Capacitation, enlargement of people's choices
1980>	Neoliberalism	Economic growth – structural reform, deregulation, liberalization, privatization
1990>	Post-development	Authoritarian engineering, disaster
2000	Millennium Development Goals	Structural reforms

Source: *Nederveen Pieterse* (2010: 7)

As an important differentiation, what is often referred to as "development theory" is in fact an interdisciplinary field that draws from a collection of theories from the disciplines of economics, sociology, politics geography and anthropology. 'Development theory' is hence not a single theory, "but its ambition is to comprehend the totality" (*Hettne* 2008b: xvi) of those different streams. In that sense, the different interpretations over time can be understood as a shift-around of the focus to the different influences.

In the ODA context, the core meaning has been closely connected to economic growth for a large part: This was true for the pioneers of development economics and the modernization-inspired concepts of the 1950s (most prominently featured in *Rostow's* (1960) *stages of growth*) as well as the subsequent wave of dependency theories

It was not until the disillusion after the end of the UN's first *development decade*[11] in 1970 that the development notion opened up and experienced a shift towards the individual, mainly driven by were *Goulet's* (1971) *basic-needs* approach, which put a stronger emphasis on personal

10 For a more finely-graded presentation, cf., e.g., *Willis* (2011: 28).

11 The *development decades* were the first four large development-planning campaigns of the *UN* (1960-1999).

values apart from income[12], and *Seers'* (1972: 22) conception of development as the "realization of the potential of human personality"[13]. It was in the wake of these concepts that *Sen* developed his approach of focusing on "capabilities" (1980: 218) of the individual rather than the mere income, thus "shifting attention from goods to what goods do to human beings" (ibid.: 219), and from income equality to "basic capability equality" (ibid.: 218).

The *UNDP* adopted these extended concepts in their *Human Development Index* (HDI) in 1990, which combined the measure of GNP with that of life expectancy at birth, as well as educational measures (literacy rate, gross enrollment ratios primary, secondary, tertiary). The first *Human Development Report* stated that "while growth in national production (GDP) is absolutely necessary to meet all essential human objectives, what is important is to study how this growth translates – or fails to translate – into human development in various societies" (*UNDP* 1990: iii).

Together with the rise of the *sustainability* notion in the 1990s, this understanding of "human development" may be seen as the most influential for the currently prevailing concept. It eventually culminated in the most recent form of a large development planning campaign, the UN's *Millennium Development Goals* (MDGs)[14], launched in 2000. It set up targets in the following eight categories (see *United Nations* 2010: 6ff.):

1. Eradication of extreme poverty and hunger;
2. Achievement of universal primary education;
3. Promotion of gender equality and empowerment of women;
4. Reduction of child mortality;
5. Improvement of maternal health;
6. Combat HIV/AIDS, malaria & other diseases;

---

12 Namely, his three basic components of development are "life sustenance" (basic needs), "esteem" (respect and independence) and "freedom" (range of choice; participation in economic and social development); see *Goulet* (1971: 87ff.).
It was the specific *focus* that was a new position, not the *desirability* of these ends. E.g., *Lewis* (1955: 420) stated previously: "The advantage of economic growth is not that wealth increases happiness, but that it increases the range of human choice."

13 He considered 'development' to be improvement in terms of income poverty, unemployment and income inequality, and stated that, if at least one of these issues have been worsening, "it would be strange to call the result 'development' even if per capita income doubled" (ibid.: 24).

14 The Post-2015 agenda (that has meanwhile received the innovative name of *Sustainable Development Goals*) now officially even includes actions by and in the donor countries (see *United Nations* 2014b: 15).

7. Ensuring environmental sustainability;
8. Building a global partnership for development.

However, while the UN are one of the key players in ODA, today's development sector also features an unprecedented amount of non-governmental and private actors on the donor side[15] and a correspondingly growing volume of budgets dedicated to 'development'. One of the more important controversies revolves around the notion of 'poverty alleviation', which is part of the MDGs and the central goal of most aid agencies' programs, including *EuropeAid* (*European Commission* 2009a: 8). E.g., *Chang* (2011a: 48) criticizes the concept altogether and argues that any development definition that focuses on poverty alleviation and does not include industrialization of production, is basically "Hamlet without the Prince of Denmark". Other criticism targets the point that a wide operationalization of 'development' such as the MDGs dilutes the original idea of poverty *alleviation* (which would require addressing the income problem) and instead promotes measures of making poverty *more bearable* (*Toro* 2014).

This controversy already illustrates how the *definition* of development is, probably more than ever, an important part of the debate around what the "fashionable ways of getting development done" (*Harrison* 2007: 672) are, i.e., around aid *effectiveness*.

2.1.2 The Current Debate Around ODA Effectiveness

The discussion around the effectiveness of foreign aid is led on three levels:

- *The macro level (country):* Is aid effective in general, and, if so, how? I.e., what are the effects on economic growth, income, income equality, political freedom?
- *The meso level.* What modes of aid are effective? I.e., separation into donors, types of donors, budget aid, program aid, sector-wide approaches, conditional aid.
- *The micro level (project):* What projects or project designs are effective? I.e., design methods such as participation, empowerment, project topics.

The terms "micro" and "macro" in this context refer to the level in the *aid system*, however they often coincide with geographical and economical

15 On the proliferation of donor organizations, see also Section 4.3.2.1.

characteristics as well. I.e., the project level naturally implies the (smaller) geographical region of a project and project-level economic data as opposed to macroeconomic aggregates.

While this study's research focus is the micro level, various aspects of the macro-level discussion of aid effectiveness interweave with this topic, as shall be laid out below.

2.1.2.1 The Macro Level

Naturally, the most fundamental debate is led on this macro level, i.e., whether or not aid is effective in general. The meso level is often part of this discussion, i.e., to further specify or differentiate the type of aid – in that sense, it may be argued that there is no real use of separating the two.

The beginning of the current wave of the effectiveness discussion is marked by the study of *Boone* (1996), who found that ODA did not have a positive effect on investment or the HDI value of the recipient country, but rather increases government spending. It was quickly followed by various counter-studies. This pattern was repeated upon the publication of another seminal study by *Burnside and Dollar* (2000) who found positive effects of aid in environments of "good policy": Their paper triggered a long wave of responses and follow-up discussions; see *Askarov and Doucouliagos* (2015: 383) for a summary of the more recent publications, and *Masud and Yontcheva* (2005: 3) for a historical overview of the aid effectiveness literature. The discussion has not come to a consensus: Contemporary positions range from the summary that growth does not seem to happen when expected, and is not explainable when unexpected, e.g., related to policy changes (*Hausmann, Pritchett & Rodrik* 2005), to the finding that "despite the questionable association between aid and growth, aid does mitigate poverty separately from the effects of aid on income" (*Alvi & Senbeta* 2012).

The inconsistent results may be partly attributed to the simple but often neglected fact that "significant amounts of aid were never intended to bring about economic growth, but rather were given to governments for geopolitical reasons" (*Wright & Winters* 2010: 63)[16]. The frequently cited figure of cumulated aid until today, meanwhile amounting to more than

16 E.g., *Dunning* (2004) finds that the effects of ODA on the level of African countries' democratization scores differ when pre- and post-Cold War era are separated.

US$4.3 trillion net ODA[17], has to be treated at least critical against this background – apart from the fact that it is not clear how much of this aid was limited to goods and services from the respective donor countries in form of *tied aid*, which is often seen as an export subsidy in disguise (*Gibson et al.* 2005: 118).

Another part of the ambiguity of the macro-level effectiveness discussion is surely indebted to the sheer complexity of the object of research, which is also reflected in the amount of publications and their plenitude of variations in datasets, time lines, estimation models, types of aid, groups of recipients, or types of indicators for constructs (e.g., policies or democratization). Additionally, measures may be tested not as dependent variables, but as *criteria* for aid flows, e.g., corruption (*Alesina & Weder* 2002)[18]. New variations provide enough potential for the publication frequency to remain at its current level. For instance, *Clemens et al.* (2012) re-test older findings with including a variable for different timings (modest positive effects of aid on growth), and one of the latest studies, *Askarov and Doucouliagos* (2015), tests aid effectiveness on growth specifically for transition countries (positive effect in average).

A popular 'proof' of aid effectiveness that is cited especially in public discussions is the success of the post-World-War-II *European Recovery Program*, popularly known as the *Marshall Plan.* A large share of scholars disapproves the Marshall Plan as a parallel to contemporary ODA: The measure lasted less than four years and never exceeded 3 percent of the GDP (*Moss et al.* 2006: 3; *Boussat* 2008: 13), recipient countries only faced one single donor (*Svensson* 2006: 128) and, most importantly, the 'aid' met environments with previously functioning legal and financial institutions and public administrations. As *Bauer* (1969: 90) noted, "[t]he economies of Western Europe had to be *restored*, while those of the present recipients have to be *developed*" (emphases in the original). On the other hand, *Barder* (2010: 22) points out that the *per-capita* levels of the Marshall Plan substantially exceeded those of today's ODA, and argues that the high growth rates of South Korea in the 1960s or Botswana in the 1980s coincide with aid at the levels of the Marshall Plan.

The most curious circumstance to outsiders of the aid debate may be the fact that the effectiveness of ODA still *is* a controversy in the first place,

---

17 See the specification on page 9.

18 As a less common example, *Arvin and Lew* (2010) have studied the relation between donor happiness and aid flows (finding a positive correlation on the donor side, but not on the recipient side).

after over six decades of its official launch[19]. Just as curiously, many features of today's discourse parallel those of its early times. The two camps of aid proponents and aid skeptics, today most prominently represented by *Jeffrey Sachs* and *William Easterly*[20], already emerged right after the introduction of the *UN's* first report on "Measures for the Economic Development of Under-developed Countries" (1951). The dispute was initiated by a critique of *Frankel* (1952) and the response of *Lewis* (1953), who was one of the document's co-authors. Their reasoning displays a striking similarity to that of today's discourse – surely attributable to the fact that a bigger part of today's ideas also goes back to the middle of the last century. This applies for the aid optimists' concept of the *big push* (*Rosenstein-Rodan* 1943) which is argued to be needed for escaping "the vicious circle of poverty" in 'underdeveloped' economies (*Nurske* 1953: 4), as well as for the claim to "help people help themselves", which politicians often cite like it is a recent invention, while it was in fact already included in the famous 'point four' speech by *Truman* (1949).

The current arguments from the side of the aid pessimists look back on an equally long history: Criticism in the technocratic planning approach had already been enunciated by *Frankel* (1952: 311); *Friedman* in 1958 (515) expressed concerns that ODA itself exerts a perverse incentive effect, and suggested to "make a final terminal grant" to developing countries – currently, this position is represented, e.g., by *Moyo* (2009: 52ff.). Also, the aid critics' allegation that the planning approach of ODA is the opposite of what created wealth in today's developed nations[21], had previously been expressed by *Friedman* (1958: 510):

19 While it may appear to go without saying that the effectiveness of a measure has to be evident before it is accepted and funded, this is often not the case in practice. This is valid not only for a large part of political actions, but a prominent example from the supposedly more efficiency-oriented private economy is the field of *print advertising*: Despite the fact that evidence for effectiveness of this channel of communication is practically nonexistent in most companies, print media cost make up for a substantial part of a company's marketing budget. However, this has radically changed with the advent of trackable online advertising.

20 One of the recent arguments is *Sachs* (2014) and *Easterly* (2014a).

21 As (*Reinert* 2007: 23) phrases it, "[w]ealthy nations have a tendency to force upon poor nations theories they themselves never have followed and probably never will".
Closely connected is the allegation that now-developed countries are "kicking away the ladder": *Chang* (2008: 47ff.) argues that nearly every developed country used protectionist policies in the course of their own development path while they are now denied to 'underdeveloped' countries. As *Reinert* (2007: 79) phrases it,

> "The striking thing is that by these tests, the United States would never have qualified as a country making an 'additional national effort' toward economic development! We have never had explicit 'measures to capture a good fraction of increases in income for the purpose of further investment.' Nor have our 'leaders' ever 'worked out an overall development program.'"

His quote implicitly addresses a feature that has been an important foundation of ODA throughout its existence: the assumption that the respective elite of the recipient country has a propensity to act in the sense of 'development' of their country. This *benevolent-leader* assumption – *Easterly* (2011) terms this the "benevolent autocrats" narrative – was already present in the 1951 *UN* document (*United Nations* 1951: 16) and the 1961 constitutional declaration of the *OECD* (documented in *Führer* 1994: 11), and it is the basis for the implementation of the current MDGs terminating in 2015. The benevolent-leader assumption can be understood as a different representation of what *Acemoğlu and Robinson* (2012b: 63) label the "ignorance hypothesis", i.e., that the reason for underdevelopment is the leaders' missing knowledge about the adequate policies: In the reverse logic of the ignorance hypothesis, a country's elite would benevolently act towards 'development', if the right knowledge was available.

The benevolent-leader hypothesis is precisely the linkage between the macro level and the project-design level of the effectiveness discussion, as many design concepts implicitly assume the cooperation of the target group and involved elite members in the way intended by the project plan.

2.1.2.2 The Micro Level

The micro or project-design level of effectiveness is the research focus of this study; the utilized empirical material are ex-post evaluation reports of individual ODA projects. In general, these reports themselves are not part of the broader effectiveness discussion – quite the contrary, they enjoy the reputation of documents that "no one reads anyway" among most parties involved, including the consultants who compose them. The way the reports are represented in the public discussion is mainly in form of summarized annual reports of the major aid agencies, which provide an overall picture of the progress and status of the current project portfolio. As opposed to the ambiguous situation on the macro-level effectiveness discus-

---

"wealthy nations keep poor countries poor based on theories postulating the non-existence of the very factors that created their own wealth."

sion, these agency reports generally present a brighter picture of the ODA measures, as the majority of projects are typically presented as successful. It was this paradox between positive aggregate micro data and missing effects on macroeconomic level that *Mosley* (1986) drew attention to as the *micro-macro paradox*. Apart from a series of biases that micro-level evaluation is subject to (see Section 5.3), one of the very simple explanations is the fact that the effectiveness notions of the micro and macro level are not congruent: The criteria used in project reports are related to the effectiveness of the project itself and only indirectly relate to macroeconomic measures[22,23,24].

This circumstance illustrates how the discussion of effectiveness on the project level is in fact split up into two separate aspects: Firstly, the (aggregated) contribution of projects to aspects of 'development', and secondly, the effectiveness of projects in reaching their respective *individual* goals *on the project level*. In the discussion, this differentiation is often diluted or not accorded adequate attention. E.g., individual project-level case studies are often used as evidence to support the rationale of aid proponents and skeptics alike. Among the more frequently encountered examples are the ITN case by *Easterly* (2006b: 12f.)[25] or the infrastructure project by *Ferguson* (1994)[26]. Project-level studies are also an attractive subject in mass media coverage, especially when new methods or topics of ODA are presented, such as the *One Laptop Per Child* campaign (*Ehlers* 2012) or the 'evergreen' of microcredits (*Provost* 2012).

As opposed to those project-level cases as an illustration for success or failure, aspects of actual *project design* have not been a substantial part of

---

22 For more details on the report structure, see the description of the empirical material in Section 5.2.3.

23 Most other explanations do not focus on the paradox itself, but effectively attempt to explain only the failure of ODA on the macro level. For a more detailed discussion of the micro-macro paradox, see *Howes, Otor and Rogers* (2011).

24 However, following the intervention logic (see Section 5.2.3), most projects are planned to ultimately contribute to macro-level effects; thus, success on the micro level should indeed convert to measurable success on the macro level.

25 *Easterly* discusses the distribution problem typical for insecticide-treated bed nets (ITNs) and cites the success of a project by *Population Services International*, in which nurses in rural antenatal clinics sold the ITNs to mothers at a small profit.

26 The project was supposed to provide farmers in Lesotho with road infrastructure for improved access to markets for selling their produce. But because the target group was not at all involved in any alleged farming activities, the project's effect was an 'improved' access to South-African mines and an expansion of state bureaucracies into the villages. See also Section 4.3.2.3.

the mainstream debate around ODA effectiveness. This has slowly been changing with the increasing popularity of randomized controlled trials.

The Impact of Randomized Controlled Trials

One of the 'hot topics' in this matter has been the introduction of the method of *randomized controlled trials* (RCTs) into the field of ODA, which has sparked a new genre of evidence-based effectiveness culture that focuses on quantitative (i.e., quanti*fied*) measures. In the typical pattern of academic discourse, the method first underwent a small hype, also thanks to the attention mass media devoted to the studies of some of the protagonists of the 'randomistas' (*Miguel & Kremer* 2004; *Banerjee et al.* 2009; *Duflo, Kremer & Robinson* 2011b) and then quickly became subject to lively critique[27]. The main issues are the binary character of treatment testing, as opposed to the synergetic character of most intervention effects in practice, and the often questionable external validity of the results: Again, as in the effectiveness debate on the macro level, the hyper-dimensionality of the design space makes it difficult to isolate decisive factors. However, the issues of external validity (and hence: reproducibility) are not exclusive to RCTs, but inherent to most evaluative actions in ODA. Not without good reason, some complain about a "double standard" (*McKenzie* 2011) in the RCT critique – indeed, one might discover a slight resemblance to the vibe of the German *Methodenstreit* of the 1960s.

The same applies to another point of criticism in RCTs: the allegation of atheoretic experimentation (*Deaton* 2010a: 442), i.e., an interest only in the 'what' or 'if' a measure is effective, but not in the 'why' or 'how'. Again, limited explanatory power can by no means be taken as an exclusive feature of RCTs; not least, the repeated failure of ODA project designs demonstrates the deficits in properly discovering the failure's underlying causes. It may well be argued that in this environment, the more systematic (i.e., experimentation) approach of RCTs has had a positive influence on the way that ODA effectiveness is discussed. E.g., *Easterly* (2002: 247) stated that to move away from a mindset of plain "good intentions", experimentation was "badly needed". Also, the numerous examples where follow-up explorations have delivered decisive insight illus-

---

27 See the miscellany by *Cohen and Easterly* (2009) for an overview of the most important positions. A substantial share of the discussion is meanwhile led in mass media (e.g., *Kristof* 2011) and blog posts (e.g., *Subramanian* 2011).

trate that the reproach of an inherent lack of interest in reasoning is inappropriate; cf. also the monograph *Poor Economics* by *Banerjee and Duflo* (2011).

The actual danger of RCTs lies in their image of being 'proper' science – a phenomenon observable for quantitative research in general, and which has been heavily criticized as a fallacy (*Rhoades* 1992). E.g., *Green* (2012b) complains that in "the tacit hierarchy of these different kinds of knowledge" (quantitative work, case studies and expert experience), "anything with a number attached" is automatically granted a privileged position, in neglect of the origin of this number. This is true even more so for RCTs, as the method's descent from the medical sciences endows it with a reputation of being the epistemic 'gold standard', or even the "hottest thing in the fight against poverty" (*Kristof* 2011). This reputation often whitewashes the previously discussed weaknesses and the fact that for identifying underlying patterns, "mimicking the natural sciences is a seductive, but often misconceived way to find them" (*Green* 2012a) – and, as *Straubhaar, Vöpel and Zweynert* (2012) highlight, may possibly deliver results that are "logically correct, but of no use or even harmful in context of reality" (own translation)[28].

But while some voices have already declared RCTs useful for "not much else" but projects of public health (*Auerswald* 2011), it seems to be more appropriate to simply call for cautious and critical, i.e., context-aware evaluation of the 'rigorous' RCT results – as it should be sensible with any research. What the discussion around randomized-controlled trial has indisputably achieved, is that it has sharpened the awareness for criteria of effectiveness research in general (cf. *Camfield & Palmer-Jones* 2013). For instance, the organization *GiveWell* is dedicated to test charities for the impact of their activities and calculate a quality index in a "change-for-your-dollar" (i.e., 'bang-for-the-buck') approach. While one of their self-proclaimed standards is the rigorousness of their evaluations, eligible evidence is not limited to quantitative measures (*GiveWell* 2015). Instead, the organization emphasizes the need for the data to be "highly *specific*, *representative* and *credible*" (ibid., emphases in the original), i.e., it is required to be falsifiable and free from publication and selection bias. This is one of the examples how the RCT movement has surely enriched the general effectiveness debate on the micro level.

---

28 Original: "logisch richtige Ergebnisse […] aber für die Wirklichkeit völlig nutzlos bis eben manchmal sogar schädlich."

Topics, Methods and Criteria in Project Design

Possibly the most important aspect how the project design level is represented in the effectiveness discourse, is that a majority of the circulating aid 'buzzwords' are concepts that ultimately relate to the project level[29]. Concepts in the ODA context are often not clearly categorized, and on the contrary often used in the paradigmatic sense of "the focus needs to be on XYZ". For a more systematic consideration, they can be separated into *methods*, *criteria* and *project topics*:

- *methods* concern the *means* of project design in order to reach a project goal. Examples: *participation*, *community-driven/community-based design*;
- *criteria* relate to the project fulfilling aspects. Examples: *sustainability*, *ownership*;
- *project topics* are simply the topics or groups of topics (sectors) that projects engage in. Examples: *microfinance*, *capacity building, governance, gender equality*.

Especially the category of 'project topics' can interweave with the aspect of 'criteria', e.g., when capacity building is a side aspect, i.e., becomes a criterion, of a transport infrastructure project. E.g., gender equality is a criterion in *EuropeAid's* ex-post evaluation reports. Additionally, the concepts may be combined freely, such as "community-based sustainable natural resource management".

The common denominator for most of those popular concepts is that they intend to tackle classical problems that hinder the effectiveness. In the majority of cases, the concepts reflect the paradigm of 'development' at the time of their creation (see Section 2.1.1). Participatory approaches, for instance, originated in the wake of the basic-needs approach of the 1970s, moving "from things to people" as *Chambers* (2013: 172) terms it; the criteria of 'sustainability' or 'governance', became popular after the 'lost decade' of the *structural adjustment* programs in the 1980s. The fact that even such longer-standing concepts are still part of the discourse around effectiveness, already underlines that they have not been a panacea to effectiveness problems; obviously, arriving at a verdict on "what works

29 The topic of 'buzzwordism' in ODA is so apparent that an entire journal issue has been dedicated to the discussion of the most common buzzwords (see *Cornwall* [2007] for an introduction), including poverty reduction, participation, empowerment, partnership, gender, right-based, sustainability, donor harmonization, capacity building, country ownership, best practice, accountability and good governance. Cf. also *Dahl* (2008) for an alternative discussion.

in development" seems to be problematic. One factor that impedes this aspiration is the effect of *concept fashion cycles*, which I hold to have a decisive influence in veiling those aspects of aid that are ignored in the effectiveness discourse.

2.1.2.3 Concept Fashions and Effectiveness

Because on the donor side, ODA is driven by the political agenda and public influence on the one hand, and the development business branch on the other, the problem-solving methodology of aid interventions is strongly subject to fashions and hypes, i.e., fashionable concepts or 'paradigms' that dominate a certain part of the discourse. Such fashions are lobbied for by those parties benefiting from the provision of the corresponding product: In the private economy, this can be observed especially in the notoriously saturated consumer electronics market, where manufacturers are under constant pressure to generate hypes around a new technology in order to make old devices appear obsolete, and generate demand for the new ones. Similar mechanisms exist in other markets: E.g., for the corporate consulting sector, *Ernst and Kieser* (2002: 65) very aptly described how the interests of the different actor groups create a cycle of "management fashions"[30,31] that is constantly perpetuated. The ODA discourse parallels their description in a remarkable way. Put simply, the interest set-up almost automatically produces all features that are needed to keep the fashion cycle moving. One key characteristic is the compatibility of the consultants' need for new concepts (to sell to the clients) and the academics' need for attention (for their ideas), which ensures that new concepts are pushed into the market. Both parties benefit from a slight vagueness of a new term: It enhances the opportunities of attention for the original authors, other researchers and media in the discourse, and at the same time creates the need for experts' (consultants') help for implementation. Because consultants as well as authors have an interest in increasing the plausibility of the new concept, this fosters the generation of a success narrative. It is supported by the circumstance that, in a complex system,

30 Original: "Management-Moden".
31 This is certainly not the first discussion of managerial fashions in general; cf. the references in the authors' article as well as the discussion in *Kieser* (1997) and in *Lang and Ohana* (2012).

the evaluation of the actual (i.e., specific) contribution of a concept to a result is a difficult task.

For the managers, in their human need to uphold control and to reduce complexity, the advent of a new concept increases the complexity and generates the need for the help of experts. In other words: The introduction of a solution itself may generate a need for this solution. With the increasing number of successful implementations, the new concept slowly becomes established as a standard, further increasing the pressure on managers who 'lag behind', and entrenching the implementation as a 'seal of quality'. Again, the media and other parties involved in the discourse support this process by creating and upholding the relevance of the concept.

As said, the similarities to the ODA industry are striking – which may not appear surprising given that the key players are almost identical: While the corporate managers are substituted by the managers from politics and aid agencies, the market for ODA implementation is dominated by consultants, and a large part of the discourse is led by academic and other research institutions (see Figure 2-1).

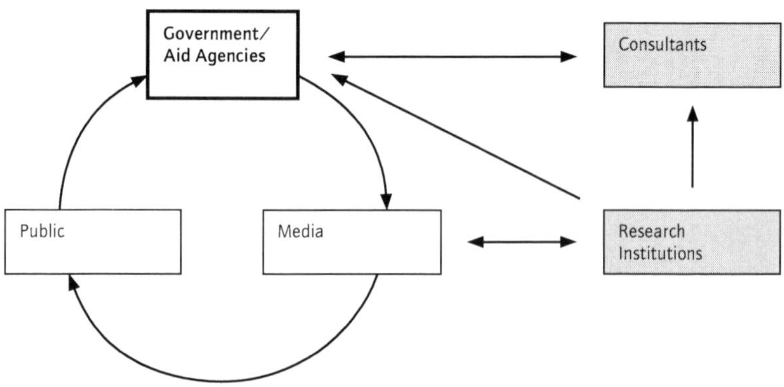

Figure 2-1: Actor groups and their dependencies in the generation of concept fashions in ODA (in the donor country)

Despite the fact that this is a very simplified picture of the more complex actor set-up of the ODA discourse[32], it does capture the principal 'layout'

32 E.g., one difference between the markets is the role of the consultants: While in the corporate market, they play a decisive part for pushing new fashions into the discourse, their role is less active in the ODA market, where the large development agencies are the main drivers of generating demand for concepts. One of the

of actors that is decisive for the dynamics of concept fashion cycles.[33] Additionally, the specific incentive structures in aid agencies often lead to increased "opportunity costs of dissidence" (*Broad* 2007: 703), thus enhancing the selective or affirmative promotion of success narratives. Concept fashions in ODA are not problematic *per se*, but become problematic when they advance a method independently of its actual effectiveness, i.e., when a method is wrongly promoted as a problem solution – or even becomes paradigmatic.

2.1.2.4 'Doing Things Right' Is Not 'Doing the Right Things'

As such, concept fashions may promote errors of two categories, which, following *Barnard* (1938: 127), could be titled "not doing the right things" and "not doing things right"[34]:

1. *Not doing the right things*: A concept is *not* a solution to the original problem but is attractive to 'sell' to the principals (donor countries governments and citizens) because the solution appears plausible and convincing. The hype here promotes the spread of a concept that is ineffective in the first place.
2. *Not doing things right*: A concept *is* a solution to the original problem, but the pressure generated from the hype lead to inflationary use of the concept as a label even for projects that do not properly incorporate the concept. The hype here promotes the spread of an originally effective concept as a buzzword and entails ineffective implementation or plain mislabeling.

---

reasons for this difference is that the agencies do not depend on shareholders, but on government budgets. Consequently, the agencies' pressure to disburse (see Section 4.3.2.2) inverts the normal market logic.

33 The parallel between organizational fashions and those in development cooperation is also noted by *Kühl* (2004), though without reference to the aspects brought up by *Ernst and Kieser*.

34 These terms are often attributed to *Drucker's* (1967: 1f.) description of effectiveness and efficiency, however, *Barnard* (1938: 127) already made this differentiation when discussing specialization: "Specialization may relate to the *kind of thing* done, where the reference is to differences in material, or it may relate to the *way* in which work is done. Often one aspect implies the other. [...] often different methods of working at the same material produce either different products or the same products more 'efficiently' or 'effectively.'" (Emphases in the original.) Note that the categories in the text above do not refer to effectiveness and efficiency directly.

Not Doing the Right Things: The "Type-Three Error"

In his work "Smart Thinking for Crazy Times", organizational scientist *Ian Mitroff* (1998) describes a behavioral pattern of problem solving which can be observed peculiarly often in the entrepreneurial world: the precise solving of the wrong problem. In reference to the terminology of the error of the first kind (erroneous assumption of significant differences/coherences) and the error of the second kind (erroneous negation of significant differences/coherences), *Mitroff* titles this phenomenon "the error of the third kind".

The idea of precise solving of the wrong problem is a popular topic in the economic literature[35] – surely because of its interesting appeal, but most likely also simply due to its universal prevalence. The development-specific literature suggests that this is valid also for the ODA context, e.g., when it is highlighted that one "should begin by asking 'what is the problem?' instead of 'which solution should we adopt?'" (*Andrews, Pritchett & Woolcock* 2012: 9), or when a NORAD handbook clarifies: "A problem is not the absence of a solution, but an existing *negative state.* [...] Example: No pesticides are available: Wrong; Crop is infected with pests: Right." (quoted in *Mikkelsen* 2005: 43).

It is important to point out again that the type-three error of "not doing the right thing" stands for the case that the *problem itself* has not been identified correctly. Consequently, a solution can be either the wrong one for an existing problem, or in the extreme, it can be a solution to a problem that does not exist.

An example for the former (wrong solution) is provided by a 2004/05 campaign of the British NGO *Christian Aid*, as discussed by *Collier* (2007: 157), which employed striking motives and headlines to oppose the reduction of trade barriers for poor countries. The campaign's claims received heavy criticism from various experts for being "deeply misleading" (ibid.: 159); *Collier* quotes an expert from the British government commenting: "They know it's crap, but it sells the t-shirts" (ibid.).

An example for the latter case (nonexistent problem) is the topic of deforestation in Madagascar: It is a well-established myth that the island had been almost entirely covered with forest prior to human colonization, and that the large part of this forest had consequently been destroyed by mas-

35 E.g., *Coase* (1998: 73) expresses his concerns about modern mainstream microeconomics with the picture of economists "having a box of tools, but no subject matter" and studying "the circulation of the blood without a body".

sive human interference. While it has been shown various times that this myth is the result of plain speculation (*Jarosz* 1993; *Klein* 2002; *McConnell & Kull* 2014), it has been perpetuated until today. Not unlikely, this is due to the too large array of environmental and development organizations which benefit from this narrative[36].

Not Doing Things Right: Implementation

One of the constitutional characteristics of a fashion is the pressure it exerts into its habitat to adopt that fashion. This is especially true for a fashion relating to the topic of problem solving, since the introduction of a 'new' concept often implicitly or explicitly makes a previous solution appear wrong – even more so in a market where the contribution of an individual factor to the overall result is difficult to evaluate. Consequently, when a concept becomes fashionable in the development discourse, the danger is that it is adopted in concept papers and project plans as a keyword just to serve the current fashion. That is, it becomes an empty label or buzzword that is just copied (mimicked) nominally, without necessarily actually incorporating its original intent. E.g., *Pritchett, Woolcock and Andrews* (2013: 9) find that such a pattern – copying form without incorporating the actual institutional function – is the major source of failure for enhancing state capacity[37]. This is the pattern also apparent in the problem of institution building (see Section 4.3.1), and the top-down mode of aid provision (see Section 4.3.2.3).

---

36 Cf. *Klein* (2002: 196) for statements implying almost-complete original forestation. Undoubtedly, Madagascar is facing various environmental problems, including uncontrolled destruction of forest assets. The above example, however, refers to statements on the *original* state of the forests (e.g., *Green & Sussman* 1990: 212).

37 They term this pattern *isomorphic mimicry* in reference to *DiMaggio's and Powell's* (1983: 150) *mimetic isomorphism*: the tendency of organizations in environments of uncertainty to imitate the structure of other successful organizations. *Ernst and Kieser* (2002: 58) draw on the same idea as one driver for the diffusion of management fashions.
Krause (2013) criticizes this terminology, as the original concept does not imply mimicry to be an imitation of form-without-function. According to him, the missing functionality is not a result of mimicry itself, but of the fact that it is externally imposed by the ideas of a donor. In order to semantically capture this top-down installation, he suggests the remarkably figurative term of *institutional ventriloquism*.

In the development literature, the improper implementation of a concept is a very frequent reasoning in effectiveness discussions. It is exactly this argument – of a concept being right *originally*, but just suffering from erroneous implementation – which is criticized for its tautological character by post-developmentalists (*Rist* 2007: 488). At the same time, there cannot be much doubt about its plausibility: When fashionable concepts are adopted in an un-differentiated, 'nominal' way, they are doomed to fail. This is specifically apparent for the treatment of elites and the concept of participation – for instance, if a project design envisages that the beneficiaries should elect a member of their own to represent their interests in the project committee, while they have no choice but to elect an existing elite actor (e.g., a slum lord), there is no point in counting the project as 'participatory' (cf. the examples in Section 3.2.1.2).

The two phenomena of 'not doing the right things' and 'not doing things right' illustrate the negative effects of paradigms that arise from the concept fashion cycle in ODA. I argue that these effects are a large part of the reason why, despite extensive discussion, 'solutions' from the discourse have not contributed to a substantial improvement of aid effectiveness: The effects veil the circumstance that the extrapolation of micro-level successes to macro-level conclusions is often a fallacy. E.g., as *Bellemare* (2014) criticizes in reference to the praised successes of the *Grameen Bank* in Bangladesh, "even if one could completely eliminate credit market failures by making small loans to the poor, many other market failures would remain that would constrain development." More precisely, as *Acemoğlu and Robinson* (2012b: 448) hint, "small market failures may only be the tip of the iceberg, the symptom of deeper-rooted problems in a society functioning under extractive institutions."

These deeper-rooted problems are part of the complex that is typically ignored, as shall be laid out in the following.

2.1.3 What Is Ignored

One apparent constant in the history of the aid effectiveness debate is its specific rhetoric of confidence, which draws through documents of most ODA agencies. E.g., *Easterly* (2003a: 35) documents how a narrative of "better times are 'just around the corner'" has been promoted for decades in *World Bank* publications. The popularity of this rhetoric is historically comprehensible for the introductory phase of ODA in the 1950s and 1960s, when the concept of dedicating part of a national budget to the development of other nations was still in need of building up political support[38]. Today, as ODA has become part of the 'establishment' in the political landscape, the rhetoric may more be interpreted as a means to support foreign aid's 'right to exist'. Additionally, it also needs to bridge the gap between the fact that aid is still existent (i.e., has not been sufficiently effective until today) and that it is still in need of continuation (i.e., that it is effective). Consequently, variations of the political classic, "much has been done, but far from enough" (in this case: *Mattsson* 2014), are a frequent encounter in development media. *Hirschman* remarked "a bias for hope" in ODA already in 1971 (253).

This 'hope' rhetoric is also reflected in the benevolent-leader narrative discussed in the previous two sections. For instance, the 1961 *Resolution of the Common Aid Effort*, a constitutional document of the *OECD*, defined the Development Assistance Committee (DAC) as "[c]onscious of the aspirations of the less-developed countries to achieve improving standards of life for their peoples" (*Führer* 1994: 11). One of the problems of this assumption is that it immanently ignores of the political component of ODA; consequently, some authors attest the technocratic aid effectiveness discourse an inherent "naivety" about politics, governance, and organizational cultures (*Kydd* 2009: 432)[39]. *Wright and Winters* (2010) hold that this applies to both aid optimists as well as pessimists:

---

38 As a curious detail to illustrate the change in perception of ODA until today: *Friedman* (1958: 501f.) refers to the 1957 US aid budget of US$4 billion, of which only half a billion was labeled "economic aid", and the vast majority "military aid" and "defense support". He comments on these proportions that "[t]he generally more favorable attitude of Congress toward direct and indirect military aid understandably leads the Administration to classify as much as possible under these two headings".

39 Interestingly, *Lewis*, who was one of the authors of the *UN's* 1951 report, already highlighted this political dimension and stated that the report was "giving the

> "Optimists appear to assume that a massive scale-up in aid will be used as economic theories predict, ignoring the possibility that governments have incentives to divert aid funds for their own purposes. The pessimists, meanwhile, argue that donors should bypass recipient governments and give aid directly to the poor [...], ignoring the political and technical difficulties of doing this. Neither perspective directly addresses the governance question, and many of the economists involved in the aid/growth debate ignore the messy world of political institutions and political decision making except to underscore that, historically, much aid has been distributed to corrupt and badly governed regimes."

Various concepts and mechanisms have been implemented to encounter such issues, such as *conditional aid* provision, bottom-up implementation through *participation* of various stakeholders, or the focus on *good governance*. However, available mechanisms have not proven to systematically cure the incentive conflicts in practice. *Birdsall* (2004: 15f.) comments that "[g]ood policy apparently cannot be imposed or even encouraged by bribe-like transfers" and that "[p]romises and 'participation' are not an adequate substitute for political ownership, and are no better than traditional conditionality as guarantees of change."

Ironically, the emphasis of 'good governance' in ODA is yet another confirmation of the benevolent-leader assumption itself: While at first glance, it may suggest an awareness of the *absence* of benevolence, it is in fact based on the assumption that the leadership will eventually understand that 'good governance' is the better or correct alternative, and 'bad governance' is a 'bad thing'[40]. But "when nations break out of institutional patterns condemning them to poverty", *Acemoğlu and Robinson* (2012b: 67) argue, "this is not because their ignorant leaders suddenly have become better informed or less self-interested or because they've received advice from better economists." Instead, the authors see the main obstacle for 'development' in the specific constraints that result from a society's political and economic institutional set-up.

---

economist's answer to the politician's question", and attested a critic an "extremely naive view of international affairs" (1953: 269) for not taking this into account.

40 It is this ignorance of the inherent repugnancies of ODA that is the target of many aid critics especially from the anthropological field, who accuse foreign aid to create a 'separate-reality agenda'. Probably the most iconic example is the notion of foreign aid as an "anti-politics machine" by *Ferguson* (1994: 180): "If the effects of a 'development' project end up forming any kind of strategically coherent or intelligible whole, it is as a kind of 'anti-politics' machine, which, on the model of the 'anti-gravity' machine of science fiction stories, seems to suspend 'politics' from even the most sensitive political operations at the flick of a switch."
Similar critique is put forward, e.g., by *Rottenburg* (2009: 81).

A popular 'battlefield' in the mainstream argument around the political dimension of aid is the state-vs.-market debate[41], in which critics see planning as the culprit for failure of development aid, as well as the associated budget orientation for measuring aid efforts. However, neither the planning approach nor the associated budget orientation are features that can be counted as a specific of foreign aid – both, instead, are inherent features of politics *in general*. Given the fact that the sector of infrastructures, which is the subject of this study, is classically controlled by 'the state' in most donor countries and operates at an acceptably high success rate there, the state-vs.-market argument does not capture the distinctive political-economy problem in this context. The actual differences to infrastructure provision via ODA culminate in two circumstances:

- Unlike with standard (i.e., intra-national) public-good provision, ODA is characterized by a geographical and political separation between the principals and the agents. The 'beneficiaries' of an ODA intervention, who would hold the role of principals in a regular setting, cannot exert any control over the donor government, which acts as the *de-facto* agent. This *broken feedback loop* (*Martens* 2002b: 154) creates severe accountability problems and thus enhances the negative effects of political planning (see Section 4.3.2.3).
- The recipient countries of ODA are typically subject to an extreme disparity of income, with political and economical activity concentrated in the hands of a comparably small elite. It appears logical that, in order for aid projects to be supported by this elite, it has to be compatible with their interests. That is to say, "what works in development", also strongly depends on a project's incentive setup from the viewpoint of the elites.

While this logic itself is rather trivial, the effect on ODA outcomes is not, as can be seen from the failure of tackling the incentive problems with existing concepts. In the mainstream discourse, however, the common system behind the prevalent incentive conflicts is rarely addressed, and the essence often does not exceed the trivial fact that 'incentives are important'. E.g., an OECD document states that it "may not be enough to tell people (and institutions) that they should co-operate because it is in their

41 This dichotomic was fuelled by *Easterly's* (2006a) "planners vs. searchers" argument. *Easterly* (2014b: 35) himself calls it "one of the biggest misunderstandings in the development debate" that the argument on planning vs. spontaneous evolution has morphed into a state-vs.-market debate, and contends that the "right debate is about individual right vs. state power" (ibid.: 254).

interest, it is necessary to identify the incentives that shape agent's [sic!] decisions and are responsible for co-operation failure" (*Bartolini* 2013: 4). Quite clearly, analyzing specific individuals' incentive setups is a difficult venture. *Robinson* (2003: 1), who tries to explore a "politician-proof policy" to overcome the structural problems of public-good provision, concludes with the disenchanted assessment that "such an approach is ultimately futile, basically because we simply do not understand the relevant political incentives".

According to *Pritchett and Woolcock* (2008), the source of the problem is to be found the development practice of "skip[ping] straight to Weber" (ibid.: 156), i.e., the paradigm that there are blueprint 'best-practice' designs of efficient bureaucracies and corresponding institutions, which can be installed in a top-down manner. This paradigm, they hold, is essentially "making development an 'engineering' problem" (ibid.: 199). *Andrews et al.* (2012) suggest replacing the top-down mode by an "iterative-adaptive" approach that promotes trial-and-error progress in implementation – and thus compensates for the restrictive institutional environment. However, while their concept contains many valid observations, it may remain questionable to "install" a culture within an environment where its absence is exactly the problem.

It is important to emphasize that there *are* working solutions for public good provision – namely those that work in most industrialized countries –, and the quest for identifying the supposedly highly specific 'incentive setups of individual actors' blurs the more important common denominator of many ODA problems: the incentive conflict that stems from the two characteristics listed on the previous page.

This study's focus on the incentive compatibility for relevant elites, which I term *elite compatibility*, aims to address this incentive conflict. As described in the introduction, it was inspired by the development theory of *Acemoğlu and Robinson*, where it is an implicit, yet central component. The next section will lay out this aspect of their framework, before the concept is then taken to the context of ODA project design.

2.2 The Model of Extractive and Inclusive Institutions

There is a vast array of publications that try to explain why the world is the way it is today – which ultimately always means an explanation for why the rich countries are rich and the poor countries are poor. The components of the frameworks vary, but they are often a mixture or variation of cultural-deterministic or geographical-deterministic approaches. More recent examples are *Huntington* (1996) or *Kennedy* (1987). Most of these works are rather disconnected from the development discourse and the context of ODA with the associated politics. This has been different for *Why Nations Fail* by *Acemoğlu and Robinson* (2012b), as the two scholars had been playing an active part in the development discussion previously, especially after their seminal contribution (*Acemoğlu, Johnson & Robinson* 2001) to the *en vogue* topic of institutions. As a result, their monograph has been receiving considerable attention not only from academia, but it also managed to bring the development discussion into mass media.

The 2012 book can be regarded as a more prosaic elaboration of their framework presented in previous publications, mainly *Acemoğlu et al.* (2001); *Acemoğlu, Johnson and Robinson* (2005) and *Acemoğlu and Robinson* (2001; 2006). One of its central motives is that of *extractive* and *inclusive* institutions, which relate to both the political as well as the economical realm. As the terminology suggests, extractive institutions are focused on the exploitation of the social, economical and physical environment in which they exist, and on protection from others gaining entry to these positions. Inclusive institutions, on the other hand, are designed to provide the opposite, i.e., ensure high political participation and permeability of society[42]. One of the key characteristics of their framework is that extractive political and economical institutions support each other reciprocally:

> "Extractive political institutions concentrate power in the hand of a narrow elite and place few constraints on the exercise of this power. […] Extractive economic institutions, in turn, enrich the same elites, and their economic wealth and power help consolidate their political dominance." (*Acemoğlu & Robinson* 2012b: 81)

More generally, political and economic institutions relate to each other as depicted in Figure 2-2, i.e., the political institutions regulate the de iure political power, but the actual economic institutions are defined in conjunction with the distribution of resources (i.e., the de facto distribution of political power). The setup of the economic institutions determines the future distribution of resources, and thus the sustainability of the status quo.

42 "To be inclusive, economic institutions must feature secure private property, an unbiased system of law, and a provision of public services that provides a level playing field in which people can exchange and contract; it also must permit the entry of new businesses and allow people to choose their careers." (*Acemoğlu & Robinson* 2012b: 74f.)

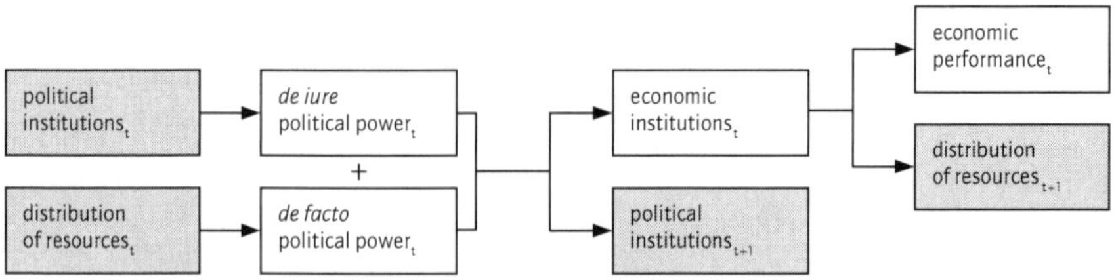

Figure 2-2: *Political and economical institutions in the framework of Acemoğlu and Robinson*
Source: *Acemoğlu et al.* (2005: 392)

The core implication is that extractive institutions generate resistance against change, because an extractive position yields higher individual returns for its owners than those resulting of a prospering 'inclusive' system. Thus, any change is blocked or opposed to by the extractive elite in the fear of erosion of their political power and economic privileges (2012b: 86), in which *Acemoğlu and Robinson* ultimately see the reason why nations fail economically (ibid.: 398). The elite, i.e., the only group that could initiate a change the institutional setup, has no incentives to do so, as any move towards more inclusive character of institutions would leave them disadvantaged. For this reason, change from extractive to inclusive institutions is *not* initiated from the elites.

This point is, in a nutshell, the authors' explanation why the mechanism which ODA relies on (the ignorance hypothesis, as described in the previous section), cannot be effective. They oppose the view that institutional change can be 'implemented' via top-down installation and contend that "You Can't Engineer Prosperity" (ibid.: 446). Instead, transitions are the product "of the interaction between existing institutions and critical junctures" (ibid.: 431), to which they count 'shocks' such as the Black Death, the opening of the Atlantic trade routes, the Industrial Revolution, or also small events that can trigger a chain of further events, such as in the case of the so-called *Arab Spring*. Where and how these shocks emerge and how the institutional set-up is re-arranged is often subject to contingency; *Acemoğlu and Robinson* repeatedly emphasize their rejection of historical determinism, and hold that their explanations are "historical, but not historically predetermined" (ibid.)[43]. These shocks re-arrange the incentive situation and exert external pressure on the elite, which they need to react to. As such, the major constraint for the elites is that they "typically live in fear of being replaced by different social groups or by other individuals within the same group. Therefore, an important issue in nondemocracies is to ensure that no group is unhappy enough to attempt to overthrow the regime, or take other political or economic actions that are detrimental to the utility of the group in power" (2006: 118). This change can also happen gradually, as successively giving in to steps of small demand is less threatening to the elite than creating "a major showdown" (*Acemoğlu & Robinson* 2012b: 317).

This is where the feature of incentive compatibility comes in, as described more explicitly also in *Acemoğlu and Robinson* (2006: 177), where large parts are dedicated to elaborate their theory into formal models: When the threat of a revolution has become too strong and cannot be encountered otherwise[44], the leadership has to make commitments to the opposing group, i.e., the citizens. Naturally, the central criterion for the effectiveness of these commitments is their credibility[45] – if a promise is not credible to the group it is given to, it is of no real value. In order for a commitment to be credible, it has to be *incentive compatible* for the committing party, i.e., the institutional setup aligns the goals of the citizens with those of the elites. This is also exactly the reason why a *policy* promise is not credible, as a policy is easily reversible and not durable, while institutions *are* durable[46] and change the incentive scheme.

Changing the institutional setup (as opposed to policy changes), thus creates what *Acemoğlu and Robinson* call a "lock-in" of participation of citizens (ibid.: 175), and makes the new situation incentive compatible for the elite, or, in my terms: *elite compatible*. This component of elite compatibility as an influence factor for the outcome of a promised commitment can be 'ported' to the effectiveness context of ODA projects.

---

43 The authors themselves acknowledge that "[n]aturally, the predictive power of a theory where both small differences and contingency play key roles will be limited." (ibid.: 434).

44 Other countermeasures are redistributive concessions or, of course, repression.

45 The original credibility-of-commitment problem is credited to *North and Weingast* (1989); for additional literature on the discussion of the commitment problem, see *Acemoğlu and Robinson* (2006: 132f.).

46 This is the aspect that they emphasize (ibid.) to contrast their institution definition to the classical variant by *North* (1990: 3). See Section 4.2 for further discussion.

Relation of the Acemoğlu and Robinson *Theory to Existing Work*

There are many parallels of this development theory to concepts of other authors, some of which explicitly mentioned – *Schumpeter's* creative destruction – some implicitly included, the most important of which likely being that of *North et al.* (2009: 2), who establish the taxonomy of *limited-access social orders* and *open-access social orders*. These concepts have been perceived to be congruent with the extractive/inclusive distinction (*Fukuyama* 2012) – an allegation which *Acemoğlu and Robinson* in turn heavily object (2012a)[47]. As stated at the beginning, the intention of this chapter is to provide the background for illustrating the elite compatibility concept and its origin; hence, I will not engage into a discussion of supposed strengths and weaknesses of the theory of *Acemoğlu and Robinson*, or of development theories in general. However, a determination worth noting is the fact that their theory is in large part compatible with results from elite studies, as will be shown in Chapter 3, but also with observable phenomena in ODA projects and their explanations given by new institutional economics, as shall be laid out in Section 4.3.2. While their 2012 work has been accused of being too conceptually diffuse (*Easterly* 2012; *Fukuyama* 2012), and invent new labels for old concepts, their notion of "extractive" institutional setups is indeed very apt and a strikingly simple conceptual summary of the incentive problem and its perpetuation, which is reflected as "rent seeking" in classical NIE terminology (going back to *Krueger* 1974) when discussed in context of government exploitation (e.g., *Fischer* 2006: 211).

2.3 Taking the Model to the Project Level: The 'Elite Compatibility' Concept

With the background of the neglected aspects in the aid effectiveness discourse, as described in Section 2.1.3, the relevance of the notion of extractive institutional setups for understanding the effectiveness of ODA projects becomes apparent, as most ODA recipient countries can be classified

47 For other issues criticized of their 2012 monograph, cf., e.g., *Sachs* (2012), *Diamond* (2012) and *Easterly* (2012), as well as the authors' response (*Acemoğlu & Robinson* 2013) to *Fukuyama* (2012) and *Gates* (2013).
For counterarguments to their 2001 and 2006 works, cf., e.g., *Rodrik, Subramanian and Trebbi* (2004), *Nunn* (2009) and *Nunn and Wantchekon* (2011).

as extractive institutional environments. E.g., for African countries, *Acemoğlu and Robinson* (2012b: 116) comment that:

> "[…] independence created an opening for unscrupulous leaders to take over and intensify the extraction that European colonialists presided over. The political incentives these structures created led to a style of politics that reproduced the historical patterns of insecure and inefficient property rights under states with strong absolutist tendencies but nonetheless lacking any centralized authority over their territories."

Naturally, attempts to implement 'good governance', 'participation' or other interventions that 'empower' currently under-represented groups are not particularly likely to receive elite support, as by definition, any form of 'empowerment' of non-elites implies a loss of privileges[48,49]. A common observation, however, is that such interventions are nevertheless officially endorsed by the elites. An important differentiation in this context is that when a project *itself* is subject to support from the elite, this does not necessarily imply the project *goals* are supported. As also pointed out by *Acemoğlu and Robinson* (2012b: 65), *formal* support of policies or projects that themselves are not compatible with elite interests is a typical pattern, and can be explained with the simple fact that the aid inflow itself *is* in the interest of the elite, even if the goals of the project are not. This phenomenon of "incentives to receive aid, but not to reform" (*Gibson et al.* 2005: 183) is discussed in Section 4.3.2.2.

Resistance Against Change as a Key

Up to this point, the concept of elite compatibility has only been taken into the context of ODA projects in so far as that it may explain the failure of interventions that focus on any type of empowerment: Following the terminology of *Acemoğlu and Robinson*, in the environment of a dominantly

48 This threatening effect of any empowerment is obviously not exclusive to extractive systems. Opportunities for extraction also exist in contemporary democratic setups that would be classified as 'inclusive', and any move towards more inclusive institutions is non-beneficial for previous 'winners'. Examples are insider trading or any form of nepotism or clientelism in general. *Van de Walle* (2012: 123) even argues that a certain level of clientelistic features is "essential and ubiquitous" for democratic regimes. See *Gigerenzer* (2007: 185ff.) for a discussion of the cultural context and Section 3.2.2 for the elite-theoretic perspective.

49 *Reno* (1998: 50ff.; 2011: 250) even holds that decimating the elite's opportunities of patronage in extractive setups will promote mechanisms of repression and violence.

extractive institutional setup, respective aid projects will never be elite compatible and thus be condemned to failure.

However, the focus of this study is the sector of infrastructures, and while respective projects may well have empowerment effects (or even include components explicitly focusing on empowerment), the above type of resistance does not appear adequate for characterizing the resistance of elites in such projects. After all, infrastructure interventions *per se* do not pose a threat to extractive positions – quite the contrary, they commonly *generate* opportunities for extraction. Consequently, the question is what the elite compatibility problems of this sector are, and what the associated forms of resistance are that impede project effectiveness. In order to be able to discuss this differentiation in more detail, the following section will provide examples of actual problem descriptions from ex-post project reports.

2.3.1 Challenges in a Typical Low-Performing Project

The following examples are descriptions of problems that typically appear in low-performing ODA projects from the infrastructure sectors. The examples are not fictional, but are quotations from an actual ex-post project report (*European Commission* 2009b) that is part of the sample used for this study. The project in question has received low ratings in all categories (relevance: C, efficiency: D; effectiveness: C, impact: C, sustainability: D)[50], and in its history unites almost the complete array of typical incentive-related problems of ODA projects, as discussed in more detail in Chapter 4.

To put these results into perspective, the project time frame fell into a difficult transition phase (the project report speaks of a "policy vacuum") from a one-party state to democracy. Project start was in 1988; after democratization movements starting in 1985, the constitution was changed in 1990 and the party system was opened. In 1995, the country was plagued by a cholera epidemic.

Other than that, the project holds classical features: a relatively high budget of €19.8 million, the implementing partner was the recipient government, the project closure had been postponed by a total of almost nine

50 The rating scale consists of four levels from A (higher than expected) to D (complete failure). The rating system and report structure are described in more detail in Section 5.2.

years. Table 2-2 shows a list of selected issues with original quotes from the ex-post Background Conclusion Sheet (BCS) and the ex-post Monitoring Report (MR) of the project documentation. All listed issues are discussed in more detail from the NIE perspective of incentives in Section 4.3.2.

Table 2-2: List of typical project-level problem types for infrastructure ODA projects

Problem type	Original description (partially summarized for better readability)
Missing or delayed policy implementation (1)	"Fundamental policies that should frame the project (poverty reduction, decentralization and environment) were only approved several years after the project started." (BCS 1.1)
Political exclusion of originally designated agencies (2)	"The Municipality […] should have been in charge but it had neither the mandate, nor the managerial, technical and financial capacity to assume the provision of water and sanitation services." (BCS 1.2)
Ineffective organizational structures (3)	"The project institutional set-up was incoherent since the beginning: The provision of water and sanitation services was taken over by a company which is now under the responsibility of the Ministry of Economy, which has no mandate in water and sanitation." (BCS 1.2)
Incoherent institutional setup (4)	"The Mid-term expenditure framework, led by the Ministério das Finanças (MF), is based on the proposals made the line ministries, given a certain expenditure ceiling previously set by the MF to each sector. As Electra depends on the Ministry of Economy, there is no dialogue between MITT and Electra in that respect. On the other hand, the MTEF does not include the expenditure made by the municipality." (BCS 5.1)
Problematic contract enforcement with external contractors (5)	"Supplies were marked by a high level of conflict between the administration bodies and the contractors (supply of inputs that were not in line with the techn. specifications, delays in the construction works, etc.)." (BCS 2.1)
High production costs; missing cost recovery of tariffs (6)	"The tariffs of the public utilities were not set in line with the real production and distribution costs, which proved to be quite unrealistic given the high production costs." (BCS 4.1)
Inadequate maintenance budget allocation (7)	"The water and sewage networks have been plagued by various technical problems since the initial phases of operation. This does not seem to derive from the lack of understanding of the technology. The available resources for Electra are insufficient to deal with all technical problems of repair and maintenance in a timely manner." (BCS 5.7)
Capacity development in bureaucracies ineffective (8)	"Managerial and technical capacity of Municipality is still weak despite support given by the project. Lack of planning marked the municipality's work over the last 15 years." (BCS 2.3)

Problem type	Original description (partially summarized for better readability)
Frequent replacement of personnel with problematic handover (9)	"The take-over of each successive town council (between opposing political parties) has always been rather contentious concerning hand-over of ongoing or outstanding dossiers." (BCS 5.4)
Institutional 'memory loss' through lack of documentation and coordination (10)	"Archives with essential documentation are nonexistent. [...] Lack of a unified management unit and coordination." (MR: 2)
Missing provision of required outputs (11)	"The PDM was never approved, there is no property and fiscal registration, no Geographic Information System (GIS) is in place, the digital imagery delivered in 1997 was obsolete based on photos taken in 1991." (BCS 2.3)
Target group (poor population) is not reached (12)	"According to planning, 70% of the plots should have been allocated to low-income families. However low-income families seem to represent a minor share of the population in the two construction plots." (BCS 3.3) "The provision of housing at reduced costs to people with a low income, through the IFH, shows a limited impact on the poorer population." (ibid.)
Infrastructure is installed, but not used (13)	"Although the water primary and secondary sewer networks were actually built, access to the above services is still limited as expressed by the relatively low level of household connections." (MR: 2)

One impression that the table already provides is that, given the extensive involvement of experts in these project types, the respective individual issues are highly unlikely to result from ignorance or 'not knowing better' – as it is also objected to by *Acemoğlu and Robinson* (2012b). Instead, the listed problems, all of which can be counted as true 'classics' of infrastructure-related ODA, display different forms of *resistance* by the involved leading actors: Issues #1-7 may be interpreted as more 'active' interference, issues #9-13 as a more 'passive' or 'negligent' form. The only issue which the project report indicated not to be attributable to resistance, was the underqualified personnel (#8)[51]. The next section will introduce an approach to classify these different forms and their implications for project design.

51 The interpretation heuristic for evaluation of the project reports is described in Section 6.3.3.

2.3.2 Elaborating the 'Elite Compatibility' Concept

As said, the elite's resistance against change, as it is described in the development theory of *Acemoğlu and Robinson*, results from the opposition against the threat of losing extractive positions. This resistance can be classified as *active*, in the sense that triggers active measures to sabotage the project's outcome. Infrastructure projects, however, *generate* opportunities for extraction, hence the resistance as reflected in the listed problems of Table 2-2 cannot be appropriately classified as 'active', even if the descriptions provide this impression at first glance. The effect of extractive institutional setups on public-good provision had already been discussed by *Bates* (1981: 113), who pointed out that selective provision of public goods is an essential part of the elite's 'toolkit' to coordinate political support – as he later termed it (*Bates* 1988b: 353), by "imposing collective deprivations, governments thus confer selective benefits". *Pritchett and Woolcock* (2008: 161) argue that the top-down approach in ODA has been so successful also because it has been favored by recipient governments – as it leaves them with direct control over supply. As such, this can be seen as a stand-off for the recipient: the project input itself may be desirable, the proper functioning of goods provision may not be – the phenomenon already described in Section 2.3 as "incentives to receive aid, but not to reform".

The main factor that is hampering effectiveness in this case is the resistance against the change that the intervention is intended to install. Given the above, I suggest differentiating between three forms of resistance.

The Three Types of Resistance Against Change

1. The first type of resistance is the *active* type, as described previously: the complete incompatibility of a project's goals with the elite's interests. The negative effects of this type are hence intentional. For infrastructure provision, however, this type is unlikely; instead, resistance can be a product not only of an active interest in failure, but also simply of a missing interest in success. From this latter reasoning derive two further types of resistance:
2. If a project generates assets that provide opportunities for extraction, making use of these opportunities is often the optimal choice for an elite actor, as in an extractive environment, deviation is a second-

order public-good problem (see page 144). In this case, it is not the complete project outcome that is opposed to, but only those project components that are 'in the way' of making use of extractive opportunities, such as organizational structures (#3 and 4 in Table 2-2) or political structures that should ensure a wider distribution of control (#2). Extractive activities by definition happen at the cost of sustainability of the respective project, thus the damage is not intentional, as in the case of the 'active' type, but can be understood as collateral damage. Measures that support project success, i.e., sustainability, in this case would produce opportunity costs for the individual actor – simply the rents from extraction. Hence, this type of resistance can be labeled as *extractive*.

3. The opportunity-cost logic is also the reason for a third type of resistance, which may apply when there is no interest by the respective actor in the outcome of the project at all: neither in extraction of project assets, nor in the success of the project. In this case, however, the project *budget* may still be diverted for other uses than investing in the project's success. Thus, again, measures to support the project produce individual opportunity costs, and are hence omitted. Because this resistance is not targeted against any specific components, but results from a general unconcern towards the project effectiveness, this type can be labeled as *passive*.

These three categories are summarized in Table 2-3. Obviously, the disjunctive character of this depiction must be a simplification:

- The actual incentive setups are more complex. E.g., in connection with *Samaritan's dilemma* situations and the incentive of a continued flow of funds, there are often positive incentives for mid-level elite actors that promote inefficient behavior and non-cooperation, such as career advancement (cf. *Andrews et al.* 2012: 6). Another example are publicly held companies such as energy producers, which may be kept in deficit on purpose to uphold their dependency on financial support by politicians.
- The (effectively) continuous flow of aid, the Samaritan's dilemma characteristic of aid, introduces a twist to the incentive setup of ODA projects that may transform even such projects that are in line with everyone's interests into projects that make extractive or passive resistance beneficial. A typical example here is maintenance: Put bluntly, there is no point in investing any resources into the sustainability of an asset if it can be rehabilitated or replaced "free of charge" after it has broken down (*Catterson & Lindahl* 1998: 145).

Table 2-3: Comparison of the three types of resistance of elite agents against ODA projects

Resistance:	Active ("intentional")	Extractive ("collateral")	Passive ("unconcerned")
Resistance against	Project goals	Project components	n/a
Reason	Empowerment of opponents	Components hinder extraction of outputs	No interest in project in total
Perception of intervention	Goals threaten extractive position in general	Outputs offer extraction opportunities: Opportunity costs of cooperation/project sustainability	Budget offers better utility in clientelistic measures: Opportunity costs of cooperation/project sustainability
Incentives for project success	Presence of negative incentives	Incentives for extraction larger than for project success	Absence of positive incentives
Extraction target	General	Project output/budget	Project budget
Reaction	Opposition/sabotage	Opposition against components impeding extraction	No active support/ diversion of budget
Examples	• Water vendors in informal settlements where fresh water provision is installed • Empowerment of weaker groups in community-based natural resource management • Anti-corruption projects	• Transport infrastructure • Electrical power production • Urban water networks	• Infrastructure in detached regions • Community-based water networks in rural areas

- The 'resistance' that is exerted by an actor may be a combination of different types, depending on the component of the project. In any case, a project will have different implications for different stakeholders and may hence trigger different types of resistance depending on the respective actor. For instance, a slum-upgrading project may be threatening to the extractive position of a slumlord, while a local politician may only be unconcerned about the project's success[52].

52 All described phenomena of this list are discussed in more detail in Chapter 4.

The differentiation of these three types is relevant for appropriately addressing elite compatibility. While effectively, there may be no difference if destructive measures are the result of intentions of sabotage or intentions of extraction, the most important implication is that extractive and passive resistance can both be addressed more easily by project design than active resistance against a project's goals in general. However, one common denominator of all categories is their origin of the extractive environment. More explicitly, it is for this reason that the extractive environment may be one of the most important sources of project failure through missing elite compatibility – the goal of this study is to identify this relevance.

How Can Elite Compatibility Be Achieved?

One frequently discussed aspect in the context of failure to cooperate is that of *accountability*. But while accountability may technically be an effective part of the incentive complex for an elite actor, it is an *ex-post* mechanism and often lacks teeth in practice, as in the context of ODA, the practical enforceability is substantially limited: Firstly, the extractive institutional setup limits accountability towards the citizens; secondly, the Samaritan's dilemma effectively diminishes accountability towards the donor. In contrast, elite compatibility is an *ex-ante* mechanism, or, in game-theoretical terms it is self-enforcing and hence a better mechanism in environments of non-cooperative behavior.

A central characteristic for operationalization of elite compatibility is the perspective of opportunity costs: In the sense of the credible-commitment criterion picked up by *Acemoğlu and Robinson*, a promise by the elite to the citizens is credible if it is incentive compatible, and it is incentive compatible when deviation is costly for the agent – i.e., opportunity costs of default. Transposed to an ODA project, this means that in order to make a project's design elite compatible, it has to effectively *transform the opportunity costs of sustainability into opportunity costs of failure* for the respective actor. This opportunity-cost perspective of the commitment problem is a common notion in the literature. For instance, *Voigt* (2004: 148) states that breaking promises "must be costly for the dictator. As long as the expected utility from carrying out one's promises is higher than that from breaking one's promises, a rational dictator can be expected to stick to his promises."[53] In this sense, elite compatibility can be understood as a form of the previously mentioned "politician-proof policy" (*Robinson* 2003), ensuring that an intervention's effectiveness will not be jeopardized by (extractive) political interference.

An Example for Elite Compatibility in an Infrastructure Intervention

A tangible example of a project design modification for the sake of elite compatibility is the BOT model. It stands for *b*uild, *o*perate, *t*ransfer, in reference to the different phases of the project path. The name implicitly highlights that the design is mainly a financing model: A principal, in most cases a public entity, gives a limited-time concession to a private contractor, who then builds the demanded infrastructure at her cost, and operates it for the limited time of the concession. The customer and thus the source of revenue for the operator is the 'general public'. After the end of the time frame, the infrastructure asset is transferred to the principal. BOT models are common practice worldwide for infrastructure provision, such as road transport or telecommunications[54] and are one form of public-private partnerships (PPPs). This design has been adopted for ODA projects as well (see *World Bank* 2014b).

However, while the BOT model is classically chosen by the side of the principal – the government – for its various alleged advantages, e.g., for lowering the financial burden on public budget, it can also be chosen as a mode for ODA project design by the donor, e.g., in order to solve incentive issues. An example is the business of *Ecotact*, a company installing and operating sanitation kiosks in Kenya (*Karugu* 2011). While their *product* design intends to address various classical incentive problems of this service genre[55], their *project* design (the BOT model) successfully solves the classical problem of maintenance provision in ODA projects:

In an extractive setting, the optimal strategy for an infrastructure project that is handed over to the public entity is often complete extraction and negligence of maintenance activities. The resources from the maintenance

53 To be clear, this logic of self-enforcement is by no means a novelty; it is a central point discussed in regulation and industrial organization, and is also the basis of *moral hazard* solutions such as the deductible for insurance contracts.

54 Recent examples in Germany are the *Herren-Tunnel* in Lübeck.

55 E.g., the kiosks feature vendors of basic goods like newspapers and press, snacks and shoeshine. The vendors are thus stakeholders who have an interest in the maintenance and cleanliness of the facilities (ibid.: 5).

budget are available for diversion, and because the structure is completely new, the negative effects from missing maintenance kick in relatively late (and more slowly) in the project course. From a monetary standpoint, the extractive option is the more attractive one for a local politician, also because his or her time in office and thus access to 'extraction' may be limited.

Putting the project into practice with the BOT model changes the incentive setup for the politician. The facilities are built and operated by *Ecotact* and only handed over to the municipality after a period of five years (ibid.: 7). By the time of transfer, the business has passed the operative stage of implementation, meaning it has been established in its environment, and acquired enough stakeholders to generate an interest group. This circumstance is beneficial because it creates both opportunity costs of change in case the service should be removed, but also generates positive incentives for political support. Secondly, the assets have passed their initial phase of the life cycle and the facilities require constant maintenance input in order to keep up their function. Thus, a politician's potential extractive (monetary) interests are aligned with the project's sustainability: Financial profit is upheld/maximized only by frequent maintenance contributions. Table 2-4 sums up the two scenarios side by side.

While this type of design is not part of 'standard' ODA, but is limited to the more specific sector of public-private partnerships (PPP), it can effectively overcome some of the typical problems resulting from political interference during the setup and implementation phase of an intervention, as it is also emphasized by *Ecotact* from the above example (*Karugu* 2011: 3).

Table 2-4: General comparison of direct handover vs. BOT model in infrastructure projects (stylized)

	Strategy A (direct handover)	Strategy B (build-operate-transfer)
Deterioration w/o maintenance	slow	fast
Revenue decline w/o maintenance	slow	fast
Profit curve (time) at handover	High initial, but diminishing marginal profit	Constant marginal profit
Resulting optimal strategy	Maximum rent extraction	Maximum life time for rent extraction
Timeframe	short-term	long-term

Making use of the terminology introduced at the beginning of this Section 2.3, this project was able to encounter and overcome two categories of resistance:

- *Passive resistance* (no interest of political actors in the topic):
  The pool of stakeholders established during the implementation and initial operation forms an interest group that changes the incentive setup for a politician and produces both positive incentives for supporting the project, as well as opportunity costs of non-support. In this sense, the successive formation of a large-enough group of stakeholders can be seen as a form of the institutional lock-in of interests that *Acemoğlu and Robinson* (2006: 175) refer to.
- *Extractive resistance* (no interest of political actors in long-term sustainability):
  For the responsible leadership, infrastructure provision through ODA projects often yields maximum rent extraction by choosing a low-effort strategy – one of the reasons of which is the fact that new assets often provide high initial returns even with levels of low (or no) maintenance. This operational phase is already overcome by the time of transfer; negligence of maintenance now produces direct opportunity cost of rent omission.

Thus, the project design established elite compatibility by aligning the incentives of the politicians with the goals of the project: Opportunity costs of sustainability were transformed into opportunity costs of failure.

As in Table 2-4 above, it must be made clear that this summary is a stylized version of reality, as it is accessible from ex-post project documentation. In particular, incentive effects that result from the continuity of the aid flow (Samaritan's dilemma, see Section 4.3.2.2) cannot be overcome on the project level – meaning that even if a project is made elite compatible as in the above example, the lowered extractive opportunities may result in 'passive resistance' (i.e., disinterest) of the respective elites if there are better opportunities available.

2.4 Summary

The effectiveness of aid has been discussed since the beginning of its existence, and the arguments and positions in today's discourse are not vastly different from aid critics and proponents of the early times in the 1950s and 60s.

The main part of the effectiveness debate revolves around the macro level, i.e., whether or not aid provision has a positive effect on 'development' in the recipient countries. While the development notion has undergone a variation in meaning over the past decades, its core focus has always been on *economic* development, and a plethora of studies circulates around this understanding of aid effectiveness. This is different for the micro level of project design: Apart from the recent rise of the movement of randomized controlled trials, especially in the health and education sector, the project level does not play a prominent explicit role in the mainstream aid debate, but is mainly represented in the form of success stories of certain project topics (e.g., microcredits), fashionable criteria (e.g., sustainability) or design concepts (e.g., community-driven designs). Because the international aid industry is subject to fashion cycles, the popularity of concepts that circulate in the aid debate are not necessarily linked to their actual effectiveness. One key aspect that has been highlighted by aid critics is that ODA until today does not aptly tackle the challenge of the incentive conflict with the elites.

With the concept of *elite compatibility*, I intend to address this feature on the project level. The concept was inspired by the development theory of *Acemoğlu and Robinson* (2012b), who differentiate between *extractive* and *inclusive* institutional setups and hold that this is the decisive difference between most modern democracies and today's recipient countries of ODA. Sustainable economic development would require a shift from extractive to inclusive institutions – however, such a transition negatively impacts the elite's opportunities of extraction, and will thus trigger their resistance against change. Instead, this change is initiated from the pressure of oppositional interest groups (including the masses), and is only granted to those groups by the elites in order to ward threats to their elite position, such as from a revolution. In this case, the elite's promises towards more inclusive institutions are only credible if they are incentive compatible for the elite, i.e., if breaking the promise entails opportunity cost.

This specific form of incentive compatibility is what I term *elite compatibility*, and apply it to the level of ODA project design. In the case of ODA, it is the same fear of loss of privileges that causes the elite's resistance against change induced by ODA projects. I term three types of this resistance, relating to different origins in the incentive setup:

- *active* resistance, resulting from intentional protection of the elite position;

- *extractive* resistance, 'collateral damage' resulting from activities of rent extraction;
- *passive* resistance, resulting from indifference about project success.

In all cases, the event of a full project success produces opportunity costs for the elite, and is thus not incentive compatible. The key criterion in order to reach elite compatibility is that these opportunity costs of success need to be transformed into *opportunity costs of failure*. An example for a design that achieves this is the BOT model. Here, the project remains with the original project management until the critical phase of project implementation and asset life cycle has been overcome. At the stage of the life cycle when it is finally transferred to the recipient entities, the opportunity cost of failure is higher than in the first phase: Opportunities for extraction quickly diminish in case of missing maintenance, and additionally, the asset has established enough stakeholders in its institutional environment to generate an interest group that is relevant enough for political consideration.

Project-level elite compatibility, nevertheless, cannot overcome incentive effects that originate from higher levels of aid provision, such as the continuity of the aid flow. A wider array of those incentive effects will be discussed in Chapter 4.

Chapter 3 Elites as a Focus in Development Research

This chapter will provide a brief overview of the origin of elite theory (Section 3.1) and then discuss the most important aspects of current elite research in the development context (Section 3.2).

Similar to the incentives concept, elites are an implicit component of any development discussion, as political leaders are always 'part of the game'; in the discussion around policies, it is the political elite who has to put those policies into practice, and after all, the budgets in ODA are shifted between the political leaders (i.e., governments) of donor and recipient country. This leads to the common practice in public communication that whenever the status or progress of a country as an entity is discussed, leaders effectively replace the intended beneficials. When "Ethiopia" receives ODA budget or implements a certain policy, it is in fact the political elite, not the beneficiaries of the country that is the subject of discussion. In the words of *Ferguson* (1994: 181):

> "When 'developers' speak of such a collectivity, what they mean is usually the government. But the government of Lesotho is not identical with the people who live in Lesotho, nor is it in any of the established senses 'representative' of that collectivity."

This situation already indirectly conveys the problematic feature that makes elites a subject for specific discussion in research: their asymmetric power position. *Ferguson* (ibid.) continues with a description of an alleged incentive problem resulting from this position in connection with the elite self-interest:

> "There is little point in asking what such entrenched and often extractive elites should do in order to empower the poor. Their own structural position makes it clear that they would be the last ones to undertake such a project."

It is this incentive problem, in combination with the key-role position of the elites for ODA effectiveness that makes 'elites' a rather interesting focus of research. As such, it has a long history – in development research, however, "it has not yet converged on a framework for understanding a key element of the development process – under what condition are the self-interested objectives of elites aligned with the development objectives of their country" (*DiCaprio* 2012: 1). Given that the discussion on the elites' incentive conflict is as old as ODA itself, this might appear slightly surprising. A classic has already been mentioned in Section 2.1.2: When the newly founded *United Nations* released their first development-themed document in 1951, the report titled *Measures for the Economic Development of Under-developed Countries*, it dedicated large parts to the causal attribution of 'progress' to the political leaders:

> "In our judgment, there are a number of under-developed countries where the concentration of economic and political power in the hands of a small class, whose main interest is the preservation of its own wealth and privileges, rules out the prospect of much economic progress until a social revolution has effected a shift in the distribution of income and power." (*United Nations* 1951: 15f.)

This "shift" is what constitutes the elites' incentive conflict, and which is addressed in *Acemoğlu and Robinson* (2012b). Ironically, the UN report does not follow up on the incentive conflict, but instead switches over to embracing the benevolent-leader logic that is still prevalent (and criticized) today:

> "But if the leaders win the confidence of the country, and prove themselves to be vigorous in eradicating privilege and gross inequalities, they can inspire the masses with an enthusiasm for progress which carries all before it." (*United Nations* 1951: 16)

Frankel (1952) attacked the report in a review in the *Quarterly Journal of Economics*, where he addressed exactly this contradiction. He questioned the narrative of leaders "eradicating privilege", and commented that the authors "do not dilate on the inconvenient problem of how privilege is to be divorced from *leadership*" (ibid.: 304, emphasis in the original). Also, he heavily criticized the "philosophy, which assumes that 'progress' is mainly a matter of 'public will'", and "the conclusion that the absence of progress must be the fault of 'the leaders.'" While *Frankel* goes as far as completely questioning the role of governments for development, his review is one of the first critiques of the narratives of modern ODA incorporating the elite incentive paradox. Interestingly, the reply by one of the report's authors, *Lewis* (1953), does not contain an answer to this paradox. Likewise, in the mainstream technocratic development debate until today, elites have not been included as a factor for success or failure of ODA. As *Kalebe-Nyamongo* (2012: 200) discusses, while "[t]he idea that politics matters in the distribution of resources in society has become widely held [...], attempts to use a political economy 'lens' with which to explore causes of poverty and strategies for poverty alleviation have largely ignored elites", or failed to focus on elites using resources for their personal gain.

Before looking at the current role of "elites" in development research, the next section will provide a short overview on the historical background of the term itself, by picking out a small selection of the most important contributions. The summaries will focus on the explanation for the elite's *position* (i.e., criteria for membership) and for the elite's *control* over the non-elite.

3.1 Theoretical and Conceptual Origin

Gaetano Mosca: Elementi di scienza politica (1896) and Vilfredo Pareto: Trattato di sociologia generale (1916)

As an explicit theoretical treatment, the concept of elites goes back to the 'Italian school' around *Gaetano Mosca* (1858–1941) and *Vilfredo Pareto* (1848–1923). The pioneering contribution of the two authors was to deliver theoretical reflections on the reasons behind and patterns of the formation of elites, its persistence or replacement, and the means of exercising power. *Mosca* (1939: 1)[1] stated that previous political scientists were rather normative than positive, i.e., focusing on recommendations rather than exploring and understanding the mechanisms behind the system. According to him, the focus was on the political success of the individual in increasing his power. *Pareto* (1935: 5/§6)[2] put a similar emphasis on being strictly scientific, assessing previous sociologists to have been too "dogmatical" and more "religion" than science. Nevertheless, both authors delivered only fragments of what from a later perspective could be termed "theory". In *Mosca's* case, this was due to a missing provision of an overall exposé of his doctrine (*Bobbio* 1972: 12)[3], and in the case of both authors, their contributions were perceived as too vague in their terminology

1 The English edition *The Ruling Class* (*Mosca* 1939) is a merger of the two different original volumes of *Elementi di scienza politica* (1896; 1923). *Parry* (1969: 38) highlights that the second volume (chapters 12-17 in *The Ruling Class*) "represents a considerable shift in Mosca's position", namely his more favorable position towards representative democracy.

2 The English edition *The Mind and Society* (*Pareto* 1935) appeared in four volumes; the Italian original *Trattato di sociologia generale* was published in 1916.

3 Neither was *Pareto* renowned for leaving behind a well-structured work. The *Trattato* is considered a difficult read and "by no means elegantly written" (*Wiese* 1936: 434, own translation, original: "dieses schwer lesbare und keineswegs elegant geschriebene Werk"); *Bobbio* (1972: 56f.) comments that "the Trattato is and remains a work which ruins weak stomachs and paralyses the strong", and that "[t]he deformity of the Trattato is so obvious that there is no need to dwell on it".

to be accepted as a basis for empirical research (*Zuckerman* 1977; *Burton & Higley* 2001). However, their work fell into "disciplinary no-man's-land between political science and sociology" (*Higley & Pakulski* 2012: 325) and thus "represents the beginning, or, if one prefers, the first outline of modern political science conceived of as objective research into political phenomena" (*Bobbio* 1972: 21) – which is precisely what the title of *Mosca's* publication (*Elementi di scienza politica*) suggested.

Other than the unity that the frequently-used term "Italian school" suggests, the two authors detested each other quite substantially[4], and engaged in a long battle about who was the originator of the idea (see *Meisel* 1958: 170ff.). However, their concepts differ from each other slightly. It was *Pareto* who established the term "élite" in this context (1935: 1421/§2026); *Mosca* used the term "classe politica" (1923: 52), which obviously translates to "political class", but instead the translation that persisted is "ruling class". While in both cases, their concept refers to a minority that exercises political power over a majority (*Mosca* 1939: 50), these different terminologies already represent the conceptual difference in their two approaches:

The French term *élite* translates to "chosen"[5] (deriving from Latin "eligere": to choose [*OLD* 1982: 599]), and is hence a value judgment on the members of that group, as it implies merit as a basis for the membership – as opposed to *Mosca's* descriptive term of 'ruling class'. Consequently, *Pareto* (1935: 1423/§2031) defines the elite as the 'best' of something, not primarily as a ruling class. These qualities are not restricted in any way; the examples given include lawyers, fraudsters and thieves, poets and chess players, or even just people with more or less wealth (ibid.: 1422/§2027). From this group of 'the best', he then distinguishes between the *governing elite* and those who have high talents, but don't have political influence (see Figure 3-1).

---

4 E.g., *Pareto* denied *Mosca* any mathematical knowledge and called him a "balloon full of hot air" (1900, quoted in *Bobbio* 1972: 12).

5 *Pareto* repeatedly refers to the publication *La circulation des élites en France* by *Marie Kolabinska*, who apparently was one of his students at the time.

Higher stratum	Élite (the "best")	Governing élite	direct
			indirect
		Non-governing élite	
Lower stratum	Non-élite		

Figure 3-1: Pareto's elite classification

His taxonomy implies that the ruling minority is indeed a sub-set of the 'best'. In other words, his understanding of the elite is a 'capacity' criterion, which *Parry* (1969: 45) terms "a psychological approach". However, Pareto does acknowledge the hereditary nature of political offices and the resulting elite affiliation "without possessing qualities corresponding to the labels they wear" (ibid.: 1424/§2035). Despite the supposed problematic background of a 'capacity' approach, "elite" has persisted as a term over *Mosca's* more neutral "political class", or even "ruling class".

In contrast, *Mosca* describes the ruling class as comprised of people best suited to govern, explicitly remarking that "such fitness by no means implies that they are the 'best' individuals intellectually, much less the 'best' individuals morally" (*Mosca* 1939: 450), and that the material, intellectual or moral superiority of an elite member over the masses may be "real or apparent" (ibid.: 53). Instead, the decisive personal qualities of political leaders are "perspicacity, a ready intuition of individual and mass psychology, strength of will and, especially, confidence in oneself" (ibid.: 450). *Mosca* himself criticized that "it is for this reason that the expression 'élite' adopted by Pareto appears inaccurate for describing what we had termed 'political class' many years ago" (*Mosca* 1953: 177, own translation)[6].

6 Original: "È per questa ragione che ci sembra inesatta l'espressione di *élite* adoperata dal Pareto per indicare quella che noi molti anni prima avevamo denominato *classe politica*." The source indicated is the second volume of the 5th Italian edi-

According to him, the elite's control derives from their capacity for organization, which is advantageous for a minority over larger groups because less coordination is required (*Mosca* 1939: 53). While *Mosca* did describe that recruitment of new elite members happens from the lower strata and that this exchange was vital for the stability of the leadership (ibid.: 65ff.), he also saw mechanisms that perpetuate the political power of the elites. I.e., he interpreted the mechanism of election as a closed circuit: As influential leaders within a structure pick the candidates for election, an individual representative is not actually freely chosen by the electorate, but a he "has himself elected" or "his friends have him elected" (ibid.: 154).

Pareto saw this differently, and described the elite as "always in a state of slow and continuous transformation" (1935: 1431/§2056), and a constant movement of new "best" members pushing 'up' into the governing elite; this is the context that the famous quote "history is a graveyard of aristocracies" derives from (ibid.: 1430/§2053). Even revolutions of lower-stratum members are led by elite members, as only they "possess the intellectual qualities required" (ibid.: 1431/§2058). The logic for the elite's composition and the style of governing is explained by human attributes that *Pareto* calls "residues" and which classify into different character types, or "classes"; within the elite, there is mainly a constant competition between a more cunning, consensus-oriented type (class I) and a more force- and integrity-oriented type (class II), which he terms "foxes" and "lions" in referral to *Machiavelli*[7].

The *residues* are one of the many concepts subject to the vagueness criticism mentioned previously that led to the reputation of *Pareto's* theses to not be empirically substantial.

---

tion, where the remark appears as a footnote to the quoted paragraph (1939: 450). It is not present in the 1939 English translation.

7 *Machiavelli* establishes these types in his *Il Principe*: "Since a ruler, then, must know how to act like a beast, he should imitate the fox and the lion, for the lion is liable to be trapped, whereas the fox cannot ward off wolves. Those who rely merely upon a lion's strength do not understand matters." (1532/1988: 61)

Robert Michels: Political Parties (1911)

This was different for the work of German-Italian sociologist *Michels* (1911)[8], who delivered the third important contribution for the beginning of elite theories. To be precise, he does not use the term 'elite' but instead refers to 'leaders' and 'leadership'; again, his central theme is that control of elite minority over the "masses" depends upon organization. The most widely known thesis of *Michels* is the "iron law of oligarchy" from the above work (ibid.: 362), that any humanly devised activity that requires more extensive forms of organization will eventually feature power structures of oligarchy. The phrase frequently quoted: "Who says organization, already says tendency towards oligarchy" (ibid.: 32) sums his 'rule' up in a (very small) nutshell.

In the second edition, *Michels* explicitly refers to *Pareto* and *Mosca* in the context of the sustainability of an oligarchy in democratic regimes. From *Pareto's* explanations, he considers "only a few links of [his] chain acceptable" (1925: 481, own translation)[9], as he describes the process of circulation "happens less as a real displacement than in a form of constant amalgamation of the new elements with the old" (ibid., own translation)[10].

His 'iron law of oligarchy' has been discussed extensively, and empirical testing delivered inconclusive outcomes; one of the most widely known studies being that of *Lipset, Trow and Coleman* (1956). *Leach* (2005: 313), who provides a very accessible discussion of the various results, concludes them to the comment that "aluminum tendency" would be a more suitable term than 'iron law'. The discourse over *Michels* also illustrates the difficulty of isolating elite theory from its very manifold links and associations to other aspects in the array of the social and political sciences. E.g., *Winters* (2011: 2) contends that the iron law of oligarchy, "when examined closely, is not a theory of oligarchy at all, but rather an analysis how elites eventually dominate all complex organizations."

However, *Michels'* analysis of leadership structures goes much further than the small excerpt that is usually subject of discussions within the scope of the 'iron law'; apart from various tracts on bureaucracy and or-

---

8 This is the first edition of the German original *Zur Soziologie des Parteiwesens in der modernen Demokratie*. The first English edition (1915) was in fact a translation of the Italian translation (1912).

9 Original: "Vielleicht sind freilich in der Kette der Pareto'schen théorie de la circulation des élites nur einige Glieder annehmbar."

10 Original: "[…] vollzieht sich weniger als tatsächliche Ablösung denn vielmehr in der Form einer beständigen Amalgamierung der neuen Elemente mit den alten."

ganizational structures, he also extensively explored mass psychology and observations of motivational phenomena of the individual vs. the group (see *Michels* 1925: 501). Most importantly, though, he discussed the sustainability of elite structures, or how "power breeds power", as *Parry* (1969: 43) puts it: Leadership controls funds and hence patronage, channels information and has the effective power of preselecting candidates for election processes (see 1925: Part II) – this is very similar to the *Mosca's* thesis of 'leaders having candidates elected' as quoted above.

C. Wright Mills: The Power Elite (1956)

Mills' study is an analysis of the society of the United States. His main argument is that the actual elite in power is an interweaved network of key positions that perpetuates itself in serving its own interests. According to *Mills*, the power elite is recruited "in substantial proportions" from the upper classes of US society (1956: 279). A complete definition of the elite term is given already in the beginning of the book:

> "The power elite is composed of men whose positions enable them to transcend the ordinary environments of ordinary men and women; they are in positions to make decisions having major consequences [...] they are in command of the major hierarchies and organizations of modern society." (ibid.: 3)

This definition covers all major aspects of his understanding of elite:

- The elite are at the top of all major hierarchies of society, they "occupy the strategic command posts of the social structure" (ibid.: 3). Namely, the three sectors are politics, military and economy (the 'big three'), the latter both financial as well as the corporate world.
- Due to this position, the elite have the ability to overview the structure as a whole, as opposed to the non-elite masses. He compares this with a military hierarchy, where "the roles men play are strictly confining; only the command posts at the top afford a view of the structure of the whole, and moreover, this view is a closely guarded official secret" (ibid.: 321).
- Their exclusive ability of overview enables the elite to "interchange commanding roles at the top of one dominant institutional order with those in another" (ibid.: 288). The 'big three' types of sectors interweave, and this reinforces elite cohesion.
- The elite can transcend, the ordinary not: The sustainability of the dominant position comes from said cohesion in combination with inability of the *masses* to transcend the milieux – since they lack the

overview that would be needed. 'Milieux' are not transcended by the ordinary, rather each is "trapped by his confining circle" (ibid.: 320).

- The mass media play a major role in manipulating the public in order to keep them in their respective 'milieux'. (ibid.)

While his interpretations may be conceived as radical or supportive of conspiracy theorists, a confirmation of his claims was famously delivered only a few years after the publication of *The Power Elite*: In US President *Eisenhower's* 1961 farewell address, he acknowledged the need for a large military "establishment"[11], but warned the American people of the dangers from the power that derives from the interweaved 'sectors':

> "Now this conjunction of an immense military establishment and a large arms industry is new in the American experience. The total influence – economic, political, even spiritual – is felt in every city, every Statehouse, every office of the Federal government. We recognize the imperative need for this development. Yet, we must not fail to comprehend its grave implications. Our toil, resources, and livelihood are all involved. So is the very structure of our society.
> In the councils of government, we must guard against the acquisition of unwarranted influence, whether sought or unsought, by the military-industrial complex. The potential for the disastrous rise of misplaced power exists and will persist." (*Eisenhower* 1961: IV)

Essentially, this is very close to the "permanent war economy" that *Mills* was fearing (1956: 215). While *Eisenhower's* famed farewell address is mainly known for only the quoted paragraph on the 'military-industrial complex', there are further passages that pick up the elite complex and appear like unintended references to *Mills*. E.g., he warns of the dangerous influence of economic power and wealth in science and fears that capital might become "a substitute for intellectual curiosity", as well as of a "scientific-technological elite" dominating public policy (*Eisenhower* 1961: IV)[12].

Apart from the radicalism of his theses regarding the degree of power concentration, *Mills'* basic framework is not too far from *Michels* (1925), who already dedicated a large fraction of his work to the analysis of elite-mass interaction. In fact, it could be interpreted as a further refinement in the sense that it adds the perspective of the 'big three' and the transcending elites – though all this in a rather dark package.

11 "A vital element in keeping the peace is our military establishment. Our arms must be mighty, ready for instant action, so that no potential aggressor may be tempted to risk his own destruction." (*Eisenhower* 1961: IV)

12 For an overview of the vast literature that picked up on this matter soon after the address, see, e.g., *Bernstein and Wilson* (2011: 4).

Robert Putnam: The Comparative Study of Political Elites (1976)

By the mid 1970s, the amount of literature that discussed elite theories had grown to a level that *Putnam* (1976) decided to take stock, and sum up the array of contributions in an "invaluable book" (*Higley & Moore* 2001: 175). The vast amount of research in the 'elite' field was also due to the fact that had split up into many different aspects and research interests from the various scholarly disciplines, such as the political effects of different elite 'compositions', motivational aspects of power, the inner structure of elites or the relationship between elites and society.

While, naturally, the research has again expanded since this publication almost forty years ago, the main contribution of *Putnam's* work is the structure it provided for the body of research. He distinguished between the topics of:

- *Social structure and elites:* socioeconomic and political stratification, education, class, ethnicity, ideology and agglutination, and their interactions and effects on elites;
- *Elite recruitment:* "channels", social permeability, selection and selectorates, leadership qualities and affiliations;
- *Motives, beliefs and their sources:* motives for power, incentives for political participation, cognitive, normative, interpersonal and stylistic orientations of elites, origins of these beliefs, effects of these beliefs;
- *The structure of elites:* elite integration (personal interaction, value consensus, social homogeneity) and its consequences
- *Elite-mass linkages:* coercion, organization, authority, opinion flow, information flow, media, interest groups, patron-client relationships
- *Elite transformation:* factors for changes in elite composition through 'circulation' (i.e., socioeconomic, social or political factors), factors for long-term changes, factors for revolutions.

The research in each of these fields continued to proliferate following *Putnam's* publication. One last important step is discussed in the next paragraph.

Further Development and 'Revival'

The latest major addition in elite theory came from the sociologists *Michael Burton*, *G. Lowell Field* and *John Higley*, who in their late 1980's publications were promoting a 'new elite framework' (*Burton & Higley* 1987b; *Higley & Burton* 1989; *Field, Higley & Burton* 1990) – which

DiCaprio (2012: 2) calls an "attempt to revive elite theory". While they picked up the major topics of the classical elitists (elite transformation, elite-mass linkages, 'inevitability' of elites), the novel component introduced was the criterion of *unity* and the differentiation into unified and disunified groups of elite. The 'consensual unity' among elites was termed 'settlement', the process from a disunified towards a unified elite was put under the wording of 'elite transitions'. While disunity is the default state, *Burton & Higley* claim that unity of the elites is not only a precondition for political stability but the decisive explanatory variable (1987a: 304). This hypothesis was tested against historical evidence in their 1989 article[13] and naturally delivered the starting point for discussion, mainly on the notorious topic of empirical value of their terms and concepts (*Cammack* 1990; response by *Higley, Burton & Field* 1990), specifically on the measurement and scale of the 'unity' variable. Further research covered various (geographical) backgrounds (*Peeler* 1992; *Higley & Burton* 1997; *Higley, Huang & Lin* 1998; *Higley & Lengyel* 2000), and is still influencing mainstream discourse today (*Gulbrandsen* 2012).

A good overview of the recent research in elite theory is provided by the monographic section of a journal edited by *Higley and Moore* (2001), as well as a journal issue dedicated to classics of the elite literature, including some new additions, e.g., *Domhoff* (2012).

Elitists' Common Denominators

The topic of elites in a wider sense interweaves with the discussion on whether or not elites are an apt concept at all – initiated by the pluralists such as *Meisel* (1958) or *Dahl* (1958) –, with the topic of social stratification such as *Dahrendorf* (1959), and generally with any field of political science that revolves around forms of government. The purpose of this Section 3.1 was to provide a brief overview of the historical path of the 'elite' term and its contexts. Despite the outlined differences, the common denominators of the elitists are rather accessible, as all argue in one way or the other that:

- elites are a minority that rules over a majority in a hierarchical structure; this unequal influence of an insider-outsider notion is the constitutive characteristic of an elite;

13 A summary of their global-historical comparative studies is provided in *Higley and Burton* (2006: 55ff.).

- the separation of a ruling elite is 'inevitable', with different explanations for formation;
- the elite position features privileges associated with the elite membership and the influence in key positions;
- the elite act in their self-interest to uphold these privileges and are cohesive;
- social access to the elite is limited; members of the elite are usually recruited from a privileged background (i.e., the upper class);
- the elite is divided in multiple levels and/or areas, usually with an important role taken by a bureaucracy;
- access to power on the different levels is competitive both within the elite stratum as well as 'into' it;
- the ruled majority is somehow 'controlled' by the elite in order to receive their support.

Needless to say, it is the individual details in the context of the respective approaches of the different authors that 'invigorate' these otherwise somewhat trivial-sounding features. Within the scope of this work, the *elite* term is used to denominate a specific 'target group' in the context of ODA projects. A current, widely accepted mainstream definition in political science is that:

> "Political elites are persons whose strategic positions in large and powerful organizations and movements enable them to influence political decision-making directly, substantially, and regularly." (*Burton & Higley* 2001: 176)

It may be similarly extended to a non-political context. As *Lasswell* already contended in 1965 (ibid.: : 4), "any single definition for such a key term as 'elite' is inadequate" and "[a]ny competent theorist can match the definition with his preferred systematics. Most simply, the elite are the influential." This definition, most simply, is the essence that is used in the context of development research as well, as will be shown in the next section.

3.2 Current Research in the Development Context

Quite logically, elite-related research in development context focuses on the role that elites' behavior plays for the 'development' of a country. The existing work can be summarized down to three aspects, as illustrated in Figure 3-2: First of all (A), how is poverty, or more broadly, development perceived by the elites and does this perception influence preferences and motivators for elite's behavior? Secondly (B), how do these preferences influence elites' behavior to act in the direction of 'development', such as pro-poor or pro-growth policies? Lastly and more fundamentally (C), what is the influence that elites' behavior exerts on 'development' at all?

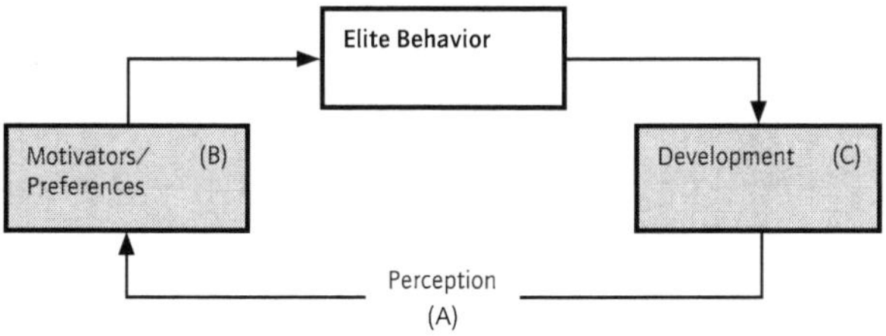

Figure 3-2: Fields of elite-related research in the context of development

Similar to the discourse on institutions and development (see Section 4.3.1), the elite research topics thus fall into a micro perspective (A and B) and a more macro-oriented perspective (C). While, naturally, the separation of the three areas is not always fully selective, the research topics may be classified as follows:

- Examples for Complex A include the discussion of the *elite-mass gap*, the social disparity between elites and non-elites and its effects on elite behavior. Other research from this complex picks up some of the aspects of the classical elite theorists (see the paragraph on *Robert Putnam* in the previous Section 3.1), such as elite formation, circulation and reproduction, and the respective effect on elite preferences. The elite incentive conflict as described in the introduction of this chapter also belongs to this category.
- Complex B comprises the phenomenon of *elite capture*. Also, the question of elite cooperation when they are part of a reform is treated in this context.
- A discussion that is somewhat positioned between B and C is the concept of *neopatrimonialism* from the field of political science, which examines the connection of predatory elite behavior and state structure.
- Complex C entails research of the growth literature that specifically explores countries' leadership as an explanatory variable.

Definitions of Elite in the Development Context

The applied definitions of the term 'elite' closely follow those of the 'original' elitists, as can be seen in Table 3-1. While the listed definitions to emphasize different aspects, the overview illustrates how all of them ultimately convey the common denominator of

- *influence* or *control* that is exerted through
- positions of *limited access*,

i.e., an asymmetric-power relationship – which is the parallel to NIE's principal-agent concept (see Section 4.2). While, e.g., neopatrimonialism mainly focuses only on the highest political elites close to the definition of *Burton and Higley* above, limited-access positions of influence (and hence power asymmetries) exist on virtually all levels of society. This circumstance is successively accounted for in recent elite research, by also addressing the low-level elites in local contexts. This has been advanced by the increasing importance of 'community-based development' and 'participation', the involvement of local-level target groups in the design process, which are also part of the popular concept of *decentralization* (*Manor* 1999).

Two patterns of behavior result from the exclusive position that are potentially antagonizing development (and in the sense of agency theory, are typical action patterns of agents):

1. actions to *secure* the position, which may include actions to limit access to it, and
2. actions of *extracting rents* from the position.

On the micro perspective, all elite-related research in the development context can be reduced to the exploration of one or both of these patterns.

Table 3-1: Definitions of the term 'elite' in development research in comparison (emphases added)

Author	Definition
'Classical'	
Mosca (1939: 50)	"...always the less numerous, performs all political functions, monopolizes power and enjoys the advantages that power brings, whereas the second, the more numerous class, is directed and controlled by the first"
Pareto (1935: 1423)	"...a class of the people who have the highest indices in their branch of activity, [...] individuals who directly or indirectly play some considerable part in government"
'Modern'	
Burnham (1941: 72)	"...a group of persons who, by virtue of special social-economic relations, *exercises a special degree of control* over access to the instruments of production and receives preferential treatment in the distribution of the product of these instruments."
Mills (1956: 3f.)	"...is composed of men [...] *in positions to make decisions* having major consequences. [...] [T]hey are in command of the major hierarchies and organizations of modern society."
Higley and Burton (2006: 7)	"...persons who are able, by virtue of their *strategic positions* in powerful organizations and movements, to *affect political outcomes* regularly and substantially."
Development Research	
Reis and Moore (2005: 2)	"...the people who occupy *commanding positions* within the set of institutions that are most salient to national *political influence and policy-making* within a country."
North et al. (2009: 18f.)	"...members of the dominant coalition" who "specialize in a range of military, political, religious, political, and economic activities [...] each of the nonmilitary elites either *controls* or enjoys privileged *access* to a vital function like religion, production, community allocation of resources, justice, trade, or education."
Robinson (2012: 31)	"...a distinct group within a society which enjoys privileged status and *exercises decisive control* over the organization of that society (though this will be a matter of degree in reality)."
Solimano and Avanzini (2012: 54)	"...individuals that *have a capacity* to save, invest, and generate knowledge technology, and creativity well *above the average* of the population."
DiCaprio (2012: 1)	"...a select set of individuals [who] influence economic development through the simple fact that they *define the social context that determines how factor endowments are used* and institutions are designed."
Amsden (2012: 19)	"...hold a *controlling interest* in property and exert power over its regulation and use."
Development Agencies	
World Bank (2008a: 1)	"Elites are actors who have *disproportionate influence* in the development process as a result of their superior social, political or economic status."

3.2.1 The Micro Perspective: Elite Behavior

3.2.1.1 The Elite-mass Gap

The *elite-mass gap* is the disparity that results from the different socialization of members of the elite versus the non-elite. *Putnam* (1976: 163) already classifies this phenomenon be specifically apparent in developing countries, as those elite members often derive from the urban upper-middle-class, and enjoy privileged education from western top schools (see also *Solimano & Avanzini* 2012), while facing a large share of the population in stark poverty. The resulting problem is twofold: The first aspect is a *capacity* issue: A too large disparity will lead to the elite being "ill equipped to respond to real problems at the grassroots, and politics tends to be court politics" *Putnam* (1976: 163). The other component is *motivational*: With a large social gap between leaders and non-elite, the role of leadership becomes merely extractive. "The elite extracts taxes and services from the non-elite but does not attempt to mobilize them for collective goals. Intra-elite conflict is personalistic and largely unrelated to broader social problems and tensions" (ibid.: 163). Put differently: The elite-mass gap lies at the root of the elite incentive problem.

As by the criterion of causality, this can be classified as the central and most important issue of elite-related development research. This is simply due to the fact that it is self-perpetuating (almost) by definition. The component of "almost" depends on whether the elites are self-interest oriented or altruistic: If they are primarily self-interest oriented, they will invest in securing and extracting their position, implying the elite-mass gap to be perpetuated. This is also a popular assumption in modeling power structures, e.g., *Acemoğlu and Robinson* (2006: 173), who expect "lower taxes, lower redistribution, and generally a range of policies favoring the rich rather than the poor" when the elites are powerful.

While one way of securing power is strengthening support from bureaucratic agents and ruling party members by corruption (*Hollyer & Wantchekon* 2014: 5), another option is augmenting the elite-mass gap. The extreme situation can be summarized to one where "the elite tries to extract as much rent as it can from the economy while trying to minimize the probability of losing political power" (*Bourguignon & Verdier* 2012: 252). At the same time, as *Hanlon and Mosse* (2010: 2) phrase the situation for Mozambique, "the leadership has had to juggle three often conflicting priorities: nationalism and development, class and self-interest, and overwhelming international pressure."

Actions to actuate the elite-mass gap have grave implications: *Easterly* (2003b), for the case of Pakistan, outlines the perverse incentives for the elites to keep literacy rates low in order to retain their elite status without being threatened by an 'empowered' population. This pattern is also mentioned by *Gibson et al.* (2005: 74), and closely linked to what *Farmer* (2004: 307; 2005) terms *structural violence*: e.g., strategic denial of basic privileges such as health care to the (poor) masses as a protective measure by the elites[14]. To *Farmer*, structural violence "is the natural expression of a political and economic order that seems as old as slavery" (2004: 317).

The elite-mass gap is not reduced to economic terms only, but is also reflected in a persistence of informal rules and social norms in everyday practice, rather than rule-of-law, leading to a state which "undermines the credibility of modern statutory law" (*Platteau* 2009: 669). Such a legal dualism in turn affects economic climate, as it promotes a phenomenon that *Voigt* (2004) terms *dilemma of the strong state*. This dilemma is due to a *hold-up* incentive for the leader: A state that is strong enough to protect private property rights and to enforce private contracts is also strong enough to expropriate private wealth. In an autocratic regime, where the law is strongly associated with the leader and credible commitments of the leader are more difficult, this may pose a problem, and the leader's hold-up incentive diminishes the investor's incentive to invest (*Feld & Voigt* 2005) – while, naturally, this incentive is not increased by a more deficient legal system.

Easterly (2014b: 159) highlights how oppressive measures by the hereditary political and economical elite block 'creative destruction' necessary for development. This situation then additionally creates more dependency on aid, and thus again enhances social disparity between the governing elites. When ODA is introduced into the game, it perpetuates the incentive problem, in a double effect: it undermines incentives for the elite to take measures for development, and at the same time, it enhances the disparity responsible for the incentive problem in the first place. *Coyne and Ryan* (2009: 28) ironically title ODA as "making the world safe for autocracy".

The reinforcing effects of the elite-mass gap as sketched out above apply only to the case of self-interest oriented behavior of the elites. If the "almost" from the statement on self-perpetuation of the elite-mass gap should come into play, i.e., poverty of the masses should be a concern for the elites, the assumption must allow for altruistic behavior, or benevo-

14 This concept was first described by *Galtung* (1969: 170).

lence[15]. One segment of research is dedicated to exploring this aspect: the motivation of elites to act deviantly from the self-interest preference as applied above. It pursues the question how the elites in developing countries perceive poverty.

Poverty Perceptions

Reis and Moore (2005: 3) define poverty perceptions as

> "a combination of cognitions (non-evaluative understanding); norms (internalized ideas about appropriate roles); and values (ideals about what might be)."

Interestingly, this definition is in fact less about *perception* than about *motivation*. The component of *knowledge* is missing in this definition; however, it plays an important role in the actual research. E.g., *Hossain and Moore* (2005) survey elites in Bangladesh and diagnose a mismatch between "their concern for the poor" (relatively high) and the "empirical knowledge about the poor" (relatively low, ibid.: 92) – all this despite other typical 'gap' factors indicating to be very low (e.g., the physical/residential segregation and linguistic differences are negligible). Nevertheless, the authors do summarize a high degree of elite interconnection. An important difference that the study discovers is between national and local elites: Local elites were far more willing to support policies for poverty reduction. *Hossain and Moore* attribute this to their higher involvement in political and bureaucratic positions, thus having "a more direct stake in the distribution of resources through government channels, and more direct responsibilities for the livelihoods of poor people" (ibid.: 96).

In a study on South-African elites, *Kalati and Manor* (2005: 159) find the exact opposite: While the awareness about the quantitative dimension of poverty is fairly accurate, the elite tended not to perceive poverty as a problematic issue for those affected by it. Additionally, the extent and gravity of *rural* poverty was not present, implying a strong difference in perception of urban vs. rural poverty (ibid.: 160). This is a pattern also found in the results of *Hossain and Moore* (2005: 97).

---

15 Given that leadership is autocratic in the majority of ODA recipient states, *Easterly and Pennings* (2014: Section 7) question the narrative that "an autocrat selected through a ruthless process of amassing power could even turn out to be benevolent".

Curiously, the latter authors also discover that a popular perception of the elite is that of the poor being responsible for their own misery themselves:

> "Our interviewees perceived a set of problems relating to the motivations and attitudes of the poor themselves: a lack of 'awareness' or 'consciousness' (chetona; shocheton), best glossed as fatalism or passivity" (ibid.: 101).

This notion is remarkable especially since it is often portrayed as a (not necessarily historical) attitude of western arrogance towards 'underdeveloped' peoples (e.g., *Chang* 2008: 182). Similar findings are made by *Reis* (2012) in her study on Brazilian elites, and *Kalebe-Nyamongo* (2012) in Malawi.

On the contrary, *Amsden* (2012) shows how development orientation is not only a matter of political will, but strongly dependent on elites' skills. Comparing Argentina, China, Korea and Taiwan, she views post-colonial changes in property rights as exogenous shocks that need to be 'managed' by the elites. She finds that it is the reaction pattern of elites that makes the difference whether or not institutional change will transform to a development-friendly' setup – thus, the relationship between institutional change and development is substantially determined by the management capacities and project execution skills of the elites.

Another segment of research targets the question how and why this pool of skills and the elite's preferences are subject to change. It is subsumed under the headline of *elite circulation*.

Elite Circulation

As an example, *Bourguignon and Verdier* (2012) pursue this question by modeling elites' incentives to increase state capacity for tax collection and redistribution. One of their main conclusions is that enhancing state capacity is strongly limited by the threat to lose power: In elite-dominated political systems, this would allow other groups to extract more rents when they get into power and thus provides strong incentives for those groups to strive for a corresponding power shift. The importance of political stability for development incentives is confirmed, e.g., by *Zang* (2012) in a study on China.

Solimano and Avanzini (2012) examine the effect of globalization on opening new paths of elite circulation (given the higher mobility of elites) and how different "channels" of circulation potentially contribute to development. They emphasize the "channel" of returning elites, and while it is evident how a globalization-enhanced mobility of *economic* elites yields returns for the home economy (in the form of importing state-of-the-art production and management methods and technology from abroad), their point for *political* elites is not really clear; foreign top-level education has been a privilege and feature of political leadership in developing countries for a long time, as already stressed by *Putnam* (1976: 163); see also *Spilimbergo* (2007: 43ff.)[16]. After all, this is one of the components of the elite-mass gap.

As one last example, according to *Robinson* (2012), elite circulation or reproduction is the explanatory factor for institutional persistence. The mode in which elites reproduce and decline defines how elites "form around a set of institutions" (ibid.: 31), and whether institutions persist over time. *Robinson* picks up the concept of *elite disunity* by *Field, Higley and Burton* mentioned in Section 3.1, as a cause for institutional change: He holds that from the direction of elites, institutional change can either be caused by this disunity, or by a change in elite's preferences[17]. He summarizes that "the key factor in institutional change will be what happens to the elite" (*Robinson* 2012: 31) – in other words, the elite's opportunity costs of change – which is the logic pursued in the elite compatibility concept of this work.

3.2.1.2 Elite Capture and 'Participation'

The phenomenon of *elite capture*[18] mainly received attention thanks to the works of *Laffont and Tirole* (1991). It refers to the rent-seeking activity of appropriation of public resources by the elite, and as such, also of aid budgets. More recently, the 'capture' term has been extended to encompass benefits in general, as the following definition by *Labonte* (2011: 91) illustrates:

> "Elite capture occurs when elites control, shape, or manipulate decision-making processes or institutions in ways that serve their self-interests and priorities, typi-

16 There is a journal version (2009) of this working paper, but it excludes the tables referenced above.

17 Robinson clearly differentiates the 'disunity' concept from 'preferences', while, in fact, disunity is nothing else but a change of preferences

18 To be clear, the elite are the grammatical subject, not the object, hence the meaning is capture *by* elites, not capture *of* elites. However, the term is not applied consistently, and is sometimes used in its object form, such as 'resource capture'.

> cally resulting in personal gain at the expense of non-elites and local communities."

This understanding is very close to popular definitions of *corruption*, such as "the abuse of entrusted power for private gain" (*Transparency International* 2011) or "the abuse of public office for private gain" (*World Bank* 1997a: 8). Indeed, the differentiation in the development literature is not always clear (and not necessarily easy to follow)[19]. From a purely semantic standpoint, the two terms can be understood as the same concept viewed from different perspectives; while 'corruption' holds a normative value statement on the result of the activity[20], 'capture' emphasizes the activity itself and is hence of positive (i.e., descriptive) nature. Both concepts involve an elite actor in the sense that they require an asymmetric-power relationship. This study will use the two terms interchangeably.

An important feature of elite capture is the acceptance by the non-elite; *Platteau* (2004: 227) describes the moral basis as follows:

> "If the intervention of the elite results in an improvement in the predicament of the poor, however small that improvement, the latter tend to be thankful to their leader(s): the new outcome represents a Pareto improvement over the previous situation and this is what matters after all."

Elite capture may in fact be implicitly promoted by donor agencies, when it is officially accepted as a trade-off for implementing preferred policies. *Hanlon and Mosse* (2010) discuss this in an interesting overview of Mozambique's political and ODA history and show how the elite became predatory "with the pressure and encouragement from international forces" (ibid.: 1).

But the phenomenon of elite capture has advanced to a relevant issue especially in the view of more 'localized' project designs. The trend for decentralization and turning to community-based approaches emerged in the 1970s on the basis of a concept for slum upgrading by *Turner and Fichter* (1972): The strategy included minimizing the involvement of government and setting on the areas' internal 'management' capacities by conceiving the beneficiaries as the 'principals'.

While community-based approaches have seen many 'revivals' and can still be found on the list of popular project designs, the method has received a lot of criticism during the years. *Werlin* (1999), in an article that he titles *The Slum Upgrading Myth*, concludes the concept to have failed

19 E.g., for *Dutta* (2009: 2), "corruption is the measurable manifestation of elite capture".

20 Deriving from Latin *corrumpere*: "to spoil" (*OLD* 1982: 450).

also due to ignoring incentive issues – firstly, with local elites (such as land tenure), and secondly within the respective communities, where "deep-rooted social and economic divisions preventing effective community participation" has largely been ill-addressed by the projects (ibid.: 1529)[21]. Put simply, the original problem that this approach intended to address was simply shifted from a high to the local level, and from the national to the local elites, and thus made elite capture an issue even harder to track.

The originally expected advantage of decentralized aid programs was exactly the opposite: First of all, an informational advantage of the beneficiaries was assumed in terms of their exact needs, as well as in terms of how objectives could be best obtained. Secondly, active participation in project design and execution aimed at a higher motivation to exert effort and increase the perceived 'stakes' in obtaining the objectives, e.g., by incorporating material contributions to the project. Localization was also assumed to ameliorate transparency and accountability (*Bardhan & Mookherjee* 2006) of involved project agencies[22].

Practical Problems of 'Participation'

Although these assumptions must appear intuitively logical in theory, they often did not hold true in project practice – which is also indicated by the ongoing discussion of elite capture in the literature (*Platteau, Somville & Wahhaj* 2014; *Panda* 2015) –, or even delivered counterintuitive results. E.g., a frequently quoted survey of *Dasgupta and Beard* (2007) found that elite capture was *restricted* in elite-controlled designs, while the community where elite capture did appear as a problem was exactly that one who had suffered domination by 'predatory' political elite, and who was now offered a strong role in the project design. This result again displays that a universal application of the participatory design does not level out local deficiencies of collective action. Some studies arrive at similar results (e.g., *Fritzen* 2007; *Banerjee et al.* 2010), while others allow to draw the conclusions expected from theory (e.g., *Björkman & Svensson* 2009).

21 For the sake of completeness: *Werlin* on the other hand draws the conclusion that authoritarian power has a positive influence on project outcome (ibid.: 1533) and thus follows the 'benevolent autocrat' concept criticized, e.g., by *Easterly* (2011).

22 The DFID labeled these elements the *CAR* framework of capability, accountability and responsiveness (*Moore & Teskey* 2006).

Gaventa and McGee (2013: S11)[23] complain of a conceptual laxness in both theory and practice: "Citizen participation tends to be under-theorized, unforthcoming on questions such as which citizens it refers to, whether they were active prior to the creation of the mechanism, where they get their information and how they act upon it, on which issues they mobilize, and whether they are well-behaved or antagonistic toward state institutions." The effect of an uncritically applied 'participatory' design is documented by *Rigon* (2014), who shows the potentially perverse outcomes of slum upgrading when the project institutionally perpetuates pre-existing power imbalances in the local community. In his study, supposed 'participation' has thus further empowered the existing elite. *Rigon* refers to a program official who claimed that no conventional monitoring mechanisms were required, "because the community, through their leaders, was directly involved" (ibid.: 274). Internal power structures of the community were hence ignored in the design[24]. *Platteau and Abraham* (2002: 106) contend that by such ill-designed community involvement, many aid agencies are actually not *tackling* elite capture, but are rather "largely contributing to *create* that problem" in the first place (emphasis added). This is supported by more recent other findings, e.g., *Gautier et al.* (2013).

'Excluding Elites' as a Solution?

A popular quick-shot response to elite problems may be the suggestion to simply circumvent elites entirely, and directly reach out to the intended beneficiaries. It should be apparent that this venture may often be both unrealistic and counterproductive: First of all, any larger group will need some sort of leadership to coordinate the actions (right in the sense of *Mosca* 1939: 53), secondly, a formerly powerful group will take measures to sustain (or regain) their position; sabotage of project material by negatively affected stakeholders is a frequent phenomenon of ODA projects.

Many studies demonstrate that the local history of the social structures remains a key factor – and could be tackled theoretically, but it just not approached properly in practice. A study by *Wong* (2012) finds that in communities where a strong dependency of non-elites to elites existed,

23 The authors provide an excellent review of the vast available literature on the topics *accountability* and *transparency*.

24 *Winters* (2010: 238) observes similar patterns in his survey and comments that it is "not yet clear that participation in this case is more than just window dressing."

participatory design could not even these out. Despite knowledge of and grievance about elite capture, the local beneficiaries rarely confronted the offenders; *Wong* quotes a villager stating that "he did not want to be seen as a trouble maker" (ibid.: 347). A recent study by *Justesen and Bjørnskov* (2014) draws a similar picture: Poverty seems to overproportionally increase the frequency of being exposed to bribes in turn for public services.

These notions concur with the findings of *Dasgupta and Beard* (2007) and illustrate the case of how sensitive community-based implementation is to the community it is based on – and that a simple nominally 'community-based' intervention will potentially do more harm than good: In their exploration of two case studies from Mozambique, *Arnall et al.* (2013) present another example of how prescriptive practices may backfire in their original intention – notably: also in the case of assuming a *malevolent* elite. They state that "community-based elites contextualized within their specific historical trajectories have varied and complex motivations that cannot be reduced to the 'timeless', static image" of community-driven development as it is usually conveyed (ibid.: 326), and call for thorough qualitative exploration of the local institutional structures and dynamics. The authors conclude with suggesting a switch from a mindset of "complete transformation of society" to one of making "the most of what is already present".

A positive verdict can be drawn from *Cantens* (2012) and *Pinhanez* (2012), who examine two administrative reforms with different modes of implementation. The comparison of the results appears like taken from the text book: While one reform was externally imposed in a typical 'top-down' approach and evoked classical problems of elite capture, the latter was designed internally by the concerned agencies involving low-level officers – and turned out to be successful in most criteria, up to the feeling of "increased, individual self-esteem" and even "new identity" (*Pinhanez* 2012: 322f.) for the involved tax officers.

These results provide a positive example for the effectiveness of two design aspects: Firstly, balancing the elite's propensity of rent seeking with the goal of improving domestic welfare – which is the idea of elite compatibility. Secondly, the empowerment of lower-elite beneficiaries with the aspiration of keeping up social influence, as it is also suggested by *Acemoğlu and Robinson* (2012b: 455) for triggering institutional change.

3.2.2 Between Micro and Macro Perspective: Neopatrimonialism

The term *neopatrimonialism* was coined by *Eisenstadt* (1973) and *Gellar* (1973: 403) in reference to *Weber* (1922: 679ff.). As opposed to the 'traditional' authority in *Weber's* concept, *neo*patrimonial authority rests on loyalty induced by material rewards and incentives[25]; as *van de Walle* (2012: 112) phrases it, "unlike more traditional patrimonial regimes, neopatrimonial systems rely on the fiscal resources of a modern state to provide the resources that are distributed following a clientelist logic". *Médard* (1979: 67) first applied the notion to the development context in a discussion of the state of Cameroon. The important component here is the bureaucracy, as "the system of exploitation is based both directly and indirectly on the public service" (ibid.: 71, own translation)[26]: Direct exploitation happens via fees, duties etc., indirect exploitation via mechanisms of corruption.

The neopatrimonialism branch has attracted attention from various disciplines of the development scene. Yet, the concept has often been mixed up with other terms of its own conceptual family: As *Médard* noted already in 1991, the term 'neopatrimonialism' had become "the common denominator for a range of practices that characterize political life in Africa, namely nepotism, clanism, 'tribalism', regionalism, clientelism, 'cronyism', patronage, 'prebendalism', corruption, predation, factionalism, which are based in social or economical exchange" (*Médard* 1991: 330, own translation)[27]. Indeed, without a concise insight into the details of the discussion, most of the named phenomena are hard to distinguish; in a wider sense they all focus on the mechanism of monetary resource provision in exchange for support, and usually on the basis of a hierarchical relationship between a principal and an agent, where material support flows downward, and political upward.

The result is, logically, a degradation or even failure of the public service landscape, as "leaders occupy bureaucratic offices less to perform

25 See *Bruhns* (2012) and *Bach* (2012b) for a more detailed discussion.

26 Original: "Le système d'exploitation repose directement et indirectement sur la fonction publique."

27 Original: "Le patrimonlialisme constitue le commun dénominateur de pratiques diverses si caractéristiques de la vie politique africaine, à savoir le népotisme, le clanisme, le «tribalisme», le régionalisme, le clientélisme, le «copinage», le patronage, le «prébendialisme», la corruption, la prédation, le factionnalisme, etc., qu'elles soient fondées sur l'échange social («parochial corruption») ou sur l'échange économique («market corruption»)."

public service than to acquire personal wealth and status" (*Bratton & van de Walle* 1994: 458). An important emphasis is that the phenomenon is not purely economical, but that "[t]he essence of neopatrimonialism is the award by public officials of personal favors, both within the state [...] and in society" (ibid.).[28] Because of this interweaving role, *Médard* (1979: 70) terms neopatrimonial bureaucracy the "bourgeoisie administrative"; similarly, *Acemoğlu, Ticchi and Vindigni* (2011: 177) speak of a "rich-bureaucrats coalition".

Van de Walle (2001: 16) traces the origin of the modern neopatrimonial state back to the colonial aftermath: "The political institutions following decolonialization were weak and endowed with little legitimacy. [...] state elites quickly came to rely on patronage and the distribution of economic rents in order to ensure political stability." This assessment is at one also with the historical-institutionalist research line led by *Acemoğlu et al.* (2001; 2009; 2012` see Section 4.3.1). *Acemoğlu et al.* (2011: 201) hold that neopatrimonial institutions are fairly stable once established, as it is the bureaucracy that will prevent a more efficient system in fear of losing the privilege of their rents. The elite theorists *Higley and Pakulski* (2012: 326) attribute the popularity of Marxist politics in developing countries during the cold-war period to motives of overcoming this established stability: "Many political adventurers in those countries were strongly attracted to Marxist theory because they could use it to justify their revolutionary seizure and wielding of government power."

Neopatrimonialism and ODA

It was exactly after the end of the cold-war period that the neopatrimonialism field was granted a role on the stage of the development debate; donor governments turned away from communist containment as a main motive of ODA politics (which had implied generous support for notoriously oppressive and cleptocratic authoritarian regimes[29]) and aid policies centered the needs of the recipient states. Similar to, or more accurately, in conjunction with the emerging focus on 'institutions' in the 1990s, it was

28 The 'essence' is formulated by numerous authors in the literature, varying in particularity. E.g., *Sandbrook* (2000: 59): "The essence of neopatrimonialism is the private appropriation of the state's powers." For *Bach* (2012a: 222), the essence is constituted by "dualism and hybrid patterns of interaction between patrimonial and legal-bureaucratic decision-making."

29 *Ganahl* (2013: 22) accurately titles this "Bad Governance as Foreign Policy".

quickly embraced by the development community in the realm of discussions on the quality of government (*La Porta et al.* 1999), under the keyword of 'good governance' (*World Bank* 1989: xii) as well as the vast topics associated with it, most prominently: corruption (*Shleifer & Vishny* 1993; *Mauro* 1995; *de Sardan* 1999). More recent voices such as *Booth* (2009) consider those post-cold war attempts to have mostly failed, and the confusion between the different concepts quoted above is just one illustrative of conceptual misunderstandings. *Van de Walle* (2001: 50) draws a sharp-edged conclusion:

> "Neopatrimonial rulers could not have resisted the pressure of international markets for two decades had they not had the assistance of the international community; large amounts of aid to the state, coupled with imperfect conditionality of reform program lending have allowed African governments to get away with partial reform. Similarly, aid has unwittingly undermined capacity for institution building. In sum, the peculiar evolution of the African political economy over the last twenty years has to be understood as the fruit of the marriage of neopatrimonialism and the international development business."

He denounces the fact that neopatrimonial phenomena in development practice were treated as "little more than an odd atavism, which a couple of additional 'capacity building' projects promoting greater administrative hygiene will soon entirely do away with" (ibid.: 127). Specifically, the conceptual laxity and uncritical use of 'clientelism' as a catch-all concept, as well as equating 'clientelism' and 'neopatrimonialism', have led to distorted outcomes, in his view.

Two Types of Clientelism

In a later publication, *van de Walle* (2012) argues that clientelism is a feature which is "essential and ubiquitous" (ibid.: 123) also in democracies, and that it is not the presence or absence of clientelistic features, but instead the distinct *type* of clientelism that will vary with the nature of the political regime. Thus, it is important to distinguish these two main types:

- *Elite clientelism:* As the term suggests, this is strictly limited to the small group of elite members. The dominant mechanism is *prebendalism*, which is the "strategic political allocation of public offices to key elites, granting personal access over state resources" (ibid.: 114). This is a popular form for authoritarian states that feature limited capacities and are resource-poor.

- *Mass clientelism:* In this form state resources are used to assign jobs and services to political clienteles. The resources are dispensed as patronage, defined as "the political instrumentalization of the distribution of public jobs and services" (ibid.: 114), and commonly involving party-organizational structures as well as electoral politics. Because of the volume of resources that systematic patronage involves, this form of clientelism requires a larger, 'healthy' state. As such, mass clientelism is also associated with western democracies.

The following table shows a comparative overview of the features of both forms.[30]

Table 3-2: Differences between elite and mass clientelism

	Key Mechanism	Dispersed by	Legality	Implication for Central State	Relationship to Democracy	Relationship to Economy
Elite Clientelism	Prebends	Presidential Network	Illegal	Undermines state capacity, legitimacy	Incompatible	Negative; undermines property rights
Mass Clientelism	Patronage	Political party	Gray area	Bias for larger state	Compatible	Depends on quality of state interventions

Source: adapted from *van de Walle* (2012: 117)

Van de Walle emphasizes that in the past, the typical African states mainly featured patterns of elite clientelism and hence prebendalism, and not patronage. Such states are non-responsive to their citizens and explicitly strive to limit non-elite participation, while, in his view, patronage does not need to be counter-indicative for effectiveness and responsiveness of the state apparatus. He concludes that, it should be considered that features of mass clientelism indicate a development away from neopatrimonial structures towards more democratic institutions. Consequently, for a successful transition of political structures, it is important to shift the focus

30 *Van de Walle* (2012: 114) provides the following rule-of-thumb illustration: "Hiring a member of one's ethnic group to a senior position in the customs office is an example of patronage. Allowing the customs officer to use the position for personal enrichment by manipulating import and export taxes is an example of a prebend."

away from an increase or decline of political corruption, and towards a change of its functions and forms.

Although *van de Walle's* analysis provides enlightening input in an environment of often uncritically applied buzzwords, empirics show that the mixed and intense forms of elite and mass clientelism which are present in many ODA recipient countries pose a great deal of challenges – and would hardly evoke feelings of delight when there is 'only' patronage present and not prebends. Additionally, neopatrimonial structures seem to not necessarily create ineffective public administration: E.g., in a comparative study that included Argentina, Venezuela, Indonesia, the Philippines, Kenya and Zambia, *von Soest, Bechle and Korte* (2011) find that the capability to raise tax revenue did not relate to the extent of neopatrimonial characteristics of the state.

As a final remark, the selectiveness of *van de Walle's* concept (that he himself acknowledges to be not as sharp in practice) is blurred even further when aid is introduced into the game: The substantial share of inward-flowing aid in the states' budgets affect the 'state capacity' variable, and thus may exert a similar effect as a natural resource (see Section 4.3.2.2). *Gibson et al.* (2005: 179) highlight how "development aid from abroad is often seen as a resource for patronage".

3.2.3 The Macro Perspective: Leaders and Growth

The discourse about the influence of elites on development is connected to the notion that for rapid economic development, authoritarian rule is advantageous over democracy, since (among other arguments) it enables a political leader to implement policy decisions that are unpopular but needed for development, without having to face voters' feedback[31,32]. Consequently, democracy should be 'postponed' until economic growth has transformed society. Specifically, the leadership of China, Singapore or early South Korea are subjects of frequent credit for their "substantial

31 This is also termed the *Lee thesis* in political science (coined by *Sen* 1999: 15; see, e.g., *Knutsen* 2010), as it was a popular statement of Singapore's first prime minister *Lee Kuan Yew*. It is a close relative to *Rostow's* stage theory (1960).

32 Other popular reasonings are the weakness of democratic structures against participatory pressures of popular demands, and the financial inefficiency of democratic households, as politicians allocate budgets to measures that increase their popularity for re-election (see *Doucouliagos & Ulubaşoğlu* 2008: 63, also for literature siding with the democracy or autocracy views).

contribution to their societies" (*Sah* 1991: 71). *Jones and Olken* (2005: 862) contend that democracy "might also have constrained the successful economic policies" in Singapore and China. Recently, the 'successes' of Rwanda or Ethiopia were added to the list (cf. *Provost* 2014; *Kushkush* 2015). Popular voices such as *Sachs* (2005) also support the idea.

The effect of the political regime type on economic growth has been examined and discussed extensively (see *Doucouliagos and Ulubaşoğlu* [2008] for a literature review), yielding inconclusive results. One of the reasons may well be the application of the term 'democracy': E.g., a high share of African countries which are labeled 'democratic' are *façade* democracies in reality, and instead more aptly fall into categories such as "competitive authoritarian" or "hegemonial electoral authoritarian", as suggested by *Diamond* (2010: xxvi). A recent study by *Masaki and van de Walle* (2014) accounts for this labeling problem and replaces the usual binary democracy variable with an ordinally scaled variable derived from the Polity IV dataset. Consequently, they find results opposing the *Lee thesis*: democracy has positive effects on growth – at least in the long run after a transition. This concurs with earlier results as well, such as *Winters* (2010)[33].

In terms of actual research on the influence of the group of *elites* on growth, the literature is more manageable. A study explicitly focused on this topic is *Jones and Olken* (2005). To account for the fact that changes in leadership are usually not exogenous but potentially driven also by the economic situation, they use "deaths of leaders while in office" to source exogenous variation in leadership. They find a strong relationship between change in leaders and growth changes, but this effect is restricted to autocratic regimes, whereas it is missing for regimes with political parties present. They interpret this result as "support for the Weberian hypothesis that leaders matter when institutions are weak" (ibid.: 858).

Besley, Montalvo and Reynal-Querol (2011) follow the above survey and investigate whether a leader's level of education affects the rate of economic growth. They extend the dataset back to 1875 and confirm both the effect of leadership change on growth change as well as leaders' education on growth. Curiously, they even find an effect of an uneducated

33 An interesting twist to the democracy-vs.-growth discourse is introduced by the question whether more democratic *donors* will be more development oriented (*Faust* 2008). The relevance of this question is driven by the allegation of China's ODA activities to solely represent measures of securing access to natural resources – which is debated (*Tull* 2006; *Bräutigam & Xiaoyang* 2011; *Bräutigam & Ekman* 2012).

leader following an uneducated leader (education in this case referring to college graduation).

Easterly and Pennings (2014) criticize the measured incident in *Jones' and Olken's* study to be extremely rare (only 57 incidents in 50 years across 100 countries), and take a new attempt, based on four different datasets. After controlling for country effects and autocorrelated errors, they find the effect of changes in autocratic leaders on changes in growth to be negligible, with substantially higher growth volatility for autocrats over democratic regimes (which is commonly agreed). In their interpretation (ibid.: Section 7), they hint to two problems that authoritarian leaders face and that support the results:

- Principal-agent problems during carrying out growth-promoting orders are not likely to be less difficult than in other organizational forms.
- The knowledge problem of getting accurate information on obstacles and opportunities from the lower levels is substantial.

They conclude to have found "little reason to believe in 'great men' – either benevolent or malevolent – driving the growth process"[34].

3.3 Summary

The actual relationship between political leaders and economical growth in ODA recipient countries is debated. While some studies find a connection, the most recent, based on four different data sets, clearly rejects this hypothesis. A larger part of the literature explores the connection of regime type and growth, and while there is a long history of discourse about the benefit of authoritarian structures for rapid growth, latest research indicates this effect to not hold true. The narrative of the benevolent authoritarian leader would thus be refuted.

As a large majority of ODA recipient countries are forms of authoritarian regimes, the most central issue in the quest for development generation is the *elite's incentive conflict*. This had already been discussed in the 1950s when the UN released their first development paper, but has not substantially changed the concept of aid provision: It is the dilemma that the elite's incentives are opposing development, both when they pursue

34 The so-called "great men" hypothesis is the interpretation that the evolution of history is largely determined by only a small number of important influential individuals.

actions to *extract rents* from their position, and actions to *secure* their position. In this situation, promoting development always implies empowering the masses and weaker groups that could endanger the own position. But an elite that benefits from social disparity between themselves and the masses (termed the *elite-mass gap*), is consequently inclined to perpetuate it.

Apart from this motivational component, the elite-mass gap also includes an informational component, the knowledge (or rather: ignorance) about poverty. Empirical research on poverty perceptions by the elite confirms this: In general, poverty is often not perceived as a real problem – even if the quantitative dimensions are usually very accurately guessed, the implications of poverty on livelihood are not present, and this is specifically true for rural poverty. On top, responsibility for poverty is often attributed to the poor themselves. These phenomena are, with some variations, rather consistent across different cultures and geographical zones.

Another common pattern is that local elites seem to show a higher propensity to promote pro-poor policies than national elites. This is attributed to the more direct involvement with their supporters.

Neopatrimonialism, a concept from political science, has provided cues for better understanding and categorizing phenomena of securing and extracting elite positions. It is argued that theoretically, patronage should be a positive indicator over prebendalism, as patronage requires higher state capacity. In the context of ODA, however, this logic is diluted, as allocated aid budgets become a resource for extraction, thus implying that patronage may well be possible even with a low state capacity.

An example of extractive actions of the elite position is the phenomenon of *elite capture*, the appropriation of (originally) public goods. One attempt to address this issue is the stronger involvement of the actual target group in the project design stage, so-called *community-based approaches* that work with the principle of *participation*. In practice, though, this often seems to simply push the problem to the lower level of the project environment – instead of empowering the beneficiaries, existing local elite structures are strengthened.

Evidence seems to suggest that perverse outcomes of community-based approaches are not due to an unrealistic institutional logic of the concept itself, but to uncritical or 'superficial' implementation; the intervention in an existing social structure seems to be a venture of higher complexity than often assumed. But empirics also show that simply bypassing the elites is not a solution. Instead, a thorough exploration of the respective institutional structures is needed to avoid perverse outcomes. Apart from a large amount of research discussing the failures, there are also studies that document the possible successes – some of which might be ‘windfall profits’, others, however, most likely due to the rigorous adaption of the implemented design. While technically, these results are just indicative, they make a good case for the need of elite compatible project designs in order to achieve the desired outcomes.

Chapter 4 Theoretical Foundation of the 'Elite Compatibility' Concept: Incentives and Incentive Compatibility

As explained in the second chapter, the term 'elite compatibility' can be understood as more specific variant of incentive compatibility from NIE, reduced to the target group of elites. The following sections shall provide a brief overview of the origin of the incentive concept (4.1; 4.2), and then discuss the role of incentives and institutions in the context of ODA (4.3).

4.1 Theoretical and Conceptual Origin

Adam Smith

It is common consent that any historical overview in economics has to start with the work of *Adam Smith* (1776). While *Simon* (1997: 5) considers *The Wealth of Nations* "not the internal world of the mind, but the external world of production and trade"[1], and comments that "within his framework, Smith has no occasion to treat human choice or decision making in any formal way", he still states that "[e]verything that psychology has learned about the processes of human choice is consistent with the view expressed by Adam Smith. (…) Their rationality is a procedural rationality" (ibid.: 8).

In one of the more recent standard volumes on the theory of incentives, *Laffont and Martimort* (2001: 8) show how *Smith* had implicitly already encompassed the phenomenon of incentives in his chapter *On the Wages of Labour*, having "recognized the contractual nature of the relationship between the masters and the workmen". However, his treatment was only implicit and rather unspecific. Most importantly, as the authors remark, *Smith* did not capture "the fundamental trade-off between incentives and the distribution of the gains from trade" (ibid.: 10). Despite all, as (1987: 49) point out, *Smith's* construct of the "invisible hand", the claim that individual pursuit of self-interest might serve the interest of society, may

1 In the contrary, *Reinert* (2007: 21ff., 40) exactly opposes this view. Cf. also *Buchanan* (1987).

easily be seen as a relative of the concept of incentives and incentive compatibility (see Section 4.2).

Chester Barnard

As an explicit object of research, the origin of incentives is often attributed to *Chester Barnard* and his work *The Functions of the Executive* (1938), in which he laid the foundations for a theory of incentives that would quickly serve as the basis for successive refinement by other researchers. *Barnard* noted:

> "The contributions of personal efforts which constitute the energies of organizations are yielded by individuals because of incentives. The egotistical motives of self-preservation and of self-satisfaction are dominating forces; on the whole, organizations can exist only when consistent with the satisfaction of these motives, unless, alternatively, they can change these motives. The individual is always the basic strategic factor in organization. Regardless of his history or his obligations he must be induced to coöperate, or there can be no coöperation. [...]
>
> Inadequate incentives mean dissolution, or changes of organization purpose, or failure of co-operation." (1938: 139)

He already differentiated between two types of incentives: those that are specific and can be offered to an individual (which he calls "specific inducements"), and those that cannot specifically offered because they are impersonal ("general incentives"). With his further specification of the limited influence of material incentives beyond physiological necessities (ibid.: 143), and his insight of the influence of opportunities for distinction, prestige and personal power (ibid.: 145), he also anticipated the basic idea behind *Maslow's* (1943) *hierarchy of needs*.

Herbert Simon

Another main protagonist in the development of incentive theory, already quoted at the beginning of this section, was organizational theorist *Herbert Simon,* starting with the *incentive-contribution theory* (*Simon* 1947), which was explicitly (ibid.: foreword) inspired by *Barnard's* work, and was later expanded by *March and Simon* (1958).

Historically, *Simon's* contribution to NIE can be seen as relatively substantial. *Wagner-Tsukamoto* (2003: 98) comments that *Simon* "could have anticipated Williamson's new institutional economics, if he had addressed various issues that conceptually plagued inducement-contribution analysis," namely the theory's focus on individual behavior and neglect of modeling interdependence of social interactions. Furthermore, "Simon did not progress beyond the aggregation logic of neoclassic economics" (ibid.: 99), since inducement-contribution analysis did not account for a nonzero-sum model of social interactions, and instead "aggregated outcomes of organizational behavior by merely adding up contributions and inducements of individual organization members". (It is, in fact, this methodological individualism that *Olson* (1965) criticized with his extension of the incentive-contribution theory; see Section 4.2.)

Bounded Rationality

Another major contribution of *Simon* is the concept of bounded rationality, which he already discussed implicitly in his early work on the incentive-contribution theory[2]. It was not until 1957 when *Simon* stated that "the concept of 'economic man' is in need of fairly drastic revision" (1957: 241), and suggested to replace it with the concept now known as bounded rationality[3]. The goal was to eliminate the complete-information assumption of the rational choice model, that implied both complete access to all information available as well as complete processing of that information, i.e., attaching concrete probabilities and payoffs to choice options. *Simon's* criticism quickly sparked the famous debate with *Milton Friedman* on the relevance of realistic assumptions for economic models. From today's perspective, the Friedman-Simon dispute is considered a classic, and yet has been continued ever since; a famous critical discussion is, e.g., *Musgrave* (1981); for a review in German, see *Erlei, Leschke and Sauerland* (2007: 10ff.).

The common reception of the bounded-rationality concept has not been unproblematic, both within the theoretical discourse[4], as well as outside,

2 He hints on "limits on [the] ability to *make correct decisions*" (1945: 39, emphasis in the original), and sees skills, values, and knowledge as limits that may "bound the area of rationality" (1945: 41).

3 In the original article, *Simon* refers to it as "'limited' rationality" (1957: 255).

4 Within the incentives discourse, one of the prominent controversies is whether the limitation is supposed to be perceived as a deficit in skillfulness (*Langlois* 1990: 691), resulting in a trade-off between effort and accuracy of the decision (*Payne, Bettman & Johnson* 1993) or there is a less-is-more effect in the sense that at a

where the utility-maximizing assumption is a notorious target of critique. E.g., the (economists') Resourceful, Evaluative, Maximizing Model (REMM) as discussed by *Jensen and Meckling* (1994)[5] triggered a sociologist's article titled "Dear Economists, Please Stop Talking About Human Nature" (*Hirschman* 2008) – a notion which is not unlikely to represent a feeling common among non-economists.[6]

There is one very large misconception about the rationality assumption in popular criticism that goes unnoticed surprisingly often: the perception that by assuming rationality, this would be a normative statement about human behavior. Firstly, rationality in the economical sense does not stand for the popular definition of the term, but simply for a fulfillment of the postulates of completeness, reflexivity, and transitivity of preferences. Secondly, instead of a normative statement, the rationality assumption can rather be understood as a 'starting point' from which diverging, (seemingly) non-rational behavior shall be explained. In other words: Rather than explaining cooperative behavior simply by assuming a certain type of altruism (and thus, delivering no explanation but simply adapting the assumptions and making the argument tautological), it is the assumption of rationality that allows for the more interesting question: Which factors could make it attractive to cooperate even under the condition that the individuals are only acting in their very own interest? The rationality assumption thus provides a 'worst case' in the spirit of *Hume* or *Mill*[7] and makes the finding more 'resilient'. This goes for normative (prescriptive) research in a mechanism-design sense of the question formulated above,

certain point, "additional information becomes detrimental, independent of costs" (*Gigerenzer & Brighton* 2011: 5).

5 Going back to *Meckling* (1976).

6 For a slightly aged, but insightful overview on the debate of economics vs. psychology, see the miscellany of *Hogarth and Reder* (1987).

7 *Hume* (1741/1903: 40) states: "Political writers have established it as a maxim, that, in contriving any system of government, and fixing the several checks and controls of the constitution, every man ought to be supposed a knave, and to have no other end, in all his actions, than private interest." At the same time he relativizes this as a precautionary principle for public goods: "[…] though, at the same time, it appears somewhat strange, that a maxim should be true in *politics* which is false in *fact.* […] men are generally more honest in their private than in their public capacity […]" (ibid.: 42)
A similar point is made by *Mill* (1861/1977: 505): "[…] the very principle of constitutional government requires it to be assumed that political power will be abused to promote the particular purposes of the holder; not because it always is so, but because such is the natural tendency of things to guard against which is the especial use of free institutions."

and the same is true for positive research interest, i.e.: For what reason could a *seemingly* irrational (*Barnard* 1938: xiii) behavior actually be rational for the individual? It is this methodical twist of the rationality assumption that makes the research worthwhile at all – in these cases.

One key point to this is that the economical influence of individual behavior, as it happens in microeconomics, does not focus on manipulating the *content* of utility functions, but rather the constraints, and it is in this aspect that infamous articles like that of *Stigler and Becker* (1977) seem to have been misunderstood by some[8]. Nevertheless, the concept has its limitations when it comes to explaining behavior; the key point, though, is that these limitations are not induced because of the rationality constraint itself, but because of the limited exogenous variables taken into account for predicting the criterion (behavior); such as prices and income in the article quoted above.

Apart from the debates that revolve around the rationality concept, bounded rationality can be (and is) considered one of the bases of new institutional economics, as sketched out in the next section.

4.2 Incentives in New Institutional Economics

As outlined above, there is a close linkage between the concepts of bounded rationality and incentives. When NIE was 'born' with the introduction of transaction costs by *Coase* (1937)[9], with an article "much cited and little used"[10], as he himself commented later (1972: 62f.), bounded rationality had already been implied by *Coase* – at least according to *Williamson*, who considers it "the cognitive assumption on which transaction cost economics relies" (1985: 45). When *Coase's* paper was finally 'used' in *Williamson's* publication that also coined the term 'new institutional economics' (1975: 1), *Williamson* consequently included the bounded

8 *Becker* was the first economist to apply economic analysis to a myriad of choice situations previously not associated with the field, such as discrimination (1957), crime (1968), or even marriage (1973). Acceptance among colleagues was mixed; the famous article *The Economics of Brushing Teeth* (*Blinder* 1974) was a parody with reference to *Becker's* work.

9 The term 'New Institutional Economics' was not intended to position NIE as a chronological successor of 'old' Institutional Economics. For a comparison and more detailed discussion of 'old' institutional economics, cf. *Rutherford* (2001), or in German *Reuter* (1994); for a historical overview cf. *Scott* (2014: chap. 1&2), or in German *Erlei et al.* (2007: 26ff.).

10 *Williamson* saw the reason for this in the article's tautological character (1975: 3).

rationality approach explicitly: He advanced *Coase's* concept of transaction costs by operationalizing it and specifying two conditions that would increase transaction costs: the (missing) availability of alternative exchange partners – while those partners available expose opportunistic behavior (ibid.: 9, 26ff.) –, and an increasing complexity and uncertainty – thus confronting the boundedly rational behavior of the individual (1975: 21ff.).

On the map of NIE[11], the explicit treatment of incentives is the subject of *principal-agent theory*, although incentives lie at the very core of NIE in general, as the common focus is the analysis of institutions in their property as incentives, which shape human behavior[12]. Since the concept of this survey adopts the concept of incentive compatibility from agency theory, the following will provide a brief overview of the history and the concept itself.

Principal-Agent Theory

Ironically, as opposed to transaction cost theory, the original agency-theory perspective assumes full rationality of the actors. The concept of incentives, nevertheless, is a direct consequence of asymmetric information and transaction costs, simply in the sense that upon introduction of information asymmetry, the optimization problem becomes nontrivial (see page 116). In the works that mark the historical path of agency theory, incentives were always a key issue, albeit the focus varied:

- The first treatment of the separation of management and ownership, which is the basis for principal-agent relationships, is often attributed to *Berle and Means* (1932: Chap. VI, particularly).
- *Samuelson's* article (1954) discussed the behavior pattern of an agent in public goods settings to "cheat" by not revealing true preferences and instead misrepresenting his true characteristics with false signals.
- The idea of *Berle and Means* was picked up by *Williamson* (1963) – although he does not explicitly refer to it; his article on the self-

11 For different taxonomies of the various fields of NIE, cf. *Erlei et al.* (2007: 41ff.), *Furubotn and Richter* (2005: 36ff.) or *Voigt* (2009: 45ff.).

12 Following *North's* popular definition of institutions as "the rules of the game in a society" and "humanly devised constraints that shape human interaction" and "structure incentives in human exchange, whether political, social, or economic" (1990: 3). For a critique and discussion, see, e.g., *Hodgson* (2006: 8).

interest motives of managers can be seen as an early description of the principal-agent problem.

- *Arrow's* model of *moral hazard* (1963) that he discovered as an insurance problem, was a consequence of information asymmetry issues, and would later serve as the basis for principal-agent theory.
- *Olson* (1965) criticized the methodological-individualistic perspective of the time (57) – which *Simon's* incentive-contribution theory was also part of; see above –, and in that way expanded incentive-contribution theory with his *Logic of Collective Action*.
- When *Akerlof* (1970) described the phenomenon of *adverse selection,* he in effect extended the opportunism pattern from a post-contractual phenomenon (moral hazard) to pre-contractual situations.
- *Ross* (1973) first formulated the agency theory, by taking up the moral hazard dilemma and elevating it to a more general context of "The Principal's Problem".
- Additional insight came from *Spence* (1973; 1974), who proposed signaling as a solution to the incentive problem in adverse selection, and *Stiglitz* (1975) who summed up earlier research into the theory of screening.
- *Holmström* (1982) combined the principal-agent approach and the free-rider problem in his team approach with one principal but multiple agents and showed how incentives, rather than monitoring, can solve the problem completely.

Meanwhile, agency theory can be differentiated into pre- and postcontractual informational problems (see Figure 4-1). In the case of post-contractual risk (moral hazard), the required incentives have the function of sharing of this risk; in the case of pre-contractual risk, their function is to induce honesty as the best option for the agent.

Notable extensions to agency theory include, among others, *Shleifer's* findings on incentive schemes based on relative performance (1985); the framework of *Bernheim and Whinston* (1985) for the analysis of one agent and multiple principals, also termed *common agency*; the analysis of collusion in larger hierarchies and the role of group incentives by *Tirole* (1986); and *Holmström and Milgrom*, who developed the multitasks principal-agent theory (1991; 1994). For a more extensive overview on the literature in principal-agent theory, see *Furubotn and Richter* (2005: 271ff.) and the recommended literature, especially *Worrall* (1990) and *Hart and Holmström* (1987), as well as *Rasmusen* (2007: 179ff.).

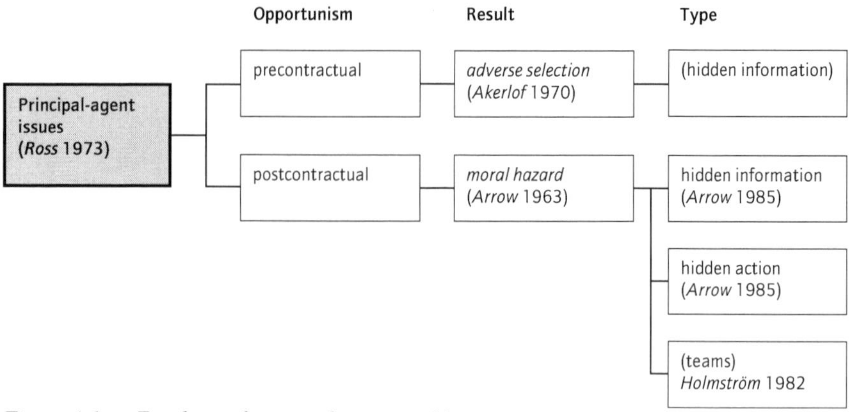

Figure 4-1: Typology of principal-agent problems

The research on the principal-agent model is vast and the theoretical discussion of the problem does get very formal and specific, mostly due to the high number of unrealistic constraints in the basic setting[13], the relaxation of which successively increases complexity. The core of the approach, however, can be reduced to a simple thought: given a hierarchical structure, the issue of a principal designing an incentive scheme to motivate the agent to act in the interests of the principal. Incentive schemes are applied by the agent as "a rule that specifies, in advance, the [principal's] behavior on the basis of his perceptions of agents' information and actions" (*Laffont & Maskin* 1982: 32). In the different branches of NIE, the term 'incentive structure' is replaced with expressions which hint to the respective context, but represent the same idea; 'contract', 'mechanism' (*Groves & Ledyard* 1987: 48), 'information structure' (*Hurwicz* 1973: 20), 'voting scheme' or 'game form' (see *Laffont & Maskin* 1982: 88). In all cases, an incentive scheme or structure is, "in effect, a promise by the planner to react in a specified way to what agents do or reveal" (ibid.: 88).

The design and choice of an incentive scheme becomes nontrivial and hence an object of research when the assumption of perfect information of the participants is given up and asymmetric information is possible. Consequently, a condition is required that will induce cooperative behavior and revealing of the true preferences of the agent; this condition is *incen-*

13 E.g., risk aversion of the actors, one good, costless contract enforcement, completeness of contract, full commitment to the contract (no renegotiation), one-shot game; see *Sappington* (1991) for an introductory overview and *Laffont and Martimort* (2001) for a more exhaustive discussion.

tive compatibility. In order for an institution to accomplish its desired goal in a group, it *requires* to be incentive compatible (see *Ledyard* 2008: 159).

Incentive compatibility

In the quest for setting institutions correctly, *incentive compatibility* is a central concept. It had already been outlined in *Barnard's* original work[14]:

> "A person can and will accept a communication as authoritative only when (…), *at the time of his decision*, he believes it to be compatible with his personal interest as a whole. (…) The existence of a net inducement is the only reason for accepting *any* order as having authority." (1938: 165f., emphasis in the original)

Hurwicz, who is considered to be the 'founder' of mechanism-design theory, coined the concept of incentive compatibility in the context of his public goods treatment (1972: 320)[15] to denote mechanisms for which "participants in the process would not find it advantageous to violate rules of the process" (*Ledyard* 2008: 158). In more general terms, incentive compatibility induces a *self-interest in cooperative behavior* for the agent. In principal-agent theory, incentive compatibility has been adopted as a constraint in the maximization aspiration of the principal. Formally, the idea is represented as follows[16]. Given the maximization function of the principal:

$$U = \beta + \alpha e - \frac{r}{2}\alpha^2\sigma^2 - C(e)$$

where

$\beta + \alpha e$ represents the expectancy value of the compensation (comprised of a fixed part and a part that varies with the output),

$\alpha^2\sigma^2$ the variance of the compensation[17],

---

14 Similar to this is the equilibrium that *Barnard* (1938: 58) describes: "The coöperative system must create a surplus of satisfaction to be efficient. If each man gets back only what he puts in, there is no incentive, that is, no net satisfaction for him in coöperation. What he gets back must give him advantage in terms of satisfaction; which almost always means return in a different form from that which he contributes."

15 Earlier mentioning of the term goes back to *Hurwicz* (1960: 28).

16 This taxonomy follows *Erlei et al.* (2007: 112ff.), for a different presentation, cf., e.g., *Laffont* (2005: 45ff.).

17 See *Erlei et al.* (2007: 112f.) for an explanation.

$\frac{r}{2}$ the risk aversion measure[18],

and $C(e)$ the costs of the efforts of the agent.

The incentive compatibly condition then is as follows:

$$\beta + \alpha e - \frac{r}{2}\alpha^2\sigma^2 - C(e) \geq \beta + \alpha e' - \frac{r}{2}\alpha^2\sigma^2 - C(e')$$

Most trivially, this implies nothing more than that the effort *e* chosen by the agent generates a higher utility than all other possible effort levels e' (*Erlei et al.* 2007: 114). In other words, the action that the principal demands from the agent has to generate at least as much return as every other possible action, and the gains for the individual are higher from cooperation. This is why *Varian* (1992: 460) calls the incentive-compatibility conditions 'self-selection constraints' in the ex-ante case.

One important specification here is that incentive compatibility does *not* imply the first-best solution for the agent, nor does it convey any statement on social desirability of the outcome. Thus, it is not necessarily fully compatible with the goals of the agent, but compatible with the principal's goal of the agent's cooperation – with the principal. An example of an incentive-compatible setting that is disadvantageous for the agent is the *prisoner's dilemma*[19], where the incentive-scheme induced cooperation with the principal means turning down cooperation on the other agent and results in an outcome advantageous for the principal, but not the agents. Another very practical example is *second-degree price discrimination*, as applied in the product design of a large array of everyday products. Incentive compatibility here ensures that the provider of a good can extract higher rents[20] from consumers that have a higher valuation for the product, or, capturing the practical application more precisely: the willingness to pay a higher price. The key factor is to differentiate the designs in the product line in such a way that transferability of demand of consumers of the higher valuation levels to the lower levels is avoided. I.e., incentive compatible product design ensures that a professional photographer will buy the 7,000-Euro camera and not the 700-Euro consumer model of the same brand, it will drive the company-paid business traveller towards the

---

18 See *Erlei et al.* (2007: 106f.) for an explanation.

19 The first written description appears to have been *Albert W. Tucker* (1950), according to *Straffin* (1983: 229).

20 The original term of this type of price discrimination refers to the monopolist situation (*Pigou* 1920/1932: 275ff., 279). However, this mechanism can be observed as a standard in many of today's polypolist markets – the term 'rent' is then not a monopoly rent.

premium fare that is more than twice as expensive as the tourist fare, and a coffee-shop visitor with a higher propensity to spend will buy a drink that has only marginally higher input cost but sells at a substantially higher price[21]. In all these examples, to say it with the words of *Miravete* (2008), "price discrimination becomes a mechanism-design problem where a non-linear tariff, charging a different unit price for each unit sold, maximizes the expected profits of the monopolist, while ensuring incentive compatibility."

Obviously, this general principle can be applied to pretty much any optimization problem, hence also to those specific to interest groups such as elites. E.g., as already described in Chapter 2, *Acemoğlu and Robinson* (2006: 161ff.) use the incentive-compatibility constraint for formulating the elite's commitment problem: Incentive compatibility for the elites in this case is a factor for a political promise to be credible to the citizens. It implies that there are incentives not to deviate from their promise in the future, either because deviation is less profitable, or because it will entail severe punishment. The credibility aspect again emphasizes one of the vital features of incentive compatibility, as already pointed out above: From the perspective of the agent, an incentive-compatible alternative really *is* the optimal alternative.

Incentives from Goods' Characteristics

While in the principal-agent situations discussed above, the incentive problems originate from diverging interests in a hierarchical relationship of two actors, the other major source for incentive issues that is treated in NIE is a good's characteristics of how its utility is acquired in a social setting. The differentiation into the types of public goods (*Samuelson* 1954; 1955), common-pool resources (*Gordon* 1954), club goods (*Buchanan* 1965) and private goods on the dimensions of consumption excludability and subtractability also indirectly classifies their incentive properties. *Ostrom and Ostrom* (1977) suggested to replace the term "club goods" as coined by Buchanan with *toll goods*, arguing that this type is provided both by private and public associations, and changed the criterion of consumption rivalry to subtractability of use (see Figure 4-2).

21 The latter example is explained in the excellent non-scientific treatment by *Harford* (2012: 33ff.). For a more in-depth survey of the topic see *Varian* (2010: 465ff.), or *Laffont, Maskin and Rochet* (1987).

Subtractability →		
	common-pool resources (*Gordon* 1954)	private goods
	public goods (*Samuelson* 1954)	club/toll goods (*Buchanan* 1965; *Ostrom & Ostrom* 1977)

Excludability →

Figure 4-2: Goods' characteristics typology
Source: adapted from *Erlei et al.* (2007: 345)

All social dilemmas associated with the goods characteristics, such as *Olson's* collective action problems and free riding (1965: 76) or *Hardin's* 'neomalthusian' *tragedy of the commons* (1968) are a result of the incentives from those properties: The common denominator for social dilemmas is that the individual player's pursuit of his own gain corrupts the outcome of the collective action. As *Green and Shapiro* (1994: 72) eloquently sum it up, social dilemmas arise "when people have opportunities to get something for nothing".

The issues in (general) collective-action and (specific) common-pool resources situations are relatives in the way that in collective action, individual input is required and not incentivized, while with common-pool resources, it is the individual's action that is to be avoided but is incentivized. Thus, the common-pool resource (CPR) problem could be seen as an inverse problem of the regular collective action situation. The key to the incentive problem is always the broken link between contribution and consumption, as seen most extremely in the free-rider case: If there is no possibility of linking the two, the incentive for free riding is high.

As demonstrated by *Ostrom* (1990) for common-pool resources, institutional designs to circumvent social dilemmas exist (see *Ostrom* 2007a: 253 for references to empirical studies). As with the incentive-compatibility definition, the term 'solution' always depends on the perspective; the previously mentioned classical *prisoners' dilemma*, for instance, may be understood as an institutional design to solve the underlying problem of the police – in the form of inducing a dilemma situation for the prisoners.

Ultimately, the incentive problems from goods' characteristics always reduce to the problem of opportunity cost: a commitment to contribution is only relevant if it is credible for the other players, and credibility is only reached if there is (some form of) accountability for the players, i.e., costs of whatever type in case of default. This is the previously mentioned credibility-of-commitment problem, as discussed by *Acemoğlu and Robinson* (2006: ch. 5), which in fact goes back to *North and Weingast* (1989). As will be explained in more detail, it is an important issue in the context of ODA provision, linking to the problem of the *broken feedback loop* treated in Section 4.3.2.

Also, the incentive effects that derive from goods' characteristics are especially important in the context of politics, as the functioning of a political system depends on the reciprocal contribution to this 'system' and many of the involved resources and taken actions become public goods (e.g., property rights) or common-pool resources: E.g., any limited resource that a politician has at his or her disposal 'becomes' a common-pool resource among those who have access to it. This is why *Ostrom* (2007a: 246) states that a "crucial problem in obtaining public goods and common-pool resources relates to the provision of the good rather than to the production of the good." In connection with ODA provision, these effects are specifically relevant in the context of patronage politics and elite capture, as will be clear in the next section.

4.3 The Role of Incentives and Institutions in ODA

It is rather tautological to state that incentives are important for ODA, as they are by definition responsible for actions, and form behavior. The decisive question is whether or not processes are analyzed with a *focus* on the incentive properties of the institutional setup, in other words, whether one puts on the right 'reading glasses'.

The role of NIE in the development discourse is rather ambivalent; on the one hand there are voices that "during the past 20 years, virtually no economic theory has had as great of an impact as New Institutional Economics" (*Lepenies* 2009: 2, own translation)[22]. However, the explicit attention that NIE has received in ODA research is surprisingly modest. In the sentence following the quote above, the author adds: "And rarely has a theory also driven [ODA] project development so noticeably, *without one*

22 Original: "Wohl kaum eine ökonomische Theorie hat in den letzten 20 Jahren so stark Einfluss auf die EZ genommen wie die Neue Institutionenökonomik."

always being aware of it"[23] (ibid., emphasis added). Indeed, the popular concepts and buzzwords that circulate in ODA documents include many that seem to have been adopted from NIE. Terms like 'institution building' or 'governance structures' clearly point towards the theory, and claims about the supposed importance of institutions are rather widespread; the statements "Institutions, institutions, institutions!" and "Institutions matter!"[24] are on the list of *bon mots* frequently encountered in the multitude of concept papers, mission statements, progress reports and similar publications. The starting point for this trend can be seen in the publications by *North* (1981; 1990) in which he discussed the importance of institutions for economical performance, and it was most notably two *World Bank* publications which introduced the subject of institutions and incentives to mainstream ODA (*World Bank* 1997b; *Burki & Perry* 1998).

However, while there seems to exist a declared consent about the importance of 'institutions', practice shows that it is exactly the institutional aspects of ODA that account for a rather respectable share of the problems of the system. This apparent paradox is explained by the fact that the discourse happens on two different perspectives:

1. The first perspective is focused on the impact of 'institutions' on the 'development' of a country, and is part of the normative discourse of what works in development. The normative claim or implication of this movement is the need for institutional reform (or policy reform, cf. *Martens* 2002a: 16) in the recipient countries in order to advance economical development. In this sense, this can be viewed as the macro-institutional perspective.
2. The second is the neo-institutional approach of analyzing incentive situations between actors, and can be seen as a micro-institutional perspective. The term "micro" does not imply a focus on the lower levels, as an analysis under incentive aspects can be applied to actors on all levels.

The differentiation into a macro and a micro perspective does not relate to macro- or micro*economics*, or to macro- vs. micro*development* (*Rodrik* 2009: 24), but to the manner how the concept of 'institutions' is utilized. The macro- and microinstitutional perspectives point to separate research

23 Original: "Und selten hat eine Theorie auch so merklich auf die Ebene der Projektbearbeitung durchgeschlagen, ohne dass man sich dessen immer bewusst ist."

24 The origins of these lines are not easily identified, but the second phrase seems to be based on *North's* (1990: 12) statement: "The most important message, one with profound implications for restructuring economic theory, is that when it is costly to transact, institutions matter."

interests: Although based on the same theoretical foundation, the quest for whether (and which) "institutions matter" for development is an entirely different field from the analysis of incentive setups. While the latter is a specific toolkit for examining interaction situations, the former is part of the effectiveness discourse of "what works" in development assistance, a discussion that includes both macroeconomic and microeconomic approaches and many more aspects than just "institutions". This explains the gap between the respectable amount of publications on the topic of "institutions" on the one side, while on the other side, actual in-depth analyses in an incentive-focused NIE perspective are not exactly a mass phenomenon. Since the two levels are theoretically connected, indeed sometimes even used interchangeably and not differentiated, both perspectives' discourses shall be briefly discussed in the following.

4.3.1 Institutions and Development: Challenges of the Macro-Institutional Perspective

The claim that "institutions matter" refers to the highest and most abstract level of the discourse, that of economic development. Institutional reforms have been part of the development toolkit for many decades, and still are today under the umbrella of *good governance*. Correspondingly, the discussion of whether or not "institutions matter" has been popular in academic research since the late 1990s and is led in a passionate manner still today. *Wallis* (2011: 591) sums up this discussion in a rather disenchanted undertone:

> "Like all political agendas, the development community requires simple messages, not nuanced and subtle ones. The development community listened to the academic community when the academics said that institutions were important. When the policy makers asked the academic community how they should go about changing institutions in a way that could be sustained, the academic community did not have any good answers."

The impression that, despite a remarkable amount of publications in the field, there are no "good answers" may be due to the inherent challenges that this research is subject to, which shall be laid out below.

The discourse is mainly divided into the *climate-cultural* view, that institutions are largely predetermined by cultural and geographical factors, and the *voluntaristic* view that institutional designs (so-called 'global standard institutions', or GSI) can be "imported" in order to kick off the prosperity path of a nation. One of the prominent critics in this matter is

Chang (2011b), also because his article initiated a discussion that filled up an entire journal issue – which provides a rather good introductory overview of the positions in the current discourse still today. *Chang* himself takes up a position that can be summarized as somewhat in the middle between the climate-cultural (that he himself calls "fatalistic", ibid.: 494) and voluntarist view, and argues against the "simplistic" (ibid.: 477) understanding of the relationship between institutions and economic development. Recently, the *historical* view, led by the works of *Acemoğlu, Johnson* and *Robinson* (2001; 2005; 2006; 2008) has been successively enriching the discourse.

As indicated, there are various issues to the concept that render the related empirical research an ambiguous venture – a circumstance that makes it likely for the discussion to be kept alive for some more time. *Voigt* (2013: 1) comments on the situation: "That 'institutions matter' is a self-evident truth for some, a mantra for new institutional economists, and a robust empirical insight for others." The key issues of the discussion are:

1. The definition of 'institutions' as an explanatory variable;
2. The measurement of the variable 'institutions';
3. The direction of causality (do institutions influence growth or vice versa?);
4. The underlying normative assumption (does market freedom lead to growth?)
5. The question of whether a concerted change of institutions is possible or not.

The Definition of the Explanatory Variable "Institutions"

One issue for empirical research is rooted in the challenge of defining the criterion "institutions" in an operational sense, in a way that would provide falsifiability for the hypothesis and render the results empirically rich in content. *Sachs* (2003: 38) has a point when he remarks:

> "The debate over the role of institutions in economic development has become dangerously simplified. The vague concept of 'institutions' has become, almost tautologically, the intermediate target for all efforts to improve an economy."

While *North's* definition of institutions (1990: 3), as given in the previous section, is a frequently quoted item in most of the literature, it does not provide a solution to the measurement problem, since it is not 'operational' and can be interpreted more or less widely. While this is what some authors even demand (*Engerman & Sokoloff* 1994: 2; or, in a different sense, *Sala-i-Martin* 2002: 17), the downside is that if a concept's definition is all-encompassing, any statement about its influence becomes trivial (*Voigt* 2013: 1) and, since there is but no falsifiability, the empirical content as an explanatory variable equals zero. As *Ostrom* (2007b: 23) puts it, "[i]t is hard to make much progress in the study of institutions if scholars define the term 'institution' as meaning almost anything."

The critique of a 'vague concept' may also be abided for another methodical aspect, as there is a decisive difference between an analysis that aims at the *quality* of the research object (i.e., the effect of the quality of institutional designs on growth or other measures), and an analysis that aims at variables of which the *presence* is to be measured (i.e., determining a connection between assumingly right institutions being 'installed' and growth). The problem begins when the variables of quality and presence are mixed in the same breath, as it is in a question "Do institutions matter?". This issue is also seen by *Chang* (2011b: 485), who discusses it as mixing variables of *forms* and *functions* of institutions. Closely related is *Jones'* (1995) critique of relating a variable relative to time (growth) to the stationary variable of "institutions", also picked up, e.g., by *Easterly* (2014b: 317).

The Measurement of the Variable "Institutions"

Ironically, it was *North*, having coined the most frequently cited conceptual definition of institutions (1990: 3), who thought:

> "We cannot see, feel, touch, *or even measure* institutions; they are constructs of the human kind." (1990: 107, emphasis added)

In order to approach the measurement of the variable "institutions", many authors rely on indices. E.g., *Acemoğlu et al.* (2001) use the "protection against risk of expropriation" index from Political Risk Services as a proxy; other examples include indices for 'degree of economic freedom' (*Gwartney, Holcombe & Lawson* 2006; *Bowman & Chand* 2007), Sachs-Warner openness-to-trade index (*Hall & Jones* 1999) or components from the World Governance Indicators[25] (*Knowles & Owen* 2010; *Tebaldi & Mohan* 2010)[26].

25 The World Governance Indicators (WGI) were introduced and are regularly updated by the World Bank; see *Kaufmann, Kraay and Mastruzzi* (2010) for more detailed methodological information.

26 For review of the existing literature, see *Pande and Udry* (2006).

However, indices themselves are only an approximation of the construct they are declared to represent. As such, they bear their own set of issues, partly due to the aggregate nature of the values, partly to the design of the indices. E.g., some widely established indices are based on subjective assessments of individuals, many of which are in fact highly likely to be *influenced* by economic growth (*Glaeser et al.* 2004: 273; *Chang* 2011b: 484) and not vice versa, thus exposing a reverse causality that consequently leads to reflexive testing.

Behar (2010) points to issues of reliability: In a comparison of different indices for the construct of "trade facilitation", he finds only a very low correlation between the indices; this phenomenon holds true even on the level of the individual dimensions of the indices, and even if they are identical, i.e., based on the same questions. An almost equal outcome is reported by *Voigt* (2012) for the "rule-of-law" concept.

Glaeser et al. (2004: 273) criticize that indices fail as an apt proxy for measuring 'institutions' because they ignore the underlying causality. E.g., a measure for risk of expropriation by the government does not differentiate the actual situation behind the risk: A dictator who *chooses* to respect property rights (not necessarily because of institutions) and a democratically elected leader who has no choice to respect it (because of institutions) will receive the same index value. On a similar track, *Boettke and Fink* (2011: 501) criticize the use of *policies* as an indicative approach to the concept of 'institutions'; institutions are by definition *in place* and hence have a first-order effect on society, while policies are by definition *imposed* and have a second-order effect[27]. *Voigt's* (2013: 8) differentiation between *de facto* and *de iure* institutions appear to relate to the same idea. As an interesting contrast to these issues, *Tebaldi and Mohan* (2010: 1048) argue that institutions can be understood as a form of index itself, measuring the typical attributes often mentioned, such as property rights protection, contract enforcement, corruption control, market openness etc.

Nevertheless, even if a valid and measureable variable can be identified, the macro-perspective quest of measuring the impact of 'institutions' must remain challenging: The complexity of the system makes it subject to isolation issues for the criterion on the one hand, and to a missing-variable bias on the other. In a well-integrated system like ODA, an isolation of the effects of certain policies on (likewise separately examined) measures or projects must be an illusion: Inhibiting characteristics are,

27 They build on *Buchanan's* (2008) distinction between constitutional and post-constitutional state of institutions.

e.g., the fact that ODA boasts a high number of donor countries and organizations, that programs are tied political conditionalities well outside the development field (e.g., UN assembly voting behavior), or that commitments are excluded from or 'generously' circumvent official conditionalities in the case of large-budget industrial deals (e.g., power plants). The literature's range of explanatory variables that have been found to be connected to growth illustrates the situation[28].

A positive (and extreme) example for a robust survey is the approach of *De Soto* (2000), who conducted an extensive empirical study to compare different nations regarding the legal steps necessary and institutions involved for standard legal procedures – if they are to be executed formally. The beauty of *De Soto's* approach derives from the objectiveness and reproducibility of the chosen indicator, but even more so from the immediate accessibility of the implied hypothesis: It is hard to question a causal relationship between a highly obstructive formal sector of a nation and a strong share of its informal sector[29].

The Direction-of-Causality Assumption

Although it may appear plausible that institutions are the cause for growth and "[e]conomic development is an institutional rather than an infrastructural or technological problem" (*Carden* 2009: 110), the assumed direction of causality that institutions influence growth (and are thus exogenous) and not vice versa (endogenous), is frequently discussed. Institutional endogeneity is a central topic in the literature (e.g., *Hall & Jones* 1999: 99; *Acemoğlu et al.* 2001: 1384; *Acemoğlu et al.* 2005: 389); *Rodrik* even holds that "institutional quality is as endogenous to income levels as anything can possibly be" (2007: 185). Because evidence shows that en-

28 As a few contemporary examples: infrastructure (*Straub* 2008; *Khandker & Koolwal* 2010), maintenance vs. investments (*Rioja* 2003), income equality (*Alesina & Rodrik* 1994), income inequality (*Forbes* 2000), foreign direct investment (*Borensztein, Gregoriob & Lee* 1998), trade (*Frankel & Romer* 1999), government consumption (*Sala-i-Martin, Doppelhofer & Miller* 2004), corruption (*Mauro* 1995), human rights (*Blume & Voigt* 2007) or democracy (*Elias & Gregorios* 2008; *Persson & Tabellini* 2009).

29 The actual achievement of *De Soto's* work are the findings about the large national volumes of the informal sector that is usually ignored in official statistics – and mostly neglected in the growth discourse until today.

dogenously evolved institutions are more persistent, *Boettke, Coyne and Leeson* (2008) refer to them as "sticky".

It is, in fact, exactly the explicit treatment of endogeneity that sparked a new 'generation' of research in the macro-institutional literature. The real contribution of the publications of *Hall and Jones* (1999) and even more so *Acemoğlu et al.* (2001) is the "ingenious solution" (*Rodrik* 2007: 185) of circumventing the measurement problem of institutions by using historical data as an instrumental variable (IV)[30,31]. In this case, their reasoning leads them to using settler mortality to capture institutional quality for property rights protection around 1500[32]. While their interpretation of the results has been both objected (e.g., *Rodrik et al.* 2004) and supported (e.g., *Easterly & Levine* 2013), their approach has influenced the field remarkably. Subsequent publications follow their path of using historical data for constructing IVs, e.g., *Feyrer and Sacerdote* (2009) use wind patterns for modeling colonialization probability. Naturally, the instrumental-variable trend did not remain without critique: *Bazzi and Clemens* (2013) question both strength and validity[33] of the IVs in many publications, although they are not counting the ones previously mentioned in this circle. However, *Banerjee* (2009: 210) points out that the historical approaches may illustrate that past "institutions matter", but that they do not

30 Instrumental-variable estimation eliminates the OLS bias in a regression when the explanatory variable is correlated with the error term of the regression; see *Murray* (2006: 111) for two illustrative examples.

31 The publications listed here are usually considered to be the initiators for the historical-instrumental-variable trend in the growth/institutions discussion. However, the invention of the IV method is attributed to *Wright* (1928), and other authors have applied them previously; e.g., *Mauro* (1995) used ethnolinguistic fractionalization as an instrument to control for endogeneity in his survey on corruption and growth. For an introduction to the historical background of IV regression, see *Stock and Trebbi* (2003).

32 The logical chain in the latter approach is as follows: If the colonizers were confronted with greater health hazards, they were less likely to permanently settle in the respective location, and as a consequence, would less likely establish institutions for property rights protection, and instead focus on extractive activities. Thus, settler mortality rates can be used as an instrument to identify the presence of said institutions. Since the diseases in question had limited effect on the indigenous population, the authors assess them unlikely to be the reason for poverty today. See *Acemoğlu et al.* (2001: 1370) for a full description.

33 The *strength* measure captures the correlation of the IV with the original variable of interest, the *validity* measure describes the causal independence of the IV from the criterion variable (naturally: other than through the explanatory variable).

provide insight whether and which particular institutions are relevant for modification today.

The Underlying Normative Assumption

A fourth point frequently questioned is the underlying normative assumption, the orthodox connection between the constructs of market freedom and development, which is a close relative of the direction-of-causality aspect. E.g., *Hausmann et al.* (2005) study periods of consecutive growth of countries since the 1950s and conclude that the vast majority of growth periods does not coincide with any major economic reforms of liberalization or opening up. *Reinert* (2007: 119) stresses how open markets are beneficial when economic development has advanced – but that historically, all now-prosperous economies had been closed markets previously; a position that is also supported by evidence from other studies, e.g., *Ackah and Morrissey* (2001) or *Rodrik* (2007)[34]. Similar points are made concerning intellectual property rights (*Chang* 2001) or also form of government: E.g., *Barro* (1996) argues that in democratic structures, the pressure for redistributive politics can have a negative impact on growth. (In contrast, *Rodrik* [2000] claims that growth volatility is more controllable by the conflict management possibilities in participatory institutions.) As an attempt to explain such findings, *Rodrik* (2007: 190) emphasizes the importance of differentiating between institutions needed for *stimulating* economic growth and those *sustaining* it, and states that the effect of institutional design is much more important for the latter.

Institutional Change

The positive research on institutions in the development context aims at identifying those institutions that are to be changed in order to generate economic growth or 'development'. This requires that they *can* be changed in the first place – which is contradictory to the definition of institutions, and as such renders the intention of 'getting the institutions right' at least questionable. *Chang* (2011b: 490) reminds that "institutions

34 The idea that different stages of a national economy demand different types of institutions is often attributed to *Gerschenkron* (1962).

are *meant* to be stable – otherwise they have no use", and highlights the paradox that

> "[d]espite their usual emphasis on scarce resource and opportunity costs, mainstream institutional economists almost entirely ignore the issue of the costs of establishing and running institutions, thus making their proposals for institutional reforms appear more attractive than what they really are." (ibid.: 494)

Indeed it must appear contradictory that one of the arguments for recommending the 'installation' of institutions is their stability: The purposeful installation would in turn either be impossible or render its alleged power a myth. For instance, *Williamson* (2000: 597) assigns a frequency of 10 to 100 years to the change in the "institutional environment", i.e., executive, legislative, and bureaucratic functions of government and the distribution of powers. He holds that "cumulative change of a progressive kind is very difficult to orchestrate" (ibid.: 598), and sharp breaks only originate from external shocks, thus in line with *Acemoğlu and Robinson* (2012b: 431). *Levine* (2009: 206) argues that institutional change requires changing the *reasons* that lead to its creation and persistence; consequently, in the context of democracy transitions and persistence, such institutional stability plays a key role. *Acemoğlu and Robinson* (2006: 30) term a democracy that is stable due to its persisting democratic institutions "consolidated democracy".

Another aspect discussed in this context is that of institutional interdependency. The phenomenon that institutional changes are not implemented because the needed complementary institutions are missing (*Aoki* 2007: 17) can also be observed in ODA practice as a frequent statement in project evaluation reports with lower quality ratings. Shortcomings of this category are summarized under the keyword of *project alignment* or *coordination* (i.e., with other interventions and activities). In this sense, institutions are seen as self-reinforcing. E.g., *Bowles* (2006) finds that poverty can be a result of institutional arrangements, but at the same time stabilize the institutions that were originally the cause for poverty. This thought is similar to the concept of *poverty traps* that is associated with the *Big Push* movement in the mainstream discourse on ODA (see Section 2.1). The 'reinforcing' narrative is also supported by the results of *Chong and Gradstein* (2007) and *Tebaldi and Mohan* (2008).

Implications

Wallis (2011: 592), who was quoted in the beginning of this section, draws the following conclusion from the macro-institutional growth discourse:

> "Ideas such as the centrality of property rights and naive beliefs in their power to solve social problems, the power of democracy to do the same, or the inability of institutional theorists to decide among themselves whether institutions are really hard or really easy to change are simplifying rules-of-thumb that reflect the lack of a coherent general theory."

While many of the publications cited in this section often deliver sophisticated approaches, they cannot fully eliminate the inherent problems that make the macro-perspective research on institutions empirically elusive. As *Rodrik* (2007: 185) holds it, "[o]ur ability to disentangle the web of causality between prosperity and institutions is seriously limited." Which is, as stated at the beginning of this section, exactly a condition that leaves room for further development and hence will most likely keep the discussion alive for quite some more time. With history as "the only laboratory available to economists" (*Reinert* 2007: xvii), the historical approach seems to be the most promising, not only due to its 'beauty at first sight' in the derivation of the IVs.

4.3.2 Institutions and Incentives: The Micro-Institutional Perspective

As discussed previously, the 'incentive' perspective differs from the macro-institutional approach not simply by the level of detail (micro vs. macro), but implies a different research interest: that of analyzing interaction situations. One of the most common objectives of institutional analysis is the explanation of an (undesirable) outcome of collective-action situations through the failure of the institutional setup, which effectively translates to a failure of the incentive scheme to generate a self-interest in the desired outcome for individual actors.

Applied to ODA, where the desired collective action outcome is the success of a project, this translates to explaining projects' failure (or that of components) through incentive structures. Apart from this descriptive (positive) approach, the research naturally also adopts a prescriptive (normative) role by trying to derive solutions for mechanism design to avoid the identified problems.

The Three Incentive Specifics of ODA

As the classic ODA sectors are infrastructure-related, a substantial share of aid projects incorporate the collective action problems of infrastructure provision, which derive from public-good characteristics and the principle-agent relationships in the delivery chain. As such, however, these issues are not specific to ODA projects. Instead, the special incentive set-up of aid that is responsible for its structural biases in outcomes is constituted by three major characteristics inherent to the ODA system:

1. *The multi-level principal-agent structure:* The addition of a donor-recipient relationship to the institutional setup expands the 'standard' set of incentive challenges associated with infrastructure and public services by an extra level. This 'level' in reality is another large multi-level principal-agent *complex* that includes the donor with its government, its bureaucracy and its public, and all external parties involved in the aid business, i.e., consultants, NGOs, and other providers of aid services. Again, each member of this additional complex introduces his or her own incentive conflicts into the system. Thus, the original institutional challenges in the recipient's country are not simply complemented, but the issues are exponentiated. In other words, while the extension of the institutional setup by the additional component of the donor level may appear like a simple step technically, it entails a giant rise in complexity in practice.
2. *The Samaritan's dilemma:* The donor-recipient relationship is characterized by the fact that the donor has a strong propensity to commit to aid again in the future – and the recipient possesses the information of this preference.
3. *The broken feedback loop:* The fact that the intervention is being controlled from outside the recipient country has an important implication for the recipient country: Whereas a government's principal are usually the voters, these are now disconnected and replaced by the donor, and the original principals do not have the possibility for any control of the external actor – the *broken feedback loop* (*Martens* 2002b: 154).

While the literature offers a plethora of different attempts to thematically structure the incentive issues of ODA, arguably *all* these issues in the recipient country can ultimately be traced back to either the Samaritan's dilemma or the broken feedback loop, whereas the multi-level principal-agent feature can be thought of as fundamental characteristic 'pervading' the entire setup. The common role of the Samaritan's dilemma and the broken feedback loop is that they practically neutralize a large part of the accountability effects that would be in place otherwise[35] – both to the side of the donor and the intended beneficiaries, as depicted in Figure 4-3.

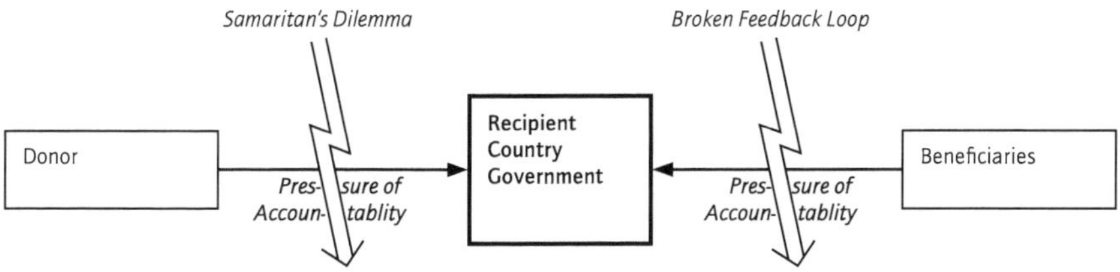

Figure 4-3: Samaritan's dilemma and broken feedback loop interrupting accountability mechanisms

Both 'sides' in fact reinforce each other reciprocally, as when the pressure of accountability is reduced on one side, this simultaneously has an effect for the bargaining power on the other side. I.e., the broken feedback loop is perpetuated by the fact that the Samaritan's dilemma of the donor keeps aid flows active, while in turn, results from the broken feedback loop ensure that the Samaritan continues to perceive the urge to 'help'. As I have argued in Section 0, the omission of effective accountability entails the lack of opportunity costs of failure for the recipient country government.

These specifics thus put incentive issues at the very core of effectiveness or ineffectiveness and make the ODA system a rather fruitful subject for institutional analyses. One of the standard works in this matter is the miscellany by *Martens, Mummert, Murell and Seabright* (2002); however, the actor level that their discussion covers is that of the ODA *system*, and it does not reach down to the level of individual projects. A study that delivers a very complete treatment of incentive issues both in the system as well as on the level of project design is provided by *Gibson, Andersson, Ostrom and Shivakumar* (2005). It is an elaboration of a previous study that had been prepared for the Swedish aid agency SIDA (*Ostrom et al.* 2001), and in this work, it serves as the basis of the coding frame for the empirical evaluation (see Section 6.3).

35 In the aid narrative, these accountability dependencies are nevertheless assumed to be in place, as documented by the periodic revival of mechanisms such as *conditional aid* (see the discussion in Section 4.3.2.2). It is this paradox that is challenged by critics such as *Marriage* (2006) or *Rottenburg* (2009: 65ff.).

Structure of the Remaining Section

As the empirical basis, this study is using ex-post reports of ODA projects. The following discussion will pick up those problems which appear in the project evaluation reports, and provide associated explanations from an incentive-oriented perspective as put forward in the literature. The starting point of the provided explanations is always the study of *Gibson et al.* (2005) mentioned above, however, the sections will also relate to other widely acclaimed literature from the discourse and include evidence from empirical studies that support the respective argumentation.

Naturally, there is no claim for the respective argumentations to be exhaustive. But while it can be doubted that incentive conflicts are always *the* one and only explanation or cause for failure, it can be doubted just as strongly that fundamental antagonisms of interest would not exert a notable impact. That is, the solution of these conflicts may not be the answer to the entire effectiveness problem, but resolving the latter without resolving the incentive conflicts must appear very unlikely.

Before discussing the concrete effects of the three categories (multi-level principal-agent, Samaritan's dilemma, broken feedback loop) below, it is crucial to lay out their common denominator, the concept of *perverse incentives*.

Digression: Perverse Incentives – at the Core of ODA

The term 'perverse incentives' describes the phenomenon of an incentive with an effect contrary to its original intention. While an anecdotal example was already given in the introduction, everyday political life holds a vast amount of perverse incentives and the effects of it[36]. Incentives are 'perverted' in the opposite direction of their original intent when a designed mechanism is not compatible with the reality of its environment, in other words: if decisive circumstances of the incentive situation have been misinterpreted or even not been taken into account at all. In ODA, these misrepresented or unaccounted-for circumstances can be found on two levels: firstly, in the nature of the aid provision system itself, i.e., the as-

36 Most conflicts over a political measure refer to this pattern, when the opposing party accuses a measure of not only being ineffective, but moreover creating perverse incentives.

pects discussed above, and secondly, in the specific environment of an intervention, i.e., the project level.

Perverse incentives are most widely known as an effect of repeated provision of free goods, such as food aid or clothing, as also frequently discussed in the mass media (*Renton* 2007; *Duffy* 2010). These interventions affect the local incentives to exert efforts, and undermine local markets (*Gibson et al.* 2005: 39), producing a crowding-out effect on intrinsic motivation. *Frey* (1997: 1046) goes even further when he argues this motivational effect to be a *general* characteristic of all external interventions[37], and notes that it "may spread to further areas, even into those where the external intervention has not been applied. There may thus be an indirect 'motivational spill-over effect', which has to be added to the direct crowding-out effect" (ibid.).

Indeed, one aspect that is frequently marginalized is the factor that ODA projects intervene with *existing* local structures of the beneficiaries, including their dependencies to the local elites, such as slumlords[38]. As a result of this ignorance, projects often 'empower' the exact opposite group of those intended (see Section 3.2.1.2). This effect is observed by *Ravallion* (2009: 53) also for higher political levels, when he remarks that "donors typically ignore the fact that their targeted poor areas exist within a government structure." Such circumstances are revealed, e.g., by *Glewwe, Kremer and Moulin* (2009) who study the free provision of textbooks in Kenya – which did not show any effect on students' performance. As the major cause, the authors discover perverse-incentive effects in the projects environment: Owing to the history of the educational system in Kenya, it is still today targeted strongly towards the elites' interests. E.g., the specific design of the school system creates an incentive situation where teachers benefit from students dropping out, and the textbook market only caters to "elite students and teachers since poorer students rarely buy textbooks" (ibid.: 133). Naturally, these unaccounted-for factors heavily contributed to an overall ineffectiveness of the project.

As simple as many of the more prominent examples appear *ex post*, exploring incentive effects and discovering perverse incentives in the project environment is not necessarily an easy task. For instance, the milestone work by *Prahalad* (2001: 207ff.) on bottom-of-the-pyramid market devel-

37 He originally discusses this effect in the context of constitutional design and material rewards.

38 *De Soto* (2000) has documented the extensive economic structures of the informal sector in his survey.

opment provides various case studies of the difficulties associated with establishing such simple products as soap. Additionally, just like in 'developed' markets, preferences of the poor do not always appear to be 'rational' from an outside view[39]. *Jensen and Miller* (2008) describe the *Giffen*-type 'flight to quality'[40], i.e., a higher availability of calories (price drop or income raise) leading to substitution with more expensive calories. Similar 'irrational' effects can be observed with the adoption of medical care or beneficial products such as insecticide-treated bed nets (ITNs). E.g., a number of studies around the randomized controlled trial (RCT) camp discovers effects that do not follow an instantly accessible logic: fertilizer that is not adopted by farmers although they see the benefits (*Duflo et al.* 2011b), nurse attendance rates dropping in a response to accountability mechanisms (*Banerjee, Glennerster & Duflo* 2008), or free public education provision increasing demand for private schools (*Bold et al.* 2011b).

A good example for the discovery of perverse effects is the latter study: The reason behind the dramatic shift towards enrollment in private schools was the selection of weaker students into public education and a crowding-out of more affluent students, with strong effects on the exam scores (*Bold et al.* 2011a).

It is an important feature that to most incentive issues in ODA recipient countries there *are* working solutions: namely those that work in the donor countries. As it was noted already in the *World Development Report* 2004, "initiatives have usually failed [...n]ot because of a lack of knowledge of what to do [...b]ut because of lack of the sustained bureaucratic, market, parental, and political pressure needed to make things work" (*World Bank* 2003: 114). While indeed, the detailed accountability structures of an informal settlement area in Nairobi may be different from those of a downtown district in Frankfurt, the underlying mechanisms are the same. The decisive difference is constituted by the distortion that is exerted by the three aid-specific characteristics named in the beginning of this section. These shall be discussed in the following.

39 For a dedicated discussion of livelihood aspects of poverty, cf. the survey of *Banerjee and Duflo* (2007).

40 This term originates from the field of financial market investments and is adopted by *Banerjee and Duflo* (2011: 24) to title the above pattern.

4.3.2.1 The Multi-level Principal-agent Nature of ODA

Murrell (2002: 76) lists five categories of actors in a typical ODA project:
1. The donor principal (superiors of the aid agency),
2. the donor agent (the aid agency)
3. the contractor (consultancy or NGO)
4. the recipient principal (political leaders of the recipient country)
5. and the recipient agent (implementation organization).

Quite peculiarly, the beneficiaries (i.e., the actual target group) are not included. The overview by *Gibson et al.* (2005: 64) adds those to the list, as well as the groups of "other donors" and "civil society organizations", resulting in the scheme depicted in Figure 4-4.

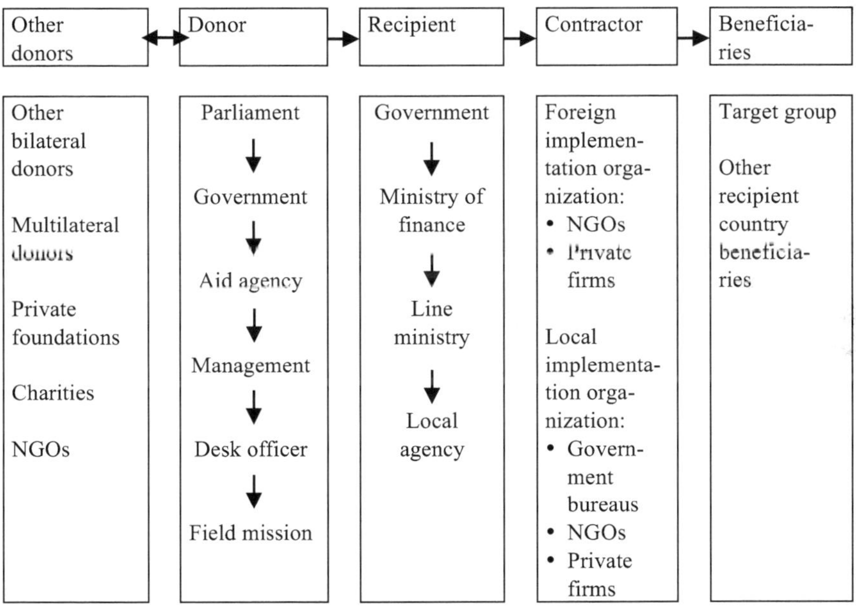

Figure 4-4: Actors in ODA delivery
Source: *Gibson et al.* (2005: 62)

Incentive issues exist on all levels of this system and in all steps of the chain. As opposed to the impression that *Murell* provides by naming each level "principal" or "agent", every actor is part of at least one principal-agent relationship with another actor[41]; additionally, these relationships extend across multiple levels and form the complex multi-level principal-agent network. As previously highlighted, it is an important feature of ODA that the entry of a donor into the action situation does not simply add a second layer, but multiplies the complexity of the original situation[42]. In that sense, a sequential presentation in form of a delivery chain as the ones above may be suited to deliver a better overview, but is indeed not accurate for depicting the network-like relations of the actor groups and should be treated with the corresponding caution. This circumstance is also pointed out by *Gibson et al.* (2005: 64), who consequently arrange the actor groups into the figure of an "international development cooperation octangle" to represent their complex interrelations.

Multiple-principal situations render the standard accountability issues of principle-agent relationships even more extensive, and the conflicting objectives more difficult to handle (see the original discussion by *Holmström & Milgrom* 1991). In addition, a multiple-principal situation is advantageous for the respective agent, in the sense that he or she can "play off different interest groups against each other, forge coalitions in support of the policies it proposes, induce collective action among members and, in general, achieve objectives that individual members would not be able to achieve on their own" (*Martens* 2005: 653). This is also valid for the side of the donor agencies, as "development bureaucrats can hide behind their consultants" (*Gibson et al.* 2005: 71) – one of the factors why accountability for results is difficult to install (see Section 4.3.2.3).

From the recipient's perspective, the network of actors does not include only one donor, but circles many donors around him: According to *Kanbur* (2006: 1579), a typical African country is the recipient of more than 20 national and multilateral donors; as of the date of their study, *Deutscher and Fyson* (2008) counted 280 bilateral donor agencies, 242 multilateral programs, 24 development banks, about 40 United Nations agencies, and an estimated amount of 340,000 development projects world-wide. Meanwhile, private foundations are contributing substantial volumes to the international aid market as well; e.g., in 2013, the *Gates Foundation* disbursed a total of over US$ 3.6 billion (*Bill & Melinda*

41 *Rottenburg* (2009: 165) provides a slightly polemic, but nevertheless sharp observation of the concrete dilemma that this situation produces especially for consultants and contractors.

42 E.g., *Werker and Ahmed* (2008) document the internal incentive problems that NGOs face due to long decision-making chains, inefficient structures and dependencies to their donors.

Gates Foundation 2014: 3) . The above effect is hence highly relevant in terms of 'competition' between donors, including both donor *countries* as well as *organizations*. The agent's bargaining power resulting from the multiple-principal setup correspondingly influences the 'carrots and sticks' of aid provision, such as conditionality, capital configuration (grant vs. loan), and selectivity. Studies by *Knack and Rahman* (2007) and *Djankov, Montalvo and Reynal-Querol* (2009), finding a positive effect of donor fragmentation on recipients' levels of corruption, support this logic empirically. Historically, this situation led to possible adverse selection of donors (*Schmidtchen* 2002: 483); however, China's recent break into the ODA donor market, with notoriously low standards for conditionality and a preference for high-volume projects, has surely changed the aid game in this matter[43].

4.3.2.2 The Samaritan's Dilemma

It is worth noting that the individual incentive issues from the complex of ODA cannot always be attributed to one of the two phenomena (Samaritan's dilemma or broken feedback loop) in a fully selective manner; this is due to the reciprocal perpetuation of the two accountability 'sides' (see page 133). Hence, the following categorization should be understood in the sense of a 'starting point' of the respective incentive perversion.

The Samaritan's dilemma (*Buchanan* 1977) is one of the fundamental roots of many notorious problems of ODA in general, and the reason why aid opponents classify aid itself as a perverse incentive – which it undeniably is. The Samaritan's dilemma is a classical microeconomic dilemma situation, with a benevolent donor ("Samaritan") and the recipient as the two actors, and options and their respective individual payoffs as depicted in Figure 4-5.

43 The impact of Chinese involvement in Africa is discussed, e.g., by *Tull* (2006), *Bräutigam and Xiaoyang* (2011) and *Bräutigam and Ekman* (2012).

		Recipient	
		Low effort	High effort[44]
Samaritan	No help	1,1	2,2
	Help	3,4	4,3

Figure 4-5: *The Samaritan's dilemma*
Source: adapted from *Buchanan* (1977: 170)

The Samaritan has a preference to help, and his individual and the total utility are maximized if the recipient cooperates and exerts high effort, but it is always higher in case of help, rendering help the dominant strategy. The recipient knows of this preference and in his choice between low and high effort (cooperation), his dominant strategy now is low effort. Applied to ODA project budgeting, this dilemma effectively cancels out the incentive effect of ODA's repeated-game design. Because the recipient player's information on the Samaritan's dilemma situation, the repeated game in effect turns into a one-shot game; no matter what the recipient player does, the Samaritan will be benevolent again in the next game. Naturally, this principle pertains only to interaction between recipients and *benevolent* (i.e., altruistic) donors[45]. However, the Samaritan's propensity to provide aid can also be constituted by characteristics other than altruism.

In ODA, the main source of the Samaritan's dilemma situation is the donor's so-called *pressure to disburse*. It results from the fact that aid commitment is commonly measured by the budget volume that is spent on projects. This alone already creates a perverse-incentive effect (*Svensson* 2003: 383), but it is further enhanced in the chain of aid delivery, as the volume disbursed is often also the performance indicator for individual career advancement of project managers (*Martens* 2002a: 20; *Seabright* 2002: 53), simply for the reason that it is a measure which can be easily monitored. Additionally, practical evidence reflects that aid agencies act in the very way that public choice theory suggests: a budget-maximizing bureaucracy, as highlighted by *Williamson* (2010: 22). But while project managers of most national aid agencies face a high pressure to allocate (disburse) their annual budget to aid projects, they at the same time only

44 The term of "high effort" in this dilemma underlines the theoretical nature. It contains the normative assumption that the Samaritan's external help is actually missing until now (ignorance hypothesis; see Chapter 2), and that it is part of the problem solution, given that the recipient invests enough effort into cooperation.

45 For a more extensive discussion of the Samaritan's dilemma in ODA, see *Pedersen* (2001); for a more theory-oriented treatment, see *Kumar* (2015).

have a limited amount of time available for managing the project portfolio.

The effects of this situation are manifold. On the donor side, it adds to the preference of maximizing expenditure volumes large, capital-intensive project types over smaller project types that involve less capital, but more staff time for project management. The need to 'move the money' can thus pervert the original intent of effective and sustainable aid projects. *Gibson et al.* (2005: 70) discuss how this can also affect the success on a project design level: One of the reasons for project failure most frequently mentioned in the evaluation reports is the application of standardized project designs without consideration of the specific project environment. However, measures for customization and adaptation fall into the category of a low-capital/high-staff-time ratio. Assuming that these measures would enhance projects' sustainability, the pressure to disburse thus effectively counteracts investing in measures that would enhance project sustainability. In this sense, one could view this effect as an adverse selection of project types.

Maintenance and Efficiency Effects

On the recipient side, the Samaritan's dilemma is one of the main reasons for the ubiquitous problem of maintenance provision, as it makes it perfectly rational to not 'lose' any resources into upkeeping. In the words of *Catterson and Lindahl* (1998: 145), "politicians cannot see the point of putting limited amounts into maintenance over time when, free of charge, they can have a totally rehabilitated or new plant within a few years." Consequently, missing or ill-designed maintenance is a frequent mention also in the ex-post evaluation reports considered in this study. As a result, e.g., the regular life span of power facilities erected by ODA is only 15 years – while under conditions of regular maintenance, an overhaul is required only every 50 to 60 years (ibid.). The irony is that not only are there missing incentives for maintenance, but even positive incentives for non-maintenance, since a deteriorated infrastructure is a good environment for attracting aid infusions[46] (*Bräutigam & Knack* 2004: 263). This moral-hazard situation for the recipient is a close relative of what is discussed as the *elite-mass gap* in elite theory (see Section 3.2.1), and it is

46 As *Blouin and Pallage* (2007: 2) phrase it: "The mere existence of aid agencies generates a need for aid."

this fundamental perverse-incentive effect of ODA that was already highlighted by early critics of ODA (*Friedman* 1958: 507 ; *Bauer* 1969: 91) and is part of contemporary criticism (*Moyo* 2009: 52ff.). With a nod to the *resource curse*[47], this phenomenon has been titled the "aid curse" (*Moss et al.* 2006; *Djankov, Montalvo & Reynal-Querol* 2008)[48], and is particularly relevant in the context of food aid and man-made famines (see *Blouin & Pallage* 2007). The 'curse of aid' will be discussed again in the context of aid dependence.

The pressure to disburse effectively implies that recipients can ignore conditions of a donor that they had agreed to prior to the funding; it creates the Samaritan's dilemma and ensures that a propensity to continued support exists, and thus can transform an originally weak bargaining position of a recipient into a strong one. This longer-term effect is combined with another effect in the short-to-medium term: Because of the high sunk costs typical for larger infrastructure projects, the donor's credibility of a threat to withdraw from a project is rather low, and creating is a strong tendency of a donor to at least finish the project. Since, as *Gardner and Waller* (2005: 97) point out, for the recipient a project mostly exposes the full benefit right after completion (especially in neglect of maintenance), this leads to a strong *de facto* power asymmetry in favor of the recipient, and eliminates possibilities for mechanisms such as reputation strategies[49] from the game.

As a result of these effects, selectivity and conditionality in aid allocation can be hard to put into practice. Indeed, a number of studies document how failed reforms on the recipients' side have not lead to sanction by the donors, or how the level of corruption or a history of failed reforms have not influenced donors' aid allocation (*Svensson* 2000; *Knack* 2001; *Alesina & Weder* 2002; *Easterly* 2006a; *Heckelman & Knack* 2008; *Coyne*

---

47 The *resource curse* entails the idea that an abundance of natural point-source resources such as oil, metals or diamonds within the territory of a nation in an low-productivity environment has an inhibiting effect on its economic growth (*Sachs & Warner* 1995). The details of explanations have been varying, but are most commonly agreed to be related to resource rents removing incentives for development and reform (cf. *Collier* 2006: 1484).
For an overview, see *Rosser* (2006); the latest empirical support is provided by *Crivelli and Gupta* (2014); however, the scheme has also been challenged recently (*Brunnschweiler & Bulte* 2008; *Murshed & Serino* 2011).

48 For a discussion of this view, cf. *Altincecik and Bearce* (2014), who also contest the existence of an 'aid curse'.

49 First discussed explicitly by *Shapiro* (1983).

& Ryan 2009; *Easterly & Williamson* 2011; *de la Croix & Delavallade* 2013)[50].

The incentive effect of the 'benevolent' Samaritan also adds an extra layer on top of the typical soft budget constraints[51] of state-owned companies, such as in energy production or service providers (*Eriksson Skoog* 2000: 2). In this case, government officials take the role of the Samaritan, and the corporate directors that of the recipient; repeated bailouts of public enterprises then resemble the repeated-game to one-shot game conversion that can be observed with ODA provision. Thus, such public-sector companies passively overuse the CPR of public budget, with the classic effect on their core business: short-run inefficiency and long-run unsustainability. This is not ODA specific, but the effect is enhanced by the institutional setup of aid provision, which adds an extra Samaritan (the donor) to the existing Samaritan (the government).

Incentives to Receive Aid but not to Reform

At least since the study of *Boone* (1996: 315), who concluded that aid had no significant impact on poverty indicators and instead increased consumption and the size of government, the topics of aid flow diversion and fungibility of aid have returned to the mainstream debate on ODA[52]. In environments where patronage mechanisms are part of the established political practice, a capital infusion is very likely to further fuel existing rent-seeking behavior[53]. Since many low-income countries are subject to clientelist[54] structures, aid in this connection can effectively serve to in-

50 In contrast, *Dollar and Levin* (2006) find a positive selectivity for multilateral aid; this is supported by the findings of *Charron* (2011). For a discussion of the effects of aid conditionality, see *Wright and Winters* (2010: 71ff.).

51 This term was coined by *Kornai* (1979: 806). For an in-depth discussion of the phenomenon from an NIE perspective, see *Eriksson Skoog* (2000).

52 See, e.g., *Marć* (2015) for a recent overview of the fungibility literature and *Panda* (2015: 50f.) for elite-capture related studies.

53 As an example from the European Union, the Spanish region of Andalusia receives the highest amount of funding in the whole EU – however, press coverage suggests that this did not increase economic activity, but instead fuelled corruption (*Pauly* 2014).

54 The terms 'clientelism', 'patronage', 'corruption' and 'elite capture' are often used interchangeably in the literature, partly due to lax definition, partly due to the inherent conceptual connection. Technically, patronage is one form of (mass) cli-

crease the pool of patronage for the elite, and can be employed to reward clients and followers, as discussed in Section 3.2.1.2. This can first of all be achieved *indirectly* by *pork-barrel* politics, i.e., steering away aid projects and associated contracts to specific regions, areas or target groups deemed as supportive. Secondly, aid can directly be utilized to maintain a 'cash-cow' system of patronage that serves the elites in charge but is substantially inefficient economically; utilities like electrical power or fresh water provision are an example for a typical good that can be "harvested" by politicians as a resource for patronage (*Gibson et al.* 2005: 190), at the expense of the 'CPR' of future budgets. As another option to divert aid, recipients can make aid fungible simply by financing activities that would have been undertaken anyway, thus freeing resources for other purposes (*Swaroop, Jha & Rajkumar* 2000: 325). And lastly, any transfer can naturally include 'fees' that are held back by the involved officials – the phenomenon mostly referred to when 'corruption' is discussed in public discourse, and aptly titled "lost in transaction" by *de Sousa and Freitas* (2011). The sheer size of transferred aid funds makes these effects almost inevitable – and a common practice in ODA (cf. *Hobbs* 2005)[55].

A large array of empirical literature documents the abundance of elite capture[56] in its various forms, e.g., in Ethiopia (*Caeyers & Dercon* 2012), India (*de Wit & Berner* 2009; *Markussen* 2011; *Panda* 2015), Malawi (*Schou* 2007), Uganda (*Reinikka & Svensson* 2004), and various sub-Sahara African countries (*Nelson & Agrawal* 2008). *Leonard et al.* (2010: 481) provide examples from different low-income countries worldwide.

Naturally, there is a strong resistance of the profiteers against change of this system; in an established system of patronage, devising rules towards reform is a classical second-order public-good problem[57]: For the individual actor, there is no incentive to cooperate (i.e., act against patronage),

---

entelism and both are phenomena of capture or corruption. The latter are in fact two different terms for the same concept; see Sections 3.2.1.2 and 3.2.2.

55 E.g., a study by the *World Bank* (2007: 345) on health projects in India found that the standard rate that contracted NGOs were charged by state officials was between 10 and 40 percent of the contract value.
A frequently cited examination of educational expenditures in Uganda by *Reinikka and Svensson* (2004: 687) found that, in the timeframe 1991–1995, an average of only 13 percent of the grants reached the schools.

56 The political economy of elite capture and corruption is not discussed here; see *Pande* (2008) for an introductory overview.

57 *Second-order* (*Ostrom* 1990: 42) refers to the circumstance that a mechanism to solve a public-good incentive problem can itself be subject to public-good problems, as first described by *Bates* (1988a: 394).

while deviation from agreeing to a new rule offers direct benefits – or put differently, there are little individual benefits and high individual cost associated with the introduction of an anti-corruption rule. In a system with a long history of established patronage mechanisms, this is likely to be valid also for the client. E.g., in the country studies of *Leonard et al.* (2010: 484), the authors report how absence of patronage links of an interest group to the political network implied that this group did not have "any effective presence in higher-level politics at all". Consequently, respective reforms can be difficult to put into practice. Nevertheless, they are often accepted by the recipient as a condition for the provision of aid – in this constellation, reforms can be understood as a "price to pay" (*Collier* 2001: 71) in order to receive aid infusion. *Gibson et al.* (2005: 183) summarize this phenomenon to the admittedly trivial yet apt tagline "incentives to receive aid but not to reform".

Additionally, from a bargaining standpoint, 'reform' components enable a clientelist political leadership to secure aid without the need for actual wholesale changes to government structures (ibid.: 204). In this situation, the ownership of a reform clearly lies with the donor, not the recipient. Quite the contrary, reforms and their extent have often been treated as concessions in negotiations between donor and recipient (*Collier* 2001: 75)[58]. This characteristic must appear evident, as policy reforms towards more accountability often hold impairment to the elite's position, implying a loss of influence. Resistance is then possible *ex-post*: When a reform has been formally accepted, the respective actors can still try to counteract this loss of influence by interfering with the configuration of the demanded political institutions, which can then lead to ill-designed institutional setups, as described in the following.

Incoherent Institutional Design

When demanded policy reforms associated with an aid project imply a loss of control over political processes and/or resources for key players, these players can try to compensate for the loss by creating dependencies

58 *Collier* (ibid.) points to another interesting feature by noting that donors often claim the credit for successful reforms "even governments that implemented reforms because they believed in them found it difficult to establish their claim to ownership with the investor community." Looking at the coverage of allegedly 'successful' leaders and the *benevolent autocrats* narrative (see *Easterly* 2011), this argument does not appear to be backed by reality, however.

in the institutional design that counteract the original reform intention. This can be the case for regulation boards for power or water provision, as in the case study provided by *Gibson et al.* (2005: 204), for the utility providers directly, or for any other bureaucratic structures. The result is an institutional setup that is often described as "wrong" or "incoherent" in project evaluation reports, but can be understood as a measure to retain compatibility with elite's interests. An example of such a setup is the following description from a *EuropeAid* report:

> "[...] the Medium Term Expenditure Framework (MTEF), led by the Ministério das Finanças (MF), is based on the proposals made by the line ministries, given a certain expenditure ceiling previously set by the MF to each sector. As Electra [the previously state-owned electricity provider] depends on the Ministry of Economy, there is no dialogue between the Ministry of Infrastructure and Telecommunications and Electra in that respect. On the other hand, the MTEF does not include the expenditure made by the municipality." (*European Commission* 2009b: BCS 5.1)

Again, deranged institutional designs and counterproductive dependencies illustrate how the actual ownership of imposed structural reforms is located on the donor's side. Settings like this are documented by the missing support of components part of a structural reform after project closure or even already during implementation, e.g., in the form of non-allocation of material, budget, personnel, or infrastructure – a form of elite capture similar to *Dutta* (2009: 8) – or replacement of key staff with little or no handover, thus erasing the organizational and institutional memory. Furthermore, another frequently encountered phenomenon can be explained with the attempt to retain influence: the political resistance against raising public service prices to a level of cost recovery. Keeping prices below this level can bind service providers to politically motivated budget transfers and thus indirectly counteract the providers' – formal – independence (*World Bank* 2003: 162).

Overstaffed Bureaucracies

One of the prime sources of patronage is awarding supporters with jobs in corporate or state-owned bureaucracies (*Knack & Rahman* 2007: 194). *Robinson and Verdier* (2013: 261) explain the prevalence of this method of redistribution with the fact that, as opposed to other patronage via public-goods distribution, it offers an incentive-compatible way of controlling the clients: Because the employment is reversible, the utility of the employee can be tied to the political success of a specific politician, or a job can even be withdrawn as a form of punishment. Similarly, according to *Acemoğlu et al.* (2011: 201), patronage through expansion of bureaucratic structures is especially attractive because a bureaucracy that is dependent on the elite will also support pro-elite policies. Others have been arguing that this type of clientelism can be best disguised against opposition (*Alesina, Baqir & Easterly* 2000), although this may be of lower relevance in political environments of low transparency and accountability.

As a result of this practice, public bureaucracies in lower-income countries often suffer from hierarchies with overstaffed lower grades and strong capacity deficits, as it is an ubiquitous description in project reports. It must appear logical that aid – as a capital infusion into this system – often cannot reduce this overhead, even if this is the project target. Additionally, for team leaders in the recipient country, a donor's ODA project often offers positive incentives for high staff count, when an increase in staff is a criterion for career advancement (*Gibson et al.* 2005: 188).

Large hierarchies with a high number of layers impede controlling of the agents, especially on a distant such as the lowest level. Under these circumstances, low effort is likely to be the optimal strategy for the respective agent; the extensive accountability chains are often the reason why notorious problems of network-dependent products such as water provision or electrical power persist, and monitoring, enforcing rules and excluding free-riding are not effectively addressed (*Gardner & Waller* 2005: 101). In other words, ODA's possibly perverse incentives that antagonize maintenance in ODA, as discussed previously, can be further aggravated when the typical CPR challenges on the ground level of execution are not solved. Especially in network infrastructure that relies on maintenance, this leads to a fast deterioration of assets, as documented, e.g., by *Gillanders* (2013), and perpetuates dependence on external support.

Sustainability of Aid Dependence

This situation thus enhances short-run inefficiency and long run unsustainability – in fact, the only sustainable component thus becomes dependence on aid: Not only because inefficiency of the system is sustained in the manner described above, but also because once this dependency has been 'established', there is a vicious circle of capital sourcing through external infusions in the form of aid. When "aid becomes a permanent soft budget constraint" (*Bräutigam* 2000: 3), it weakens the incentives for political leaders to identify alternative revenue sources for increasing the tax base (*Rajan & Subramanian* 2007), or more concretely, for inducing policies promoting development. With no dependency on or accountability towards taxpayers, motivation to cater to this group (or to 'govern well') is correspondingly low, as when "the flow of revenue is little affected by government efficiency, there is little incentive to improve state capacity" (*Bräutigam & Knack* 2004: 265). As such, aid may adhere to keeping up the *elite-mass gap* discussed in Section 3.2.1.

This sustainability of aid dependence is also discussed as one aspect of the "curse of aid", as mentioned at the beginning of this section. *Collier* (2006: 1484) describes how a constant flow of "sovereign rents" influences the political toolkit in a (formally) democratic setting. He differentiates two strategies of electoral competition: patronage or public-goods provision. A too large ratio of available sovereign rents over scrutinized revenues such as tax income may "tip the balance" of which strategy for gaining votes is the more efficient alternative. In his eyes, the availability of rents can even *determine* the political outcome:

> "Sovereign rents are that part of public revenue over which there is no effective scrutiny. Given political pressures to raise finance for patronage, the government will be driven to use sovereign rents in this way. Political leaders who attempt to resist these pressures take a risk of being replaced by those willing to do what is necessary to maximize electoral support." (ibid.)

Many authors view aid to have a 'sovereign rent' effect similar to that of natural resources (cf. *Wright & Winters* 2010: 69f.), though the empirical findings are not as clear as one might expect (see *Altincecik & Bearce* 2014: 18 for an overview and the latest contribution). The main argument of aid-curse critics is that aid does not feature the constancy over time, the fungibility and the unconditionality of natural resources such as oil[59] and thus "lacks some of the key properties necessary to produce this effect" (*Altincecik & Bearce* 2014: 19). However, as the effectiveness of aid conditionality as well as the (in)fungibility are strongly debated, so is this argument. *Bräutigam* (2000: 25) emphasizes how "[a]id as a source of revenue parallels other 'non-earned' revenue sources, particularly the

59 In the previously quoted article, *Collier* assesses aid conditionalities to be effective, as "aid comes with various donor-imposed mechanisms of scrutiny, which […] substitute for reduced pressure from citizens" (2006: 1485). On a side note, this is contrary to earlier statements such as in *Collier* (2001).

rents from mineral extraction. 'Rentier' states face fewer internal pressures to improve state capacity and accountability."

Consequently, when an infrastructure is notoriously plagued by missing cost recovery, deterioration and resistance against fixing the underlying causes, potential private investors are crowded out of the market and the dependency on external capital infusion is perpetuated. *Kanbur* (2006: 1579) points out the effect that such a crowding out exerts on the orientation of public bureaucracies, as when the bureaucracy's focus of revenue is external aid[60], the bureaucratic capacities are driven away from its own people:

> "But perhaps as important than the sheer time use is that these senior technocrats and politicians become oriented towards convincing the aid agencies to keep the aid flow going, rather than towards listening to the domestic population and the local development agenda."

Similarly, *Moss et al.* (2006: 10) emphasize the critical role of taxing capacities for development, as "[r]eliance on citizens for raising public revenues [...] is considered an essential ingredient to establishing accountability between the state and society" or can be understood as "the exchange of tax revenues (for the state) for institutionalized influence over public policy (for citizens)" as *Moore* (2008: 36) phrases it[61].

It is these effects of aid dependency that create an incentive paradox for project purposes of capacity building or 'good governance'. This logic is largely supported by empirical evidence that finds a negative relationship between net ODA inflows and tax revenues of recipient countries (*Bräutigam & Knack* 2004; *Gupta et al.* 2004; *Remmer* 2004); the most recent studies again confirm the effect to be valid for grants but not for loans (*Benedek et al.* 2014; *Thornton* 2014).

The perverse incentives of foreign aid that have been discussed in this section are all created or perpetuated by the Samaritan's dilemma and its negative effect on the accountability of the recipient to the donor. As described in the introduction, aid creates an accountability gap also to the other side, that of the recipient government to its own people: the broken feedback loop.

---

60 Cf. *Easterly's* (2002) discussion of the extensively bureaucratic processes in ODA.

61 This construct of the accountability function of taxation is supported, e.g., by *Broms* (2014), who examines sub-Saharan survey data and finds how taxpaying citizens display a higher political interest.

4.3.2.3 The Broken Feedback Loop: Disconnected Principals

Effectively, the phenomenon of the *broken feedback loop* (*Martens* 2002a: 15) is two-fold: The voters of the recipient government cannot deliver feedback to the agent providing the projects in their own environment; on the other side, the voters in the donor country are the principals over their aid agencies, but cannot see the results of the interventions that they are principals of, as they happen elsewhere.

This geographical and political separation reverses the principal-agent order in the recipient country and takes away the power from beneficiaries (the voters) over their government – it should be precisely for this reason why the keyword of *beneficiary ownership* has made it into the agenda of ODA in the first place. The effect is a severe accountability problem, and just as with the multiple-principle setup in aid delivery, the actors can always blame the other involved party for problems of default, as it has happened frequently (*Collier* 2001: 76). In other words, from the beneficiaries' perspective, 'broken feedback' can be interpreted in two levels, both to their own government, as well as to the donor government.

The Credibility-of-Commitment Problem

As explicated in Section 2.2, the notion of the *credibility of commitment* was first discussed by *North and Weingast* (1989), and is now widely seen as a central factor for the quality of a respective institutional setup. For *Acemoğlu et al.* (2005: 394), the credibility of commitment is at "the heart" of their framework.

'Credibility' in this case translates to nothing else but *incentive compatibility* for the committing party (cf. *Henisz & Zelner* 2001: 127); according to *North* (1990: 57), "creating an institutional environment that induces credible commitment entails the complex institutional framework of formal rules, informal constraints, and enforcement that together make possible low-cost transacting". As the respective environment of many ODA recipient countries is substantially weak concerning these features (see *Laffont* 2005: Ch. 1)[62], this credibility is notoriously low – a problematic feature for many actors, leading to *hold-up* situations between the political

62 E.g., high cost of public funds, missing institutional arrangements like government audits, supreme courts and independent media; weakness of the rule of law, corruption and less stringent monitoring of illegal activities (ibid.).

elite on the one side and investors and citizen groups on the other (*Acemoğlu et al.* 2005: 430). Resistance of political elites against any change of this status is summarized by *Acemoğlu et al.* (2005: 437) in that "[t]hey may be better off with a large slice of a small pie"[63].

The broken feedback loop strongly affects the credibility-of-commitment problem, since it destroys the elite's credibility of political promises for reform to the 'disconnected' voters. This is one of the reasons why the proposal of big-push solutions for development tends to be treated critically from an incentive-oriented perspective. E.g., *Winters* (2010: 238) contends that big-push concepts "will amount to little more than throwing money down the rat's hole if proper accountability procedures are not in place." Broken-feedback effects can also exist locally, the most prominent example is in connection with the mode of provision of a good or service: E.g., if a good is provided for free, the missing fee takes away a basis to hold the provider accountable and constrains his or her credibility of commitment to the contract.

Vermillion (2001: 188) gives the example of a farmers' protest in the Philippines in the early 1990s, when politicians promised to provide irrigation for free to the farmers in the pre-election phase as a bait to gain votes. Unfortunately for the political candidates, the targeted farmers thought differently. "The protestors said that their payment of the fee was their only basis for demanding an acceptable irrigation service from the government. In their minds payment of the fee established their right to an acceptable service" (ibid.) – the fee was their guarantee that they could hold the service provider accountable. This logic is also apparent in the inverse mechanism of fines, as demonstrated by the adverse effects discovered in an experiment of *Gneezy and Rustichini* (2000): The introduction of a "tardy fee" for late-coming parents in a children day-care center significantly *increased* the rate of parents showing up after official closing time. The authors see this as a result of the previously incomplete contract then providing the agents (the parents) with a price information for the 'product' – as opposed to the previous uncertainty gap resulting from the contract leaving consequences in the open, it now defined an explicit compensation (ibid.: 10ff.). Put differently: The fee provided the parents with the *right* for the 'provision' of the good (the kid being taken care of after the official closing time), while this provision had previously been provided on the basis of a *favor*.

63 For the comparison of inclusive vs. extractive institutional setups, *Easterly* (2014b: 168) uses the analogy of "growing the pie vs. fighting over it".

However, accountability and provider motivation represent only one aspect of the extensive debate around fees (and subsidies) and their positive or negative incentive effects. E.g., proponents of user fees point out that a positive price for a product or service screens out low-valuation consumers and reduces product diversion (e.g., the use of ITNs as fishing nets), while the sunk-cost effect additionally increases the actual use rate after the product has been acquired[64]. Yet, while these arguments may be easily comprehensible in the context of utility provision, there appears to be a different picture especially for the sectors of healthcare and education, where the results of empirical studies cast strong doubt that the above effects hold true. Instead, the financial barrier that the fee creates often dominates and reduces the product's take-up (cf. the overview of *Kremer & Holla* 2009; *Gaarder, Glassman & Todd* 2010; *Dupas* 2014). In a study of *Fafchamps and Minten* (2007) on school enrollment and healthcare services in Madagascar, fee abolishment simply lead to an increase of the adoption rate without any negative effects on the quality of provision.

Nevertheless, the educational sector is often indeed subject to substantial accountability problems that demonstrate a local broken feedback loop. Aid projects that do not tackle this complex are likely to worsen the issue and instead fuel rent seeking. And while empirical results suggest that fees are not a solution to accountability problems in the educational system (*Bold et al.* 2011a: 44), they also demonstrate how more direct accountability mechanisms[65] can fix the broken feedback loop and exert a substantial impact on teacher attendance and performance (*Duflo, Dupas & Kremer* 2011a).

Output Over Outcome

The broken feedback loop also affects the side of the donor – after all, in the ODA setup, the donor is one of the agents to whom the feedback loop is labeled 'broken'. Despite the important role that evaluation officially is stated to take in the ODA cycle (see Section 5.2.2), no one is systematical-

64 Another issue discussed in connection with subsidies to promote adoption of a 'new' product, such as medication or ITNs, is the *framing* effect (going back to *Tversky & Kahneman* 1981): Subsidization may be effective in the short term, but often negatively affects long-run adoption, as the beneficiaries might 'anchor' around the subsidized price and then be unwilling to later pay more for the product (*Dupas* 2014: 221).

65 E.g., locally hired contract teachers and parent-run monitoring committees.

ly held accountable for the actual outcomes of ODA projects (*Svensson* 2003: 117).

It is a typical feature of public-sector agencies that the focus is drawn on inputs instead of actual outputs and outcomes (see *Lane* 2005: 59). In ODA, this is true for the macro level, as aid is commonly measured and compared on the basis of capital disbursed (see Section 2.1), and can also be observed on the project level (*Seabright* 2002: 64). However, as "focusing on results" has become a popular tagline in reports and other public documents of ODA agencies, the attention bias on project level does not only happen between 'outputs' and 'inputs', but also between out*puts* vs. out*comes*. The distance created by the broken feedback loop drives the focus away from the *actual* results (outcomes) and towards the more measurable factors of project output, e.g., not the amount of people actually reached and benefitting from fresh water provision, but the amount of kiosks or connections built. In reference to the terminology applied also by *EuropeAid*, I summarize this as the *output-over-outcome* phenomenon[66].

This pattern is part of many 'classic' examples given by ODA critics. One of these is *Easterly's* (2006b: 11) case of ITNs which had been financed, bought, transported to the target area but did not include a plan on actually getting them in the hands of the target group, and, more importantly, getting the target group to using them correctly. (*Easterly* is a proponent of charging subsidized prices for solving the various allocation problems; this is one of the heavily contested mainstream topics, cf. *Cohen and Dupas* [2010].)

Another example that has advanced to a citation classic is that of *Ferguson* (1994: 180), where a project in Lesotho was supposed to provide transport infrastructure to connect the beneficiary target group to markets to sell their produce. As the target group had in fact never been involved into any farming activities, the roads were not enhancing the connection to the market, but rather had inward effects on the region, as they enabled institutions of state bureaucracy to expand into the villages.

Output-over-outcome results like these are fostered by the inherent incentive structures of typical ODA bureaucracies for the project level; when 'output' measures as the dominant success criterion are strongly incentivized, the practical implication often is that the opposite is the case for 'outcome' measures. *Whittle* (2013: 6) reports how activities to im-

66 This is similar to the "'expenditures = outcome' mentality" discussed by *Easterly* (2006a).

prove 'outcome' measures are perceived as too "messy and time consuming" for ODA agencies, as they would involve redesign, renegotiation with the government or even project closure of unsuccessful projects. More importantly, all these activities would happen at the cost of 'output' measures such as the number of new project preparations and capital disbursed. *Pritchett* (2002) sums up these incentive structures as "It pays to be ignorant". The output-over-outcome phenomenon is very connected to another important characteristic of ODA, the top-down mode of provision.

Top-down Mode of Provision

With the ideological shift towards more human-centered approaches beginning in the late 1970s, ODA provision has seen the introduction of different measures to soften the effects of top-down implementation. Most notably, these were community-based and participatory approaches, which are intended to work 'bottom-up' from the beneficiaries. From a technical standpoint, these measures do not change the fundamental design character of the ODA system of top-down provision, as the separation of the donor and beneficiaries and the aid-inherent broken feedback loop persists.

As discussed in the previous Section 4.3.2.2, the disconnection of recipient government and its voters fosters an extension of the top-down mentality of governance into the recipient country, e.g., by the orientation of public bureaucracies towards external revenue sourcing and the impediment of the government's fiscal accountability towards its own citizens. *Pritchett and Woolcock* (2008: 156) refer to ODA's top-down delivery pattern as the "needs-supply-civil service solution" paradigm (needs as problem, supply as solution, civil service as instrument), where all problems are treated "as amenable to the logic of policies and programs" and accountability flows upward instead of towards the citizens.

The deficit in institutional structures dwarfs the voters' "capacity for analysis", as *Collier* (2001: 77f.) labels it: The lack of information (and of the capacity for making use of this information) and the lack of government transparency in general are perpetuated in a system that is geared towards top-down orders. At the same time, this environment facilitates the capture processes of the project implementation and manipulation of organizational setups, as described in the last section. As such, aid often has the effect of maintaining or even promoting existing asymmetric-power relationships.

Results from elite research (see Section 3.2.1.2) suggest that there may be little public resistance, as in social environments with a long history of elite dependence, people accept low accountability and feel strong norms of conflict avoidance (*Abbink & Ellman* 2010: 1328; *Wong* 2012: 347). But, as *Pritchett and Woolcock* (2008: 158) point out, the top-down delivery of aid impairs observability not only between the recipient and the beneficiaries. It is also a concern between the recipient and the donor, who can be kept in the dark about actual beneficiary reach – thus enabling local recipient agencies to create 'ghost' project sites and divert budget to other uses (*Whittle* 2013: 5).

The information problems of top-down delivery pose strong challenges to projects that require the input of *local knowledge*, which is the case for solving most public-good and common-pool resources problems at the operational level (*Gibson et al.* 2005: 41). In connection with elites, this is specifically apparent in projects targeting the interaction between elites and local communities, such as the very common project sector of *community-based natural resource conservation*. The existing elites in charge often hold a monopoly for extraction of the natural (common-pool) resource, and have no primary interest in devolving ownership to local users; since local users in turn have no share in the commercial value of 'their' resource, they do not have an interest in sustainability either (*Gibson et al.* 2005: 177). In a setting like this, community projects are predestined to fail, and frequently have (see *Nelson & Agrawal* 2008: 558), as they often cannot level out the strong incentives for the elites to maintain control when valuable resources are involved (ibid.: 578). The asymmetric-power relationship of the original situation is maintained or even enhanced, and the attempt to build capacities in the local community are likely to fail due to the strong resistance of the existing bureaucracy.

Lastly, the broken accountability mechanisms also explain the difficulty of putting institutional reforms into practice, as institutions cannot simply be 'installed' (see Section 4.3.1). *Easterly* (2008: 96), for instance, refers to the post-soviet "shock therapy" approach, which attempted to convert institutions of communism into those of capitalism, as "one of the most notorious failures of top-down reform". As such, top-down institutional reform underlies the repugnancy similar to that of fighting of corruption by capital infusion. Still, as *Rodrik* (2008: 100) points out, especially multilateral aid is often skewed toward the idea of universal "best-practice" (i.e., *ex-ante*) designs for institutional reform, leading to "institutional monocropping", as *Evans* (2004: 31) acutely remarks. *Andrews et al.* (2012: 5f.) argue that this practice in fact facilitates "the perpetuation of dysfunction" and acts as a driver to the same capability problems that it is supposed to solve – because it constrains local experimentation, similar to the local knowledge problem. Formally, the impossibility and the perverse effects of institutional reform through 'installation' are meanwhile acknowledged by donors (e.g., *OECD* 2012a: 10), yet this does not imply that the concept is likely to disappear very soon in actual ODA practice, given the incentive structures in place.

4.4 Summary

It has been popular for quite a while to point out the importance of incentives and institutions for development – from development economist *Lewis* (1953: 273) stating that one of the three "most urgent needs for economic development are social institutions which promote incentives", up to the contemporary and ubiquitous "institutions, institutions, institutions!" However, claiming that incentives are important for action outcomes is a rather tautological statement (as this is their definition), and the question is less *whether* they matter, but *how* they matter. NIE provides the framework corresponding to this research interest.

The first explicit treatment of incentives goes back to the late 1930s and the work of *Chester Barnard*. Initially, the concept mainly received attention from organizational theory and psychology, before it was adopted also by the research branch that later received the label of *New Institutional Economics*. Incentive effects are at the core of the neo-institutional perspective; they are the reason for problems in collective-action situations as well as for the 'market failures' of public and common-pool goods. Within NIE, the explicit treatment of incentives is part of *principal-agent theory*, which is also the branch that the concept of *incentive compatibility* derives from. It stands for the idea that in a hierarchical relationship, the incentive provided by the principal has to be subjectively compatible with the desired effort that the agent is expected to invest. This concept can be ported to any other interaction situation, and is applied, e.g., in product design to realize *second-order price discrimination*. In this study, the idea of incentive compatibility is adopted and reduced to the group of elites in the ODA project environment.

Despite the ubiquitous assertion that "institutions matter" for development, actual neo-institutional studies are rather rare in the ODA context. This is due to two different research interests behind the concept of 'institutions', resulting in a macro- and a micro-institutional branch. The *macro-institutional view* intends to investigate the role that institutions play for development. The results here have been inconclusive, also due to a number of methodical problems with untangling the concept into operative research models. The most promising work that emerged from the discussion is the 'historical institutionalist' line around *Acemoğlu and Robinson*, who also picked up the interesting approach of using historical data as an instrumental variable.

As opposed to this view, the *micro-institutional perspective* looks at the institutional arrangements in terms of their incentive mechanisms. The ODA system is a very fruitful object of investigation, as it is subject to a plethora of *perverse incentives*. This is due to the specific setup of ODA that effectively combines several sources of such issues: Those of the *multi-level principal-agent structure* of ODA provision, and those perverse incentives resulting from the external intervention into existing institutional structures – all this from a foreign government not accountable to the actual target group, the so-called *broken feedback loop*. Additionally, this foreign government faces a *Samaritan's dilemma* in providing aid to the recipient government. The latter is one of the most fundamental incentive problems in aid provision, as it effectively turns aid into a one-shot game regarding the recipient accountability, while preserving the recipient's benefits of a repeated game (which it is). Some of the elite-related incentive effects observable in ODA are:

- Recipient playing off different interest groups against each other (attributable to: *multi-level principal-agent*)
- Missing incentives for maintenance (*Samaritan's dilemma*)
- Soft-budget constraints in state-owned enterprises (*Samaritan's dilemma*)
- Aid as a resource for patronage, exploitation of rent-seeking opportunities and fungibility of aid/food aid (*Samaritan's dilemma*)
- Non-adoption of well-known solutions to market failure problems, perpetuation of missing cost recovery, crowding-out of private investors (*Samaritan's dilemma*)
- 'Sustainably' overstaffed recipient bureaucracies; failure of capacity development (*Samaritan's dilemma*)
- Incoherent institutional design of bureaucratic structures (*Samaritan's dilemma*)
- 'Empowerment' measures cementing skewed power structures in target communities (*broken feedback loop*)
- Motivational crowding-out by external interventions (*broken feedback loop*)

- Output-over-outcome phenomenon; project outputs are more important than results (*broken feedback loop*)
- Top-down mode of provision and public-service delivery (*broken feedback loop*)
- Failure of community-based natural resource management (*broken feedback loop*)

The core incentive problem of ODA can ultimately be reduced to the question of *accountability* – one of the main challenges in the interaction between actors in the recipient countries. The incentive effect of accountability is also a key aspect in the historical-institutionalist model that sparked the idea to this research, as it assures that political promises of any sort (more technically: the commitment to contribution) are credible. If a mechanism is incentive compatible for the elite, it is a signal of credible commitment to contribution. Phrased in colloquial terms: If the committing party has something to lose in the game, their commitment is more easily taken seriously.

Interim Summary of the Research Focus

After the presentation of the conceptual outline in Chapter 2 and the theoretical backgrounds in Chapter 3 and 4, the following provides a brief summary of the research focus for better clarity.

The construct of 'elite compatibility' that is used in this survey is based on the concept of incentive compatibility, reduced to a specific target group of elite actors in the ODA project environment, assuming the 'elite' definition of recent development research that includes elites of the local level.

Important classifications of this research are:

1. *Informal, not formal:* As opposed to the formal surveys in the field of incentive compatibility and agency theory, this work adopts the framework of NIE as an informal way of thinking and not to build a formal model.

   The goal of this survey is to empirically test the relationship between an elite-compatible project design and the performance of ODA projects. The evaluation of qualitative data is followed with categorization and quantitative testing.
2. *Micro-institutional, not macro-institutional:* The incentive effects of institutional arrangements and not at the 'body' of institutions; it is hence an entirely separate research interest from the macro-institutional discussion of the influence of institutions on growth and economic development.
3. *Project design level, not on the level of aid provision:* Focus is on incentive issues between actors on the project design level, not on the general level of the design of aid provision.
4. *Actors in the recipient country, not donor actors:* As implied by the project design level, donor actors are not part of the focus.
5. *Elites in a functional sense, not in a sociological:* Elites, as used in this work, are defined as actors from the recipient country who assume leadership roles in the context of the respective project. This includes national-level politicians, actors from adjacent political entities such as regulation agencies, as well as local-level elites, such as mayors or other local-level politicians.

The following Chapter 5 will provide background information on the empirical material, before Chapter 6 discusses the method and the results.

Chapter 5 Background on the Empirical Material of Evaluation Reports

The empirical material used for this study is ex-post evaluation data and qualitative ex-post reports from *EuropeAid*. The material itself is described in more detail in Chapter 6. This chapter provides brief background information on EuropeAid as a donor (5.1), describes the specific processes and terms of evaluation (5.2) and discusses challenges and limitations of evaluation (5.3).

5.1 EuropeAid as an Actor in ODA

EuropeAid is the donor organization of the European Commission and as such acts as the donor organizations of individual countries. The main mode of aid provision is in form of grants. With a net ODA volume of US$12.1 billion in 2013, it ranked among the top five largest donors in worldwide, after the United States (US$32.2 billion), the United Kingdom (US$17.5 billion), Germany (US$13.3 billion), and Japan (US$ 13.0 billion) (*OECD* 2014c)[1]. *EuropeAid* covers all geographical regions and operates in all classical aid sectors, such as infrastructure (water and sanitation, transport, urban development), environment (forestry, climate change, biodiversity), food security, agriculture and rural development, energy, health and education, economic growth (private sector development, trade, regional integration, employment), and human rights.

5.2 Procedure and Terms of the Evaluation Process in ODA

The following overview of the terms and procedures in this section is based on *EuropeAid's* own material. Most of these procedures follow established standards of ODA practice and use the standard terms as commonly applied in the majority of international donor agencies. A criti-

1 The cited figures are the total net disbursements ODA bilateral and multilateral grants, excluding non-grants.

cal discussion is not part of this section, but instead is the subject of Section 5.3.

5.2.1 Actors

The actors in *EuropeAid* practice correspond to the common organizational setup which is also presented by *Gibson et al.* (2005: 62); see Figure 4-4. Since the detailed internal organizational structure on the donor side is not relevant for the research as conducted by this study, this aspect is not elaborated here. For more details on the actors in the management of the evaluation procedure, see *European Commission* (2012: 24ff.).

5.2.2 The Project Cycle

The project management at *EuropeAid* splits the project life cycle into five phases. This scheme and the associated management activities is referred to as *Project Cycle Management (PCM)* and is compatible with common development practice (cf. *Binnendijk* 2000: 12; *Mikkelsen* 2005: 264). Figure 5-1 lays out the phases and their respective key documents.

Figure 5-1: The EuropeAid project cycle and selected key documents of each project phase
Source: adapted from *European Commission* (2004: 19)

The programming phase (1) is the strategic stage of the cycle and not yet project-specific. The ex-ante stage of the project itself starts with the identification of problems (2) and the formulation of the intervention plan (3), involving feasibility studies as well as stakeholder and target group analyses and ultimately leading to the *financing agreement*, which is the legal commitment of *EuropeAid* and the partner government to the project. After the implementation (4) and project closure, the evaluation by external experts takes place (5). Internally, the same unit managing ex-ante quality assessment is also responsible for the coordination of post-implementation activities of monitoring and evaluation, with the aim of further integrating the different steps of quality assurance (*European Commission* 2012: 26).

Monitoring and evaluation underlie a specific terminology at EuropeAid that differs from common practice: Commonly, *monitoring* refers to the ongoing stage of the project implementation and mainly focuses on the efficiency and resource use, while *evaluation* denotes the ex-post assessment with a clear focus on cause-effect relations of the intervention (e.g., *World Bank* 2008b: 21; cf. *Mikkelsen* 2005:265 for an overview).

Contrary to this, monitoring at *EuropeAid* is not restricted to resource use, but involves a rather extensive tool that covers all five OECD evaluation criteria (see next section), and is consequently titled *results-oriented monitoring* (*ROM*). The same tool is also the basis for the ex-post assessment, leading to the somewhat contradictory term of *ex-post monitoring* for the process of project evaluation. In contrast, the term *evaluation* is not applied to the project level, but exclusively refers to assessments above project level, such as sectors, countries, programs or financing instruments (*European Commission*: 8f.). The total amount of such 'evaluation reports'[2] published each year by *EuropeAid* varies between 6 and 20 (cf. *European Commission* 2014c).

In other words, external *project-level* quality assessment always involves the ROM tool, both for ongoing missions (projected results), as well as for ex-post missions (actual results).

EuropeAid's Result-Oriented Monitoring Tool

For monitoring of ongoing projects, the ROM mission is required to take place between 6 months after project start and until 6 months before the end of the project, while ROM missions for ex-post assessment should be carried out 1-2 years after project closure. The project selection mainly focuses on projects with a budget larger than €1 million (*European Commission* 2012: 38); in 2013, more than 1,500 projects have been assessed by an ongoing or ex-post ROM mission, covering roughly a third of the total funding portfolio (*European Commission* 2014a: 135).

The ROM missions are executed by independent (i.e., external) monitoring experts who visit the project sites and conduct interviews with project or program staff as well as with key stakeholders and beneficiaries. The reporting follows a standardized process that leads to a corresponding standardized set of documents, the most important of which is the so-called *Background Conclusion Sheet*, or *BCS*. Of all documents generated from a ROM mission, the BCS contains the most detailed information on the monitor's assessments of the project quality, separated into several criteria in a highly standardized format which is intended to ensure a high

2 For the sake of simplicity, this study will employ the common terminology outside of this section, i.e., the term *evaluation report* refers to the document that contains an ex-post project assessment, and not to evaluation reports in the *EuropeAid* terminology as described above.

comparability of the gathered data (*European Commission* 2012: 8). As the BCS is the document format that is used as the empirical basis for this study, the specific structure and contents of these reports is discussed in Section 6.1.3. The appraisal is guided by the questions from the ROM tool and involves the review of key project documents; one of the most important foundations is the *intervention logic* of the project.

5.2.3 The Intervention Logic and Evaluation Criteria

The term *intervention logic* describes the cause-effect relationships that a project design is based on, i.e., the measures taken in order to generate a specific result that contributes to addressing a specific problem. When assessing the success of a project, this logical chain is tested in reverse order. The intervention logic can be separated into a micro and a macro perspective: On the micro level, it should be assessed whether the applied project design is an apt measure for reaching the defined overall project goals, i.e., in how far the measures and incentive components of the projects work out. This is the interpretation in which the term 'intervention logic' is used in evaluation. Additionally, it can also be interpreted from a more macro perspective: Taking a step back in the causal chain, the intervention logic reflects the question of whether or not a project's *goals* are actually suited measures for targeting an existing problem. Another step back could furthermore discuss the question whether the problem itself was correctly identified in the first place – although this question is not part of a project's evaluation process.

Figure 5-2 shows this hierarchy of objectives and the relationships between the different levels of objectives and the evaluation criteria. In the context of project design and evaluation, the different levels of goals are differentiated into the *overall objective,* the *project purpose,* the *outcomes, outputs, activities* and *means/inputs*, ordered from general to specific. Each of these levels is connected in a (hypothetical) if-then relationship from bottom to top, which combines to the overall narrative of the intervention.

The five evaluation criteria relate to the fulfillment of these objectives and encompass the following:

1. The *relevance* criterion incorporates both the relevance for the strategic objectives of the EU development policy, as well as the relevance of the project to address an actual problem that the beneficiaries are facing. In the structure of the evaluation reports, it also encompasses

the *design* aspect, i.e., the quality of the design to address this problem and deal with the specific circumstances in the project environment (a more detailed description of the report contents is provided in the discussion of the qualitative data in Section 6.1.3).

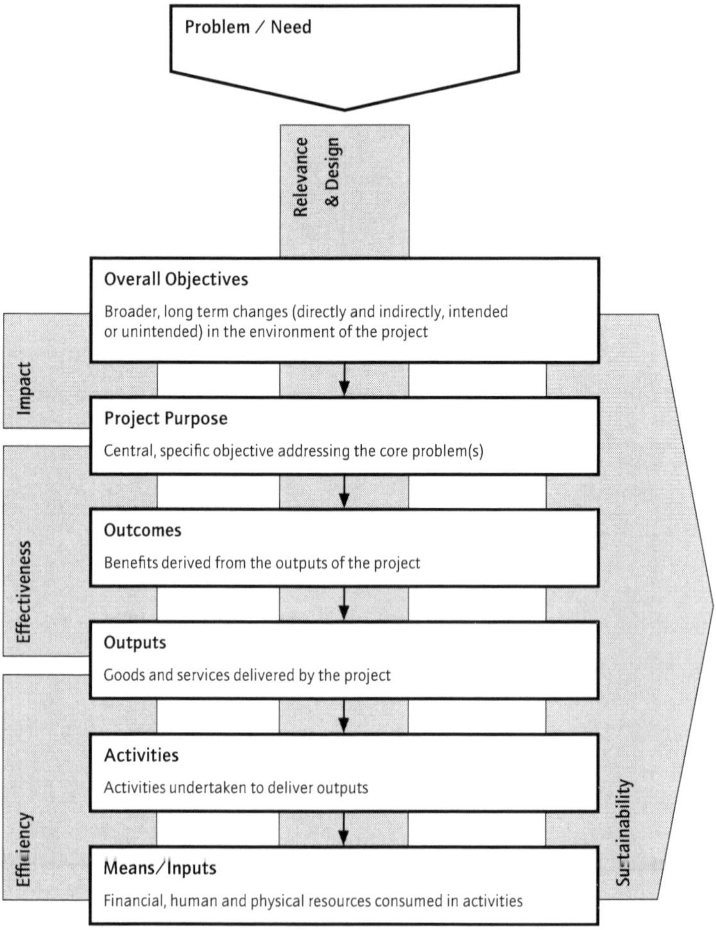

Figure 5-2: Hierarchy of the intervention logic (logical framework, white) and the five evaluation criteria (gray) of EuropeAid
Source: adapted from *European Commission* (2012: 32)

2. *Efficiency* captures the relationship between inputs and outputs, while

3. *effectiveness* measures how well the project's planned outputs have been achieved and how they have contributed to the project purpose. Thus, the two criteria follow the classic definition[3] of efficiency as a measure of the utilization of means, and effectiveness as a measure of target achievement. Within this level of objectives, the differentiation between *outputs* and *outcomes* is crucial: While outputs are the goods that a project is intended to produce, the actual benefits are the outcomes that derive from the outputs. E.g., if a planned amount of schools have been built (output), this does not imply that children are actually attending school (outcome) and benefit from the intervention. This differentiation is not common ODA practice, although some donors share it (e.g., *UNDG* 2011: 16).
4. *Impact* captures the degree to which a project fulfilled its original purpose – the solution of the previously defined problem, or, in the language of the hierarchy as depicted above, the achievement of the *overall objective*. Thus, the 'impact' measure can be seen as the most central criterion of ODA success or failure. In colloquial language, the term 'aid effectiveness' often actually refers to the impact of aid projects, not to the effectiveness measure as described above.
5. *Sustainability* describes the likelihood of continued project success after support of the donor has ended. Generally, it can relate to either impact (i.e., was the targeted problem actually solved, or was it only cured temporarily) or to effectiveness. *EuropeAid* defines sustainability as "the continuation in the stream of benefits produced by the project" (*European Commission* 2012: 32), which in the objectives hierarchy above relates to the *effectiveness* criterion.

The Logical Framework Approach

The process of laying out the intervention logic into the chain of objectives, outputs, means and activities, as described above, is referred to as the *logical framework approach* (LFA). In order to assess the project's success with regards to fulfilling the individual steps of this chain, each objective of the chain is assigned an indicator which has the requirement to be *objectively verifiable* in a consistent way and at acceptable cost (*European Commission* 2004: 80). To be able to capture the change induced by the intervention, the specification for each indicator needs to include a

3 *Barnard* (1938: 127); see also the discussion on page 26.

'before and after' value, or in more official wording, a *baseline* level (as measured before the intervention) as well as a *target* level (the level to be reached after the intervention). For the specification of those targets, there are a number of additional requirements that are commonly agreed on (*Gasper* 2000: 17); *EuropeAid* uses the acronym *SMART* as a mnemonic for *s*pecific, *m*easurable, *a*chievable, *r*ealistic and *t*ime-bound (*European Commission* 2012: 68).

The presentation of all these components for a specific project is termed *logical framework matrix*: It lays out the hierarchy of inputs, activities and objectives, as described above, on the vertical dimension, and on the horizontal dimension assigns the objectively verifiable indicators to each of the objectives, specifies the baseline and target levels and includes risks and assumptions (*European Commission* 2012: 30). The resulting matrix (or table) sums up the intervention logic in a compact presentation format.

As mentioned previously, most of the above terms of the logical framework approach are not specific to *EuropeAid*, but derive from the original application (cf. *Coleman* 1987: 252) and are commonly used in ODA, although their adaption can vary substantially between individual aid agencies (cf. *Bakewell & Garbutt* 2005: 4ff.; *Lamhauge, Lanzi & Agrawala* 2012: 19ff.). The approach itself derived from *Drucker's* (1954: 126) *Management by Objectives*, and has been present in development planning since the early phase of ODA in the 1960s (*Dale* 2003: 57), when it was adopted by USAID. It arrived in European aid agencies in the 1980s and eventually became established as a required standard; *EuropeAid* made the use of the approach mandatory for project planning in 1993 (*European Commission* 2012: 31).

However, this refers to development *planning* – systematic application in the stage of *monitoring and evaluation* is of younger date (*Gasper* 2000: 18), a circumstance that is also apparent from the empirical material used in this study: Reports relating to projects of earlier planning dates often refer to different standards at the time of project planning, and hint to indicators not having been clearly defined, not fulfilling the criterion of being objectively verifiable, or missing baseline values. Despite criticism in the LFA, e.g., the warnings of narrowing focus in evaluation (*Gasper* 2000: 22, see also the discussion in the next section), this illustrates the benefit that the approach brings to monitoring and evaluation in ODA: the basis for a more structured and results-based appraisal that avoids subjective, arbitrary judgments.

5.3 Challenges and Limitations of Evaluation: What Is Evaluated in Evaluation?

While aid evaluation is supposed to unveil successes and failures in order to enable learning and improvement of provision and implementation, there are various factors that impede this procedure. One component is that evaluation takes a difficult position within the influence of interest groups; secondly, the evaluator's concrete activity of gathering information 'in the field' is not straightforward; and thirdly, the measurement of part of the relevant data itself is challenging.

5.3.1 The Difficult Role(s) of Evaluation

The effectiveness of aid is the central justification of its existence, and as such, evaluation is a central component for providing this proof. The evaluation of aid projects, a standard procedure today for all bi- and multilateral ODA aid agencies, emerged only in the 1970s, after a decade with a disappointing track record for ODA. With the consequential upcoming 'aid fatigue' among the public, organizational interest for evaluating aid effectiveness arose – strengthening public support for aid was explicit topic when aid evaluation was first systematically discussed by the DAC (*OECD* 1993: 8).

In its function of demonstrating effectiveness and proof-of-concept, one role of evaluation is the delivery of success narratives – the other is that evaluation *itself* serves as a narrative to demonstrate effectiveness as the primary goal of ODA, and perpetuate the axiomatic value of aid. *Bauer* hinted to the underlying paradox already in 1969 (88):

> "This interpretation is a corollary of treating foreign aid as axiomatically beneficial. Once it is so treated, either progress or retrogression can be advanced in support of the continuation or expansion of aid; the former as evidence of its success, the latter as evidence of the need for its reinforcement."

Naturally, the broken feedback loop discussed in the previous chapter (Section 4.3.2.3) also creates classical asymmetric information situations for evaluation, i.e., in the principal-agent relationships between the donor, the (donor's) taxpayers and the aid agencies' contractors. Very generally, the common denominator for all actors involved in the aid process (including the evaluators), is that the demonstration of *in*effectiveness is *not* incentivized. Because of this role that aid evaluation takes in this context, it is sometimes referred to as "ritualistic" (*Mikkelsen* 2005: 44); harsher critics even contend that evaluations "have to be organized in such a way that they do not reveal the inevitable inconsistencies of institutional organizations." (*Rottenburg* 2009: 71).

Rigor

It appears logical that evaluation should focus on results of the intervention that is evaluated. Correspondingly, the language of international aid organizations strongly features "results" as a focus of their work, especially in reports for public availability. The strong emphasis of "focusing on results" (*DFID* 2014: 117) in documentation practice and headlines of reports, is nevertheless often not met in practice; instead, the focus on inputs persists (*Barder* 2009: 5).

Additionally, 'rigorous' evaluation requires good baseline measures and data (*CEDAP* 2008: 120), which is often not the case. In the sample of this study, 25 of the 34 project reports did not confirm the existence of a baseline study, 9 reports even mentioned the non-availability explicitly. This phenomenon is not restricted to selected donors; even 'lighthouse' or 'best-practice' projects such as the *Millennium Villages*[4] do not live up to standards of rigorous evaluation and are often dominated by subjective choices and missing baselines (*Clemens & Demombynes* 2010).

Paradigm maintenance

Aid agencies have an organizational interest in promoting concepts that are considered 'correct' or that they offer 'solutions' to; *Pritchett* (2002) argues that too much knowledge collection is in the way of collecting political support for corresponding programs. For the behavior resulting from this effect, *Broad* (2007. 702) utilizes the term of "paradigm maintenance", and, e.g., attests the research department of the World Bank to have played "a critical role in the legitimization of the neo-liberal 'free-trade' paradigm over the past 25 years".

In a similar vein, *Andrews et al.* (2012: 6) point out that, in the donor-recipient relationship, the proposed reform ideas represent "scripts" of

4 The Millennium Villages are part of the *UN's* MDG campaign and are supposed to be a 'proof-of-concept' for the MDGs. Selected districts (not villages, as the name suggests) receive a multitude of interventions.

acceptable reform, and recipient organizations "like finance ministries or central banks gain legitimacy by agreeing to adopt such reforms, regardless of whether they offer a path towards demonstrated success in a particular context." In a setting like this, evaluation will simply document the compliance with those scripts. Consequently, this focus on compliance with a certain 'form' may veil the actual 'function', and makes evaluation particularly ambitious, as it may lead to superficially excellent results, while the actual core problem has not been tackled and remains unaltered, as documented by *Pritchett et al.* (2013: 5f.). As such, evaluation may promote the typical *error of the third kind*, as discussed previously in Section 2.1.2.4.

Feedback loops

Organizational learning requires feedback loops and knowledge collection, i.e., learnings from evaluation reports would need to be considered for future projects. But while these feedback links are officially proclaimed by most aid agencies, they often do not exist in practice, and evaluation reports are rarely studied by more than a very small number of an agencies staff members (*Gibson et al.* 2005: 150)[5]. This is especially problematic since it hampers the long-term effectiveness of programs and projects. *Gibson et al.* (2005: 30) contend that without systematic learning it is impossible to reach sustainable solutions to incentive conflicts in ODA projects. Much more important, nevertheless, is the fact that there are strong incentives against organizational learning *itself*.

Failure Motive

The Canadian chapter of the NGO *Engineers without Borders* (EWB) publishes an annual "Failure Report" (*EWB* 2014) to encourage organizational learning from past mistakes – a rather unique case in the landscape of ODA. The problem is that, as opposed to the rhetoric of aid organizations, the institutional setup of these aid organizations typically offers few rewards for systematically seeking out failures (*CEDAP* 2008: 101). This

5 In interviews with the author in 2013, three managers from large German donor organizations confirmed that there is no effective link between the evaluation results and the actual planning of new projects.

is a typical feature of large organizational structures with multiple principal-agent relationships, for which *Dörner* (2008: 266) delivers an interesting psychological explanation. He describes this *Logic of Failure*[6] with the "ballistic" control behavior of the individual actor: Similar to a cannon ball, which cannot be influenced anymore after it has been fired, ballistic behavior refers to the pattern of not caring about the effective result of a measure, once the measure has been induced – the inducement itself is seen as the problem solution. Consequently, the actor can maintain his own "illusion of competence" if the measures are not evaluated thoroughly. In situations with a high level of uncertainty, the propensity to act 'ballistically' increases.

Additionally, if the discrepancy of actions and own values increases, such as in the case of external 'shocks', unexpected changes in the project environment, ex-post revision of the own behavior is limited in order to avoid cognitive dissonance and keep up the illusion of competence (ibid.: 269). In the ODA context, this may be applicable, e.g., to corruption or difficult political situations that the project is embedded in.

This may explain rationalization of mistakes (such as "the right measure, just not implemented correctly"), or in the more extreme form, setting up constructs of reality: E.g., again from the Millennium Villages, *Munk* (2013: 197) cites a case of a water project where the borehole was attested to be "the most reliable water source in the region" by the reports, but was a great fail in practice due to repeated draughts and floodings and repeated breakdown with long periods until repair by a remote expert.

Pritchett (2002: 251) sums up this incentive situation for knowledge collection in ODA with the words: "It pays to be ignorant". This avoidance and disinterest in the failure motive is also apparent on the in-the-field level of the evaluator.

5.3.2 In-the-Field-Reality of Evaluation

The monitoring missions for the reports used in this study usually last between 5 and 10 days, during which stakeholders are interviewed and selected sites are visited; on-site visits should total four days (*European Commission* 2012: 46). Naturally, the monitor cannot gain in-depth insight of the complex environment of a project. Additionally, various other fac-

6 Own translation, original: "Die Logik des Misslingens".

tors are in the way of investigating a realistic impression of the project assessment. To name but a few examples:

- Project stakeholders may not accept the monitor as an interview partner 'on par', but perceive him or her as someone without much connection to practical problems of in-the-field reality. E.g., in interviews with the author, monitors repeatedly reported that they were often viewed as "that person from the capital".
- Project stakeholders may just be 'playing along' for the interviews, and not reveal actual problems, in fear of losing support altogether. *Marriage* (2006: 481ff.) gives examples for this behavior of beneficiaries facing elite capture problems.
- Similarly, project managers and other expert staff project managers and experts may have no interest in sharing their knowledge, as they feel it is their competitive 'asset', and too much explication of this knowledge will make their position obsolete.
- Naturally, a bias may also be induced intentionally by the monitor, as a result of his or her incentive situation as described in the previous section.
- The prescribed focus on information that is measurable may veal the exploration of important interrelations. E.g., in their responses from SIDA staff, *Gibson et al.* (2005: 151) received the comments that evaluations "cover only tangible, readily available and measurable information from a project rather than trying to get at deeper reasons for successes or failures." In other words, this is a specific case of the format of the tool not fitting the problem.

It should be noted, however, that many design components of today's project planning and evaluation, such as the use of logical frameworks, 'objectively verifiable indicators' or the SMART criterion for project targets[7], are all measures in the endeavor to make evaluation more objective and reproducible. Thus, the above critique has to be taken in this context. Put differently: Taking the focus away from measurable indicators would most likely invoke corresponding criticism.

5.3.3 The GNP and Other Rough Estimates: Measurement Problems

In a 2010 paper, *Deaton* closes with a "final note on measurement":

---

7 Targets should be "specific, measurable, achievable, realistic, time-bound" (*European Commission* 2004: 81).

> "The basic facts of economic development, such as the growth rates of GDP, come from measures that ought to be much more deeply debated than is the case. GDP is a poor measure of welfare to start with, and many important developing countries, China and India being only the leading examples, have weak statistical systems that are most likely overstating their rates of growth" (*Deaton* 2010b: 14).

It appears as a peculiar issue that, while official aid effectiveness studies rely heavily on both macro-level data and survey-based data, the accuracy of these data is rarely questioned. Especially two factors seem to suggest that it should be. The first is *completeness*: In his seminal monograph, *De Soto* (2000) showed the vast proportions of the unofficial market in LDCs, a part which is never accounted for in official statistics. Nevertheless, his findings have not been receiving any serious attention in the context of international income statistics. A similar problem of incompleteness exists for statistics on national spendings such as education or specific projects: As *Reinikka and Svensson* (2004: 679) point out, official budget data do not reflect the actual spendings that reach the target (e.g., schools/education), simply because it is not clear how much of that total amount has been "lost in transaction" (i.e., diverted by actors in the transaction path; cf. *de Sousa & Freitas* 2011).

The second factor is that of *reliability*: *Easterly* (2006b: 194) recounts from his first visit to The Gambia, where he witnessed how the balances of the central bank consisted of pencil writings in a ledger book, with signs of having been erased and recalculated several times. He comments that since this incident, his "faith in central bank accounting suffered". *Jerven* (2013: x) describes the case of Zambia in 2010, where the national income statistics were prepared by one man alone. But the problem is not an anecdotal one. *Jerven's* work, e.g., is an entire monograph dedicated to the reliability issue of African development statistics, providing a plethora of other examples[8]. As reliability may be considered the most fundamental criterion for data usability, this is not merely a side issue – in strong contrast to the absence of this notion in the mainstream debate.

It is, however, not a new one: The usability of official statistics in LDCs had already been critically discussed by *Usher* (1968: xi), and was later picked in a 'classic' argument between *Péter Bauer* and *Nicolas Stern*. *Stern* (1974: 197) argued that "[o]ne is prepared to share [*Bauer's*] caution over the accuracy of the data, but at present they are all we have".

8 See also *Devarajan* (2013), who discusses the effect of different accounting standards on African GDP measures. E.g., Ghana's GDP saw an increase of over 60 percent after the adoption of the UN 1993 standard in 2010 (ibid.: S10).

This was heavily contested by *Bauer* (1975: 405), who stated that "[i]nsistence on the usefulness of national income statistics of LDCs on the ground that they are all we have is a notable instance of the belief in indiscriminate quantification". He considered these practices "damaging both because they conceal the radical shortcomings of the underlying data, and also because they divert attention from other ways of reasoning and of collecting and interpreting evidence".

This measurement issue is relevant not only on the macro level, but also in the context of project evaluation and effectiveness assessment, where aggregate data is used for baseline and progress measurement. E.g., child mortality, one of the key values addressed by health projects and one of the MDGs, is a field where "rates are notorious for their imprecise measurement" (*Easterly* 2014b: 125). The same applies to measures of infrastructure projects such as traffic accident statistics, which are a standard for road transport projects (cf. *European Commission* 2010): Reliability and completeness of such data must appear at least critical to anyone who has witnessed accident practice in many LDCs.

The persistence of the problem until today is attributable both to reasons of capacity, as well as to missing incentives, which *Hirschman* (2003: 230) considers to be "one of the most intractable and vexing problems in the way of good quality information". *Laffont* (2005: 247) even concludes that "[s]erious empirical studies in LDCs are not really feasible today".

5.3.4 Relation of This Study to the Limitations

As this study's interest in the contents of the reports is the attribution of success and problem factors, the above limitations naturally impact the quality of this venture. Firstly, the report contents underlie a form of 'publication bias' for evaluations, in the sense that just because a problem is not mentioned, it does not imply that it did not exist. Secondly, the incentive situation may impose a special form of 'investigator bias', when a report author does not portray things as drastic as they are.

However, there is no viable way of controlling for the discussed effects within the scope of this study. Hence, the reports' descriptions have to be assumed as 'correct', or treated 'as is' – a position which may be justified with the famous quote often attributed to *Keynes* but going back to *Carveth Read* (1898: 272), who stated that "[i]t is better to be vaguely right than exactly wrong." Nevertheless, the exclusive focus on the *problems* of evaluation in this section should not distract from the fact that, within the amount of data available and usable for this research interest, the quality of the sourced reports is on a rather high level. This will be laid out in Section 6.1.4.

5.4 Summary

The ex-post project reports used for empirical evaluation in this study were collected from *EuropeAid*, which ranked among the top five largest donors worldwide with a net disbursed ODA volume of US$ 12.1 billion in 2013, covering all geographical regions and all classical aid sectors. For project design, *EuropeAid* applies the *logical framework matrix*, a standard tool which structures the intervention logic into a hierarchy of objectives, resulting activities and inputs, and which serves for both project planning as well as monitoring during project management. The reports relate to this logic with the five evaluation criteria of *relevance*, *efficiency*, *effectiveness*, *impact* and *sustainability*, again an international standard appointed by the OECD.

Project evaluation underlies various challenges that counteract its original intention of unveiling and documenting successes and failures to promote organizational learning. This results from the situation that virtually none of the actors involved in ODA – including the evaluators – have an interest in documenting 'too much' failure. Some of the most important challenges are:

- Rigorous evaluation is often impossible, as baseline studies are not available.
- Serious feedback loops between evaluation reports and future project planning often do not exist.
- The prescribed focus on measurable items in evaluation may hinder the exploration of important deeper interrelations for failure or success.
- The evaluation may only document the compliance with paradigms of institutional solutions, and not reveal solution of the actual core problem, thus promoting the 'error of the third kind: precise solution of the wrong problem.
- Individuals in a large organizational structure like that of ODA often expose a propensity for 'ballistic' behavior, where the inducement of a measure is more important than the actual outcome.

- The monitor in the field may face the problem of non-cooperation of his interview partners, not only by said 'ballistic' actors trying to avoid cognitive dissonances: Project managers may not want to reveal knowledge they perceive as a personal 'asset' for their career, and also beneficiaries and other stakeholders may just 'play along' in fear of losing future support.
- Finally, the reliability of data is often critical in environments where serious documentation is nonexistent. This applies both to macro data such as the GDP, as well as to micro data such as accident rates or child mortality.

However, the reports provide a very good data source for the research interest of this study. Additionally, the structure of the tool and the reports renders a rather high data quality, as will be discussed in Section 6.1.4 of the next chapter.

Chapter 6 Evaluation of the Empirical Material

The goal of this research is to empirically test the relevance of the construct of elite compatibility (independent variable, or predictor) for the project outcome (dependent variable, or criterion). The elite-compatibility (EC) construct has been explained in Chapter 2, concrete examples of its representations in ODA practice have been provided in Section 4.3.2. The actual evaluation of the empirical material is presented in this chapter; Figure 6-1 illustrates the procedure.

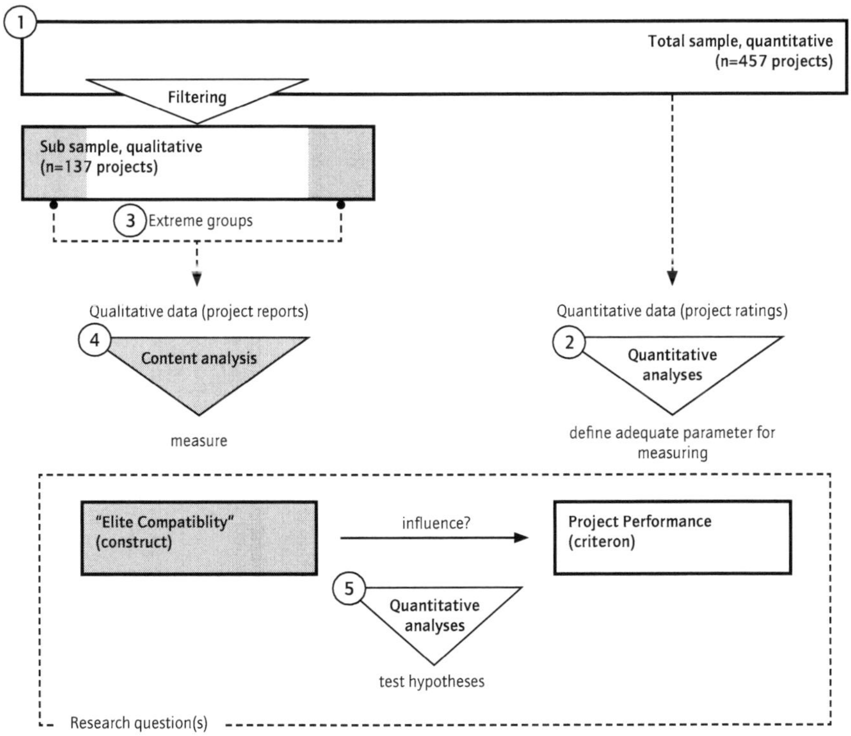

Figure 6-1: The research procedure

Following the logic of the above figure, this chapter is structured as follows:

1. The empirical basis for this are ex-post evaluation project data from *EuropeAid*: A data set of n = 457 projects containing quantitative data, including project ratings in the five OECD categories. For a subset of n = 137 projects, qualitative ex-post evaluation reports are available after applying filter criteria. Section 6.1 describes the empirical material regarding the sample selection, contents and quality of the sample, and the homogeneity of sample and sub sample is demonstrated.
2. For the criterion of project performance, the five quantitative ratings from the reports may be used. Since the study uses an extreme-group design, an apt measure, i.e., one *single* measure, for forming the extreme groups needs to be identified. For the total sample of n = 457 projects, quantitative analyses are run to explore patterns within the ratings. T-tests and χ^2-tests ensure that the total sample and sub sample are homogenous regarding the respective variables. These analyses are presented in Section 6.2.
3. The project performance criterion is then used to form extreme groups from the n = 137 sample. Not only does this design reduce the number of cases to a more manageable amount, but it also ensures a more clear-cut separation of high- and low-performing projects, which is beneficial given the subjective nature of the rating process.
4. In order to examine the EC of the projects, the qualitative data of the reports are extracted using the method of manual content analysis in its interpretative form: The reports are reviewed for descriptions that indicate EC issues, these issues are then extracted (i.e., collected), interpreted and coded. Various measures are taken in order to ensure the interpretation and coding to be reliable. Section 6.3 describes the operationalization of the EC construct and the setup of the coding scheme, as well as the concrete steps of the coding procedure.
5. The results of these qualitative analyses are presented and discussed in Section 6.4, including quantitative testing of hypotheses.
6. The last section (6.5) discusses the classical quality criteria of the research design.
7. There is no summary in this chapter, instead, the results will be summarized in the last chapter, which concludes this study.

Concerning the discussion of data and measurement quality, it is important to differentiate that for this study, there are effectively two measurements taken: One is the evaluation of the *projects* themselves, leading to the data documented in the project reports. The second is the evaluation of the *reports* themselves, to collect data for testing the research hypotheses of this study. The quality aspects of the first (original) measurement are discussed in the section on the data quality of the empirical material (6.1.4). The quality of the second step is a component of the operationalization of the construct which is to be tested and is hence discussed in the respective context (Section 6.5.1).

6.1 Description of the Sample and Sub-sample

As illustrated above, the sample consists of two sets: A large sample of *quantitative* ex-post project data, and a sub-sample of projects for which *qualitative* ex-post project reports are available. All data were obtained from the project data bank of EuropeAid, which is referred to internally as *CRIS* (*c*ommon *R*ELEX *i*nformation *s*ystem, RELEX being in turn the abbreviation for 'external relations'). The sample can be summarized as follows:

- Time frame: 2006-2013
- Regions: all regions but Europe/Russia
- Sectors: all sectors of infrastructures (details in the next section)
- Project status: final, ex-post data available

The following section provides an explanation for the above selection criteria.

6.1.1 Selection Criteria for the Total Sample

Time Frame (Report Dates)

There was no specific filter for the report dates, and the time frame is a simple result of the availability of data: The standardized report format, as used in this research, was introduced to EuropeAid evaluation practice in 2005 (*European Commission* 2012: 23), and it took until the following year for data to be available in this format. 2013 was the latest available data as of the last request to *EuropeAid* office.

Regions

EuropeAid also manages European Neighborhood Programs; since the focus of this study is on classical ODA, European and Russian projects were excluded from the sample.

Sectors

For the sector selection, the goal was to concentrate on classical ODA sectors – which can be summarized as infrastructure in a wider sense: The filtering of the reports included all sectors so-called *economical infrastructures* (electrical power, gas, water/sanitation, telecommunications, transportation and public utilities), also referred to as *hard* infrastructure due to its physical nature, as well as sectors of the so-called *social infrastructures* (education and health care), also referred to as 'soft' infrastructure due to the institutional nature[1].

Additionally, since the sectors of *agriculture* and *urban development* in practice often contain infrastructure projects, these sectors were included as well to increase the number of cases (193 additional projects for the total sample resulting in 62 projects for the sub-sample).

All sectors not related to infrastructure have been eliminated from the sample. Namely, projects from the sectors of *population policies*, *emergency relief*, *financial services*, *trade policy*, *industry*, *business*, *food aid* and *refugees* have been excluded.

Infrastructure sectors account for a large share of EuropeAid's ODA and hence deliver a sufficient amount of material. Additionally, these sectors can be considered very 'attractive' from a theoretical standpoint, as one common denominator of all hard infrastructure is the network character of the assets, making them subject to classical incentive issues from NIE (see Section 4.3.2), similar effects exist for soft infrastructure.

---

1 This represents the classification commonly used in the literature (e.g., *Laffont* 2005: 1). In the taxonomy of the DAC codes by the *OECD* (2012b), the sector *water/sanitation* (DAC code 140xx) belongs to the social infrastructures (DAC code 1xxxx), most likely following the logic that access to water and sanitation is viewed as a basic social right.

Project Status: Final/Ex-post Data Available

The report format that is used in this study is available for different project stages, i.e., the framework is not only used for ex-post evaluation reports, but also for monitoring reports of ongoing projects (see Section 5.2.2). Since the interest of this study is the final result of a project, no reports from ongoing missions have been included, but only those from the ex-post project evaluation mission. (While surely the integration of ongoing vs. final reports could deliver interesting insight, this would constitute a different research focus.) Not all projects necessarily have reports available in the database; this is due to technical reasons, as well as the simple circumstance that only a fraction of approximately 10 percent of all projects receives a final evaluation of this type.

6.1.2 Comparison of Total Sample and Qualitative Sub Sample

From the total sample (n = 457), the amount of projects available for qualitative evaluation is reduced to a subsample of n = 137 by two factors:

- *Availability of report documents:* For projects evaluated prior to 2008, the large reports as used for this study were not always available from the EuropeAid document system (only summaries in a more compact document format[2]). Hence, qualitative sample contains only a very limited amount of projects evaluated in 2006 or 2007.
- *Report Language is English:* Only reports written in English were included for evaluation in this study. Reports can be written in English, French, Spanish or Portuguese; in the majority of cases, the language of choice is the official language of the recipient country. I.e., excluding Spanish reports from the sample implies a dropout of a large proportion of projects in Latin America.

However, apart from the distribution of geographical regions, the exclusive selection of English reports as well as the limited availability of 2006 and 2007 reports did not have a negative effect for the intercomparability of the n = 457 (quantitative) total and the n = 137 (qualitative) sub sample

2 In *EuropeAid* terminology, these summaries are termed *Monitoring Reports*. These two-to-four-page documents provide a consolidation of the more extensive documents reviewed in this study, and are viewed as an "executive summary" (*European Commission* 2012: 59).

concerning the distribution of the variables *sector*, *project budget* and *ratings*:

Table 6-1 shows the distribution of the *sector* variable in the sub sample compared to n = 457-137 (the total minus sub sample).

Table 6-1: Distribution of the sector variable for the sub sample versus the total sample

	Agri-culture	Commu-nications	Edu-cation	Energy	Health	Trans-port	Urban & Rural Dev.	Water/ Sani-tation
n=137	33	1	9	9	17	10	32	26
n=457–137	54	16	45	8	33	46	74	44

A χ^2-test for the *sector* variable shows that the differences in distribution are random and hence can be assumed equal at a very high significance level of α=0.001 (for details, see Appendix A).

Table 6-2 compares the distributions of the two samples regarding the variable *project budget*. Both the means as well as the variances do not differ systematically, as a t-test and an F-test for the comparison of variances show; the distribution can hence be assumed as equal, again at a level of α=0.001 (see Appendix A).

Table 6-2: Distribution of the project budget variable for the sub sample vs. the total sample

Sample	Observations	Minimum	Maximum	Mean	Std. deviation
n=137	137	430,000	61,000,000	5,565,802	9,172,433
n=457–137	320	92,099	95,242,949	6,628,618	11,021,590

The homogeneity of the total and sub sample is also given regarding project ratings; this is discussed in Section 6.2 in the context of the criterion of project performance.

6.1.3 Structure and Contents of the Reports

The ex-post evaluation reports[3] follow a standardized structure. The reports are set up as Microsoft-Excel files, with a separate sheet for each of

3 The material referred to as "evaluation reports" throughout this study has a different naming in official *EuropeAid* terminology, where it is termed *Background*

the five OECD evaluation criteria, as presented in Table 6-3. Each criterion is again structured into four sub criteria ("prime issues" in *EuropeAid* terminology), covering different aspects.

Table 6-3: General structure of the project evaluation reports

	Criteria				
	Relevance/ Design	Efficiency	Effectiveness	Impact	Sustainability
sub criteria	1.1 Level of relevance of the project (lifetime/today)	2.1 Management quality of availability and usage of means and inputs	3.1 Achievement of planned results (outcomes)	4.1 Direct impact of project at overall objectives level	5.1 Financial / economic viability
	1.2 Appropriateness of design for reaching objectives	2.2 Management quality of implementation of activities	3.2 Achievement of project purpose	4.2 Indirect positive and/or negative impacts (social, cultural, gender and economic)	5.2 Level of ownership by target groups today
	1.3 Stakeholder support	2.3 Achievement of project outputs			5.3 Level of policy support/degree of interaction between project and policy level
	1.4 Consideration of cross-cutting issues	2.4 Contribution/ Involvement of partners			5.4 Contribution to institutional and management capacity

In each of these sub-criteria, the report template contains between two and six questions that further specify each prime issue. Table 6-4 gives an example of these contained questions. The full set of questions and a screenshot of an actual report section can be found in Appendix B and C.

Conclusion Sheet (BCS) and is a product of the ex-post *ROM* (results-oriented monitoring) mission. On the contrary, the term "evaluation report" in EuropeAid terminology refers to a different document that is the product of a more extensive evaluation mission applied on program level. It commonly involves a larger team of experts, a longer timeframe in the field, and a substantially larger budget. These reports vary between 50 and 150 pages in length. (See also Section 5.2.2.)

These questions are merely provided as a guide and are not compulsory – as the *ROM* handbook states, the template "is not a questionnaire" (*European Commission* 2012: 63). Neither should the monitor's assessments for each prime issue be limited to the questions, nor do all questions need to be answered (ibid.). Consequently, the entries in the completed reports vary in length. In a typical report, the responses total up to 8-12 standard pages.

Table 6-4: The guiding questions for sub-criteria 2.1 and 2.2 of the Efficiency sheet

Sub criteria (*prime issues*)	Guiding questions
2.1 How well was the availability/usage of means/inputs managed?	To what degree were inputs provided / available on time and at planned cost to implement activities from all parties involved? Point out and briefly comment on reasons for major delays and deviations (at project's end), if any. Were inputs monitored regularly to encourage cost-effective implementation of activities? By whom were they monitored? Were project resources managed in a transparent and accountable manner? Has a final audit been carried out? If yes, what were the conclusions? Were all contractual procedures clearly understood and did they facilitate the implementation of the project?
2.2 How well was the implementation of activities managed?	At project's end, to what extent were activities implemented as scheduled and with the planned committed funds? If not, please briefly comment on reasons for major deviations. How well were activities monitored? Was the log-frame or similar tool used as a management tool? If not, why not? If an exit strategy was defined, how well was it implemented? Was any other monitoring tool used by the project's management and/or other relevant parties (e.g., activity or resource schedule, others)? If appropriate, how flexible was the project in adapting to changing needs? If appropriate, how did the project co-ordinate with other similar interventions to encourage synergy and avoid overlaps?

In each of the sub-sections the monitor has to fill in the full-text field as well as decide for a rating of the project quality regarding the respective aspect. The scale ranges from A to D (see Table 6-5); at first glance, this may be perceived as a scale eliminating a median option and thus forcing the monitor to decide for a tendency towards a good (B) or problematic (C) rating. However, a closer look reveals that the scale is in fact a symmetric three-step scale: B represents the 'neutral' middle (expectations are met), and A and C the deviations from the expectations (exceeded or undermatched). The fourth step (D) is merely an addendum and represents the extreme of a complete fail of the project.

The low number of grades means that each grade corresponds to a clear assessment, thus potentially enhancing the reliability of the rating and positively impacting inter-comparability of the project reports (cf. Section 6.1.4).

Table 6-5: Grades of the rating system used for the sub-sections of the evaluation reports

Grade	Qualitative	Description	Summary
A	very good	The situation is considered highly satisfactory, largely above average and potentially a reference for good practice. Recommendations focus on the need to adopt these good practices in other operations.	Performance exceeds expectations
B	good	The situation is considered satisfactory, but there is room for improvements. Recommendations are useful, but not vital for the operation.	Performance meets expectations
C	problems	There are issues which need to be addressed; otherwise the global performance of the operation may be negatively affected. Necessary improvements however do not require major revisions of the operations' strategy.	Performance undermatches expectations
D	serious deficiencies	There are deficiencies which are so serious that, if not addressed, they can lead to failure of the operation. Major adjustments and revision of the strategy are necessary.	Problems dominate or project even has negative impact

Source: adapted from *European Commission* (2012: 64)

The overall rating for each of the five evaluation criteria is then automatically calculated as a weighted average from the ratings in the sub-sections (see Appendix B). Each project thus receives five overall ratings; there is no total average rating. Instead, *EuropeAid* uses four performance categories (I to IV) to classify project performance into an overall value. These performance categories intend to translate intuitive quality statements into concrete rating patterns, as presented in Table 6-6. In the following, I will be using the term "grade class" to refer to these categories.

Table 6-6: Overall performance grade classes of EuropeAid

Grade Class	Quality statement	Criteria
I	"very good performance"	• at least three A ratings • no C or D ratings
II	"good performance"	• no more than two C ratings • no D rating
III	"performing with problems"	• more than two C ratings • no D rating
IV	"not performing/major difficulties"	• any project with a D rating

Source: adapted from *European Commission* (2009c: 63)

The most remarkable feature of these categories is that any D rating will imply the project to be classified into the last grade class IV, no matter what the remaining ratings are. In other words, if the project is subject to major failure in any criterion, it is considered a failed project in total. Correspondingly, on the other end of the quality scale, a project that is labeled "very good performance" cannot contain any ratings lower than B, or, following the descriptions from Table 6-6, cannot undermatch expectations in any quality criterion. The logic of this performance categorization appears to be rather plausible and provides a promising approach for forming extreme groups of high and low performers from the n = 137 sample. This will be discussed in the context of the exploration of a project performance criterion in Section 6.2.

6.1.4 Critical Discussion of the Data Quality

For this research, the two main issues of the data are the *comparability* as well as the *completeness*: Logically, for a research design that is based on comparing specific aspects of the contents of a data source, the actual comparability of these reports must be a minimum criterion in order to be able to draw any meaningful conclusion. Completeness may be seen as a sub-criterion of the aspect of comparability.

As the evaluation reports are written by various authors with different perceptions and writing styles, and additionally underlie the phenomena described in Section 5.3 to various extents, the comparability of the report data may appear highly questionable *prima facie*.

In operative terms, inter-comparability of the reports translates to *inter-observer reliability*, i.e., different monitors need to apply the same measures for their assessment and would need to arrive at similar, or ideally even the same assessments if evaluating the same project. Additionally, the measurements should be *consistent* for each monitor, i.e., he or she should apply the same standards for the assessment if the same monitor evaluates different projects, yielding intra-observer reliability. These criteria apply for both the qualitative descriptions as well as the quantitative project ratings. It is impossible to statistically test this reliability measure because there are simply no ex-post data available from different assessors on the same project[4]. However, reliability can be discussed by looking at design aspects of the data collection:

Inter-Comparability of the Qualitative Data

An aspect that enhances the comparability of the data is the high level of standardization of the data collection format. As described in the previous section, the report templates follows a rather tight structure of 16 sections, each covering a specific aspect to be evaluated by the monitor, and each section accompanied by guiding questions. This design reduces one of the major causes of missing inter-observer reliability: the disagreement on the operational definition of a construct regarding both the selection of sub aspects as well as their individual weightings (*Wirtz & Caspar* 2002: 31). Instead of having to freely assess, e.g., the efficiency of the project, the monitor is guided by the respective questions and concrete sub-aspects as listed in the previous section. This highly structured framework for the evaluation reports reduces the error variance from individual interpretation, and enhances inter-observer reliability, or comparability of the various reports – which has been one of the explicit intentions of the design (*European Commission* 2012: 8).

Inter-Comparability of Quantitative Project Ratings

The same challenges mentioned for the qualitative assessments in the previous paragraph apply to the quantitative project ratings: While in their result, the project ratings are 'hard' quantitative data, they are assigned in

4 Since the medium-term monitoring reports are prepared in the same format as the ex-post evaluation reports, and both are usually drafted by different monitors, an approach could be to compare ongoing and ex-post reports per project. However, it would be unclear how the involved biases should be controlled for.

the process of the report writing by the monitors, and are thus subject to the same discussed issue of inter-observer reliability. Two factors in the design help to address this:

With only four possible ratings (see Table 6-5), the scale is rather compact and reduces the latitude of subjective gradation for the assessor. While more graduated rating scales (e.g., the German *KFW Development Bank* uses a 6-step scale) often convey the character of an interval scale, the *EuropeAid* rating system features a clear and differentiating statement assigned to every grade, thus transforming a quasi-continuous item into a discrete, ordinal scale, which leaves less room for subjective nuances[5,6].

Additionally, as discussed in the previous section, the monitor does not assess the five ratings directly, but instead rates the individual sub-aspects, and the overall ratings are then a weighted average of the respective sub-aspect ratings (see Appendix B for the weighting scheme). This subdivision of the individual rating criteria has the same effect as described for the qualitative statements: The predefinition of sub-criteria reduces error variance from the differences of raters' individual (i.e., subjective) operative definitions of the criteria, such as of 'efficiency'.

Naturally, the set weightings may induce 'adaptive' rating, i.e., the monitor may feel inclined to modify individual ratings in order to obtain a specific overall category rating score. This behavior is known by *EuropeAid* and explicitly prohibited in the *Monitoring Handbook* (*European Commission* 2012: 64). Nevertheless, such a behavior does not need to necessarily impose a bias on reliability: After all, each rating is not an objective measure but a subjective assessment, and if a monitor feels a project deserves a specific overall category rating score, this may well be the case for a reason.

5 Interval scaling requires equidistance of the intervals, while ordinal scaling does not. As explained in the previous section, the scale can be understood as a three-step scale (performance higher than, equal, lower than planned) with en extra step on the low end (failure of the project with possible negative impact).

6 The application of finer gradation for the rating scales often turns out to be more of a cosmetic feature: In practice, the higher resolution is later reduced as intervals are often grouped for analysis and presentation.

Rating Consistency

Inter-project consistency (i.e., the consistency of the assessments of one monitor for different projects) is catered to by the same design aspects as those discussed above for the reliability criterion.

Conclusions on *intra*-project inconsistencies in the ratings can be drawn from the compatibility of a monitor's qualitative statements with the ratings he assigns to the project. I.e., if the qualitative explanations describe a substantial amount of problems and unsolved challenges, but these issues are not reflected in corresponding ratings (or vice versa), the assessments have to be treated critically. In a first batch of reports that were used for the pilot study for this research, this issue had indeed been a problem. For the main study, this aspect therefore has been covered with a dummy variable in the data collection (consistency of quantitative and qualitative assessments) with the intention to remove affected projects from the sample. However, no reports had to be eliminated because of this criterion.

Completeness of Information

Completeness may in fact be viewed as a specific form of reliability: the reliability that those observed circumstances that the monitor deems relevant are recorded in the report. (Naturally, this presumes the actually relevant information to be observed and deemed relevant by the monitor in the first place.) Both the quantity and quality of the descriptions provided in the reports vary substantially, and both do not necessarily coincide; there are both reports with a high volume of text but a rather descriptive style and little information, as well as reports with concise comments and explanations that are presented in a rather compact exterior. This phenomenon cannot be ignored and does potentially produce a bias to the intercomparability. However, for the sample of the extreme groups, only one report contained too little data for meaningful interpretation, and was excluded manually.

6.2 Definition of the Project Performance Criterion

With the five quantitative performance ratings contained in each project report, a potentially apt measure for the variable of project performance already exists. However, for the formation of extreme groups, a *single* measure is needed to select the actual reports for evaluation.

6.2.1 Quantitative Exploration of the Large Dataset

The first obvious idea would be to calculate the arithmetic mean of the five ratings to arrive at an overall project rating. In order to explore the adequacy of this measure, quantitative analyses of the total n = 457 sample are conducted, i.e., to test to what extent the arithmetic mean discards critical information of the individual ratings. Table 6-7 shows the results of a Pearson correlation analysis: The individual ratings show high inter-correlation values with the maximum per variable between 0.43 and 0.62, which is remarkable given the large n.

Table 6-7: Correlation matrix (Pearson n-1) of the five rating categories for the total (n=457) sample

Variables	RELV	EFCY	EFCT	IMPT	SUST
RELV	1	0.435	0.432	0.376	0.351
EFCY	0.435	1	0.611	0.443	0.343
EFCT	0.432	0.611	1	0.623	0.449
IMPT	0.376	0.443	0.623	1	0.538
SUST	0.351	0.343	0.449	0.538	1

All values different from 0 at a significance level of α=.001

A Principal Component Analysis confirms this impression (see Table 6-8) and shows that the total variance of the ratings (i.e., the monitor's rating conduct) is almost completely explained by only one factor: The first factor has a substantially high eigenvalue of 2.857 and a contribution to variance explanation of over 57%. The eigenvalues of the remaining factors are all clearly below 1. This result is stable for the n = 137 sub sample, as seen in Table 6-9.

Table 6-8: Principal Component Analysis of the five project ratings of the total (n=457) sample

	F1	F2	F3	F4	F5
Eigenvalue	2,857	0,739	0,635	0,453	0,317
Variability (%)	57,135	14,780	12,691	9,050	6,344
Cumulative %	57,135	71,915	84,606	93,656	100,000

Table 6-9: Principal Component Analysis of the five project ratings of the qualitative (n=137) sample

	F1	F2	F3	F4	F5
Eigenvalue	3,054	0,726	0,663	0,309	0,247
Variability (%)	61,089	14,516	13,268	6,177	4,949
Cumulative %	61,089	75,605	88,873	95,051	100,000

These results suggest that it may indeed be perfectly sensible to reduce the five rating values to their arithmetic mean. For the sake of completeness, the arithmetic mean correlates with the PCA's factor 1 scores at a coefficient of $r_s = 0.993$ ($\alpha = 0.001$).

Possible Explanations for the Results

The results of high intercorrelation of the five project ratings may be explained by two approaches:

1. A psychological explanation would be the classical *halo effect*, as first described by *Thorndike* (1920)[7]. This is a cognitive bias where judgments on individual personality aspects are influenced by an overall impression of a person. As a consequence, existing impressions or previously formed judgments influence following assessments; one classical illustration is that of rating student tests (*Kahneman* 2011: 83), where tests with decreasing quality of answers receive a more favorable rating than such with increasing answer quality. *Kahneman* (ibid.: 82) complains that despite its importance and pervasiveness, the effect is still not commonly known or represented in everyday language. In context of ODA project evaluation, a high intercorrelation of the individual ratings may be driven by such an overall impression that then influences the assessments of individual project performance aspects – both positively and negatively.

7 *Thorndike* used the term "error of the 'halo'" (ibid.: 28).

2. A second explanation is the inherent logic of the rating criteria: The individual categories relevance, efficiency, effectiveness, impact and sustainability are intrinsically interdependent. E.g., sustainability and impact are dependent on effectiveness in the performance logic (only an effective project can unfold any impact, and only if there is any impact can this be sustainable), while an irrelevant project is very unlikely to be effective in the first place. Finally, effectiveness is the logical precondition for efficiency, as defined by *Barnard* (1938: 127) and later *Drucker* (1967: 1f.)[8].

Most likely, the high intercorrelations of the five ratings in question are attributable to the combined force of these two effects.

Testing for Differences Between Total and Sub Sample

Since the formation of extreme groups will be conducted with the cases of the smaller sub sample, it is important that the distribution of the criterion is homogenous for the two samples. Table 6-10 shows the distribution of the variable *rating arithmetic mean* for the n = 137 sub sample versus the n = 457-137 total minus the sub sample.

Table 6-10: Distribution of Rating Arithmetic Mean for the total and sub sample

	4-3.6	3.4	3.2	3	2.8	2.6	2.4	2.2	2	1.8-1
n=137	8	10	15	22	27	12	14	14	5	10
n=457-137	16	15	18	73	54	40	36	29	24	15

Both samples do not differ systematically concerning their distribution of the *rating arithmetic mean* and *grade class* variables. These results are valid at a significance level of $\alpha = 0.001$ for all tests: *Rating arithmetic mean* was tested using a two-sample t-test for the n = 457-137 and the n = 137 samples and a comparison of variances, treating the variable as quasi-metrically scaled. Also, if the variable is treated as (ranked) nominal with categories (similar to the 'grade class' variable), the result holds true when the two samples are compared using a χ^2-test (see Appendix E for detailed results).

8 See Footnote 34 on page 49.

6.2.2 Formation of Extreme Groups

This study uses an extreme-group approach, i.e., selects only the extreme high- and low-value cases of the criterion in order to arrive at a stronger contrast[9,10]. In this study, this procedure is sensible for two reasons:

- The measured representations of the EC construct are only an approximation and as such subject to random measurement error. The same is true for the quantitative values of the criterion, which are based on subjective assessments of the monitors. Eliminating the middle-value cases from the comparison produces a stronger contrast for the criterion and increases statistical power.
- Because of the high volume of qualitative data per case, the amount of cases has to be reduced to a feasible level. Extreme group sizes are commonly chosen on the basis of sample quantiles; for this study, the top and bottom octile of the qualitative n = 137 sample was included, resulting in two groups with 17 cases each. This cutoff provided enough cases for meaningful evaluation, while at the same time ensuring the within-group homogeneity of the 'project performance' criterion, which is one of the assumptions for the extreme-groups approach (*Preacher* 2015: 1189). Using quartiles as the cutoff would have compromised on the within-group homogeneity: It would have implied including a third *grade class* level (see page 188) in the bottom group and a fifth rating level to the top group, and thus would not have been suited for this sample.

The project performance was ranked using a lexicographic approach of the grade class variable and the rating arithmetic mean: The projects were ordered by grade class first, and rating arithmetic mean second. As there are not enough cases in the top and bottom grade class (I and IV), the highest performers (by rating arithmetic mean) of grade-class IIa projects as well as lowest performers of grade-class III projects were additionally included. This results in a range of 'rating arithmetic mean' values between 4 and 3.2 for the top group and 2.2 and 1 for the bottom group (a complete listing of the cases is provided with the presentation of the results in Section 6.4).

---

9 See *Preacher et al.* (2005) for a discussion of the extreme groups approach and related literature.

10 The extreme groups were formed after the sourcing of the primary data; nevertheless, as the sample formation preceded the actual evaluation of the reports, it does not classify as *post hoc* subgrouping.

Extreme-groups designs imply that the requirements for parametric tests such as t-tests are not met and only non-parametric testing is adequate (*Bortz & Döring* 2006: 494). Within the scope of this study, this does not pose a limiting factor, as the construct's representation are contingencies of symptom descriptions, and the differences between the two groups are tested for by using χ^2-tests.

Manual Elimination of Reports from the Sample

Finally, a total amount of 12 reports, of which 5 in the top group and 7 in the bottom group, was excluded from the extreme groups manually during the selection, for the simple reason that the respective descriptions did not provide a sufficient level of quantity and/or quality needed for meaningful text analysis. For a total of seven cases (2 in the top group, 5 in the bottom group), this was due to the respective projects being part of a larger program, which made it difficult to clearly separate the influence factors in the reports' descriptions.

These cases were skipped and replaced by the adjacent case in the sorted list. However, as no selection criteria of the total sample were violated by the respective cases, they have not been excluded from the total sample (i.e., no post-hoc corrections of the above calculations).

6.3 Operationalization of the 'Elite Compatibility' Construct Into a Research Design

For the empirical evaluation, the central hypothesis to be tested is the correlation of EC and project success. Further exploration seeks to identify patterns and coherences in order to find out in what context EC is of relevance, and whether and how it can be influenced. This section will explain how the construct is operationalized, i.e., translated into concrete measurement techniques.

6.3.1 Methodology

The central goal of this study's empirical evaluation is to measure the presence of EC phenomena in ODA projects, and elaborate on the specific type and context. With ex-post project evaluation reports as the empirical material, the approach is to identify those problem (or success) descriptions in the reports that are congruent with descriptions from theory. In order to do so, each report is reviewed and all problem and success descriptions are extracted, then compared to a coding scheme whether they match any of the descriptions, and coded with the respective information about the problem type and additional sub-criteria. The coding frame for this study has been prepared based on the descriptions provided in the monograph by *Gibson et al.* (2005). Both the data collection as well as the building of the coding frame will be laid out in more detail below. This procedure, which is illustrated in Figure 6-2, is a form of what is referred to as *content analysis*.

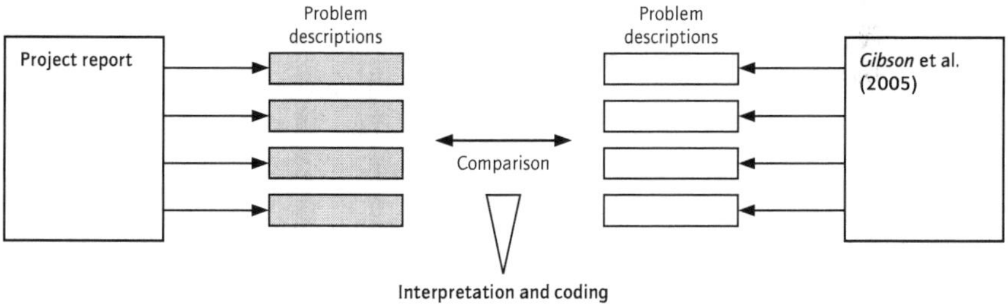

Figure 6-2: The basic logic of the empirical evaluation

The method of content analysis is often reported to have been pioneered by *Harold Lasswell* in his dissertation on propaganda in mass media (1927/1971)[11]. This heritage is noticeable also in today's assortment of applications of content analysis, where the field of public media still remains a key research subject, alongside with the application to interpersonal and political communication (cf. *Neuendorf* 2002: 191ff.). *Berelson* (1952) was the first specific monograph on content analysis and as such delivered the first 'official' definition as "objective, systematic and quantitative" (ibid.: 18). In its basic form, content analysis may simply deliver a quantitative analysis of the incidences, e.g., of certain words, phrases etc., which is also how it was used in *Lasswell's* work. The method used for this study, however, requires the interpretation of the qualitative data of the project reports prior to their coding, and hence may classify as the type of *qualitative content analysis* that was systematically described by *Mayring* (1983).

11 For a historical overview of the roots of the method of content analysis, see, e.g., *Krippendorf* (2013: 10ff.) and the literature cited there, as well as, in German, *Früh* (2011: 11ff.).

This dichotomous taxonomy is one of the strongly debated aspects of the method. E.g., while *Mayring* (2010: 18) classifies all analyses based on nominal-scale measures as qualitative, *Krippendorf* (2013: 22) contends that "ultimately, all reading of texts is qualitative, even when certain characteristics of a text are later converted into numbers". Applying the latter logic, one could certainly argue the contrary: All content analysis is ultimately quantitative, *because* the measured characteristics are later converted into numbers. I.e., this research is quantitative in the sense that the goal is capturing the frequency of incidences, but with a qualitative element in between, as the coding requires interpretation of the data[12].

Due to the "constructivist" nature (cf. *Oleinik* 2010: 860) of this inductive component, the method of qualitative content analysis is sometimes criticized for the "highly subjective character". But while it is often seen as an ambiguous venture to apply the classical quality criteria of objectivity, reliability and validity to general qualitative research (cf. *Flick* 2006: 429), this should not distract from the fact that for the framework-oriented approach of content analysis, a central goal needs to be minimizing the extent of subjectiveness of the interpretation, in order to make the results reproducible and replicable. Thus, reliability indeed *is* an essential criterion that needs to be attended to, and in fact, most of the commonly postulated requirements for content analysis research design cater to this criterion. These requirements will be discussed together with the explanations in the following. A critical discussion of the overall research design will be provided in Section 6.5 at the end of this chapter. The next section will address the formation of the coding frame.

6.3.2 The Coding Frame for Content Analysis

The coding frame is based on the monograph by *Gibson et al.* (2005). As discussed previously, their work is based on in-depth case studies of five different types of projects, and presents a rather compact, yet complete discussion of the incentive-related problem complexes of ODA. The coding frame is simple and straightforward: All problem phenomena that feature an incentive-oriented explanation have been collected and assigned an identification code. Each item contains information on the observable

12 It is for this reason that authors such as *Früh* (2011: 67) decline the taxonomy as "inappropriately dichotomizing" (own translation, original: "diese unzutreffend dichotomisierenden Bezeichnungen").

phenomenon and the underlying incentive situation or problem as provided by the authors, and additional information including the references as well as the case study incidence.

As an important addition, the items are enhanced with the taxonomies previously set in this study: the classification of which elite level it relates to (national-level elite, agency elite, local-level elite; see Section 6.3.3), as well as which type of resistance it indicates (active, extractive/project assets, extractive/project output, passive). An exemplary excerpt is shown in Table 6-11 below. A full list can be found in Appendix F.

While the research presented in this study was preceded by pilot studies, the symptom IDs of the coding frame remained fixed, as they are based on a fixed theoretical framework. Thus, other than sometimes seen as a requirement (*Schreier* 2014: 173), the coding frame has not been adapted or modified in its categories. This is also due to the fact that it refrains from using a hierarchical structure and as such was not in need of this type of adaptation[13].

13 In fact, the pilot design of this research applied a type of hierarchical structure, however, the concept was discarded again because of the associated epistemological problems: Such a design would have involved causal inferences that may appear face-valid, but are not actually provided by the reports.

Table 6-11: Examples of items from the coding frame

ID	Elite level			Resistance				Observable phenomenon			Underlying incentive situation	Inci-dence
	national	agency	local	active	extractive-p	extractive-o	passive		Ref theory	Ref case		
20	y	n	n	n	y	n	n	No governmental support of an agency (e.g., regulation agency) part of a previously accepted reform; Agency dependent on donor support	113	204, 207	Donor conditions as the "price" of aid support: 1. Meeting the donor's demand for institutional change without wholesale changes to government structures (institutions can be designed to ensure influence) 2. Regulation authorities provide the government with a "buffer" from public criticism generated by rate hikes or privatization actions.	Energy Regulation Board, Zambia
08	y	y	y	n	y	y	n	Local communities are not accorded privileges of ownership, although they possess the largest stake in responsible management of their natural resources	101	177, 181	Local governmental departments are provided legal monopoly in protecting (i.e., excluding) and raising revenue from local resources. Departments oppose devolving ownership and resist increased participation.	Orissa Forest Management, India

The inferences involved in the coding, i.e., the matching of a description from a report to a problem description from the coding frame, rely on *indicators*. Those are passages that are not problem descriptions but deliver additional background information which may support conclusive interpretation; this will be explained in more detail in the next section. The coding frame thus meets the common requirements of the categories to be exhaustive and mutually exclusive (*Neuendorf* 2002: 118ff.; *Schreier* 2014: 175): The labels are exhaustive in the sense that they include problems that are not EC-related, as well as a category for non-specified issues. Secondly, as will be laid out in the description of the data collection process in Section 6.3.3, mutual exclusiveness is given as indicator passages are collected from the texts and help distinguishing inconclusive descriptions; in case a single description contains multiple components or aspects, it is separated and coded individually.

6.3.3 The Data Collection and Coding Procedure

The heart of this research is the collection and coding of symptoms from the project reports; these symptoms may describe successful aspects as well as aspects of failure for the project and its components. It appears trivial that low-performing projects are very likely to feature a higher frequency of problem descriptions, and high-performing projects a higher frequency of success descriptions. However, the interest behind this research is not the mere amount of problems, but the relevance of a specific *type* of problems. Consequently, the goal of the coding is to assign the required information to each item to allow for this analysis. The logic of this procedure will be laid out below.

As explained before, in a first step, all relevant descriptions of a report are extracted into a dataset; in order to include all available information, all five sections of each report (i.e., relevance, efficiency, effectiveness, impact, sustainability) are taken into account. In a next step, every item is then coded. Figure 6-3 illustrates the steps of this procedure.

In the coding process, the statements in the material are taken 'for granted', i.e., the monitor's reliability and credibility are not doubted. While this may be criticized as "epistemologically naive" (*Schreier* 2014: 181), there is simply no way of consistently assessing the verdict of the reports' authors. The upside of this approach is that it positively affects reliability, as it avoids another component of subjective interpretation.

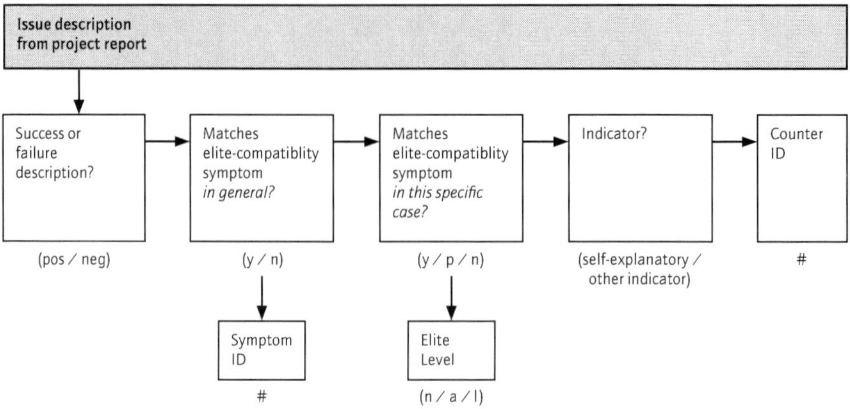

Figure 6-3: Steps of the data interpretation and classification of elite-compatibility issues

In more detail, the coding procedure is as follows:

Positive vs. Negative

Every extracted description is rated either as *negative* (*neg*), for a description that denotes a problem presence, or *positive* (*pos*) for a description that denotes a success (or the absence of a possible problem). Examples:

> "The district offices received full support from the Ministry of Transportation, budgets were approved in a timely and transparent manner." → *rated as* pos.

> "Envisaged budgets were not approved by the Ministry and maintenance works could repeatedly not be executed." → *rated as* neg.

This variable does not yet specify the *type* of problem, but simply classifies the issue as a description of the presence or absence of a problem for project success. The interpretation of each description into a type is then separated into two steps, general and specific:

General Problem Type: Elite-compatibility Related?

The description is compared with the list of problems that has been extracted from *Gibson et al.* (2005), and dummy-rated (*y*/*n*) whether or not it resembles an issue which holds a theoretical explanation that makes it an issue of EC. This rating refers to the un-specific appearance of the issue, i.e., whether the description from the report matches a problem description from the list *in general*. If this is the case (*y*), the problem ID from the list is assigned. Example:

> "Envisaged budgets were not approved by the Ministry and required maintenance works could repeatedly not be executed." → *This refers to the problem of maintenance (symptom ID #50), and is rated as general* yes.

> "An unplanned gap in programming led to suspension of the project over a time frame of 4 months, causing a breakdown of carefully built-up trust among stakeholders." → *This refers to a problem on the donor side; general* no */ no symptom ID.*

Specific Problem Type: Elite-compatibility Related?

However, the mere description of a problem, i.e., of an outcome, does not automatically imply that the incentive-theoretic explanation is the correct underlying cause of this outcome. This is accounted for by the second dummy that captures whether or not this problem can be interpreted as 'EC-related *in this specific case'*. This interpretation may be possible from the description itself or from a separate passage of the report that hints to circumstances that indicate EC presence or absence. The variable may have three values:

- Yes (*y*), if EC relation is clearly indicated from the report;
- possibly (*p*), if EC relation is likely, but not explicitly indicated in the report;
- no (*n*), if the report *contraindicates* the issue to be EC-related.

In case of y or n, it is also recorded whether the interpretation is based on the problem description itself (*self-explanatory*) or a different passage that is used as an indicator (*indicator*). Example:

> "The regulation agency suffered from staffing with substantially underqualified personnel, which hampered their capacity and contributed to its ineffectiveness."

In general, this can be classified as problem ID #20 (denial of support for a regulation agency). Without any further indication, this problem will receive a [neg|y|p] rating, as it is possibly EC-related but lacks explicit attribution. For a classification as [neg|y|y], i.e., that the problem is generally *and* specifically EC-related, the report needs to provide a clear indication, such as:

> "The regulation agency was subject to different support issues from the Ministry of Energy. This concerned both the approval of required funds as well as the provision of requested information."

However, the underqualified personnel may also be attributable to mere availability problems. If this is mentioned in the report, such as:

> "The staffing proved to be a constant problem for the entire project timeframe, since the availability of qualified staff is a notorious country-wide issue."

With this contraindicator, the previous problem will be rated as [neg|y|n], a problem exists, but is *not* EC-related.

Elite Level

elite level If a description matches a symptom type of EC, it is coded which elite level the description refers to. Possible levels are *national-level* (political) elite, *agency* elite and *local-level* elite. The term 'agency' does not refer to the implementing partner or the aid agency, but to those organizational entities within the political structure that are accorded a separate position dedicated to the management of a specific task or resource. This may be a regulation agency, an authority specifically responsible for a certain road infrastructure or departments in charge of protecting (and extracting) natural resources. Multiple entries are possible. This coding will later allow the analysis to take into account the different spheres of action of the different project types.

Indicator Passages

The indicator passages that serve for the above interpretation are also extracted from the reports. Whether a description is marked as an indicator or problem description, depends on if it explicitly refers to the project management or just describes circumstances or design aspects. Examples:

> "The design contains a high quality logframe which clearly reflects the connections between the different elements of the intervention." → *This is a mere description of a design component; collected as an indicator.*

> "The logframe however was not used later on as a management tool and there was no interest in assessing the progress of the project." → *This contains an assessment of the project management quality; collected as a problem description.*

Counter variable

The goal of the data collection and interpretation is both the analysis of the problem *types* as well as the *amount*, i.e., the number of incidences in the projects. As mentioned above, the type of issue is captured by the problem ID. In order to enable a quantitative analysis on the *amount* of issues mentioned in the report, each issue is numbered with a counter variable. If a description refers to a same or similar issue that has already been coded, it receives the same counter, in order to avoid counting the same issue twice.

Qualitative Variables Collected for Further Analyses

While the majority of project reports provide sufficient information for the above interpretation, i.e., the presence or absence of EC issues, they rarely provide insight as to *why* a project was elite compatible or not. In order to explore possible correlations of project features with the amount of EC issues, an array of additional qualitative variables was collected, as listed in Table 6-12. These variables relate to the qualities of the project design and of project implementation, as well as the type of implementing partner, which may be, e.g., the public administration of the recipient country, an NGO, or a profit-oriented organization. All values were generated from the written content of the project reports.

Table 6-12: Additional qualitative variables collected per project

Qualitative Variable	Values		
LQ (Logframe quality)	y – high	n – low	0 – not available
AQ (Assumptions quality)	y – high	n – low	0 – not available
AC (Assumptions correct)	y – yes	n – no	0 – not available
AG (Ambitiousness of project goals)	y – ambitious	n – realistic	0 – not available
BE (Baseline study existent)	y – existent	n – not existent	0 – not available
FD (Flexibility of project design)	y – flexible	n – not flexible	0 – not available
MQ (Internal monitoring quality)	y – high	n – low	0 – not available
PD (Participatory design)	y – yes	n – no	0 – not available
RM (Resource managed by...)	g – government entities	s – local stakeholders	0 – not available/ applicable
IP (Type of implementing partner; coding adopted from *EuropeAid* taxonomy)	00 – not available 01 – International NGO/CSOs/Universities (at EU and international level) 02 – Local NGOs/CSOs/Universities (at Partner country level) 03 – Profit-oriented organizations (companies, think-tanks, institutes) 04 – International governmental organizations (non UN) 05 – UN family organizations (incl. WB) 06 – Partner countries' public administration (ministries, municipalities, etc.) 07 – European countr. public administration (ministries, municipalities, etc.) 08 – European governmental organizations/EU agencies 09 – Regional bodies (MERCOSUR, SADEC, ASEAN, etc.) 10 – Hybrids (mix of different partners)		

6.3.4 Code Types for Symptoms Collected From the Reports

The classification of the extracted issues in terms of 'general' and 'specific' congruence with EC explanations results in eight different possible types of symptoms, as are listed in Table 6-13. (The types of [|n|y] and [|n|p], while technically possible, do not render sensible categories and are not listed.)

Table 6-13: Code types of data interpretation

Pos/Neg	General	Specific	Description	Explanation
pos	y	y	Elite-compatibility problem absence, *confirmed*	
	y	p	Elite-compatibility problem absence, *likely*	
	y	n	Elite-compatibility problem absence *contraindicated*	EC-related problem does not exist, but elite-compatibility issue is not solved
	n	n	Positive factor, *not* elite-compatibility related	Other positive factors, such as weather, economic factors, etc.
neg	y	y	Elite-compatibility problem, explanation *confirmed*	
	y	p	Elite-compatibility problem, explanation *likely*	
	y	n	Elite-compatibility problem, e xplanation *contraindicated*	Problem exists, but other reasons than elite-compatibility issues.
	n	n	Problem, but *not* elite-compatibility related	E.g., problems resulting from donor-sided issues

An important specification is that if the EC relation of a description is not confirmed, the result will be a [|y|p] rating and not a [|y|n] rating. The type of [|y|n] does not denote that a description's EC relation is unconfirmed, but that it is *contraindicated.*

As can be seen, the simple two-step rating procedure of problem or success descriptions results in a taxonomy that also includes other problem types than just those of EC. It is thus possible to analyze the importance of EC in relation to those other problem complexes. EC issues are captured by the [|y|y] and [|y|p] types (i.e., both *pos* and *neg*), while [|n|n] and [neg|y|n] capture problems that are not related to EC. This does not imply that there is no underlying incentive-theoretic explanation, but simply that there is not an *elite-related* explanation; an example are donor-sided problems.

A Symptom Types 'Scale'

In order to render the different code types more intuitively accessible, I suggest the following ordinal scale as a mental model to describe their relations. Figure 6-4 presents this scale, including colloquial summaries of each code type.

I	II	III	IV	V	VI	VII	VIII
[pos|n|n]	[pos|y|y]	[pos|y|p]	[pos|y|n]	[neg|y|p]	[neg|y|y]	[neg|y|n]	[neg|n|n]
Other success factors	"elite compatibility *confirmed*"	"elite compatibility *possible*"	"looks like elite compatibility solved, but isn't"	"elite incompatibility *possible*"	"elite incompatibility *confirmed*"	"looks like elite incompatible, but is other reasoning"	Other problem factors
← successes →			← problems →				
	Elite-compatibility symptoms, of which:						
	confirmed	← possible →				confirmed	

Figure 6-4: The different code types in an 'ordinal scale'

On the left (type I-III) are the success descriptions, on the right (IV-VIII) the problem descriptions. Again, it is important to note that [pos|y|n] (type IV) effectively denotes a problem, despite its association with the 'positive' category. The categories relating to EC issues, and hence of main interest for this study, are types II-VI.

Notation

Above, to denote the different symptom types, the standard triple notation of

$$[\alpha|\beta|\gamma] \text{ with } \alpha = \{\text{“pos”}; \text{“neg”}\},\quad \beta = \{\text{“y”}; \text{“n”}\} \text{ and } \gamma = \{\text{“y”}; \text{“p”}; \text{“n”}\}$$

was used. In the following, I will use a simplified notation for the sake of better readability. I choose a scheme where "PosYY" denotes [pos|y|y] issues and "NegNN" replaces [neg|n|n], for instance. This notation avoids characters that could be confused with operators, as well as spaces, and yet retains a relatively quick visual 'accessibility'. In the following tables, the code types are used as labels for columns containing contingency counts. Again for the sake of readability and unification, the simplified notation is also used in for labeling simple mathematical operations to calculate ratios. E.g., the ratio of:

NegYY / (NegYN + NegNN)

denotes

n([neg|y|y]) / (n([neg|y|n]) + n([neg|n|n])) with $n \longrightarrow \{ \mathbb{N} \}$ as the number of contingencies

Lastly, the TOTAL values draw a total of all unspecified characteristics, i.e., "TOTAL Pos" cumulates the contingencies of [pos| |], and TOTAL YY denotes the count for [|y|y].

6.4 Results of the Evaluation

6.4.1 Distribution of Elite Compatibility Issues

Table 6-14 shows an overview of the results for the two contrast groups of high- and low-performing projects. The symptom types are ordered in the logic described in Figure 6-4. EC-related issues are located in the gray columns; the light gray columns contain 'possible', i.e., likely but unconfirmed factors, dark gray denotes 'strict' (i.e., [|y|y] factors that are *explicitly* confirmed.

The right area of the table provides the total frequencies for all positive and negative factors (bold values), and the ratio of positive vs. negative factors. The dark gray columns focus on EC: The 'strict' ([|y|y]) factor counts are repeated and the total of only those strict factor incidences is drawn. The last column calculates a ratio of the EC problems ([neg|y|y]) to all other problems ([neg|y|n]; [neg|n|n]).

Table 6-14: Distribution of incidences of success and problem factors in the evaluated projects

#	Grade CLASS	Rating MEAN	Budget	PosNN	PosYY	PosYP	PosYN	NegYP	NegYY	NegYN	NegNN	*TOTAL Pos*	*TOTAL Neg*	*TOTAL*	TOTAL Pos / TOTAL Neg	PosYY	NegYY	*TOTAL YY*	NegYY / (NegYN + NegNN)
1	I	4	584,798	7			1	2			2	7	4	11	1.8				0
2	I	3.6	430,000	1	6	1		1			3	8	4	12	2.0	6		6	0
3	I	3.6	1,541,640	3	4			2	3	1	1	7	7	14	1.0	4	3	7	1.5
4	I	3.6	1,005,030	2	9				1		2	11	3	14	3.7	9	1	10	0.5
5	I	3.6	663,032	2	6	1			1		5	9	6	15	1.5	6	1	7	0.2
6	IIa	3.4	1,521,402	3	8						2	11	2	13	5.5	8		8	0
7	IIa	3.4	2,550,000	5	4	1	1				2	10	2	12	5.0	4		4	0
8	IIa	3.4	1,500,000		3	1	1			1	1	4	2	6	2.0	3		3	0
9	IIa	3.4	1,356,100	1	4					1	2	5	3	8	1.7	4		4	0
10	IIa	3.4	1,000,000	2	5			1		1	2	7	4	11	1.8	5		5	0
11	IIa	3.4	2,715,502		3		2	2	1		3	3	6	9	0.5	3	1	4	0.33
12	IIa	3.4	882,198	1	7					1		8	1	9	8.0	7		7	0
13	IIa	3.2	749,977	2	5	4		1			6	11	7	18	1.6	5		5	0
14	IIa	3.2	5,000,000		6	1	2	1	3	2	1	7	7	14	1.0	6	3	9	1
15	IIa	3.2	14,100,000		7				1	1	1	7	3	10	2.3	7	1	8	0.5
16	IIa	3.2	1,124,655		7	1		1			2	8	3	11	2.7	7		7	0
17	IIa	3.2	1,740,125		6				1	1	3	6	5	11	1.2	6	1	7	0.25
1	III	2.2	1,981,000	2		1		1		4	3	3	8	11	0.4				0
2	III	2.2	1,152,474		1			3	1	1	6	1	11	12	0.1	1	1	2	0.14
3	III	2.2	4,900,000			1	3		10			1	10	11	0.1		10	10	n.def
4	III	2.2	24,823,049	1				4	4			1	8	9	0.1		4	4	n.def
5	III	2.2	1,680,000		6	1	1	2		4	5	7	11	18	0.6	6		6	0
6	III	2	22,000,000		2			5	9	1	2	2	17	19	0.1	2	9	11	3
7	III	2	1,110,000		2			4		5	9	2	18	20	0.1	2		2	0
8	IV	2.2	14,465,710		3			2	1	5	5	3	13	16	0.2	3	1	4	0.1
9	IV	2.2	59,883,921		1			2	6		1	1	9	10	0.1	1	6	7	6
10	IV	2	1,272,126		3			2	1	3	1	3	7	10	0.4	3	1	4	0.25
11	IV	1.6	19,800,000					1	11		1		13	13	0		11	11	11
12	IV	1.6	750,000						1	1	9		11	11	0		1	1	0.1
13	IV	1.6	61,000,000					4	4	2	6		16	16	0		4	4	0.5
14	IV	1.6	15,000,000		1			2	2	4	5	1	13	14	0.1	1	2	3	0.22
15	IV	1.2	6,000,000				2		9		4		13	13	0		9	9	2.25
16	IV	1.2	921,480					2	8		5		15	15	0		8	8	1.6
17	IV	1	1,673,950					2	9		1		12	12	0		9	9	9

The results are discussed below. Unless otherwise indicated, the tests for differences between the groups have been performed using χ^2-tests.

General Distribution of Success vs. Problem Incidences

Concerning the distribution of the problem and success descriptions in general (TOTAL Pos; TOTAL Neg), the following features can be observed:

- First of all, while the problem type of PosYN (symptoms that *appear* to have EC problems solved, but the solution is contraindicated) appeared as an interesting category during the empirical evaluation, is not of high actual relevance from an overall viewpoint. Because of its specific (i.e., difficult) predication, it has also not been included in the TOTAL values and is discarded from further discussion.
- The general tendency is as expected: The top group features a higher amount of success descriptions than problem descriptions (TOTAL Pos/TOTAL Neg > 1), vice versa for the bottom group. The difference between the two groups, as shown in Table 6-15 is very highly significant at $\alpha = 0.001$ and render a moderate correlation of $\Phi = 0.56$.

Table 6-15: Contingency table of the TOTAL Pos and TOTAL Neg descriptions

	TOTAL Pos	TOTAL Neg	Total
Top Group	129	69	198
Bottom Group	25	205	230
Total	154	274	428

- One prominent result is that both the top as well as the bottom group feature success as well as problem factors. The fact that challenges are always contingent even in highly successful projects (where those challenges have obviously been dealt with effectively), illustrates that their success is likely not a matter of pure luck but indeed does coincide with a higher management capacity. In fact, the top group has no cases without problem descriptions, while in the bottom group, there are cases with no success factors.
- Failed projects have more problem descriptions than successful projects feature success factors. This is natural because it is common and expected for the reports to identify problems and their attributions, while successes are not only harder to attribute, but are also not expected to be attributed in the same detail as problems.
- The total amount of descriptions (positive and negative) is significantly higher in the bottom group.

Elite Compatibility

The category of 'unconfirmed' issue descriptions (PosYP; NegYP), as denoted in the light gray columns, enabled an important differentiation during the coding procedure. In order to arrive at meaningful conclusions, the further discussion will ignore the contingencies of this category and concentrate on the 'strict' categories only (YY symptoms), which are summarized in the last columns in dark gray.

- Firstly, the above difference in general success and problem descriptions is also true for the symptoms relating to EC. The difference in distribution, as listed in Table 6-16 is very highly significant at $\alpha = 0.001$ and renders a high correlation of $\Phi = 0.70$.

Table 6-16: Contingency table for elite-compatibility symptoms

	PosYY	NegYY	Total
Top Group	90	11	101
Bottom Group	19	76	95
Total	109	87	196

- EC symptoms are present as success factors in *all* but one projects of the top group, while they are *not present in all* projects in the bottom group as problem factors. In other words, while all successful projects appear to be elite compatible in at least some aspects, not all failed projects display EC problems.
  What this suggests for the bottom group is that, while elite *in*compatibility appears to be the main reason for failure in many cases (#3; 4; 6; 9; 11; 13; 15-17), other factors may well lead to failure despite the absence of EC problems (#1) or even symptoms of EC (#5; 7; 8; 10; 14).
  In numerical terms, this situation is apparent in a much higher variance of elite- compatibility problems (NegYY) in the bottom group over the successes (PosYY) in the top group (Table 6-17). This difference is significant at $\alpha = 0.05$ (F-test).

Table 6-17: Comparison of the variances (n-1) of elite-compatibility related symptoms

Variance (n-1)	PosYY	NegYY
Top Group	4.721	0.993
Bottom Group	2.735	16.515

Verbalized, these "other features" leading to failure may be, e.g., a weak project design, external factors such as low capacity of involved government entities, or donor-related problems such as delays, unrealistic timeframes, or complications introduced by the consultant.

- The importance of EC-related problems over other problems is indicated by the value in the very right column, the ratio NegYY / (NegYN + NegNN). In the top group, this value is generally low, with only one exception > 1 (#3). In the bottom group, in contrast, the value is > 1 for 8 of the 17 cases (# 3; 4; 6; 9; 11; 15-17). However, much more interesting about this is the fact that the other 9 of 17 projects feature a ratio < 1, at a generally very low level (arithmetic mean = 0.15). Meaning, there is a clear dichotomy between failure that is clearly EC-related and failure that is clearly *not* EC-related.
- Looking at the latter group of low-performing projects where EC was not the main reason for failure (last column value < 1), four projects (# 5; 7; 8; 10) even show more EC-related successes than failures. This supports the previous observation that EC may be a necessary but not sufficient condition for success.
- When successful and failed projects are tested for their difference concerning all 'other' problem categories, i.e., successes *not* related to EC (PosNN) vs. problems not related to EC (NegYN + NegNN), this difference returns a very high significance ($\alpha = 0.001$), albeit only a moderate correlation of $\Phi = 0.45$. This demonstrates the lower importance of 'other' over EC aspects ($\Phi = 0.70$, as seen in Table 6-18) for project success.

Table 6-18: Contingency table for symptoms not related to elite-compatibility

	PosNN	NegYN + NegNN	Total
Top Group	29	47	76
Bottom Group	3	93	96
Total	32	140	172

Donor-related issues

Besides external factors such as unfavorable development of currency exchange rates, or meteorological conditions, the category of 'other' problems often related to the side of the donor. The most frequent problems of this category were:

- Bureaucratic procedures leading to delays in funding;
- consultant-donor principal-agent problems (*Gibson et al.* 2005: 72);
- failure of or delays caused by the consultant;
- poor programming (overambitious goals, unrealistic timeframe);
- poor (implausible) logical framework;
- poor terms of reference or indicators for monitoring, weakening the potential of good project management and qualified decision making;
- coordination problems when extending, merging or adapting a project design.

Summary

These general results confirm the relevance of the concept of EC in the sense that they expose a significant connection between EC and project performance. The distribution shows that EC seems to be a necessary but not sufficient condition for project success, and EC-related issues have a substantially higher correlation to project success than other factors unrelated to EC.

Nevertheless, the overview from Table 6-14 cannot provide any insight as to the reasoning behind the EC situation in the individual projects. As mentioned previously, neither is this possible from the original qualitative data from the reports, as the respective information is provided only very rarely in order to be suited for systematic induction. To explore possible causal patterns and elaborate the general findings, it is necessary to analyze the collected additional data. Namely, these data are the differentiation into the elite levels, the quantitative project data, the collected qualitative variables, and finally, the contingencies of the concrete issue codes from the coding frame. Each of these aspects will be discussed in the following sections.

6.4.2 Elaboration: Elite Levels

As explained in Section 6.3.3, each success or problem factor was coded either to the national-elite level (high-level politics, ministries etc.), agency-elite level (regulation agencies, authorities and departments dedicated to resource or asset administration), or local-elite level (district and local departments, local politicians). Table 6-19 again lists both extreme groups and their contingencies of 'strict' EC-related success (PosYY) and problem (NegYY) descriptions (gray columns). In the right columns, the elite levels of the compatibility issues of each project are differentiated. Additionally, the table contains the type of implementing partner, the sector, the target country of the intervention (ZONE), and the project budget.

Table 6-19: Breakdown of the levels (national, local, agency) of elite-compatibility issues

#	Grade CLASS	Rating MEAN	Implementing PARTNER	SECTOR	ZONE	BUDGET	PosYY	NegYY	PosYY national	PosYY agency	PosYY local	NegYY national	NegYY agency	NegYY local
1	I	4	010	Agriculture	Tajikistan	584,798								
2	I	3.6	001	Rural Dev.	Laos	430,000	6			1	5			
3	I	3.6	001	Energy	Cambodia	1,541,640	4	3	2	1	1	2		1
4	I	3.6	001	Agriculture	Timor Leste	1,005,030	9	1	3		7			1
5	I	3.6	001	Agriculture	Afghanistan	663,032	6	1			6	1		
6	IIa	3.4	002	Agriculture	W.Bank/Gaza	1,521,402	8		2		6			
7	IIa	3.4	001	Agriculture	Pakistan	2,550,000	4		1	2	3			
8	IIa	3.4	002	Rural Dev.	Bangladesh	1,500,000	3		1		3			
9	IIa	3.4	003	Energy	Uzbekistan	1,356,100	4		3	1				
10	IIa	3.4	001	Rural Dev.	Afghanistan	1,000,000	5		5	1	1			
11	IIa	3.4	001	Water/Sanit.	East Timor	2,715,502	3	1		1	2	1		
12	IIa	3.4	001	Rural Dev.	Tajikistan	882,198	7			1	6			
13	IIa	3.2	001	Water/Sanit.	Laos	749,977	5		1	1	3			
14	IIa	3.2	004	Rural Dev.	Afghanistan	5,000,000	6	3	3		4	1	1	1
15	IIa	3.2	006	Water/Sanit.	Ghana	14,100,000	7	1	2	2	5			1
16	IIa	3.2	001	Agriculture	Malawi	1,124,655	7				7			
17	IIa	3.2	001	Agriculture	Mozambique	1,740,125	6	1	1	2	4	1		
TOTAL TOP GROUP									24	13	63	6	1	4
1	III	2.2	009	Agriculture	Cook Islands	1,981,000								
2	III	2.2	005	Water/Sanit.	P.N.Guinea	1,152,474	1	1		1		1		
3	III	2.2	006	Water/Sanit.	P.N.Guinea	4,900,000		10				9		2
4	III	2.2	n/a	Water/Sanit.	Jamaica	24,823,049		4				4		
5	III	2.2	006	Agriculture	Vanuatu	1,680,000	6		3	3				
6	III	2	006	Water/Sanit.	Angola	22,000,000	2	9	1			5	5	
7	III	2	006	Water/Sanit.	Jamaica	1,110,000	2		1	1				
8	IV	2.2	006	Education	Botswana	14,465,710	3	1	2		1			
9	IV	2.2	n/a	Transport	Ethiopia	59,883,921	1	6				6		
10	IV	2	002	Energy	Namibia	1,272,126	3	1	3	3	3	1		
11	IV	1.6	006	Water/Sanit.	Cape Verde	19,800,000		11				9	1	
12	IV	1.6	001	Agriculture	Timor Leste	750,000		1						1
13	IV	1.6	006	Transport	Ghana	61,000,000		4				3	2	1
14	IV	1.6	006	Water/Sanit.	Nigeria	15,000,000	1	2	1			2	2	
15	IV	1.2	006	Agriculture	P.N.Guinea	6,000,000		9				8	8	
16	IV	1.2	006	Agriculture	Turkmenistan	921,480		8				8		
17	IV	1	003	Water/Sanit.	Turkmenistan	1,673,950		9				9	9	9
TOTAL BOTTOM GROUP									11	8	4	65	27	13

The above subdivision into different levels of elites now reveals an important detail: While in the top group, the PosYY factors are concentrated on the level of local elites, the NegYY factors in the bottom group are most frequent on the national level. I.e., successful projects seem to be elite *compatible* primarily with local elites, while in the low-performing projects, elite *in*compatibility issues mostly seem to arise with national-level elites.

The emphasis of the *national*-level *in*compatibility (NegYY) in the bottom group is very apparent: Out of the 11 projects that feature elite incompatibility issues, eight cases have their mode on the national level, and only three cases (#13; 15, 17) are an exception to this.

In the top group, this emphasis of *local*-level EC (PosYY) is rather strong in the 7 of 17 of cases (#2; 5; 6; 13; 15-17), and slightly weaker in others (#3; 4; 7; 8; 12; 14). Only two cases (#9; 10) do not have their modes in the local-level but in the national-level category. At the same time, these projects do not display any EC conflicts (NegYY) on the national-level either. Table 6-20 summarizes the incidences.

Table 6-20: Contingency table of elite-compatibility symptoms, breakdown by elite level

	PosYY			NegYY			
	national	agency	local	national	agency	local	Total
Top Group	24	13	63	6	1	4	110
Bottom Group	11	8	4	65	27	13	128
Total	35	21	66	71	28	17	238

To confirm the above observation, the top group's successes (PosYY) distribution can be tested against the bottom group's problems distribution (NegYY), as compiled in the reduced Table 6-21. The difference identifies as very highly significant ($\alpha = 0.001$), and the effect size of the 'group' variable is high ($V = 0.53$).

Table 6-21: Elite levels of top group's success descriptions vs. the bottom group's problem descriptions

	national	agency	local
Top Group PosYY	24	13	63
Bottom Group NegYY	65	27	13

The distribution illustrated in the above table – successful projects being elite-compatible on the local level, failed projects being elite incompatible on the national level – can be labeled a key finding for the differences between the top and bottom group. It suggests a simple interpretation: The vast majority of the successful projects in the top group may have been elite compatible on the local level because the project did not involve national-level elites in the first place, in the sense that higher-level political support was not required. In contrast, the projects in the bottom group displayed a high amount of EC problems on the national level because they were dependent on the support mainly from this level of elites. Consequently, the hypotheses that arise from the above analysis are:

- The projects differ in scope *a priori* – and it is this difference that is decisive for their different situation of EC ("first hypothesis" in the following).
- The EC issues which projects in the top group have solved are not the same issues that the bottom group failed to solve. This is an important distinction because it implies that the respective problems could not have been solved by 'better' project management or by striving for 'local' EC ("second hypothesis").

The next section investigates whether the additional data support or refute these assumptions.

6.4.3 Evaluation of Additional Project Data

Two variables that serve as good proxies for the project scope are the type of implementing partner and the project budget. Both already listed in Table 6-19, and they do differentiate the top and bottom groups significantly, as treated below.

6.4.3.1 Type of Implementing Partner

While there are 10 possible types of implementing partners (see Table 6-12 on page 206), the top and bottom group difference is already highly apparent:

- The group of successful projects features 11 cases of 'International NGO' implementation (001), and 2 of 'Local NGO' implementation (002), totaling in 13 out of 17 projects. Only one case each was implemented by 'profit-oriented organizations' (003), 'international governmental organizations' (004), the partner country's public administration (006), and multiple partners (010).
- In contrast, the low-performing group contains only two NGO-implemented projects (#10; 12), which additionally are not subject to

EC problems. The strong majority, 10 out of 17 projects, has been implemented by partner countries' public administration (006). The remainder is one case each with UN (005), 'regional bodies' (009), and 'profit-oriented organizations' (003).

This stark variation is summarized in Table 6-22 below. Naturally, it is very highly significant at $\alpha = 0.001$, and the correlation is at a strong $\Phi = 0.77$.

Table 6-22: Contingency table for implementing partner; NGOs vs. recipient countries' public administration

Implementing Partner	NGOs (001+ 002)	Publ. Adm. (006)	Total
Top Group	13	1	14
Bottom Group	2	10	12
Total	15	11	26

While this difference is significant for the extreme groups, NGO-implemented projects are not specifically known for a significantly higher effectiveness at *EuropeAid*. Unfortunately, it cannot be determined whether this difference would hold for the total n = 457 sample, the 'implementing partner' variable had to be compiled manually and is not available for the total sample. However, a test that was run with a different *EuropeAid* dataset of n = 648 projects between 2010 and 2012 ('ROM Workbooks'), does return a slightly higher rating average for the NGO-implemented projects over the group implemented by partner countries' administrations (006). The difference is very highly significant ($\alpha = 0.001$), yet it amounts to a value of only 0.156, which renders only a small effect size ($g_{Hedges} = 0.33$).

Nevertheless, the illustrated distinction between the extreme groups supports the hypothesis of different project scopes. The same would then be expected for the BUDGET variable.

6.4.3.2 Budget

The project budget is another variable that significantly differentiates the groups of successful and failed projects: The arithmetic mean is around €2.3 million for the top group and €14.0 million for the bottom group. This difference is highly significant ($\alpha = 0.01$) when tested using a non-parametric two-tailed *Mann-Whitney* test, with a medium effect size of r = 0.44. (As discussed in Section 6.2.2, it is not viable to conduct parametric between-group comparisons in extreme-group designs.)

It appears plausible that lower-budget projects offer fewer opportunities for extraction, and hence may be a factor influencing EC issues, and ultimately project success. Nevertheless, this interpretation does not hold when looking at the total (n = 457) sample, which shows no correlation ($\Phi = 0.07$) between the project budget and project success: The distribution of the BUDGET variable of the total sample is reverse-J shaped with an extreme slant towards the low budget classes ($\gamma_1 = 3.62$), excluding a strong correlation with the approximately-normally distributed 'rating arithmetic mean' variable ($\gamma_1 = 0.37$ towards the higher ratings); see Appendix I for details.

What is safe to assume, on the other hand, is that the BUDGET variable is simply a different means of illustrating the difference in implementing partners. A lower budget inherently correlates with the implementing partner type of NGOs (as the types of projects that are NGO-implemented generally have a lower project budget)[14]; this circumstance is also visible in the Table 6-19 on page 216. As such, this significantly higher budget of the failed bottom-group projects confirms their larger scope over the lower-budget top-group projects. While there is no other quantitative variable available that represents this 'scope', the reports' qualitative information supports this impression. Thus, the 'implementing partner' and BUDGET variables both clearly support the first hypothesis of significantly different project scopes of the successful and failed projects.

As previously stated, the bottom group's dichotomic distribution of EC problems offers a good opportunity for further analysis. Interestingly, of the 8 projects in the bottom group with a lower budget (below €2 million), 6 had no or just 1 incidence of EC problems (NegYY). The statistical difference is moderate (significant at $\alpha = 0.05$ [Fisher's exact test], moderate effect size of $\Phi = 0.65$), owing to the low n and the correspondingly low expectancy values below 5 (3.29).

14 As mentioned previously, the total n = 457 sample used in this study does not have 'implementing partner' data available. Nevertheless, the connection is evident, e.g., for the 'ROM Workbooks' dataset cited above: The BUDGET difference between implementing partner of NGOs (001+002) and 'other' yields a very high significance ($\alpha = 0.001$) in a two-tailed *Mann-Whitney* test.

Table 6-23: Budget vs. NegYY incidences in the bottom group

	> €2m	≤ €2m	Total
NegYY > 1	8	2	10
NegYY ≤ 1	1	6	7
Total	9	8	17

6.4.3.3 Qualitative Variables

Lastly, the qualitative variables described in Section 6.3.3 may be taken into account. The distribution of the collected variables is depicted in the following Table 6-24. For the sake of completeness, the right columns list the EC issues. The codes refer to:

- LQ logframe quality
- AQ assumptions quality
- AC assumptions correct
- AG ambitiousness of project goals
- BE baseline study existent
- FD flexibility of project design
- MQ internal monitoring quality
- PD participatory design
- RM resource managed by...

All values have been collected manually, i.e., coded from the qualitative descriptions in the reports, as they are not available as quantitative data. These variables were collected without specific *a priori* hypotheses; the original intention was to be able to correlate commonly available information on aspects of project design and management quality project performance and EC contingencies, in order to explore differences behind otherwise similar results or explain differences such as the almost dichotomic importance of EC problems in the bottom group.

Table 6-24: Distribution of the collected qualitative variables

#	GCLASS	RMEAN	BUDGET	LQ	AQ	AC	AG	BE	FD	MQ	PD	RM	PosYY	NegYY
1	I	4	430,000	y	y	y	-	n	-	y	-	-		
2	I	3.6	1,541,640	y	y	y	-	y	-	y	y	-	6	
3	I	3.6	1,005,030	n	-	-	n	-	y	y	-	-	4	3
4	I	3.6	663,032	y	y	y	n	-	-	y	y	s	9	1
5	I	3.6	1,521,402	y	y	y	y	y	y	y	y	s	6	1
6	IIa	3.4	2,550,000	y	y	y	n	y	-	y	y	s	8	
7	IIa	3.4	1,500,000	y	y	y	n	y	y	y	y	-	4	
8	IIa	3.4	1,356,100	y	y	y	n	y	y	y	y	s	3	
9	IIa	3.4	1,000,000	y	y	y	n	-	-	-	n	g	4	
10	IIa	3.4	2,715,502	-	-	-	n	-	y	y	n	s	5	
11	IIa	3.4	882,198	y	-	-	y	-	y	y	y	s	3	1
12	IIa	3.4	749,977	y	y	y	n	-	y	y	n	s	7	
13	IIa	3.2	5,000,000	y	y	y	n	-	-	y	y	-	5	
14	IIa	3.2	14,100,000	n	-	-	n	y	-	y	y	s	6	2
15	IIa	3.2	1,124,655	-	-	-	n	n	y	n	y	s	7	1
16	IIa	3.2	1,740,125	y	-	-	n	-	-	y	y	s	7	
17	IIa	3.2	1,981,000	-	n	-	y	y	y	y	-	-	6	1
1	III	2.2	1,981,000	y	y	y	n	n	n	y	y	-		
2	III	2.2	1,152,474	n	y	y	n	-	y	n	n	s	1	2
3	III	2.2	4,900,000	y	y	y	n	n	n	-	n	g		10
4	III	2.2	24,823,049	-	-	-	-	-	-	-	n	g		5
5	III	2.2	1,680,000	n	-	-	y	n	y	y	n	g	6	
6	III	2	22,000,000	y	n	-	n	y	n	n	n	g	2	9
7	III	2	1,110,000	n	-	-	y	n	n	n	n	g	2	
8	IV	2.2	14,465,710	y	-	-	y	-	n	n	n	g	3	1
9	IV	2.2	59,883,921	-	n	n	n	-	n	n	n	g	1	7
10	IV	2	1,272,126	y	-	-	y	-	y	y	n	-	4	
11	IV	1.6	19,800,000	n	n	n	-	n	-	-	n	g		12
12	IV	1.6	730,000	n	n	n	y		n	n	y	s		1
13	IV	1.6	61,000,000	n	-	-	-	n	n	-	n	g		4
14	IV	1.6	15,000,000	n	-	-	y	n	n	n	n	-	1	
15	IV	1.2	6,000,000	y	y	-	y	y	y	y	n	g		9
16	IV	1.2	921,480	-	n	n	y	-	n	-	n	g		9
17	IV	1	1,673,950	n	n	n	-	-	n	n	n	g		8
Missing values top group				3	6	7	1	8	7	1	2	5		
Missing values bottom group				3	7	9	4	8	2	5		3		
Missing values total				6	13	16	5	16	9	6	2	8		

During the coding, it became apparent that some variables would prove to be more difficult in interpretation than expected: First of all, due to the small group sizes, missing values (when reports were lacking the respective information) carry overproportional weight and meaningful comparison and interpretation is quickly rendered unrealistic. Specifically, this is true for the variables on the assumptions quality (AQ), correctness of assumptions (AC), the baseline study existence (BE), with over 10 missing values each. (For higher clarity, the missing values in the table are denoted by a dash.) Secondly, the usability of some variables successively turned out to be limited with regards to definition – this was the case for the logframe quality (LQ) – or because of the 'endogeneity' of the assessment – which was the case for the ambitiousness of project goals (AG) and the flexibility of the project design (FD); both will be explained below.

In the following, all variables with less than 10 total missing values will be briefly discussed, both with regard to project performance (top and bottom group), as well as to how the different project scope determined in the previous sections is reflected by the respective aspects. The differences between the groups are χ^2-tested, using Yate's continuity correction because of the low n (*Bortz & Döring* 2006: 169). The general requirement of an expected value ≥ 5 is fulfilled for all variables but design flexibility (FD) and internal monitoring quality (MQ); here, *Fisher's exact test* results will be used.

Logframe Quality

The quality of the logical framework is a standard subject of commentary in most reports. This value was collected as a proxy for project design quality. The logframe is assessed in terms of plausibility and realistic causal assumptions given the environment of the intervention. Ideally, these assumptions should implicitly also include aspects of EC (and other actors), however, during the data collection, it turned out that in many reports, the logframe has also been assessed favorably in cases with low effectiveness, implicitly pointing to an interpretation as pure *ex-ante* plausibility, and less as a contextual assessment. Also, as can be seen from the full table, there is no substantial correlation with contingencies of EC issues.

Table 6-25: Contingency table of the LQ variable

LQ	y	n	Total
Top Group	12	2	14
Bottom Group	6	8	14
Total	18	10	28

For the above distribution, difference between the groups is only significant at $\alpha = 0.05$, and the correlation is at a low $\Phi = 0.447$ and is hence not relevant.

Ambitiousness of Project Goals (AG)

This variable was collected to include an indicator for donor-sided expectations, but also proved to be ambivalent in interpretation, which can be attributed to the *ex post* nature of the assessment: Labeling the project goals as 'ambitious' or 'realistic' from an ex-post perspective may not be an actual appraisal of the project goals, but may effectively just be a synonym for 'failure' or 'success': I.e., if goals were not reached, they were too ambitious, if they were met, they were realistic.

Table 6-26: Contingency table of the AG variable

AG	y	n	Total
Top Group	3	12	15
Bottom Group	8	5	13
Total	11	17	28

From a statistical point of view, this variable is also not considerably valuable: For the above distribution, the correlation is low at $\Phi = -0.424$ and the difference between the groups is not significant ($p = 0.063$).

Flexibility of the Project Design (FD)

This variable was supposed to capture one aspect of project management quality.

Table 6-27: Contingency table of the FD variable

FD	y	n	Total
Top Group	9	0	9
Bottom Group	4	11	15
Total	13	11	24

The above distribution shows a high correlation of $\Phi = 0.713$ and the groups' difference is highly significant at $\alpha = 0.01$, although at a rather high amount of 10 missing values. Despite these missing values, it is nevertheless remarkable that the group of successful projects contains *only* cases where flexibility of the project design has been explicitly mentioned in the reports. The bottom group contains more project designs that have been commented to not be specifically flexible.

An obvious interpretation is that more flexibility in the project design leads to higher success because it can adapt to unforeseen circumstances (including elite-related issues). While this is very likely correct, the above result has to be considered in the context that the vast majority projects of the top group involved a participatory design or component (as discussed below), which by definition implies flexibility – simply because the project needs to adapt to the results from participatory input. Thus, this variable may again not provide the information that it was originally supposed to.

Internal Monitoring Quality (MQ)

Of the discussed variables, this is the first that delivered usable results and did not pose problems with regards to meaning or with a too high amount of missing values. The quality of the internal monitoring is another aspect of project management, in this case focusing on an aspect on efficiency. This variable can be used to confirm or, more importantly, contraindicate the general concept of EC: For a *y* value (i.e., high quality), the *absence* of EC problems should be a precondition, as extractive activities by elites impede efficient project management.

Table 6-28: Contingency table of the MQ variable

MQ	y	n	Total
Top Group	15	1	16
Bottom Group	4	8	12
Total	19	9	28

For the above distribution, the correlation is at a moderate $\Phi = 0.64$ and the difference is highly significant at $\alpha = 0.01$. More insight is provided by looking at the contingencies in context of Table 6-24, as they draw a picture similar to the overall distribution of EC successes and problems discussed in Section 6.4.1: While a high quality of internal monitoring is indicated for almost the entire top group, the failed projects in the bottom group divides up into two thirds of the cases with low-quality monitoring, and a third with positive entries. So again, while this aspect of project management seems to be an inherent feature of successful projects, it does not necessarily prevent failure. This seems trivial, as efficient budget management cannot compensate for wrong project design or negative external factors. What is remarkable, though, is that the failed projects with a high monitoring quality are the same projects that lack EC problems (#1; 5; 10) – one somewhat mysterious exception being a project that, in the qualitative descriptions, in fact contains the most extortionate extractive elite behavior of the whole sample (#15).

Apart from this one case, there is thus no contraindicator for the EC concept: All cases with a high amount of EC problems feature *n* values, and there are no cases with *y* values that feature substantial EC problems.

Participatory Design (PD)

The main intentions of participatory design approaches have been the creation of better opportunities to solve collective-action problems, but also the reduction of top-down effects, both from the donor, as well as from the elites in the project environment (see Section 3.2.1). Participatory design should thus have a positive effect on EC, i.e., all *y*-rated projects should display a low importance of EC-related problems.

Table 6-29: Contingency table of the PD variable

PD	y	n	Total
Top Group	11	3	14
Bottom Group	2	15	17
Total	13	18	31

For the above distribution, the between-group difference is of very high significance at $\alpha = 0.001$, and renders a moderate correlation of $\Phi = 0.67$. Again, it cannot be concluded that participation is a decisive factor for success, but the contingencies are another indicator of the more local focus of the top group's projects. Interestingly, only two projects with participatory design in the bottom group feature a participatory approach (#1; 12), and just as with the IM variable, these projects display no (#1) or just one (#12) contingency of EC problems. Thus, in this study's small sample, the participatory design approaches correspond perfectly to theoretical expectations (and those of ODA practice).

Resource Managed by...

To include an aspect of 'ownership', this variable captures whether the resource that was part of the project output (e.g., transport infrastructure, water or sanitation infrastructure, managed funds etc.) was managed by governmental structures (*g*) or by the local stakeholders (*s*), such as local communities, the associations or organizations of the beneficiary groups, etc. An *s* entry should positively influence EC, as it implies the exclusion (i.e., irrelevance) of high-level elites.

Table 6-30: Contingency table of the RM variable

RM	g	s	Total
Top Group	1	10	11
Bottom Group	11	3	14
Total	12	13	25

As can be seen in Table 6-30, this distribution separates the two groups very clearly, though again at a high number of 9 missing values. The difference is very highly significant at $\alpha = 0.001$ and yields a correlation coefficient of $\Phi = - 0.69$. It is remarkable that almost all listed cases in the top group carry a 'local-stakeholder managed' value, which confirms the previously assumed distance to national-level elites also considering the 'ownership' aspect. The single exception (#9) is a project in which the elites were in fact the only beneficiaries; it will be discussed in the conclusion. The 3 cases of *s* values in the bottom group (#2; 5; 12) correlate with a low project budget (cf. page 216), and all display a low importance ratio of EC problems over other problems.

Summary

The three qualitative variables that include usable data for interpretation differentiate the top and bottom group at high or very high significance. While naturally, there can be no assumption of causality, the results can be used to analyze whether they confirm or contradict the previous assumptions, i.e., the general concept of EC (MQ variable), and the second hypothesis (see page 218) that low contingencies of EC-related problems can be attributed to the irrelevance of national-level elites (PD and RM).

The three variables, which (individually) highly correlate with the criterion of project success, should logically also display a high intercorrelation. While this could not be tested[15], the individual distributions as such are confirmatory towards the previously presented presumptions. Due to their effect directions as previously described, all variables should effectively follow the same logic: Any case with a positive (y) value should display zero or a low amount of EC problems (NegYY). Even in the bottom group, this is true for all three variables, and the results are thus conform with this study's concept of EC; there is no contraindicator except for one case (#15) which features a high monitoring quality despite being the most 'extractive'. As the PD and RM variables imply a local project focus, the result is also in line with the hypothesis that the top group was successful because national-level elites were not involved[16].

15 Due to the missing values, a Principal Component Analysis, for instance, does not return usable results. While the missing-data problem could be treated using methods such as *multiple imputation*, I regard these approaches critical given the small amount of *n*.

16 This follows the same logic: All cases with a *y* value imply exclusion of national-level elites and should therefore display low amount of EC problems (NegYY).

6.4.3.4 Rating Category Values (Sustainability, Impact, etc.)

Lastly, it would be obvious to test the amount of elite compatibility symptoms against the project ratings in their individual dimensions. However, due to the high intercorrelation of the ratings in their individual categories, as demonstrated in Section 6.2.1, these tests would not deliver any usable results.

6.4.4 Elite-Compatibility Issue Codes

Apart from the classification of symptom types into EC issues and 'other' issues, as discussed until now, the evaluation process of the reports also involved the coding of the specific symptom IDs, i.e., the matching of the extracted description with a description from the coding frame. Thus, it is possible to extend the analysis to the concrete *content* of the EC symptoms, the majority of which has been discussed in Section 4.3.2.

This is specifically interesting concerning the second hypothesis: The results in Section 6.4.2 found the EC successes (PosYY) of the top group to be related to the local-elite level and the problems (NegYY) of the bottom group to be related to the national-elite level. This situation should also be visible in the distribution of the concrete symptom codes: The top group's success descriptions should reflect substantially more local-level symptoms, and the bottom group's problem descriptions should center around symptoms relating to national-level elites. In concrete contingencies, this should manifest in symptoms with a strongly asymmetrical incidence distribution, i.e., high in the top group's PosYY count and low in the bottom group's NegYY count, and vice versa.

Table 6-31 lists the contingencies of the most frequent symptoms by their ID number (the corresponding descriptions will be provided below, a full list of all issues can be found in the coding frame in Appendix F), including all symptoms with more than 2 incidences per entry; the full overview can again be found in Appendix K.

Table 6-31: Contingencies of the different elite-compatibility symptoms

Symptom ID #	01	08	11	14	15	16	17	21	23	27	32	33	35	50	57
Top Group															
PosYY	3	3	9	3	14	7	5	1	11	1	8		4	2	2
NegYY		1	1		2				1		2		1		
Bottom Group															
Pos YY	1		2	1	1	1	4	1	2	1	1	1			
NegYY	6	1	8	3	2	6		3	9	12	11	4		6	3

In the following, all symptoms with counts ≥ 5 will be discussed. In Table 6-31, four symptoms are subject to the asymmetry described above. These are #15 and 17, with a stronger emphasis in the top group, and #27 and 50, with an imbalance towards the bottom group:

#15: No Support for Initiatives for Local Development

This phenomenon is a classical case of individuals in elite positions exerting resistance against measures that could strengthen or bring about local leadership capabilities, which may be threatening to their own position. In general, this may affect any intervention of empowering previously underprivileged target groups, from enhancing local economic infrastructures, down to any measure “facilitating ways for citizens to make their voice effective” (*Gibson et al.* 2005: 74). Resistance may originate from both from national as well as local-level elites, as actions to secure the own position and limit access to it may be sensible for elite members of any level.

This category shows a very high count (14) of success descriptions for the top group, and only 2 problem incidences in the bottom group. As the top group mainly consisted of local-level interventions with participatory designs that focused on local development, it appears inherently logical and thus not surprising that the projects feature this phenomenon as solved. It is worth pointing out that the high count does not only represent the mere absence of resistance, but means that the reports contained explicit mentions of the support by local and/or national-level elites.

More noteworthy, nevertheless, is the low amount of incidences in the bottom group (both as success or problem descriptions): It shows the low relevance of this type of EC for the interventions *not* targeted at development in a local scope.

#17: Agency Cooperation Despite no Interest in Change

This symptom indicates a form of extractive behavior, in this case with the resource of the project budget, and it relates to elites in agencies, departments or specific authorities. Paradoxically, it is a frequent issue in projects aiming at structural reform: While the demanded change in existing structures may be threatening to members of the respective agency, the increase in staff and budget associated with an aid project may offer "incentives to receive aid but not to reform" (*Gibson et al.* 2005: 183), i.e., to officially commit to reform, despite no actual interest, and consecutively not provide support for the project's actual goals.

Again, the distribution of success incidences is pronounced in the top group (5). An explanation could be that on the local level, an empowerment of local activity could be perceived as an opportunity to expand influence and thus political importance. As such, the reaction is thus strongly dependent on the agency's situation prior to the intervention – in this sense, this symptom may not be selective or differentiated enough to draw meaningful conclusions.

As with the previous item #15, more revealing is the low relevance of this symptom in the bottom group, in a double sense: Not only are there no incidences of problem descriptions, but even 4 incidences of this symptom as 'solved', i.e., concrete descriptions of the respective agency showing interest and support for the required changes imposed by the intervention. For these lowest-performing projects of the sample, the contribution of this form of EC to project success was apparently neglectable, though.

#27: Low Efforts in Monitoring and Rules Enforcement

This symptom refers to one of the typical and omnipresent problems of infrastructure ODA projects, that measures of monitoring, enforcing rules and excluding free-riding are not put into practice in an effective manner. This is explained by a large amount of layers in hierarchical structures and a strong top-down oriented architecture of organization, making low effort the better strategy choice for agents on the lower levels. Larger hierarchies, in turn, are often the result of job positions being part of the patronage 'toolkit' as a measure of reward, leading to overstaffed bureaucracies with low accountability. The problem of low monitoring efforts is one of the explanations for high inefficiency through clandestine connections in water or electrical power networks, or for speeding or overweight problems in transport infrastructure.

The distribution here is in line with theory, as well as with the previous explanation of EC distribution: The bottom group, with projects of larger scope and higher budgets, features a high problem count of 12 incidences. The top group, on the other hand, does not contain a corresponding amount as successes (only 1 success description) and thus confirms the irrelevance of this aspect for the successful projects: With the majority of projects intervening on the local level and with participatory approaches, a type of problem that results from large distances in hierarchies does not arise in the first place.

#50: Continuous Underfunding of Maintenance

The problem of the failure of maintenance can be considered another classic, not only because of its high prevalence, but also because it is a perfect representation of the Samaritan's dilemma. It is strongly associated with extractive activities of large infrastructure facilities such as electrical power, water provision, or transportation, and as such is associated especially with projects of correspondingly high budgets. The values are surprisingly low in this sample. While it is a frequent, if not the most frequent problem in infrastructure projects, the bottom group only counts 6 incidences – despite the fact that 11 of the 17 cases are infrastructure-related, and 9 cases feature a budget above €4 million.

Similarly, for the top group, a higher value than the 2 success incidences could have been expected, as one of the strengths of successful participatory designs and beneficiary involvement is the solution of the collective-action problem of maintenance on the local level.

Both the asymmetric distribution of this symptom type, as well as its relatively low relevance in general cannot be counted as support for the second hypothesis; however, neither do these features provide counterevidence.

Explaining Symmetric Distributions of Symptoms

The types of the symptoms discussed above are in line with the second hypothesis of asymmetric EC symptoms between the top and bottom group. Much more frequent, though, are symptoms with a symmetric distribution, i.e., a similar count in both the top group's success factors as well as the bottom group's problem factors. At first sight, this simply implies that successful projects managed (or happened) to solve EC issues, while the same issues posed problems and remained unsolved in the bottom group. This does not contradict the concept of EC itself – however, the subject of investigation here is the *causality* behind the EC situation in the successful and the failed projects, and a symmetric distribution for a symptom *does* contradict the previous hypothesis that top-group projects did not solve the same problems that bottom-group projects failed at. On the other hand, following up on the analysis of elite levels in Section 6.4.2, it could be possible that it is these 'symmetrically' distributed symptoms that are not subject to the same level of elites.

A clearer picture of these items may be obtained when the respective contingencies are again broken down into elite levels. Table 6-32 shows this differentiation for all symptom IDs that feature counts higher than 5[17]. Note that, because a single description extracted from a project report may be assigned multiple levels at the same time in the coding process, the breakdown may contain more incidences than the total.

Table 6-32: The most frequent success descriptions of the top group and problem descriptions of the bottom group, and their differentiation into elite levels (national, agency, local elite)

Symptom ID	01			11			15			16			23			27			32			50		
Levels	n	a	l	n	a	l	n	a	l	n	a	l	n	a	l	n	a	l	n	a	l	n	a	l
Top PosYY																								
Total	3			9			14			7			11			1			8			2		
Levels	3		2	3	1	7	5		10	3		5	3	1	9	1				2	6			2
Bott. NegYY																								
Total	6			8			2			6			9			12			11			6		
Levels	6			8	2					6			9			8	4	2	10	5		5	2	

The general impression that issues in the top group are more frequent on the local-elite level, and in the bottom group, more frequent on the national-elite level, should not be surprising, as it is logically coherent with the breakdown previously provided in Section 6.4.2. This tendency is also valid for the symptom IDs discussed previously. The remaining – symmetrical – symptoms (#01; 11; 16; 23; 32) are now addressed below.

17 Due to space restrictions, #17 was not included; this issue has been discussed above and is by definition relevant for the agency level only.

#01: Strong Political Control Over an Agency

This problem refers to the phenomenon that politicians exert strong control over operations of an agency that is in charge of regulation, generation, administration or distribution of a public utility such as electrical power, transport infrastructures, financial infrastructures etc. The provided reason is that the control over the agency enables the control over the distribution of the respective good as means of patronage. Selective distribution of public goods and public utilities is seen as one of the central measures of elites in an extractive economic environment to secure political power.

With the total incidence count at a moderate level, after all there are 6 problem incidences in the bottom group, all relating to national-level elite. The top-group distribution features more national-level than local level incidences, and as such contradicts the second hypothesis; however, at a low count of only 3 descriptions, it is not particularly relevant as a success factor.

#11: Strong Political Control Over Project Implementation

This symptom is closely related to the above, though with the project (budget) as the source of patronage. Political control over implementation allows politicians to reward supporters and punish detractors, e.g., by controlling or interfering with the selection of project sites (target locations), contractors, or contract scopes. The political control can stem from both national- or local-level politics, although naturally, the attractiveness increases for higher-level politicians because of the correspondingly higher budgets of associated projects.

The symptom has a high count both as success factor in top group (9) as well as problem incidence in bottom group (8). As expected, all problems in the bottom group are related to the 'national' elites, of which 2 additionally concern the 'agency' level. As a success factor in the top group, the 7 of the 9 incidences related to the local level, however, 3 involved national-level elites. Again, it has to be emphasized that an incidence in the PosYY category does not only represent an absence of a problem (e.g., "There was no interference from the Ministry"), but a description of explicit support (e.g., "The ministry provided the requested materials in a timely and accurate manner."). Hence, despite the low value, the incidences are a (weak) contraindicator for the hypothesis of the irrelevance of national-level elites for the top group.

#16: Government Cooperation Despite no Interest in Change

This issue is technically the same as #17, only that it refers to governmental entities instead of agencies, both on the national as well as the regional and local levels. The mechanism is the same: An ODA project targeting structural reform is accepted for the sake of budget extraction, while the actual goals of the project are against the interest of the respective entities. Again, the target of the reform is often an extractive structure of an institutional setup, and again this setup is required to maintain patron-client relationships, e.g., in the form of selective distribution of goods. While there is no interest in changing this setup, ODA budget inflow is seen as a resource to help sustaining the pool of patronage.

There is a moderate count of 7 incidences in the top group and 6 in the bottom group. The latter is completely related to national-level elites, in the top group, the success incidences are slanted towards the local level (5). The count of 3 incidences on the national level again implies a contra-indication for the second hypothesis, however, again at a very low manifestation.

#23: Failure in Enhancing Capabilities of Officials or Beneficiaries

When interventions include a component of (explicit or implicit) capacity building for officials in ministries, agencies, or local or regional governments, the effectiveness of these measures can be strongly confined by pronounced top-down structures in the recipient's bureaucratic structures. This may be even more pronounced if the respective target entity of the capacity building component is subject to aid dependency, and thus also depends on the goodwill of the higher hierarchies for allocation of these aid budgets. Additionally, this dependency reduces fiscal accountability and consequently overall accountability towards the citizens – the reinforcement of which ironically is often the exact goal of the intervention or component. As such, this problem originates from the same paradox that is also observable for anti-corruption interventions, where an aid infusion into a rent-seeking environment enhances the pool of patronage and may yield a perverse effect.

This symptom has strong incidence both as a success factor in the top group (11) as well as a problem factor in bottom group (9). The latter amount is concentrated entirely on national-elite level, the top group incidences are clearly slanted towards the local level (9), but nevertheless include 3 incidences relating to national elites. While those 3 entries contradict the second hypothesis, the 9 local-level successes are a confirmation in a double sense: Not only do they indicate the level of action, but, by definition of this symptom, also explicit independence from higher-level politics[18].

#32: Output-over-outcome Phenomenon

This symptom relates to the circumstance that wherever there is a budget transfer, in this case: aid, there is the opportunity for extraction. Politicians involved in the tendering process and the selection of sites, measures, and contractors may take a direct cut of the project, e.g., in the form of 'success fees' from contractors or other partners. This leads to the phenomenon that I have termed 'output-over-outcome' in Chapter 4, and that is not exclusive to ODA: The budget transfer becomes the central motivation for the politician and is thus prioritized, leading to increased importance of output of a project over the actual outcome. A common representation is a built network with missing follow-up on the actual connections to the network. Also, obviously-bad planning and wrong design with respect to the intended end-user purpose are often the results of an output prioritization.

The contingencies of this problem in the bottom group are high (11), which corresponds to the fact that this issue, just like that of maintenance provision (#50), is notoriously common in ODA projects, especially for larger budgets. Accordingly, the problems are all categorized to the 'national-level' (10) and 'agency' (3) category. The top group's success descriptions (8) are clearly slanted towards the local level (6), with 2 counts in the agency level and none on the national-elite level. This symptom again confirms the irrelevance of national-level elites for the top group, which in this case is allegeable to the dominating type of implementing partner being NGOs (see Section 6.4.3.1): Often times, the budget in this

18 The problem by definition arises from dependence on top-down hierarchies; if this problem is solved on the local level, this logically implies independence from higher-level hierarchies.

case is directly transferred to and spent by the NGO. Additionally, the majority of the top group's projects follow participatory design approaches, which are naturally not exposed to the problem as much.

Summary

The goal of the analysis of the concrete symptom types' distributions was to identify support or counterevidence of the second hypothesis from Section 6.4.2. All symptom contingencies relevant for discussion (with a count > 5) support the hypothesis. They can be differentiated into three types of distribution:

- An asymmetric distribution with a high count as a success factor in the top group, but a low count as a problem factor in the bottom group, meaning that the respective symptoms have been solved in the successful projects, but were of no relevance for the failed projects. Two issues are subject to this distribution: 'no support for initiatives of local development' (#15) and 'agency cooperation despite no interest in change (#17). The first issue clearly relates to local-scope interventions and thus supports the hypothesis. The latter is more difficult to interpret, but a possible explanation is that on the local level, agency empowerment is perceived as an opportunity to expand influence and thus political importance.
- An asymmetric distribution with a low count as a success factor in the top group, and a higher count as a problem factor in the bottom group – meaning that while the respective symptom was an important problem in failed projects, it was of low or no relevance for the success of the top projects. The classical 'maintenance' issue (#50) shows this distribution, which is slightly surprising, however it does not contradict the hypothesis. Supportive is the issue of 'low efforts in rules enforcement' (#27), as this is a typical problem resulting from large distances in hierarchies, i.e., larger-budget projects with a larger scope.
- The more frequent case, however, is that of symmetrical distribution, i.e., a high count both as a success factor for the top group as well as a problem factor for the bottom group. Nevertheless, when broken down into the elite levels, all respective symptoms (again) show the same pattern: The top group projects' successes all have a higher count on the local level (with low counts on national-level elites), the problems in the failed projects have no contingencies on the 'local'

level (with only one exception among the 9 symptoms being 'failed capacity building' (#23).

The second hypothesis is thus confirmed also by consideration of the concrete content of the individual EC symptoms. Counterevidence is found in the contingencies of the top group's success descriptions in the 'national elite' level; however, these are always at a lower value than the 'local elite' entry (with one exception), and at a low count in general.

6.5 Critical Discussion of the Research Design

This section refers to the quality of the evaluation of the reports; the data quality of the reports themselves has been discussed in Section 6.1.4.

6.5.1 Objectivity, Reliability, Validity

6.5.1.1 Objectivity

This study used the method of content analysis with a component of that required the interpretation of qualitative data. Thus, the evaluation cannot fulfill the criterion of objectivity, which, as discussed previously, is subject to critique (see *Oleinik* 2010: 860). However, to ensure reproducibility of the results, the research design can aim at minimizing the extent of subjectiveness in the coding process by making the coding more reliable.

6.5.1.2 Reliability

As the measurement in the context of content analysis is the coding, the two main measures of reliability *inter*-coder reliability and *intra*-coder reliability (*Schreier* 2014: 178).

The latter simply translates to consistency of the coding, i.e., whether the same coder arrives at the same results if the coding procedure is repeated at a later stage (i.e., without memory of the first coding results). This procedure is uncommon in practice of qualitative analysis (*Mayring*

2010: 117)[19] and was also not pursued in this study: A second cycle of coding could have only been performed at the 'cost' of a lower amount of total cases considered.

Measuring *inter-coder reliability* would go even further, as it logically involves the coding by additional coders of equal or similar expertise in regard to the respective topic. For economic reasons, this procedure was not feasible within the scope of this study. Realistically, the individual coding behavior will vary with the coder's familiarity with the coding frame – which is also why the importance of the intercoder reliability criterion is sometimes seen as critical other than for very simple coding frames (see *Mayring* 2010: 117).

However, one important endeavor in the design of the coding process indeed has been the aspect of reliability. The symptom rating is split up into multiple aspects that translate the interpretation into a step-by-step procedure, the individual steps of which represent clearer questions and involve less subjectivity than an all-in-one interpretation. Additionally, the 'double-opt-in' coding approach (of 'general' and 'specific' description matching) enables the separation of 'unconfirmed' impressions and 'safe' assessments in the later evaluation of the results. This takes the pressure off the coder to immediately and compulsorily assign a description with a final verdict: For instance, a problem or success description can be rated as [general: yes | specifically: possibly] until an indicator allows a revision of the 'possibly' assessment into a 'yes' or 'no' value.

Since, as stated, it was not feasible to take on multiple coders for this study, the aspect of intercoder reliability has to be assumed (taking into account the above remarks).

6.5.1.3 Test Validity

The conventional array of test validity measures of the social sciences is also often cited for the method of content analysis (e.g., *Neuendorf* 2002: 11ff.; *Früh* 2011: 196): face validity, criterion validity (predictive, concurrent), construct validity (discriminant, convergent), and content validity. Due to the exploratory nature of this study, only a minority of these criteria applies:

---

19 For *quantitative* content analysis, it is common practice to select a subset of the main analysis sample for re-coding that is 10-20 percent the size of the total sample (*Neuendorf* 2010: 283).

Face Validity

Basically, the construct of EC was defined as a specific subset of incentive compatibility; corresponding problem descriptions were taken from an existing survey and put into a coding frame, and the content of the reports was then reviewed for incidences of these descriptions. By definition, this construct thus represents the theory it was built on and the setup measures what it is intended to measure, in a plausible and thus *face-valid* nature.

Criterion Validity

As there is no intention of estimating a criterion of any sort, neither in a concurrent, nor a predictive nature, the aspect of criterion validity is of no relevance.

Construct Validity

Also due to the explorative purpose of this study and the resulting logic described above, convergent or discriminant aspects of the construct validity are of no relevance.

Content Validity

An aspect that *is* of relevance is that of *content validity*[20], i.e., whether all relevant aspects of the construct are captured by the measurement. While the coding frame did deliver useable results, it is in the nature of data aggregation that it introduces simplification and cannot represent the complex reality that is inherent especially to incentive situations. Notable limitations that became apparent during the data collection concerned the following aspects:

- *Multiple regions:* Large projects may comprise several sub-projects in different regions, which then may vary in quality of implementation. In this case, if the characteristics of one component diverge from the rest, they may 'disappear' in the overall impression of the respective

20 Content validity is an aspect of construct validity, but is treated separately here for better clarity.

project. This is both valid for its performance, as well as its EC symptoms. In this study's sample, this was not an issue, but the problem was apparent in the pilot study.

- *Multiple components:* The same is true for projects with multiple components. In this study, it was applicable for one project (#2 of the top group).
- *Policy environment:* A project itself may receive full support from national-level elites, also in terms of the policy environment, while at the same time, other plans may undermine the future of the project. E.g., again in case #2, there was the apprehension that parts of the national elite supported plans of foreign investors for large-scale agricultural projects which would effectively jeopardize the project's local initiatives and even harm rural population in general. As opposed to the relevant destructive potential of this factor, on the quantitative level this is only reflected with one entry in the "possible problem" category (NegYP), and the report's *B* rating for 'sustainability'.
- *Post-hoc intervention of politics:* Similarly, post-hoc interventions may endanger the future of the project, e.g., when politicians 'appropriate' project results and claim the project to be the initiative of a specific party. This was the case for one project (#4), where local politicians additionally started to hand out goods for free to woo voters, and endangered project success. Again, in quantitative measures, this is only represented by one problem entry, and a *B* rating in the 'sustainability' category.
- *Agency situation:* Finally, the 'agency elite' level proved to be not detailed enough for meaningful interpretation and differentiation of the results. Future studies should possibly separate the 'agency' category into a national and local level.

It should be kept in mind that it is in the nature of aggregation that information is reduced and details are omitted. While these cited aspects should serve for consideration in future studies, the impact of the above limitations was moderate for this study, and I assess the content validity to be at a high level for the construct and the purpose of this research.

6.5.1.4 Internal and External Validity of the Empirical Results

Bortz and Döring (2006: 33) contend that "ultimately, internal and external validity are the most important quality differences between empirical research and everyday experience."[21]

Internal Validity

The most critical aspect for this study is that of its *internal validity*, i.e., how valid the causal explanation of the independent variable for the dependent variable is.

The goal of this work is to explore the importance of the EC concept for the effectiveness of aid projects, or, more precisely, the influence of EC on project performance. While the results presented in this chapter are of mostly very high significance, this naturally cannot be taken as a proof for a cause-effect relationship between the construct and the criterion – a general problem for all non-experimental studies, and a debated topic also in the context of RCTs (see Section 2.1.2.2).

However, following the logic of probabilistic causality (*Humphreys* 1989), as described by *Westmeyer* (2015: 596), probability for a causal relationship increases with a) the distribution of the explanatory variable corresponding to expectations; b) the grade of homogeneity of the expected distribution and c) the degree of absence of counterevidence. For this study:

- The distribution of the construct (predictors) is as expected, with a high effect size (see page 212).
- A high level of *homogeneity* is given for the 'solved' issues (PosYY) in the top group, but not for the problem issues (NegYY) in the bottom group. With this pattern (a homogenously high count of solved EC issues in the top group, and a dichotomous importance of EC problems in the bottom group), it can be deduced that EC is a necessary, but not sufficient condition for project success.
- With the category of 'other' success and problem factors, a direct comparison is possible. Support for a higher importance of EC-related problems is given by the result that both the total amount as well as

21 Own translation; original: "[…] sind interne und externe Validität letztlich die wichtigsten Qualitätsunterschiede zwischen empirischer Forschung und Alltagserfahrung."

the effect size of other non-EC-related issues for project success is lower than for those related to EC.

- *Counterevidence* (for the interpretation of EC as a necessary but not sufficient condition for project success) would emanate from cases in the top group with no relevance of EC issues. Indeed, there is one project with EC issues completely absent (no PosYY, no NegYY). The project report explicitly mentions the project's complete independence from local and national political elite[22]; in this sense the case could even be counted as supportive of the EC hypothesis – in any case, not as counterproof.

The situation is similar concerning the hypotheses of the local scope and the consequential lower relevance of national-level elites as the underlying cause for the higher EC. Here, almost all differences between the successful and failed projects are of both very high significance and high effect sizes. This is not only true for the distribution across elite levels in the top and bottom group, but also for the qualitative variables that can support or contraindicate this thesis:

- The variables PD, RM and 'type of implementing partner' projects, all of which constitute a local-level field of operation and an involvement into local incentive structures, separate the successful and failed projects at very high significance and with high effect sizes.
- *Counterevidence*, more importantly, can potentially be identified from the bottom group. Here, the dichotomic distribution of EC problems (relevant/not relevant) can be used to falsify the hypothesized effect of the above features on EC. However, there is not one case of falsification: No project with the features [NGO implementing partner], [stakeholder-managed resource] or [participatory design] counts more than 1 incidence of NegYY, i.e., no project that has any one of these features has high relevance of EC problems.

Finally, an interesting question would be whether there are cases in the bottom group that hold low relevance of EC problems *without* carrying any of the above features. This is the case for one project (#9) in the top group and two (#7; 8) in the bottom group. The former will be addressed in Section 7.2.3 of the last chapter.

22 "This project had the advantage of being completely independent of local and national administrations; consequently the sustainability of its results does not rely on financial support from these sources." (*European Commission* 2011b: BCS 5.1)

From these circumstances as described above, I estimate the internal validity of the results to be at a satisfactory level.

External Validity

Lastly, the *external validity*, i.e., the generalizability of the results towards the defined population, is given by the unbiased availability of data (see below) and the clear sampling procedure (see Section 6.1). As the evaluation depends on the content of the reports, this validity can naturally only be assumed for projects of the same report type (i.e., *EuropeAid* projects), and that are congruent with the applied selection criteria, i.e., infrastructure sectors.

The effective sample size of projects included for the analysis is at a fairly low n = 34. Given the limitations discussed above, one could polemically argue that as such, the study combines the disadvantages of qualitative research (low n due to inefficient processing) and quantitative research (information loss through aggregation). Though this is a matter of individual assessment, I term the results usable on a level that goes beyond anecdotal evidence or case-study-level n. The often very high significance with moderate to large effect sizes, as well as the clear overall picture that the results connect to, are supportive of this assessment.

As discussed in Section 6.2.2, increasing the quantiles in this sample would dilute homogeneity of the groups regarding the project performance criterion, as it would include too many additional rating levels. In future studies, to increase the size of the extreme groups without compromising on their homogeneity, a larger total sample would hence be recommended (given a similar distribution of the project performance variable).

A clear strength of the sampling in this study is the availability of data: While, as previously discussed, only a fraction of the total projects at *EuropeAid* receive an ex-post evaluation, these evaluations are assigned randomly (and not based, e.g., on project performance). The two extreme groups thus represent *EuropeAid's actual* top- and lowest-performing projects within the selection criteria of the sample and do not underlie the issue of non-random sampling in smaller-scale studies (cf. *Reynolds* 2012: 552) which is often the result of a publication bias in favor of more successful cases.

6.5.2 Geographical Regions and the Blank Slate Approach

In a strict sense, the following aspect also relates to external validity, but, to its importance in relation to ODA discourse, shall be discussed under a separate headline:

The sample of this study takes all projects into consideration regardless of their geographical region, thus assuming the universality of the EC concept. This could be interpreted as a form of *Blank Slate* approach, which is heavily criticized, e.g., by *Easterly* (2014b: 26), for "homogeniz[ing] otherwise diverse countries" in a one-size-fits-all manner, ignoring specific cultural differences.

The question of the impact of geography and culture has been a debated field in the development discourse for a long time. Especially the high appeal of cultural factors as the explanatory value for a society's economic situation may be due to its plausibility. Famously going back to *Weber's Protestant Work Ethic* (*Weber* 1920), the cultural-deterministic view in the development discourse had already been criticized by *Bauer and Yamey* (1957: 68)[23]. One of the prominent contemporary critics is *Chang* (2008: 186), who contends that culture-based explanations for economic development "offered a very convenient excuse [...] – neo-liberal policies have not worked very well, not because of some inherent problems but because the people practicing them had 'wrong' values that diminished their effectiveness." *Chang* gives the example of historical descriptions of supposedly inherent Japanese and German national cultures, documenting how they once carried the exact opposite of their image of diligence and precision which is perpetuated today (ibid.: 182). Similarly, *Acemoğlu and Robinson* (2012b: 57ff.) rebut a number of frequently cited (asserted) determinants of economic development (e.g., the protestant work ethic, African, Latin, Confucian and Chinese values, 'specific' national cultures such as English or European, or contemporary share of indigenous culture), and conclude that cultural factors are "mostly an outcome of institutions, not an independent cause" (ibid.: 57). *Zweynert* (2009: 347) warns that the common understanding of culture in economics as an exogenous and homogenous factor may turn the concept into "a 'catch-all' explana-

23 They cite the alleged connection between religious reformations and economic changes in 16th-century Europe and confront this by pointing to the compatibility of traditional attitudes and social relationships with the rapid economic change in Japan.

tion for the differences between societies that cannot be explained otherwise“ and that may lead to “cultural fatalism”[24].

It should be clear that the refusal of cultural-deterministic views does not correspond to an endorsement of the Blank Slate approach, as both complexes relate to completely separate issues: While the former refers to an explanatory factor for (economic) development, the latter denotes an understanding in the context of project *implementation*. The Blank Slate view here represents the notion of universality of institutional solutions, and translates to the promotion of ‘best-practice’ (i.e., blueprint) institutional designs, as already discussed in Section 4.3.1. In the Blank Slate view, cultural factors are deemed dispensable for implementation, and cultural differences are hence ignored.

However, I hold that the research interest of EC represents exactly the *contrary* of this form of universalist mindset, as it seeks to reveal underlying incentive situations; incentive compatibility (and thus: EC) in this context serves as a mere analytic category. What I do implicitly assume to be universal is the tendency of elite members to a) secure their position and to b) extract rents from the position. This is in line with elite theorists until today as well as with results from elite research in the context of development (cf. *Amsden et al.* 2012), specifically elite capture (*Wong* 2012).

The implementation of interventions, in contrast, is a separate issue from this, and following *Acemoğlu's and Robinson's* above understanding of culture being the outcome of institutions, it (i.e., culture) naturally represents an important factor of the institutional environment in this context. *Zweynert* (2009: 349) picks up the metaphor of culture as a “toolkit”:

> “This toolkit so to speak provides the ground on which competing political actors as cultural entrepreneurs can play in order to push through their interests and political agendas, both constraining them and enabling them to engage in bounded innovation. Thus, culture turns into an important strategic factor of policy-making.” (ibid.: 357)

The need for different ‘tools’ upon implementation is supported also by illustrative findings such as that by *De Jong* (2011: 526), that the degree of centralization of political and private organizations in a country correlates with the country's score on *Hofstede's* power distance[25] index. A

24 Thus perfectly in line with *Chang* (2011b: 494), who refers to cultural determinism as “unduly fatalistic”.

25 The *Hofstede* indices establish six dimensions of national cultures, for which data are available from 93 countries (*Hofstede, Hofstede & Minkov* 2010: 35). The

study by *Arnall et al.* (2013) shows how the effective measure for tackling elite capture varies even intranationally, depending on the specific local institutional arrangements and power configurations – and is often not congruent with prescriptive practices of the involved agencies. The relevance of these local specificities may vary: E.g., *Banerjee* (2009: 214) points to the results from several RCTs in completely different cultural settings (Kenya and India), and highlights that there are both interventions that have been perfectly replicated, and those that have not.

In this sense, I argue that the EC approach rejects both the cultural-deterministic as well as the Blank Slate view. Or, in other words: While market failure and dilemmas work the same everywhere, their individual solution requires different tools.

original study was based on a very large cross-national database of opinion surveys in a multi-national corporation, and has been expanded multiple times since. For a critique, see, e.g., *McSweeney* (2002).

Chapter 7 Summary and Conclusion

This study introduced the concept of elite compatibility (EC), which I define as a specific form of incentive compatibility, reduced to the target group of elites – more precisely, the incentive compatibility of the goals of ODA project designs with political elites of recipient countries. It is an inherent problem of ODA that, under standard circumstances, this compatibility is exactly *not* given.

The awareness of this paradox is not new in the discourse of aid provision. In fact, the foundation of this paradox was already taken up by the first ODA document of the UN in 1951, when it stated that

> "under-developed countries where the concentration of economic and political power [lies] in the hands of a small class, whose main interest is the preservation of its own wealth and privileges, rules out the prospect of much economic progress until a social revolution has effected a shift in the distribution of income and power." (*United Nations* 1951: 15)

From the very beginning of the ODA effectiveness debate, the incentive compatibility problem has also been one of the central arguments of most aid critics. For the more radical fraction, both historical (*Frankel* 1952: 304; *Friedman* 1958: 515; *Bauer* 1969: 91) and contemporary (*Moyo* 2009: 52ff.), it has been the reason to demand the termination of aid altogether. *Acemoğlu and Robinson* (2012b: 86) pick up the incentive paradox as a central point in their development theory and arrive at a similar conclusion (ibid.: 447). Others, such as *Collier* (2006: 1485), acknowledge the problem, but argue that a conclusion to end ODA "is as wrong as would be a proposal to close hospitals".

Authors specifically focusing on an incentive-theoretic analysis of ODA similarly broach the issue of the inherent incentive conflict (*Catterson & Lindahl* 1998: 145; *Bräutigam & Knack* 2004: 263; *Moss et al.* 2006: 4). In the mainstream effectiveness discussion, however, while the importance of the elite's incentive situation is sometimes acknowledged (*Angeles & Neanidis* 2009: 133), it is regularly overlooked when it comes to project design, and actors are generally assumed to be benevolent (*Williamson* 2010: 19).

The novelty of the EC concept in this context is the *explication* of the problem complex by subsuming associated phenomena into a new heading, and thus pointing out its high relevance, i.e., its explanatory value for project performance. The goal of this study was to verify this explanatory value empirically. The results are summarized in the next section. Section 7.2 briefly discusses the results and possible implications for project design. The last section draws a conclusion.

7.1 Summary of the Results

For the empirical evaluation, extreme groups from a sample of n = 137 project reports were used, resulting in a top group of the 17 highest-performing projects and a bottom group of the 17 lowest-performing projects[1]. The data collection included problem and success descriptions, which were coded regarding relation to EC (y/n) and their specific symptom type. Additionally, various qualitative variables were collected that related to aspects of project management quality and project design features. The results for these variables will be discussed in their respective context.

General Distribution of Problem and Success Factors

- The general tendency is as expected: The top group features a significantly[2] higher amount of success descriptions than problem descriptions, vice versa for the bottom group.
- Nevertheless, problem factors appear also in the top group (and success factors in the bottom group), illustrating that success is likely not a matter of pure luck, but seems to coincide with a higher capacity of project management.
- Failed projects count more problem descriptions than successful projects feature success factors. This is not surprising, as the identification and attribution of problems in case of failure is commonly more important than that of successes in case of high performance. Consequently, the total amount of descriptions (i.e., positive and negative) is significantly higher in the bottom group.

---

1 This corresponds to octiles; in the sample, increasing the group sizes (e.g., to quartiles) would have compromised on the within-group homogeneity regarding the criterion.

2 For better readability, "significant" in this chapter refers to very high significance ($\alpha = 0.001$), unless specified otherwise.

Relevance of Elite Compatibility

When looking at the successes and failures that are supposed to be related to EC, the two groups again differ significantly:

- EC successes are substantially more prevalent in the top group, EC failures are more prevalent in the bottom group. The correlation of project performance to EC problem/success distribution is at a high $\Phi = 0.70$.
- All but one case of the top group feature EC successes. However, not all projects of the bottom group actually feature EC problems – some even feature symptoms of solved EC.

This situation is very similar to a comment from an OECD report that summarizes the results from a series of case studies:

> "Perhaps the most striking feature of the case studies is that the commonalities observed among successfully converging regions are far more apparent than those seen among regions that are losing ground. The latter are characterised by greater variety of conditions with respect to the variables under study. Their experience brings to mind the opening line of Tolstoy's *Anna Karenina*: 'Happy families are all alike, but every unhappy family is unhappy in its own way.' […] There are more 'recipes' for failure than for success." (*OECD* 2012a: 266)

A likewise summary could be drawn for the distribution of EC issues in this study:

- Approximately half of the failed projects are not subject to substantial problems of EC, and instead show a high count of 'other' problems. In other words, there is an almost equal dichotomy between failure that is clearly EC-related and failure that is clearly *not* EC-related. Because the top group is rather homogeneous regarding EC, the bottom group's distribution offers a good opportunity for further identification of factors that may be connected to EC and those that are not.
- However, for the other half, the amount of EC-related problems is substantial. Additionally, comparing it to the count of success and problem descriptions *not* related to this concept, EC-related problems have a stronger correlation to project performance.
- None of the cases with EC problems has a high internal monitoring quality. As extractive activities are in the way of efficient project management, this appears logical: the *absence* of EC problems should be a precondition, as extractive activities by elites impede efficient project management.

These general results expose a significant connection between EC and project performance; the overall distribution pattern suggests EC to be a necessary, but not sufficient condition for project success. Thus, the EC concept proves to be a highly relevant problem category and offers a fruitful 'search domain' for problem solving in ODA project design.

Project Scopes and Elite Levels

Further investigation shows that there is a significant difference between the successful and the failed projects:

- The bottom group's elite-related problems predominantly refer to the *national-level* elite, while the successful projects' solved symptoms are mainly slanted towards the *local*-elite level.
- The additional project data reveal that this distribution is not random: The groups substantially differed in their scope, as the top group almost entirely consists of projects that intervened on the local or regional level, while the failed projects mainly operated on the national level. This is apparent from the significant differences in both the type of implementing partner (13 of 17 projects in the top group were NGO-implemented, vs. only 1 in the bottom group; 10 of 17 projects of the bottom group were implemented by recipient's public administration), but also in the project budgets (an arithmetic mean of €2.3 million in the top group and of €14 million in the bottom group, differing at $\alpha = 0.01$).

Significant differences between successful and failed projects are also identified with regard to two aspects of project design:

- Of the top-performing projects, 11 followed a *participatory design approach*, while only 2 of the low performers did. Interestingly, these projects display no (#1) or just one (#12) contingency of EC problems. Thus, in this study's small sample, the participatory design approaches correspond perfectly to theoretical expectations (and those of ODA practice), as the inclusion of the project's stakeholders in the design process is supposed to solve collective-action problems and reduce top-down effects.
- Another variable captured an aspect of ownership: when the project output included a resource, such as water or electrical power, whether this resource was foreseen to be managed by government entities or by local stakeholders. All of the top group's designs were 'stakeholder managed' with only one exception, the bottom group only included 3 cases – all of which again display a low importance of EC problems over other problems.

These results illustrate that the irrelevance of national-level elites is most likely attributable to the more local scopes of the interventions in the top group, and the resulting higher distance to the elites of the national level.

The Most Relevant Elite-Compatibility Symptoms

The different relevance of national-level elites for the high- and low-performing projects is confirmed also when examining the concrete symptom types, i.e., the actual content of the EC issues. Comparing the top group's success factors and the bottom group's problem factors, the following patterns are apparent:

- The problem with the highest contingency in the failed group (12 incidences) was that of low efforts in monitoring and rule enforcement – a result of large distances in hierarchies with top-down control structures. At the same time, it had only one incidence as a success factor of the top group, and hence was of very low relevance in the first place, i.e., the project did not have to cope with large hierarchies.
- The opposite is true for the problem of missing support for local development: This is the highest contingency (14 incidences) of all 'solved' issues in the successful projects, while it is practically irrelevant as a problem in the bottom group, with only 2 incidences. This irrelevance illustrates the distance of the bottom group from the local level.
- Lastly, there are also symptoms with high counts both as solved problems in the top group as well as unsolved problems in the group of failed projects. The common feature of all these cases[3] is that the bottom group's failures are all related to national-level elites, while the top group's solved issues mainly relate to the level of local elites. The most important symptom was the failure to enhance capabilities of officials or beneficiaries (11 'solved' incidences in the top group/9 'unsolved' incidences in the bottom group), again a problem that derives from top-down orientation in hierarchies. Other symptoms were the 'output-over-outcome' phenomenon (8/11) that is a result of politicians cutting a share of the contract budgets; political control over implementation (9/8); no cooperation of government for implementing change (7/6).

3 The only (insignificant) exception is success factor #1: Of the three total incidences, 3 distribute to the national, 2 additionally to the local-elite level.

So while the *overall* distribution of EC-related successes and problems already significantly separates the successful and the failed projects, the specific distribution by concrete EC symptoms shows that the top group did not solve the same problems that were those of the failed projects. Instead, the vast majority of successful projects had a completely different scope; they were operating on the local level and successfully solved incentive problems with local elites, while national-level elites were not involved to a decisive extent.

In other words, from the results of the samples, EC was significantly *solved* on the local level, and elite incompatibility was significantly *problematic* on the level of national elites. Generalizing this result, one could arrive at the conclusion that EC in aid projects is solvable only on the local level, but not on the higher political level of national elites. Naturally, this is deliberately overstated for the sake of discussion.

7.2 Discussion: Solving Elite-Compatibility Problems

Similarly to the discussion of test validity in Section 6.5.1.3, it would be slightly tautological to assess the general results for their congruence with theory, as the coding frame for the report evaluation was built on existing incentive-theoretical explanations. The results seem to confirm the belief that incompatibility of standard ODA project goals with national-level elites is inherent to the aid system. As stated at the beginning of this chapter, this notion is shared among many of the aid critics, as well as authors who have been examining development aid with the lens of NIE, and there is no reason why these incentive problems can be solved at more than a random level. Various solutions that have been implemented as an answer to effectiveness problems of ODA (see *Pritchett & Woolcock* 2008), have not been successful on a substantially systematic level.

Instead of a theoretical exhaustion, this section will discuss possible solutions for EC problems, in three aspects: possible implications from the results of this study (7.2.1); solutions from the general aid discourse in the literature (7.2.2); project-level solutions (7.2.3).

7.2.1 Possible Implications From the Results of This Survey

The results of this study provide a rather clear picture of characteristics that significantly differentiate successful from failed projects, and more specifically, projects that displayed a high EC from those that did not: the implementing partner type of NGO, and the adoption of a participatory design approach. I have previously argued that neither is necessarily causally related to project success *directly*, but that instead, both represent the underlying factor of project scope. The question is whether a 'reduction' of the project scope can be a solution for EC, and how these two characteristics relate to this.

NGO Implementation

NGOs are generally regarded as an advantageous complement to official aid actors, mainly due to their supposed independence from political interests, more needs-based targeting and thus higher efficiency (see *Dreher et al.* 2012: 1450). Typically, their 'competitive advantage' is especially seen for interventions involving public-goods transfer, i.e., social or 'soft' infrastructure, while for physical or 'hard' infrastructure such as transport, this is the case for profit-oriented actors (ibid.). The NGO-implemented projects in this study mostly involved a combination of both.

Despite their good public image, NGOs do not necessarily live up to the supposed standards. Firstly, the independence from political entities is often not given, as many organizations rely on public funding sources (*Kilby* 2000: 48f.). Because official funding tends to increase administrative costs (*Nunnenkamp & Öhler* 2012), the efficiency of operations strongly varies with this funding source and the availability of funds. More importantly, the bureaucracies of larger NGOs are prone to the same incentive conflicts as other bureaucratic structures (*Williamson* 2010: 22), so the general supposition of a more "altruistic" (see *Dreher et al.* 2012: 1449) behavior is not an apt assessment. Quite the contrary, the organization may pursue its own agenda, with incentive effects decoupled from actual effectiveness (cf. footnote 6 below), often leading to "reality gaps" (*Arnall et al.* 2013: 326) between NGO aspiration and in-the-field situation. Thus, the quality and effectiveness of NGOs may vary dramatically, *inter alia* depending on the ability to cope with these deficiencies[4].

Also, the ownership structure of NGO-implemented projects varies depending on whether, how many and which contractors are involved in the

4 *Werker and Ahmed* (2008: 87) summarize the problematic effect of an increasing number of NGO players in the aid system as "too many actors, too many chiefs, too much mission".

implementation. In this sense, the commonplace statement of a measure not being a 'magic bullet' is especially true here, as the 'NGO' label of implementing partner does not stand for a standardized project design or management quality.

However, what it *does* stand for are the organizational characteristics which provide NGOs with the potential to bypass higher-level elites and target local groups directly – which is not exactly unquestionable from an ethical standpoint (*Kilby* 2000: 52). This feature alone does not warrant project success; instead, how well the local collective-action problems are tackled seems to depend much more on acquaintance with the existing local institutions and not so much on the mere aspect of community-based design: Deploying *existing* leadership structures often yields better results for reaching the poor than the 'universal' solution of distributing power evenly (*Dasgupta & Beard* 2007: 244). As, on community level, leadership structures with bottom-up forms of control may already exist (*Arnall et al.* 2013: 327), knowledge of and familiarity with these structures is a key for successful implementation.

Summarized, the success of the NGO-implemented projects is a combination of a potential organizational advantage in operating at the community level, and the actual familiarity of the local implementing staff with these local structures. In this sense, the implementing NGOs of the sample were successful not because they were NGOs, but more importantly because they were good at what they were doing.

Participatory Approaches

Despite the frequently discussed problems of participatory approaches, especially with regards to elite capture, the projects in this study are textbook-style successes that demonstrate the potential strengths of the designs in effectively solving local-level incentive problems. One of the success factors is a characteristic that has already been highlighted by *Gibson et al.* (2005: 13): In community-based designs, the 'ownership' of the output (or parts of it) is with the beneficiaries directly, and the standard separation of ownership and responsibility, which lies "at the heart of the incentive problem in development" (ibid.) can thus be resolved. As discussed in the previous paragraph, though, a key aspect seems to be that the pre-interventional distribution of power and potential asymmetries are taken into account by the design – which is often a problem in practice (*Rigon* 2014: 272).

Generalizing from the success of local-scope project designs in this study, one obvious idea for implementation would be to avoid large-scale national-level interventions and instead break projects down into local-level units that are independent from national-level politics. Apart from a myriad of challenges associated with this concept[5], the most central problem would be the fact that the extractive institutional environment in which these projects would need to be embedded, is not changed – resulting in vulnerability towards later political interference from higher levels. The probability of such interference may vary with the physical or institutional distance between beneficiaries and politicians, however, the attractiveness for interference rises with the size of the targeted population and the (economic) success of the intervention. This is already evident in some of the (otherwise successful) projects of this sample. E.g., one report states that "[u]nfortunately, apart from capacity building, which is a long-term affair, there is little that the project can do to avoid opportunistic preying on its groups by people with other agendas than the welfare of the groups" (*European Commission* 2011a: BCS 4.2)[6].

In other words, designs that are not 'resistant' against their extractive environment may not offer a true, i.e., long-term and sustainable solution, and effectively underlie the same mistake as the notorious top-down installation of institutions. As *Huber, North and Weingast* (2003) state, history offers "no case of a well-developed market system that was not embedded in a well-developed political system. Even under apartheid, South Africa prospered – relative to the rest of Africa – because of the rule of law (however unpalatable and discriminatory some laws were)." As such, carefully crafted local-level interventions share the problem of said institutional reform interventions: The political equilibrium, in this case of

5 To start with, not every larger intervention is suited for splitting and decentralizing to the local level, e.g., power plants. Secondly, this would imply a substantial increase in the ratio of personnel vs. disbursed capital – which is a problematic feature in the current system of ODA provision (see Section 4.3.2.2). Thirdly, the topic of decentralization is itself subject to extensive discussion (cf. *Fritzen & Ong* 2008; *Gadenne & Singhal* 2014: 582f.).

6 Interestingly, the report also includes uncoordinated aid interventions as a threat: "The project has had to fight against a certain dependency mentality that too many projects with too many handouts have created. This fight has been relatively successful but, as the final evaluation states, a major danger for what the project has been doing is that another government organization or NGO arrives and starts to give money or food – or other inputs – to the farmers, to erode the nascent self-reliance of the groups - which seems to be exactly what is happening" (ibid.: BCS 3.2).

their higher-level environment, is not altered. Even further, the absence of higher-level elites in participatory designs may be just superficial. As *Kumar and Corbridge* (2002: 94) point out, higher-level politics often support corresponding interventions precisely *in expectation* of capture by lower-level elites; the projects are then used as an indirect tool of patronage. In this sense, community-based designs may even indirectly support the extractive institutional setup which they are meant to exclude. This underlines the upshot contended by critics of participatory approaches, that circumventing elites is not an actual solution, but only postpones the EC problems[7].

So while participatory, NGO-implemented project designs were significantly (and explicably) characteristic for solving EC problems in this study, a generalization seems problematic from a standpoint of the empirics documented in the literature.

7.2.2 Alternative Solutions From the Aid Discourse

One of the central reasons for the elite's incentive conflict is the insufficient separation between political and economic power. As *Zweynert* (2009: 343) describes for *North's* theory of the state,

> „[e]stablishing a well-defined borderline between the political and the economic game enables each of the systems to develop its own rationality. However, once such a borderline has been established, the ruler is no longer able to influence directly the flow of material resources to own and followers' benefit."

It is this influence and its potential loss that causes the elite's resistance against change, as also picked up by *Acemoğlu and Robinson* (2012b: 86). For the context of ODA, I termed three types of this resistance, relating to different origins in the incentive setup:

- *active* resistance, resulting from intentional protection of the elite position;
- *extractive* resistance, 'collateral damage' resulting from activities of rent extraction;
- *passive* resistance, resulting from indifference about project success.

7 However, as a positive effect, an empowered group of beneficiaries may be more capable of generating relevant resistance against extraction – which is the idea of empowerment measures in the first place, and one of the reasons for *Acemoğlu and Robinson* (2012b: 455) to assess them as "a better prospect" than traditional aid.

In all cases, full project success (by the criteria of the donor) produces opportunity costs, and is thus not elite compatible. In order to reach EC, these opportunity costs of success need to be transformed into opportunity costs of failure. This section will briefly discuss some of the suggested solutions from the current discourse with regard to their capability to achieve this and thus create higher EC.

Project, Budget and Conditional Aid

One approach to create these costs of failure is reflected in the aid debate's focus on the modalities of provision, i.e., project aid vs. budget aid (*Klasen* 2009; *Hemmer* 2010), program aid (*Leiderer* 2012), and attached conditionalities. Moving away from individual project to budget aid or program aid, for example, is intended to reduce transaction costs and enhance ownership for the recipient government. An embedded part of this discussion is always aid conditionality, be it in an explicit form that a specific budget is provided on the condition of a larger-scale policy reform, or in the implicit form that an intervention requires certain changes in institutional practice to be effective, such as in public utility provision. With the notoriously questionable track record of conditionality (*Collier* 2007: 67; *Temple* 2010: 4468ff.), another focus of the discussion has been on possible solutions for the problems of coordination and credibility on the donor side. Suggestions include converting more of the bilateral to multilateral aid (*Birdsall* 2004: 10), or budget pooling of multiple donors (*Kanbur, Sandler & Morrison* 1999; *Svensson* 2003: 399).

The inherent conflict of this complex of aid provision is the trade-off between recipient ownership and accountability, which is reflected in the fact that, e.g., for budget aid, contrary to its goal of increasing recipient discretion over budget allocation, one of the most frequently discussed issues is the reduction of fungibility effects (cf. *Leiderer* 2012: 3). As such, the complex underlies the same implicit paradox as the topic of 'good governance'[8,9].

8 Which is in fact part of the debate around conditionality, cf. *de Sousa and Freitas* (2011: 489).

9 Aid conditionality has been criticized to be intrusive due to the limitations it imposes on recipient discretion. *Kilby* (2000: 54) provides a very tangible analogy to illustrate the ethical problem.

The main weakness of the approach of engineering aid modalities is that it will not yield *ex-ante* mechanisms: While *ex-ante* incentive compatibility is self-enforcing – hence commitments to respective institutional arrangements are termed "credible" (also) by *Acemoğlu and Robinson* (2006: 177) –, accountability is an *ex-post* mechanism. Its effect in the context of the Samaritan's dilemma of ODA is at least ambiguous; consequently, the limited success of these instruments cannot be counted as particularly surprising from the perspective of opportunity cost of failure.

Results-based Aid/Cash-on-delivery Aid

More recent concepts that are summarized under the headline of *results-based financing*[10], intend to shift the focus away from conditionalities associated with reforms and policies to conditionalities associated with targeted project outcomes – from "buying development" to "buying things" (*Birdsall et al.* 2011: 3). As the name suggests, the idea is to bind the conditionality of the budget transfer to the achievement of the actual output or outcome of the agreed intervention; payments are made successively according to the measured units of progress. Again, these concepts tackle the incentive problem from the side of accountability towards the donor and hence require a substantial amount of monitoring efforts – which is also one of the main challenges (*World Bank* 2014a: 19). Meanwhile, variants have been adapted into aid practice by, e.g., the UK's DFID as well as the World Bank (*Anderson* 2015), mainly in the healthcare and education sectors.

The original idea of the concept as described by *Birdsall et al.* (2011: 19) is for the donor to be completely hands-off, leaving the recipient with full discretion and responsibility. This should include the choice over design and planning, as well as "whether to have a plan" (ibid.). Thus, the approach implicitly aims at incentivizing a trial-and-error procedure that the conventional system of aid provision is notoriously lacking (see *Pritchett & Woolcock* 2008). More importantly, this idea represents the promotion of conditions for '*creative destruction*', which many authors in the development debate, including *Acemoğlu and Robinson* (2012b: 84,

10 The terms 'results-based financing' vs. 'results-based aid' are sometimes used synonymously, sometimes differentiated (*Grittner* 2013: 7).

430), view as essential for progress in the sense of innovation and sustainable economic growth[11].

An advantage of this approach regarding the effect on EC is that by 'slicing' the disbursements proportional to agreed stages of output, it combines the mechanism of ex-post accountability with the recipient discretion of budget aid to an instrument that produces rather direct opportunity costs of failure – at least on the theoretical level. However, it remains to be seen whether this step-by-step conditionality proves realistic in aid practice. This also applies to the conceptual aspiration of a hands-off donor and a fully sovereign recipient, as both stand in sharp contrast to the historical importance of tied aid[12] (see *Clay et al.* 2009), and the often politically charged donor-recipient relationships (see *Kilby* 2013).

The biggest problem will always remain the issue of donor coordination: Any design that generates opportunity costs of failure by focusing on the accountability side, ultimately represents a conditionality (which limits the possibilities for extraction). Naturally, it will be avoided if other, 'less conditional' donors are available for pitching in, to then offer aid budgets without opportunity costs of failure attached.

Problem-Driven Iterative Adaption

Andrews et al. (2012) suggest an approach which they term *problem-driven iterative adaption*. It explicitly aims at solving traps in building state capacity, and is supposed to be an answer to the standard "needs-bureaucracy supply approach" (*Pritchett & Woolcock* 2008: 160) and its deficiencies. These are seen mainly in blueprint adoption of 'best practice' solutions, the linear processes in ODA provision, the focus on inputs, and the top-down implementation. They contend that, in order to escape the capability trap, an organizational environment is needed that promotes experimentation and involves learning and iterative feedback. In order for solutions to be politically supportable and practically implementable, a broad set of agents needs to be engaged. But while their analysis and their proposed responses are very apt, their treatment does not address the

11 Just as the inherent incentive conflict of ODA, the importance of creative destruction has already been highlighted in the UN report (*United Nations* 1951: 13).

12 *Tied aid* refers to transfers that are granted to be spent on goods and services from the donor country. The share of tied aid has meanwhile fallen from an estimated 54 percent of total bilateral aid in 1999-2001 (*Clay, Geddes & Natali* 2009: 8) to 18 percent in 2014 (*OECD* 2014b: 261).

origin of the missing incentives – the complex of elite capture, limiting public goods provision and patronage politics. This is illustrated, e.g., when they state:

> "It is a process that […] must be accommodated by *system-wide mechanisms* that allow non-linear, frustrating (sometimes even contentious) processes of change that are liable to produce idiosyncratic (perhaps odd-looking) solutions." (*Andrews et al.* 2012: 14` emphasis added)

The change of these system-wide mechanisms is indeed exactly the problem, as there are no incentives for this change to happen. In their description, *Andrews et al.* highlight the need to move from an orientation of solution adoption to that of problem identification, i.e., "begin by asking 'what is the problem?' instead of 'which solution should we adopt?'" (ibid.: 9). The central incentive is supposed to stem from this problem orientation, as it emphasizes organizational performance and "encourages contributions from leaders and front-line workers to work for change" (ibid.: 12). While this incentive might positively impact process ownership by the individual actors *once the process is existent*, it fails to address the opportunity cost transformation that would help create the process in the first place.

As such, their solution seems sensible for an organizational environment where the need for change has already been acknowledged in principle, such as a company or corporation; but in the context of aid flows to extractive institutional environments, this is exactly *not* the case. Put bluntly, it appears slightly paradox to strive for solving the problem of a top-down implementation culture with the top-down implementation of a more open culture – or to 'install' an environment of experimentation and 'creative destruction' at all.

Charter Cities

A rather radical approach of putting the 'creative destruction' idea into practice is the *charter cities* concept, which has been suggested by *Paul Romer*, famous for his paper in which he integrated technological change into growth theory (*Romer* 1990; 1994). A charter city (*Romer* 2010) is a special economic zone, erected on a territory that is leased to a foreign power which is then mandated with its administration. The protectorate should be open to citizens from the 'host' country and thus feature classical *vote-with-your-feet* characteristics[13]. In Madagascar, the approach had already been on its way of being put into practice, before the country saw a coup in the beginning of 2009 (*Mallaby* 2010: 98). The latest promotion had been about Honduras setting up a charter city led by Canada (*Fuller & Romer* 2012), where *Romer* resigned from his consultant position after disputes over implementation. Naturally, public reception of this neo-colonial concept has not been very favorable (*Chakrabortty* 2010). Interestingly, the core characteristics of the charter-city idea are very similar to the example that was previously given in Chapter 2: the *build-operate-transfer* model (BOT).

Build-Operate-Transfer

This design could in fact be viewed as a 'micro' or project-level translation of charter cities. Here, a public entity grants a private party the concession to construct and operate an asset for a limited time frame, before ownership is transferred to the public entity. This design is a standard financing model for infrastructure world-wide (e.g., roads, tunnels, bridges etc.), and within ODA, leads an off-mainstream existence under the *public private partnership*[14] headline (cf. *BMZ* 2011). The role of BOT models here is that it is chosen as a design between a recipient and a private third party, and then funded by the donor (*Hartig* 2008: 3; *OECD* 2011: 133). Also, in the semi-private sector of 'emerging-markets' development, as promoted, e.g., by the *UNDP* (2008), business models have been applying this design (*Karugu* 2011).

An approach could be to devolve this mode of implementation to general projects, in the sense that the transfer from the donor to the recipient is not final upon completion of construction, but after an appointed time of operation – providing the benefits outlined in Chapter 2, mainly reducing the possible extent of rent extraction and effectively building up a mechanism for opportunity costs of failure. However, while this model sounds appealing in theory, the practicability of this idea is most likely negligible.

---

13 Going back to *Tiebout* (1956: 418).

14 In ODA, this category is two-fold: Aside from financing public-private partnerships in the recipient countries, it may also refer to such partnerships on the donor side, i.e., the support of private companies for activities that generate 'development impact' (see *GTZ* 2010).

One of the obvious downsides is that the government does not build up any capabilities in public service provision, as the entire solution is effectively taken over by the grantee of the concession – not only for this reason, privatization of public services is subject to heavy debate in general. In this sense, the above scheme of cash-on-delivery aid at least theoretically appears more promising.

A valuable impulse from the essential idea behind the BOT model, though, is the focus on asset lifecycle and resulting incentives for maintenance: A possible implication could be to explicitly support maintenance – in separate projects and prior to the state where infrastructure assets require rehabilitation. This shift would not necessarily eradicate extraction (i.e., capture) of the projects, however it would exactly for this reason align elite's incentives with positive economic effects of maintenance over building new infrastructure[15].

7.2.3 Solving Elite Compatibility on the Project Level

Finally, while the above concepts require a redesign of the mode of aid provision in one way or the other, a higher compatibility with elite's incentives may also be established by other, smaller-scale solutions that concern the project level. As *Barder* (2009: 2f.) holds:

> "We are reaching the limits to what can be achieved by better planning to improve aid. Greater use of market and network mechanisms, by contrast, would help to alter the incentives and political constraints faced by aid agencies."

A classic example of *Paul Romer* (*Mallaby* 2010: 96) tangibly illustrates the effect of market versus misguided incentives: *Romer* uses a photograph of Guinean teenagers sitting over their homework under streetlights and points out that, while the type of youths depicted in the photo generally own and use cell phones (a rather cutting-edge technology), they obviously do not have electric light at home (a 100-year-old technology) – otherwise they would not be working under street lights at the side of the road. Despite his illustration having been slightly 'over-cited' in mass media, it is indeed a pointed comparison; not only because of the paradox

15 In the frequently cited *World Development Report 1994*, the *World Bank* (1994: 4) estimated that, in Africa during the then-previous decade, an additional US$12 billion spent on timely road maintenance could have saved US$45 billion spent in reconstruction.
Cf. also the analysis of *Rioja* (2003) and the literature discussed there.

of technology maturities, but also because both technologies share the characteristic that they are network-based, and thus underlie similar challenges in provision. But while the provision of electrical power often suffers from textbook-style failure of EC, the incentive situation for mobile telecommunication providers has been solved often even in remote regions (see also *Etzo & Collender* 2010).

Very good examples for the effect of market mechanisms to create EC are in fact provided by two projects from the top group of this study's sample, both of which explicitly featured extraordinary support from national-level elites:

- #9 (Uzbekistan): This project was neither NGO-implemented nor participatory in design, and the resource was government-managed. However, the support is easily explained: The project purpose was the assistance for harmonization of standards and practices of the national gas infrastructure with the requirements of the EU – in other words, the project opened up the European market for the Uzbek gas producers. Ownership and responsibility were located with the same agents – as the national-level elites were both recipient and beneficiary.
- #3 (Cambodia): The project purpose was the implementation of a national wood energy policy and the setup of a local infrastructure for production and distribution of improved cooking stoves. This project received extraordinary support from national-level politics, and the report explicitly mentions the reasoning: the interest in the carbon credits revenue that the project was set up to generate. The feature that made this project elite compatible were those opportunity costs of failure.

It is the original idea behind carbon credits to make carbon dioxide savings incentive compatible by internalizing external effects, so there is no novelty in the project design itself; it merely made use of an existing market-based mechanism that already aligned the incentives. Unfortunately, not every project purpose offers an 'easy' solution like this. At the same time, solutions with 'big' impact are not necessarily 'big' themselves. A case cited by *Reinikka and Svensson* (2004: 700) gives an example of another simple solution in Uganda: To fight local elite capture of a large school-grant program, the monthly transfers of public funds were published in local newspapers; the schools were thus informed about the original volume and were empowered to hold local elites accountable for the full amount. This simple measure increased the average ratio that the schools received of their original entitlements from 20 percent to 80 percent.

7.3 Conclusion

The problem of the incompatibility of project success and elite interests is inherent to the aid system. The empirical results of this study are clear and unambiguous in confirming the importance of EC as a necessary but not sufficient condition for project success. The way aid delivery is organized, however, most popular solutions do not address this complex according to its importance, and instead often try to engineer solutions and assuming ignorance as the central problem, thus committing the "error of the third kind" (*Mitroff* 1998: 13): precise solving of the wrong problem. My central argument is that, in order to align ODA project goals with elite interest, the elite's opportunity cost of aid success has to be transformed into opportunity costs of failure. Classical solutions like aid modalities and conditional approaches do not adequately achieve this change, although more recent suggestions like Aid on Delivery appear more promising in this respect.

While this study identifies a clear-cut profile of success (locally-intervening participatory designs, and NGO implementation), it becomes clear from empirics in the literature that both approaches solve EC only on the local, but not on higher elite levels, and thus simply delay EC problems, hampering project sustainability. Instead, I conclude that on the project level, market mechanisms may be the best design to introduce opportunity costs of failure and thus achieve EC. The study's sample offers two prominent examples of this design, resulting in active support also by national-level elites.

That the identification of effective solutions will most likely remain an immanent part of the economic discipline also for the nearer future, is nicely illustrated by the following quote by a famous economist:

> "The complicated analyses which economists endeavor to carry through are not mere gymnastic. They are instruments for the bettering of human life. The misery and squalor that surround us, the injurious luxury of some wealthy families, the terrible uncertainty overshadowing many families of the poor – these are evils too plain to be ignored. By the knowledge that our science seeks it is possible that they may be restrained."

The quote is from the 3rd edition of *Arthur Pigou's* "Economics of Welfare" (ibid.: vii), which was published in 1929. Insofar, as for the quest to identify the correct solutions, the timeless quality of the above quote aptly substantiates the point of *Acemoğlu and Robinson* (2012b: 460) when they hold: "The honest answer of course is that there is no recipe". However, the provided examples show that the appropriate mechanism may sometimes be quite simple. A valuable search domain can therefore be offered by the concept of elite compatibility and the opportunity costs of failure.

References

Abbink, K. and M. Ellman (2010). The Donor Problem: An Experimental Analysis of Beneficiary Empowerment. Journal of Development Studies 46(8): 1327-1344.

Acemoğlu, D., C. García-Jimeno and J. A. Robinson (2012). Finding Eldorado: Slavery and long-run development in Colombia. *Journal of Comparative Economics* 40(4): 534-564.

Acemoğlu, D., S. Johnson, J. A. Robinson and P. Yared (2009). Reevaluating the modernization hypothesis. *Journal of Monetary Economics* 56(8): 1043-1058.

Acemoğlu, D., S. H. Johnson and J. A. Robinson (2001). The Colonial Origins of Comparative Development: An Empirical Investigation. *The American Economic Review* 91(5): 1369-1401.

Acemoğlu, D., S. H. Johnson and J. A. Robinson (2005). Institutions as the Fundamental Cause of Long-Run Growth. In: P. Aghion and S. Durlauf: *Handbook of Economic Growth. Vol. 1A*. New York, NY: North Holland. 385–472.

Acemoğlu, D. and J. A. Robinson (2001). A Theory of Political Transitions. *The American Economic Review* 91(4): 938-963.

Acemoğlu, D. and J. A. Robinson (2006). *Economic Origins of Dictatorship and Democracy*. Cambridge, UK: Cambridge University Press.

Acemoğlu, D. and J. A. Robinson (2008). Persistence of Power, Elites, and Institutions. *American Economic Review* 98(1): 267-293.

Acemoğlu, D. and J. A. Robinson (2012a). "Acemoglu and Robinson Answer Your Questions." Published 2012-04-20 on *Freakonomics Blog*. Available from http://freakonomics.com/2012/04/20/acemoglu-and-robinson-answer-your-questions/

Acemoğlu, D. and J. A. Robinson (2012b). *Why Nations Fail: The Origins of Power, Prosperity, and Poverty*. New York, NY: Crown Publishers.

Acemoğlu, D. and J. A. Robinson (2013). "What Bill Gates Got Wrong About Why Nations Fail." Published 2013-03-12 on *Foreignpolicy.com*. Available from http://www.foreignpolicy.com/articles/2013/03/12/what_bill_gates_got_wrong_about_why_nations_fail

Acemoğlu, D., D. Ticchi and A. Vindigni (2011). Emergence and Persistence of Inefficient States. *Journal of the European Economic Association* 9(2): 177-208.

Ackah, C. and O. Morrissey (2001). *Trade Liberalisation is Good for You if You are Rich*. CREDIT Research Paper 07/01. Nottingham: University of Nottingham.

Akerlof, G. A. (1970). The Market for "Lemons": Quality Uncertainty and the Market Mechanism. *The Quarterly Journal of Economics* 84(3): 488-500.

Alesina, A., R. Baqir and W. Easterly (2000). Redistributive Public Employment. *Journal of Urban Economics* 48(2): 219-241.

Alesina, A. and D. Rodrik (1994). Distributive Politics and Economic Growth. *The Quarterly Journal of Economics* 109(2): 465-490.

Alesina, A. and B. Weder (2002). Do Corrupt Governments Receive Less Foreign Aid? *American Economic Review* 92(4): 1126-1137.

Altincecik, C. and D. H. Bearce (2014). Why There Should Be No Political Foreign Aid Curse. *World Development* 64: 18-32.

Alvi, E. and A. Senbeta (2012). Does Foreign Aid Reduce Poverty? *Journal of International Development* 24(8): 955-976.

Amsden, A. H. (2012). Elites and Property Rights. In: A. H. Amsden, A. DiCaprio and J. A. Robinson: *The Role of Elites in Economic Development*. Oxford, UK: Oxford University Press. 19-28.

Amsden, A. H., A. DiCaprio and J. A. Robinson, Eds. (2012). *The Role of Elites in Economic Development*. Oxford, UK: Oxford University Press.

Anderson, M. (2015). "World Bank announces $5bn drive to improve quality of global education." Published 2015-05-18 on *TheGuardian.com*. Available from http://www.theguardian.com/global-development/2015/may/18/world-bank-education-quality-5bn

Andrews, M., L. Pritchett and M. Woolcock (2012). *Escaping Capability Traps through Problem-Driven Iterative Adaptation (PDIA)*. CGD Working Paper 299. Washington, D.C.: Center for Global Development.

Angeles, L. and K. C. Neanidis (2009). Aid effectiveness: the role of the local elite. *Journal of Development Economics* 90(1): 120-134.

Aoki, M. (2007). Endogenizing institutions and institutional changes. *Journal of Institutional Economics* 3(1): 1-31.

Arnall, A., D. S. G. Thomas, C. Twyman and D. Liverman (2013). NGOs, elite capture and community-driven development: perspectives in rural Mozambique. *The Journal of Modern African Studies* 51(2): 305-330.

Arrow, K. J. (1963). Uncertainty and the Welfare Economics of Medical Care. *The American Economic Review* 53(5): 941-973.

Arvin, B. M. and B. Lew (2010). Does Happiness Affect the Bilateral Aid Flows Between Donor and Recipient Countries? *European Journal of Development Research* 22(4): 546-563.

Askarov, Z. and H. Doucouliagos (2015). Development Aid and Growth in Transition Countries. *World Development* 66: 383-399.

Auerswald, P. E. (2011). "Why Randomized Controlled Trials Work in Public Health...and Not Much Else." Published 2011-09-07 on *The Coming Prosperity*. Available from http://thecomingprosperity.blogspot.de/2011/09/why-randomized-controlled-trials-work.html

Bach, D. C. (2012a). Conclusion: neopatrimonial and developmental – the emerging states' syndrome. In: D. C. Bach and M. Gazibo: *Neopatrimonialism in Africa and Beyond*. Abingdon, UK: Routledge. 221-224.

Bach, D. C. (2012b). Patrimonialism and neopatrimonialism: comparative receptions and transcriptions. In: D. C. Bach and M. Gazibo: *Neopatrimonialism in Africa and Beyond*. Abingdon, UK: Routledge. 25-45.

Bakewell, O. and A. Garbutt (2005). *The Use and Abuse of the Logical Framework Approach*. Stockholm: Swedish International Development Cooperation Agency.

Banerjee, A. V. (2009). Big Answers for Big Questions: The Presumption of Growth Policy. In: J. Cohen and W. Easterly: *What Works in Development? Thinking Big and Thinking Small*. Washington, DC: Brookings Institution Press. 207-221.

Banerjee, A. V., R. Banerji, E. Duflo, R. Glennerster and S. Khemani (2010). Pitfalls of Participatory Programs: Evidence from a Randomized Evaluation in Education in India. *American Economic Journal: Economic Policy* 2(1): 1-30.

Banerjee, A. V. and E. Duflo (2007). The Economic Lives of the Poor. *Journal of Economic Perspectives* 21(1): 141-167.

Banerjee, A. V. and E. Duflo (2011). Poor Economics: A Radical Rethinking of the Way to Fight Global Poverty. New York, NY: Public Affairs.

Banerjee, A. V., E. Duflo, R. Glennerster and C. Kinnan (2009). *The miracle of microfinance? Evidence from a randomized evaluation*. IPA Working Paper. New Haven, CT: Innovations for Poverty Action.

Banerjee, A. V., R. Glennerster and E. Duflo (2008). Putting a Band-Aid on a Corpse: Incentives for Nurses in the Indian Public Health Care System. *Journal of the European Economic Association* 6(2/3): 487-500.

Barder, O. (2009). *Beyond Planning: Markets and Networks for Better Aid*. CGD Working Paper 185. Washington, D.C.: Center for Global Development.

Barder, O. (2010). An Open Letter To Aid Skeptics. *The Forum* (Spring): 21-27.

Bardhan, P. and D. Mookherjee (2006). Decentralisation and Accountability in Infrastructure Delivery in Developing Countries. *The Economic Journal* 116: 101-127.

Barnard, C. I. (1938). *The Functions of the Executive*. Cambridge, MA: Harvard University Press.

Barro, R. J. (1996). Democracy and Growth. *Journal of Economic Growth* 1(1): 1-27.

Bartolini, D. (2013). *The Role of Incentives in Co-operation Failures*. OECD Regional Development Working Paper 2013/09. Paris: Organisation for Economic Co-Operation and Development.

Bates, R. H. (1981). Markets and States in Tropical Africa: The Political Basis of Agricultural Policies. Berkeley, CA: University of California Press.

Bates, R. H. (1988a). Contra Contractarianism: Some Reflections on the New Institutionalism. *Politics & Society* 16(2/3): 387-401.

Bates, R. H. (1988b). Governments and Agricultural Markets in Africa. In: R. H. Bates: *Toward a Political Economy of Development: A Rational Choice Perspective*. Berkeley, CA: University of California Press. 331-358.

Bauer, P. T. (1969). Dissent on Development. *Scottish Journal of Political Economy* 16(1): 75-94.

Bauer, P. T. (1975). N.H. Stern on Substance and Method in Development Economics. *Journal of Development Economics* 2(4): 319-416.

Bauer, P. T. and B. S. Yamey (1957). *The Economics of Under-developed Countries*. London, UK: James Nisbet & Co.

Bazzi, S. and M. A. Clemens (2013). Blunt Instruments: Avoiding Common Pitfalls in Identifying the Causes of Economic Growth. *American Economic Journal: Macroeconomics* 5(2): 152-186.

Becker, G. S. (1957). *The Economics of Discrimination*. Chicago, IL: University of Chicago Press.

Becker, G. S. (1968). Crime and Punishment: An Economic Approach. *Journal of Political Economy* 76(2): 169-217.

Becker, G. S. (1973). A Theory of Marriage: Part I. *Journal of Political Economy* 81(4): 813-846.

Behar, A. (2010). Do managers and experts agree? A comparison of alternative sources of trade facilitation data. CSAE Working Paper 2010-29. Oxford, UK: University of Oxford.

Bellemare, M. F. (2014). "Development Bloat: How Mission Creep Harms the Poor." Published 2014-01-05 on *Foreign Affairs Online.* Available from http://www.foreign affairs.com/articles/140624/marc-f-bellemare/development-bloat

Benedek, D., E. Crivelli, S. Gupta and P. Muthoora (2014). Foreign Aid and Revenue: Still a Crowding-Out Effect? *FinanzArchiv: Public Finance Analysis* 70(1): 67-96.

Berelson, B. (1952). *Content Analysis in Communication Research.* Glencoe, IL: Free Press.

Bergmann, J. (2003). Operation Saubermann. *brand eins* (05/2003): 36-41.

Berle, A. A. and G. C. Means (1932). *The Modern Corporation and Private Property.* New York, NY: Commerce Clearing House.

Bernheim, B. D. and M. D. Whinston (1985). Common Marketing Agency as a Device for Facilitating Collusion. *The RAND Journal of Economics* 16(2): 269-281.

Bernstein, M. A. and M. R. Wilson (2011). New Perspectives on the History of the Military-Industrial Complex. *Enterprise and Society* 12(1): 1-9.

Besley, T., J. G. Montalvo and M. Reynal-Querol (2011). Do Educated Leaders Matter? *The Economic Journal* 121(554): F205-F227.

Bill & Melinda Gates Foundation (2014). *2013 Annual Report.* Seattle, WA: Bill & Melinda Gates Foundation.

Binnendijk, A. (2000). Results Based Management in the Development Co-operation Agencies: A Review of Experience. Paris: DAC Working Party on Aid Evaluation.

Birdsall, N. (2004). *Seven Deadly Sins: Reflections on Donor Failings.* CGD Working Paper 50. Washington, D.C.: Center for Global Development.

Birdsall, N., W. D. Savedoff, A. Mahgoub and K. Vyborny (2011). *Cash On Delivery: A New Approach to Foreign Aid.* 2nd Ed. Washington, D.C.: Center for Global Development.

Björkman, M. and J. Svensson (2009). Power to the People: Evidence From a Randomized Field Experiment on Community-Based Monitoring in Uganda. *The Quarterly Journal of Economics* 124(2): 735-769.

Blinder, A. S. (1974). The Economics of Brushing Teeth. *Journal of Political Economy* 82(4): 887-891.

Blouin, M. and S. Pallage (2007). *Addressing the Food Aid Curse.* CIRPÉE Working Paper 07-17. Montréal: Université du Québec à Montréal.

Blume, L. and S. Voigt (2007). The Economic Effects of Human Rights. *Kyklos* 60(4): 509-538.

BMZ (2011). *Forms of Development Cooperation Involving the Private Sector.* Strategy Paper 05/2011e. Berlin: Federal Ministry for Economic Cooperation and Development.

Bobbio, N. (1972). *On Mosca and Pareto.* Geneva: Librairie Droz.

Boettke, P. and A. Fink (2011). Institutions first. *Journal of Institutional Economics* 7(4): 499-504.

Boettke, P. J., C. J. Coyne and P. T. Leeson (2008). Institutional Stickiness and the New Development Economics. *American Journal of Economics and Sociology* 67(2): 331-358.

Bold, T., M. Kimenyi, G. Mwabu and J. Sandefur (2011a). *Does Abolishing Fees Reduce School Quality? Evidence from Kenya.* CSAE Working Paper 2011-04. Oxford: University of Oxford.

Bold, T., M. Kimenyi, G. Mwabu and J. Sandefur (2011b). *Why Did Abolishing Fees Not Increase Public School Enrollment in Kenya?* CGD Working Paper 271. Washington, D.C.: Center for Global Development.

Boone, P. (1996). Politics and the effectiveness of foreign aid. *European Economic Review* 40: 289-329.

Booth, D. (2009). *Elites, governance and the public interest in Africa working with the grain?* APPP Discussion Paper 6. London, UK: Overseas Development Institute.

Borensztein, E., J. D. Gregoriob and J.-W. Lee (1998). How does foreign direct investment affect economic growth? *Journal of International Economics* 45(1): 115-135.

Bortz, J. and N. Döring (2006). *Forschungsmethoden und Evaluation.* 4th Ed. Heidelberg: Springer.

Borzello, A. (2001). “Uganda's Museveni leads in 'rigged' elections.” Published 2001-03-14 on *The Guardian.* Available from http://www.theguardian.com/world/2001/mar/14/2

Bourguignon, F. and T. Verdier (2012). The Simple Analytics of Elite Behaviour Under Limited State Capacity. In: A. H. Amsden, A. DiCaprio and J. A. Robinson: *The Role of Elites in Economic Development.* Oxford, UK: Oxford University Press. 251-280.

Boussat, G. (2008). The Marshall Plan: History and Legacy. In: E. Sorel and P. C. Padoan: *The Marshall Plan: Lessons Learned for the 21st Century.* Paris: OECD Publishing. 13-28.

Bowles, S. (2006). Institutional Poverty Traps. In: S. Bowles, S. Durlauf and K. Hoff: *Poverty Traps.* Princeton, NJ: Princeton University Press. 116–138.

Bowman, C. and S. Chand (2007). *Size Matters: The Impact of Aid on Institutions.* UNU-WIDER Working Paper 2007/25. Helsinki: United Nations University.

Bratton, M. and N. van de Walle (1994). Neopatrimonial Regimes and Political Transitions in Africa. *World Politics* 46(4): 453-489.

Bräutigam, D. (2000). *Aid Dependence and Governance.* Stockholm: Almqvist & Wiksell.

Bräutigam, D. and S.-M. S. Ekman (2012). Rumours and Realities of Chinese Agricultural Engagement in Mozambique. *African Affairs* 111(444): 483-492.

Bräutigam, D. and T. Xiaoyang (2011). African Shenzhen: China's special economic zones in Africa. *The Journal of Modern African Studies* 49(1): 27-54.

Bräutigam, D. A. and S. Knack (2004). Foreign Aid, Institutions, and Governance in Sub-Saharan Africa. *Economic Development and Cultural Change* 52(2): 255-285.

Broad, R. (2007). 'Knowledge Management': A Case Study of the World Bank's Research Department. *Development in Practice* 17(4-5): 700-708.

Broms, R. (2014). Putting Up or Shutting Up: On the Individual-Level Relationship between Taxpaying and Political Interest in a Developmental Context. *The Journal of Development Studies*: 1-17.

Bruhns, H. (2012). Weber's patrimonial domination and its interpretations. In: D. C. Bach and M. Gazibo: *Neopatrimonialism in Africa and Beyond.* Abingdon, UK: Routledge. 9-24.

Brunnschweiler, C. N. and E. H. Bulte (2008). The Resource Curse Revisited and Revised: A Tale of Paradoxes and Red Herrings. *Journal of Environmental Economics and Management* 55(3): 248-264.

Buchanan, J. (1987). *Economics Between Predictive Science and Moral Philosophy.* College Station, TX: Texas A&M University Press.

Buchanan, J. M. (1965). An Economic Theory of Clubs. *Economica* 32(125): 1-14.

Buchanan, J. M. (1977). The Samaritan's Dilemma. In: J. M. Buchanan: *Freedom in Constitutional Contract*. College Station, TX: Texas A&M University Press. 169-180.

Buchanan, J. M. (2008). Same players, different game: how better rules make better politics. *Constitutional Political Economy* 19(3): 171-179.

Burki, S. J. and G. E. Perry (1998). *Beyond the Washington Consensus: Institutions Matter*. Washington, D.C.: World Bank.

Burnham, J. (1941). The Managerial Revolution: What Is Happening in the World. New York, NY: John Day.

Burnside, C. and D. Dollar (2000). Aid, policies, and growth. *The American Economic Review* 90(4): 847-868.

Burton, M. G. and J. Higley (1987a). Elite Settlements. *American Sociological Review* 52: 295-307.

Burton, M. G. and J. Higley (1987b). Invitation to Elite Theory: The Basic Contentions Reconsidered. In: G. W. Domhoff and T. R. Dye: *Power Elites and Organizations*. Newbury Park, CA: Sage. 219-238.

Burton, M. G. and J. Higley (2001). The Study of Political Elite Transformations. *International Review of Sociology* 11(2): 181-199.

Caeyers, B. and S. Dercon (2012). Political Connections and Social Networks in Targeted Transfer Programs: Evidence from Rural Ethiopia. *Economic Development and Cultural Change* 60(4): 639-675.

Camfield, L. and R. Palmer-Jones (2013). Three 'Rs' of Econometrics: Repetition, Reproduction and Replication. *Journal of Development Studies* 49(12): 1607-1614.

Cammack, P. (1990). A Critical Assessment of the New Elite Paradigm. *American Sociological Review* 55(3): 415-420.

Campbell, D. (2006). "Uganda hit by violence as opposition claims election fraud." Published 2006-02-26 on *The Guardian*. Available from http://www.theguardian.com/world/2006/feb/26/uganda.deniscampbell

Cantens, T. (2012). Is it Possible to Reform a Customs Administration? The Role of the Customs Elite on the Reform Process in Cameroon. In: A. H. Amsden, A. DiCaprio and J. A. Robinson: *The Role of Elites in Economic Development*. Oxford: Oxford University Press. 281-306.

Carden, A. (2009). Can't Buy Me Growth: On Foreign Aid and Economic Change. *The Journal of Private Enterprise* 25(1): 105-123.

Catterson, J. and C. Lindahl (1998). The Sustainability Enigma: Aid Dependency and the Phasing out of Projects. The Case of Swedish Aid to Tanzania. Stockholm: Almqvist & Wiksell.

CEDAP (2008). Improving Democracy Assistance: Building Knowledge Through Evaluations and Research. Washington, D.C.: The National Academies Press.

Chakrabortty, A. (2010). "Paul Romer is a brilliant economist – but his idea for charter cities is bad." Published 2010-07-27 on *TheGuardian.com*. Available from http://www.theguardian.com/science/2010/jul/27/paul-romers-charter-cities-idea

Chambers, R. (2013). *Revolutions in Development Inquiry*. London, UK: Earthscan.

Chang, H.-J. (2001). Intellectual Property Rights and Economic Development – Historical Lessons and Emerging Issues. *Journal of Human Development* 2(2): 287–309.

Chang, H.-J. (2008). *Bad Samaritans*. New York, NY: Bloomsbury Press.

Chang, H.-J. (2011a). Hamlet without the Prince of Denmark: How development has disappeared from today's 'development' discourse. In: S. Khan and J. Christiansen: *Towards New Developmentalism: Market as Means rather than Master*. Abingdon: Routledge. 47-58.

Chang, H.-J. (2011b). Institutions and economic development: theory, policy and history. *Journal of Institutional Economics* 7(4): 473-498.

Charron, N. (2011). Exploring the Impact of Foreign Aid on Corruption: Has the "Anti-Corruption Movement" Been Effective? *The Developing Economies* 49(1): 66-88.

Chong, A. and M. Gradstein (2007). Inequality and Institutions. *Review of Economics and Statistics* 89(3): 454-465.

Christensen, P. W., H. Doucouliagos, M. Paldam, M. Kold and J. B. Sørensen (2010). *Master List of the AEL: The Aid Effectiveness Literature*

Christopher, W. (1993). *The United States and Africa: A New Relationship*: Remarks by Secretary of State Warren Christopher at the 23rd African-American Institute Conference, Reston, VA, 21 May 1993.

Clay, E. J., M. Geddes and L. Natali (2009). Untying Aid: Is it working? An Evaluation of the Implementation of the Paris Declaration and of the 2001 DAC Recommendation of Untying ODA to the LDCs. Copenhagen: Danish Institute for International Studies.

Clemens, M. A. and G. Demombynes (2010). *When Does Rigorous Evaluation Make a Difference? The Case of the Millennium Villages*. CGD Working Paper 225. Washington, D.C.: Center for Global Development.

Clemens, M. A., S. Radelet, R. R. Bhavnani and S. Bazzi (2012). Counting Chickens When They Hatch: Timing and the Effects of Aid on Growth. *The Economic Journal* 122(561): 590-617.

Coase, R. H. (1937). The Nature of the Firm. *Economica* 4(16): 386-405.

Coase, R. H. (1972). Industrial Organization: A Proposal for Research. In: V. R. Fuchs: *Economic Research: Retrospect and Prospect, Vol 3: Policy Issues and Research Opportunities in Industrial Organization*. Cambridge, MA: National Bureau of Economic Research. 59-73.

Coase, R. H. (1998). The New Institutional Economics. *The American Economic Review* 88(2): 72-74.

Cohen, J. and P. Dupas (2010). Free Distribution or Cost-Sharing? Evidence from a Randomized Malaria Prevention Experiment. *Quarterly Journal of Economics* 125(1): 1-45.

Cohen, J. and W. Easterly, Eds. (2009). *What Works in Development? Thinking Big and Thinking Small*. Washington, D.C.: Brookings Institution Press.

Coleman, G. (1987). Logical framework approach to the monitoring and evaluation of agricultural and rural development projects. *Project Appraisal* 2(4): 251-259.

Collier, P. (2001). Consensus Building, Knowledge, and Conditionality. In: B. Pleskovic and N. Stern: *Proceedings of the Annual World Bank Conference on Development 2000*. Washington, D.C.: World Bank. 67-83.

Collier, P. (2006). Is Aid Oil? An Analysis of Whether Africa Can Absorb More Aid. *World Development* 34: 1482-1497.

Collier, P. (2007). The Bottom Billion: Why the Poorest Countries are Failing and What Can Be Done About it. New York, NY: Oxford University Press.

Cornwall, A. (2007). Buzzwords and Fuzzwords: Deconstructing Development Discourse. *Development in Practice* 17(4-5): 471-484.

Cornwall, A. and K. Brock (2005). What do buzzwords do for development policy? A critical look at 'participation', 'empowerment' and 'poverty reduction'. *Third World Quarterly* 26(7): 1043-1060.

Coyne, C. J. and M. E. Ryan (2009). With Friends Like These, Who Needs Enemies? Aiding the World's Worst Dictators. *The Independent Review* 14(1): 26-44.

Crivelli, E. and S. Gupta (2014). *Resource Blessing, Revenue Curse? Domestic Revenue Effort in Resource-Rich Countries.* IMF Working Paper 14/5. Washington, D.C.: International Monetary Fund.

Dahl, G. (2008). Words as Moral Badges: A Flow of Buzzwords in Development Aid. In: B. Hettne: *Sustainable Development in a Globalized World: Studies in Development, Security and Culture. Vol. 1.* Basingstoke: Palgrave Macmillan. 172-199.

Dahl, R. A. (1958). A Critique of the Ruling Elite Model. *The American Political Science Review* 52(2): 463-469.

Dahrendorf, R. (1959). *Class and Class Conflict in Industrial Society.* Stanford, CA: Stanford University Press.

Dale, R. (2003). The logical framework: An easy escape, a straitjacket, or a useful planning tool? *Development in Practice* 13(1): 57-70.

Dasgupta, A. and V. A. Beard (2007). Community Driven Development, Collective Action and Elite Capture in Indonesia. *Development and Change* 38(2): 229-249.

De Jong, E. (2011). Culture, institutions and economic growth. *Journal of Institutional Economics* 7(4): 523-527.

de la Croix, D. and C. Delavallade (2013). Why corrupt governments may receive more foreign aid. *Oxford Economic Papers* 66(1): 51-66.

de Sardan, J. P. O. (1999). A moral economy of corruption in Africa? *The Journal of Modern African Studies* 37: 25-52.

De Soto, H. (2000). The Mystery of Capital: Why Capitalism Triumphs in the West and Fails Everywhere Else. New York, NY: Basic Books.

de Sousa, L. and R. Freitas (2011). Lost in transaction. Ensuring the deliverables in development aid. *Crime, Law and Social Change* 58(5): 483-494.

de Wit, J. and E. Berner (2009). Progressive Patronage? Municipalities, NGOs, CBOs and the Limits to Slum Dwellers' Empowerment. *Development and Change* 40(5): 927-947.

Deaton, A. (2010a). Instruments, Randomization, and Learning about Development. *Journal of Economic Literature* 48(2): 424-455.

Deaton, A. (2010b). Understanding the Mechanisms of Economic Development. *Journal of Economic Perspectives* 24(3): 3-16.

Della Porta, D., Ed. (1997). *Democracy and Corruption in Europe.* London, UK: Pinter.

Deutscher, E. and S. Fyson (2008). Improving the Effectiveness of Aid. *Finance & Development* 45(3): 15-19.

Devarajan, S. (2013). Africa's Statistical Tragedy. *Review of Income and Wealth* 59: S9-S15.

DFID (2014). *Annual Report and Accounts 2013-14.* London: Department for International Development.

Diamond, J. (2012). "What Makes Countries Rich or Poor?" Published 2012-06-07 on *The New York Review of Books*. Available from http://www.nybooks.com/articles/archives/2012/jun/07/what-makes-countries-rich-or-poor/

Diamond, L. (2010). Introduction. In: L. Diamond and M. F. Plattner: *Democratization in Africa: Progress and Retreat*. 2nd Ed. Baltimore, MD: John Hopkins University Press. ix-xxviii.

DiCaprio, A. (2012). Introduction: The Role of Elites in Economic Development. In: A. H. Amsden, A. DiCaprio and J. A. Robinson: *The Role of Elites in Economic Development*. Oxford, UK: Oxford University Press. 1-15.

DiMaggio, P. and W. W. Powell (1983). The Iron Cage Revisited: Institutional Isomorphism and Collective Rationality in Organizational Fields. *American Sociological Review* 48: 137-160.

Djankov, S., J. G. Montalvo and M. Reynal-Querol (2008). The curse of aid. *Journal of Economic Growth* 13(3): 169-194.

Djankov, S., J. G. Montalvo and M. Reynal-Querol (2009). Aid with multiple personalities. *Journal of Comparative Economics* 37: 217-229.

Dollar, D. and V. Levin (2006). The Increasing Selectivity of Foreign Aid, 1984–2003. *World Development* 34: 2034-2046.

Domhoff, G. W. (2012). An Invitation to a Four-Network Theory of Power: A New Viewpoint Compatible with Elite Theory. *Historical Social Research* 37(1): 23-37.

Dörner, D. (2008). Die Logik des Misslingens: Strategisches Denken in komplexen Situationen. 8th Ed. Reinbek: Rowohlt.

Doucouliagos, H. and M. A. Ulubaşoğlu (2008). Democracy and Economic Growth: A Meta-Analysis. *American Journal of Political Science* 52(1). 61-83.

Dreher, A., P. Nunnenkamp, S. Thiel and R. Thiele (2012). Aid Allocation by German NGOs: Does the Degree of Official Financing Matter? *The World Economy* 35(11): 1448-1472.

Drucker, P. (1954). *The Practice of Management*. New York, NY: Harper & Row.

Drucker, P. (1967). *The Effective Executive*. New York, NY: Harper & Row.

Duffy, P. (2010). "Lessons From Haiti: How Food Aid Can Harm." Published 2010-08-31 on *TheAtlantic.com*. Available from http://www.theatlantic.com/health/archive/2010/08/lessons-from-haiti-how-food-aid-can-harm/62252/

Duflo, E., P. Dupas and M. Kremer (2011a). Peer Effects, Pupil-Teacher Ratios, and Teacher Incentives: Evidence from a Randomized Evaluation in Kenya. *American Economic Review* 101: 1739-1774.

Duflo, E., M. Kremer and J. Robinson (2011b). Nudging Farmers to Use Fertilizer: Theory and Experimental Evidence from Kenya. *American Economic Review* 101(6): 2350-2390.

Dunning, T. (2004). Conditioning the Effects of Aid: Cold War Politics, Donor Credibility, and Democracy in Africa. *International Organization* 58(2): 409-423.

Dupas, P. (2014). Short-Run Subsidies and Long-Run Adoption of New Health Products: Evidence From a Field Experiment. *Econometrica* 82(1): 197-228.

Dutta, D. (2009). *Elite Capture and Corruption: Concepts and Definitions*. NCAER Working Paper. New Delhi: National Council of Applied Economic Research.

Easterly, W. (2002). The Cartel of Good Intentions: The Problem of Bureaucracy in Foreign Aid. *Journal of Policy Reform* 5(4): 223-250.

Easterly, W. (2003a). Can Foreign Aid Buy Growth? *Journal of Economic Perspectives* 17(3): 23-48.

Easterly, W. (2003b). The Political Economy of Growth Without Development: A Case Study of Pakistan. In: D. Rodrik: *In Search of Prosperity: Analytic Narratives on Economic Growth*. Princeton, NJ: Princeton University Press. 439-472.

Easterly, W. (2006a). Planners versus Searchers in Foreign Aid. *Asian Development Review* 23(2): 1-35.

Easterly, W. (2006b). The White Man's Burden: Why the West's Efforts to Aid the Rest Have Done So Much Ill and So Little Good. New York, NY: Penguin Press.

Easterly, W. (2008). Institutions: Top Down or Bottom Up? *American Economic Review* 98: 95-99.

Easterly, W. (2011). *Benevolent Autocrats (preliminary draft)*. Working Paper. New York, NY: New York University.

Easterly, W. (2012). "Book Review of: Why Nations Fail." Published 2012-03-24 on *The Wall Street Journal Online*. Available from http://on.wsj.com/1w3j4yk

Easterly, W. (2014a). "Aid Amnesia." Published 2014-01-23 on *Foreign Policy Online*. Available from http://foreignpolicy.com/2014/01/23/aid-amnesia/

Easterly, W. (2014b). *The Tyranny of Experts*. New York, NY: Basic Books.

Easterly, W. and R. Levine (2013). *The European Origins of Economic Development*. NYU Working Paper. New York, NY: New York University.

Easterly, W. and S. Pennings (2014). *How Much Do Leaders Explain Growth? An Exercise in Growth Accounting*. NYU Working Paper. New York, NY: New York University.

Easterly, W. and C. R. Williamson (2011). Rhetoric versus Reality: The Best and Worst of Aid Agency Practices. *World Development* 39: 1930-1949.

Ehlers, F. (2012). Das Wunder von Wonchi. *Der Spiegel* 2012(52): 98-101.

Eisenhower, D. D. (1961). *Farewell address by President Dwight D. Eisenhower, January 17, 1961 (Press Release)*. Abilene, KS: Eisenhower Library/National Archives and Records Administration.

Eisenstadt, S. N. (1973). Traditional Patrimonialism and Modern Neopatrimonialism. Beverly Hills, CA: Sage.

Elias, P. and S. Gregorios (2008). Democratisation and Growth. *Economic Journal* 118(532): 1520-1551.

Engerman, S. L. and K. L. Sokoloff (1994). Factor Endowments, Institutions, and Differential Paths of Growth Among New World Economies: A View from Economic Historians of the United States. NBER Working Paper 66. Cambridge, MA: National Bureau of Economic Research.

Eriksson Skoog, G. (2000). The Soft Budget Constraint: The Emergence, Persistence and Logic of an Institution. Dordrecht: Kluwer.

Erlei, M., M. Leschke and D. Sauerland (2007). *Neue Institutionenökonomik*. 2nd Ed. Stuttgart: Schäffer-Pöschel.

Ernst, B. and A. Kieser (2002). Versuch, das unglaubliche Wachstum des Beratungsmarktes zu erklären. In: R. Schmidt, H.-J. Gergs and M. Pohlmann: *Managementsoziologie: Themen, Desiderate, Perspektiven*. Munich/Mering: Rainer Hampp Verlag. 56-85.

Esteva, G. (2010). Development. In: W. Sachs: *The Development Dictionary: A Guide to Knowledge as Power*. 2nd Ed. London: Zed Books.

Etzo, S. and G. Collender (2010). The mobile phone 'revolution' in Africa: Rhetoric or reality? *African Affairs* 109(437): 659-668.

European Commission (2004). Aid Delivery Methods, Vol. 1: Project Cycle Management Guidelines. Brussels: European Commission.

European Commission (2009a). Annual Report 2009 on the European Community's Development and External Assistance Policies and Their Implementation in 2008. Brussels: European Commission.

European Commission (2009b). *Cape Verde: Aménagement De La Ville De Praia*. EuropeAid Ex-Post Monitoring Report (BCS) MR-123501.01. Brussels: European Commission.

European Commission (2009c). *Results Oriented Monitoring Handbook*. Brussels: European Commission.

European Commission (2010). *Lesotho: Road Transport Infrastructure Programme*. EuropeAid Ex-Post Monitoring Report (BCS) MR-000529.06. Brussels: European Commission.

European Commission (2011a). *From Hunger To Health: Strengthening Community Capacity And Resilience For Food Security in Oecusse, Timor Leste*. EuropeAid Ex-Post Monitoring Report (BCS) MR-112620.04. Brussels: European Commission.

European Commission (2011b). *Support to food processing enterprises in Tajikistan*. EuropeAid Ex-Post Monitoring Report (BCS) MR-131993.02. Brussels: European Commission.

European Commission (2012). *ROM Handbook: Results-oriented Monitoring*. Brussels: European Commission.

European Commission (2014a). Commission Staff Working Document accompanying the 2014 Annual Report on the European Union's Development and External Assistance Policies and Their Implementaton in 2013. Brussels: European Commission.

European Commission (2014b). Evaluation Matters: The Evaluation Policy for European Union Development Co-operation. Brussels: European Commission.

European Commission (2014c). "Evaluation Reports." *EuropeAid Website*. Available from http://ec.europa.eu/europeaid/how/evaluation/evaluation_reports/index_en.htm

Evans, P. (2004). Development as Institutional Change: The Pitfalls of Monocropping and the Potentials of Deliberation. *Studies in Comparative International Development* 38(4): 30-52.

EWB (2014). 2014 Failure Report: Monitoring, Evaluation, and Adapting to Failure. Toronto: Engineers Without Borders Canada.

Fafchamps, M. and B. Minten (2007). Public Service Provision, User Fees and Political Turmoil. *Journal of African Economies* 16(3): 485-518.

Farmer, P. (2004). An Anthropology of Structural Violence. *Current Anthropology* 45(3): 305-325.

Farmer, P. (2005). Pathologies of Power: Health, Human Rights, and the New War on the Poor. Berkeley, CA: University of California Press.

Faust, J. (2008). Are More Democratic Donor Countries More Development Oriented? Domestic Institutions and External Development Promotion in OECD Countries. *World Development* 36: 383-398.

Feld, L. and S. Voigt (2005). How Does Judicial Independence Affect the Investment Climate? In: G. Kochendörfer-Lucius and B. Pleskovic: *Investment Climate, Growth, and Poverty*. Washington, D.C.: World Bank.

Ferguson, J. (1994). The Anti Politics Machine: "Development" and Bureaucratic Power in Lesotho. *The Ecologist* 24: 176-181.

Feyrer, J. and B. Sacerdote (2009). Colonialism and Modern Income: Islands as Natural Experiments. *The Review of Economics and Statistics* 91(2): 245-262.

Field, G. L., J. Higley and M. G. Burton (1990). A New Elite Framework for Political Sociology. *Revue européenne des sciences sociales* 28(88): 149-182.

Fischer, P. (2006). Rent-seeking, Institutions and Reforms in Africa: Theory and Empirical Evidence for Tanzania. New York, NY: Springer Science.

Flick, U. (2006). Qualität in der Qualitativen Evaluationsforschung. In: U. Flick: *Qualitative Evaluationsforschung: Konzepte, Methoden, Umsetzung*. Reinbek: Rowohlt. 424-443.

Forbes, K. J. (2000). A Reassessment of the Relationship Between Inequality and Growth. *The American Economic Review* 90(4): 869-887.

Fox, S. (2014). The Political Economy of Slums: Theory and Evidence from Sub-Saharan Africa. *World Development* 54: 191-203.

Frankel, J. A. and D. Romer (1999). Does Trade Cause Growth? *The American Economic Review* 89(3): 379-399.

Frankel, S. H. (1952). United Nations Primer for Development. *The Quarterly Journal of Economics* 66(3): 301-326.

Frey, B. S. (1997). A Constitution for Knaves Crowds Out Civic Virtues. *The Economic Journal* 107(443): 1043-1053.

Friedman, M. (1958). Foreign Economic Aid: Means and Objectives. *The Yale Review* 47: 500-516.

Fritzen, S. A. (2007). Can the Design of Community-Driven Development Reduce the Risk of Elite Capture? Evidence from Indonesia. *World Development* 35: 1359-1375.

Fritzen, S. A. and P. W. Ong (2008). Decentralization in Developing Countries. In: E. M. Berman: *Encyclopedia of Public Administration and Public Policy. Vol. 2*. Boca Raton, FL: CRC Press. 498-503.

Früh, W. (2011). *Inhaltsanalyse*. 7th Ed. Konstanz: UTB.

Führer, H. (1994). A History of the Development Assistance Committee and the Development Co-Operation Directorate in Dates, Names And Figures. OECD Paper GD(94)67. Paris. Organisation for Economic Co-Operation and Development.

Fukuyama, F. (2012). "Acemoglu and Robinson on Why Nations Fail (Book Review)." Published 2012-03-26 on *The American Interest.* Available from http://www.the-american-interest.com/2012/03/26/acemoglu-and-robinson-on-why-nations-fail/

Fuller, B. and P. M. Romer (2012). *Success and the City: How Charter Cities Could Transform the Developing World.* Working Paper: Macdonald-Laurier Institute.

Furubotn, E. G. and R. Richter (2005). *Institutions & Economic Theory: The Contribution of the New Institutional Economics*. 2nd Ed. Ann Arbor, MI: The University of Michigan Press.

Gaarder, M. M., A. Glassman and J. E. Todd (2010). Conditional cash transfers and health: unpacking the causal chain. *Journal of Development Effectiveness* 2(1): 6-50.

Gadenne, L. and M. Singhal (2014). Decentralization in Developing Deconomies. *Annual Review of Economics* 6: 581-604.

Galtung, J. (1969). Violence, Peace, and Peace Research. *Journal of Peace Research* 6(3): 167-191.

Ganahl, J. P. (2013). Corruption, Good Governance, and the African State: A Critical Analysis of the Political-Economic Foundations of Corruption in Sub-Saharan Africa. Potsdam: Potsdam University Press.

Gardner, R. and C. J. Waller (2005). A Formal Analysis of Incentives in Strategic Interactions Involving an International Development Cooperation Agency. In: C. Gibson, K. Andersson, E. Ostrom and S. Shivakumar: *The Samaritan's Dilemma: The Political Economy of Development Aid.* Oxford, UK: Oxford University Press. 87-111.

Gasper, D. (2000). Evaluating the 'logical framework approach' towards learning-oriented development evaluation. *Public Administration and Development* 20(1): 17-28.

Gates, B. (2013). "Why Nations Fail: The Origins of Power, Prosperity, and Poverty (Book Review)." Published 26 February 2013 on *The Gates Notes.* Available from http://www.thegatesnotes.com/en/Books/Personal/Why-Nations-Fail

Gautier, D., T. A. Benjaminsen, L. Gazull and M. Antona (2013). Neoliberal Forest Reform in Mali: Adverse Effects of a World Bank "Success". *Society & Natural Resources* 26(6): 702-716.

Gaventa, J. and R. McGee (2013). The Impact of Tranparency and Accountability Initiatives. *Development Policy Review* 31(S1): S3-S28.

Gazibo, M. (2012). Introduction. In: D. C. Bach and M. Gazibo: *Neopatrimonialism in Africa and Beyond.* Abingdon: Routledge. 1-6.

Gellar, S. (1973). State-Building and Nation-Building in West Africa. In: S. N. Eisenstadt and S. Rokkan: *Building States and Nations, Volume II: Analyses by Region.* Beverly Hills, CA: Sage. 384-426.

Gerschenkron, A. (1962). *Economic Backwardness in Historical Perspective: A Book of Essays*. Cambridge, MA: Harvard University Press.

Gibson, C. C., K. Andersson, E. Ostrom and S. Shivakumar (2005). *The Samaritan's Dilemma: The Political Economy of Development Aid.* New York, NY: Oxford University Press.

Gigerenzer, G. (2007). Gut Feelings: The Intelligence of the Unconscious. New York, NY: Viking.

Gillanders, R. (2013). Corruption and Infrastructure at the Country and Regional Level. *Journal of Development Studies* 50(6): 803-819.

Giné, X. and D. Karlan (2014). Group versus individual liability: Short and long term evidence from Philippine microcredit lending groups. *Journal of Development Economics* 117: 65-83.

GiveWell (2009). "Agriculture-focused aid (international)." Published 2009 on *GiveWell.org.* Available from http://www.givewell.org/international/economic-empowerment/agriculture

GiveWell (2015). "GiveWell: a medium-depth overview." *GiveWell.org.* Available from http://www.givewell.org/about/givewell-overview

Glaeser, E. L., R. La Porta, F. Lopez-de-Silanes and A. Shleifer (2004). Do Institutions Cause Growth. *Journal of Economic Growth* 9(3): 281-303.

Glewwe, P., M. Kremer and S. Moulin (2009). Many Children Left Behind? Textbooks and Test Scores in Kenya. *American Economic Journal: Applied Economics* 1(1): 112-135.

Gneezy, U. and A. Rustichini (2000). A Fine Is a Price. *Journal of Legal Studies* 29(1): 1-17.

Gordon, H. S. (1954). The Economic Theory of a Common-Property Resource: The Fishery. *Journal of Political Economy* 62(2): 124-142.

Goulet, D. (1971). The Cruel Choice: A New Concept in the Theory of Developnent. New York, NY: Atheneum.

Green, D. (2012a). "Comment on: Lant Pritchett v the Randomistas on the nature of evidence – is a wonkwar brewing?" Published 2012-11-21 on *Oxfamblogs.org*. Available from http://oxfamblogs.org/fp2p/lant-pritchett-v-the-randomistas-on-the-nature-of-evidence-is-a-wonkwar-brewing/#comments

Green, D. (2012b). "Lant Pritchett v the Randomistas on the nature of evidence – is a wonkwar brewing?" Published 2012-11-21 on *Oxfamblogs.org*. Available from http://oxfamblogs.org/fp2p/lant-pritchett-v-the-randomistas-on-the-nature-of-evidence-is-a-wonkwar-brewing/

Green, D. P. and I. Shapiro (1994). Pathologies of Rational Choice Theory: A Critique of Applications in Political Science. New Haven, CT: Yale University Press.

Green, G. M. and R. W. Sussman (1990). Deforestation History of the Eastern Rain Forests of Madagascar from Satellite Images. *Science* 248(4952): 212-215.

Grittner, A. M. (2013). Results-based Financing: Evidence from performance-based financing in the health sector. Discussion Paper 6/2013. Bonn: German Development Institute.

Groves, T. and J. O. Ledyard (1987). Incentive Compatibility Since 1972. In: T. Groves, R. Radner and S. Reiter: *Information, Incentives, and Economic Mechanisms*. Oxford, UK: Basil Blackwell. 48-111.

GTZ (2010). *develoPPP.report: Fortschritt durch Vielfalt* 30/2010. Eschborn: Gesellschaft für technische Zusammenarbeit.

Gulbrandsen, T. (2012). Elite Integration – An Empirical Study. *Historical Social Research* 37(1): 148-166.

Gupta, S., B. Clemens, A. Pivovarsky and E. R. Tiongson (2004). Foreign Aid and Revenue Response: Does the Composition of Aid Matter? In: S. Gupta, B. Clements and G. Inchauste: *Helping Countries Develop: The Role of Fiscal Policy*. Washington, D.C.: International Monetary Fund. XX.

Gwartney, J. D., R. G. Holcombe and R. A. Lawson (2006). Institutions and the Impact of Investment on Growth. *Kyklos* 59(2): 255-273.

Haber, S., D. C. North and B. R. Weingast (2003). "If Economists Are So Smart, Why Is Africa So Poor?" Published 2003-07-30 on *The Wall Street Journal Online*. Available from http://online.wsj.com/news/articles/SB105952321523586100

Hall, R. E. and C. I. Jones (1999). Why Do Some Countries Produce So Much More Output Per Worker Than Others? *The Quarterly Journal of Economics* 114(1): 83-116.

Hanlon, J., D. Hulme and A. Barrientos (2010). *Just Give Money to the Poor: The Development Revolution From the Global South*. Sterling, VA: Kumarian Press.

Hanlon, J. and M. Mosse (2010). *Mozambique's Elite – Finding its Way in a Globalized World and Returning to Old Development Models*. UNU-WIDER Working Paper 2010/105. Helsinki: United Nations University.

Hardin, G. (1968). The Tragedy of the Commons. *Science* 162: 1243-1248.

Harford, T. (2012). The Undercover Economist: Exposing Why the Rich Are Rich, the Poor Are Poor - And Why You Can Never Buy a Decent Used Car! 2nd Ed. New York, NY: Oxford University Press.

Harrison, E. (2007). Corruption. *Development in Practice* 17: 672-678.

Hart, O. D. and B. R. Holmström (1987). The Theory of Contracts. In: T. F. Bewley: *Advances in Economic Theory*. Cambridge, MA: Cambridge University Press. 71-155.

Hartig, P. (2008). Financing Urban Infrastructure: Innovative Financial Instruments for Cities. Working Paper. Frankfurt a. M.: KFW Entwicklungsbank.

Hausmann, R., L. Pritchett and D. Rodrik (2005). Growth Accelerations. *Journal of Economic Growth* 10: 303-329.

Heckelman, J. C. and S. Knack (2008). Foreign Aid and Market-Liberalizing Reform. *Economica* 75(299): 524-548.

Hemmer, H.-R. (2010). *Ein Plädoyer für die Projekthilfe: Totgesagte leben länger*. KFW Development Research Working Paper. Frankfurt a. M.: KFW Entwicklungsbank.

Henisz, W. J. and B. A. Zelner (2001). The Institutional Environment for Telecommunications Investment. *Journal of Economics & Management Strategy* 10(1): 123-147.

Hettne, B. (1995). Development Theory and the Three Worlds: Towards an International Political Economy of Development. 2nd Ed. Harlow: Longman.

Hettne, B. (2008a). Development Discourses in History. In: B. Hettne: *Sustainable Development in a Globalized World: Studies in Development, Security and Culture. Vol. 1*. Basingstoke: Palgrave Macmillan. 172-199.

Hettne, B., Ed. (2008b). Sustainable Development in a Globalized World: Studies in Development, Security and Culture. Vol. 1. Basingstoke: Palgrave Macmillan.

Higley, J. and M. G. Burton (1989). The Elite Variable in Democratic Transitions And Breakdowns. *American Sociological Review* 54(1): 17-32.

Higley, J. and M. G. Burton (1997). Types of Political Elites in Postcommunist Eastern Europe. *International Politics* 34: 153-168.

Higley, J. and M. G. Burton (2006). *Elite Foundations of Liberal Democracy*. Lanham, MD: Rowman & Littlefield.

Higley, J., M. G. Burton and G. L. Field (1990). In Defense of Elite Theory: A Reply to Cammack. *American Sociological Review* 55: 421-426.

Higley, J., T.-y. Huang and T.-m. Lin (1998). Elite Settlements in Taiwan. *Journal of Democracy* 9(2): 148-163.

Higley, J. and G. Lengyel, Eds. (2000). *Elites After State Socialism*. Oxford, UK: Rowman & Littlefield.

Higley, J. and G. Moore (2001). Political Elite Studies at the Year 2000: Introduction. *International Review of Sociology* 11(2): 175-180.

Higley, J. and J. Pakulski (2012). Elite Theory versus Marxism: The Twentieth Century's Verdict [2000]. *Historical Social Research* 37(1): 320-332.

Hirschman, A. O. (1971). *A Bias for Hope*. New Haven, CT: Yale University Press.

Hirschman, D. (2003). Aid Dependence, Sustainability and Technical Assistance. *Public Management Review* 5(2): 225-244.

Hirschman, D. (2008). "Dear Economists, Please Stop Talking About Human Nature." Published 2008-06-12 on *asociologist.com.* Available from http://asociologist.com/2008/06/12/dear-economists-please-stop-talking-about-human-nature/

Hobbs, N. (2005). *Corruption in World Bank Financed Projects: Why Bribery is a Tolerated Anathema.* DESTIN Working Paper 05-65. London: London School of Economics.

Hodgson, G. M. (2006). What Are Institutions? *Journal of Economic Issues* 40(1): 1-25.

Hofstede, G., G. J. Hofstede and M. Minkov (2010). Cultures and Organizations, Software of the Mind: Intercultural Cooperation and its Importance for Survival. New York, NY: McGraw-Hill.

Hogarth, R. M. and M. W. Reder, Eds. (1987). *Rational Choice: The Contrast Between Economics and Psychology*. Chicago, IL: University of Chicago Press.

Hollyer, J. R. and L. Wantchekon (2014). Corruption and Ideology in Autocracies. *Journal of Law, Economics, & Organization*(Online First, 2014-10-22).

Holmström, B. (1982). Moral hazard in teams. *The Bell Journal of Economics* 13: 324-340.

Holmström, B. and P. Milgrom (1991). Multitask Principal-Agent Analyses: Incentive Contracts, Asset Ownership, and Job Design. *Journal of Law, Economics, & Organization* 7(Special Issue): 24-52.

Holmström, B. and P. Milgrom (1994). The Firm as an Incentive System. *The American Economic Review* 84(4): 972-991.

Hossain, N. and M. Moore (2005). So near and yet so far: elites and imagined poverty in Bangladesh. In: E. P. Reis and M. Moore: *Elite perceptions of poverty and inequality*. Cape Town: David Philip. 91-126.

Howarth, R. B. (2002). Sustainable Development: Principles. In: A. S. Goudie: *Encyclopedia of Global Change: Environmental Change and Human Society*. Oxford, UK: Oxford University Press. 405-408.

Howes, S., S. Otor and C. Rogers (2011). *Does the World Bank have a micro-macro paradox or do the data deceive?* Development Policy Centre Discussion Paper 5. Canberra: Australian National University.

Hume, D. (1741/1903). *Essays: Moral, Political and Literary*. London, UK: Grant Richards.

Humphreys, P. W. (1989). Scientific Explanation: The Causes, Some of the Causes, and Nothing but the Causes. In: P. Kitcher and W. C. Salmon: *Scientific Explanation*. Minneapolis, MN: University of Minnesota Press. 283-306.

Huntington, S. P. (1996). *The Clash of Civilizations and the Remaking of World Order*. New York, NY: Simon & Schuster.

Hurwicz, L. (1960). Optimality and Informational Efficiency in Resource Allocation Processes. In: K. J. Arrow, S. Karlin and P. Suppes: *Mathematical Methods in the Social Sciences, 1959: Proceedings of the First Stanford Symposium*. Stanford, CA: Stanford University Press. 27-46.

Hurwicz, L. (1972). On Informationally Decentralized Systems. In: C. B. McGuire and R. Radner: *Decision and Organization*. Amsterdam: North Holland. 297-336.

Hurwicz, L. (1973). The Design of Mechanisms for Resource Allocation. *The American Economic Review* 63: 1-30.

Hynes, W. and S. Scott (2013). *The Evolution of Official Development Assistance: Achievements, Criticisms and a Way Forward.* OECD Development Co-operation Working Paper 12. Paris: Organisation for Economic Co-Operation and Development.

Jarosz, L. (1993). Defining and Explaining Tropical Deforestation: Shifting Cultivation and Population Growth in Colonial Madagascar (1896-1940). *Economic Geography* 69: 366-379.

Jensen, M. C. and W. H. Meckling (1994). The Nature of Man. *Journal of Applied Corporate Finance* 7: 4-19.

Jensen, R. and N. Miller (2008). Giffen Behavior and Subsistence Consumption. *American Economic Review* 98(4): 1553-1577.

Jerven, M. (2013). Poor Numbers: How We are Misled by African Development Statistics and What to Do about It. Ithaca, NY: Cornell University Press.

Jones, B. F. and B. Olken (2005). Do Leaders Matter? National Leadership and Growth Since World War II. *The Quarterly Journal of Economics* 120(3): 835-864.

Jones, C. I. (1995). Time Series Tests of Endogenous Growth Models. *The Quarterly Journal of Economics* 110(2): 495-525.

Justesen, M. K. and C. Bjørnskov (2014). Exploiting the Poor: Bureaucratic Corruption and Poverty in Africa. *World Development* 58: 106-115.

Kahneman, D. (2011). *Thinking, Fast and Slow*. New York, NY: Farrar, Strauss and Giroux.

Kalati, N. and J. Manor (2005). Elite perceptions of poverty and poor people in South Africa. In: E. P. Reis and M. Moore: *Elite perceptions of poverty and inequality*. Cape Town: David Philip. 156-181.

Kalebe Nyamongo, C. (2012). Mutual Interdependence between Elites and the Poor. In: A. H. Amsden, A. DiCaprio and J. A. Robinson: *The Role of Elites in Economic Development*. Oxford, UK: Oxford University Press. 200-230.

Kanbur, R. (2006). The economics of international aid. In: S.-C. Kolm and J. M. Ythier: *Handbook of the Economics of Giving, Altruism and Reciprocity. Vol. 2.* Amsterdam: North-Holland. 1559-1588.

Kanbur, R., T. Sandler and K. M. Morrison (1999). *The Future of Development Assistance: Common Pools and International Public Goods*. Washington, D.C.: John Hopkins University Press.

Karugu, W. (2011). *Ecotact: Affordable sanitation services in pleasant surroundings*. GIM Case Study. New York: United Nations Development Programme.

Kaufmann, D., A. Kraay and M. Mastruzzi (2010). *The Worldwide Governance Indicators: Methodology and Analytical Issues*. Working Paper 5430. Washington, DC: World Bank.

Kennedy, P. M. (1987). *The Rise and Fall of the Great Powers*. New York, NY: Random House.

KFW (2009). *Kenia: Slumrehablitierung Matahare 4A*. Ex-Post-Evaluierungsbericht BMZ-Nr. 1996 656 88. Frankfurt a. M.: KFW Entwicklungsbank.

Khandker, S. R. and G. B. Koolwal (2010). How Infrastructure and Financial Institutions Affect Rural Income and Poverty: Evidence from Bangladesh. *Journal of Development Studies* 46: 1109-1137.

Kieser, A. (1997). Rhetoric and Myth in Management Fashion. *Organization* 4(1): 49-74.

Kilby, C. (2000). Sovereignty and NGOs. In: K. Stiles: *Global Institutions and Local Empowerment*. Basingstoke: Macmillan. 48-64.

Kilby, C. (2013). The political economy of project preparation: An empirical analysis of World Bank projects. *Journal of Development Economics* 105: 211-225.

Klasen, S. (2009). *Ein Plädoyer für die Budgethilfe*. KFW Development Research Working Paper. Frankfurt a. M.: KFW Entwicklungsbank.

Klein, J. (2002). Deforestation in the Madagascar Highlands – Established 'truth' and scientific uncertainty. *GeoJournal* 56: 191-199.

Knack, S. (2001). Aid Dependence and the Quality of Governance: Cross-Country Empirical Tests. *Southern Economic Journal* 68: 310-329.

Knack, S. and A. Rahman (2007). Donor Fragmentation and Bureaucratic Quality in Aid Recipients. *Journal of Development Economics* 83(1): 176-197.

Knowles, S. and P. D. Owen (2010). Which Institutions are Good for Your Health? The Deep Determinants of Comparative Cross-country Health Status. *Journal of Development Studies* 46: 701-723.

Knutsen, C. H. (2010). Investigating the Lee thesis: how bad is democracy for Asian economies? *European Political Science Review* 2(3): 451-473.

Kornai, J. (1979). Resource-Constrained versus Demand-Constrained Systems. *Econometrica* 47(4): 801-819.

Krause, P. (2013). Of institutions and butterflies: is isomorphism in developing countries necessarily a bad thing? ODI Working Paper April 2013. London, UK: Overseas Development Institute.

Kremer, M. and A. Holla (2009). Pricing and Access: Lessons from Randomized Evaluations in Education and Health. In: J. Cohen and W. Easterly: *What Works In Development?* Washington, D.C.: Brookings Institution Press. 91-119.

Krippendorf, K. (2013). *Content Analysis: An Introduction to Its Methodology*. 3rd Ed. Thousand Oaks, CA: Sage.

Kristof, N. D. (2011). "Getting Smart on Aid." Published 2011-05-18 on *The New York Times Online*. Available from http://www.nytimes.com/2011/05/19/opinion/19kristof.html

Krueger, A. O. (1974). The Political Economy of the Rent-Seeking Society. *The American Economic Review* 64: 291-303.

Kühl, S. (2004). Moden in der Entwicklungszusammenarbeit: Capacity Building und Capacity Development als neue Leitbilder von Entwicklungshilfeorganisationen. *Soziale Welt* 55: 231-262.

Kumar, A. (2015). Samaritan's Dilemma, Time-Inconsistency and Foreign Aid: A Review of Theoretical Models. In: M. Arvin: *Handbook on the Economics of Foreign Aid*. Cheltenham, UK: Edward Elgar. Forthcoming.

Kumar, S. and S. Corbridge (2002). Programmed to Fail? Development Projects and the Politics of Participation. *Journal of Development Studies* 39: 73-103.

Kushkush, I. i. (2015). "Ethiopia, Long Mired in Poverty, Rides an Economic Boom." Published 2015-03-03 on *The New York Times Online*. Available from http://nyti.ms/1CsJ4Yd

Kydd, J. G. (2009). A New Institutional Economic Analysis of the State and Agriculture in Sub-Saharan Africa. In: J. F. Kirsten, A. R. Dorward, C. Poulton and N. Vink: *Institutional Economics Perspectives on African Agricultural Development*. Washington, D.C.: International Food Policy Research Institute. 429-460.

La Porta, R., F. Lopez-de-Silanes, A. Shleifer and R. Vishny (1999). The Quality of Government. *Journal of Law, Economics, & Organization* 15(1): 222-279.

Labonte, M. T. (2011). From patronage to peacebuilding? Elite capture and governance from below in Sierra Leone. *African Affairs* 111(442): 90-115.

Laffont, J.-J. (2005). *Regulation and Development*. Cambridge, UK: Cambridge University Press.

Laffont, J.-J. and D. Martimort (2001). *The Theory of Incentives: The Principal-Agent Model*. Princeton, NJ: Princeton University Press.

Laffont, J.-J. and E. Maskin (1982). The theory of incentives: an overview. In: W. Hildenbrand: *Advances in Economic Theory*. Cambridge, MA: Cambridge University Press. 31-94.

Laffont, J.-J., E. S. Maskin and J.-C. Rochet (1987). Optimal nonlinear pricing with two-dimensional characteristics. In: T. Groves, R. Radner and S. Reiter: *Information, Incentives, and Economic Mechanisms*. Oxford, UK: Basil Blackwell. 256-266.

Laffont, J.-J. and J. Tirole (1991). The Politics of Government Decision-Making: A Theory of Regulatory Capture. *The Quarterly Journal of Economics*: 1089-1127.

Lamhauge, N., E. Lanzi and S. Agrawala (2012). *Monitoring and Evaluation for Adaptation: Lessons from Development Co-operation Agencies*. OECD Environment Working Paper 38. Paris: OECD Publishing.

Lane, J.-E. (2005). Public Administration and Public Management: The principal-agent perspective. London: Routledge.

Lang, G. and M. Ohana (2012). Are Management Fashions Dangerous for Organizations? *International Journal of Business and Management* 7(20): 81-89.

Langlois, R. N. (1990). Bounded Rationality and Behavioralism: A Clarification and Critique. *Journal of Institutional and Theoretical Economics* 146: 691-695.

Lasswell, H. D. (1965). Introduction: The Study of Political Elites. In: H. D. Lasswell and D. Lerner: *World Revolutionary Elites: Studies in Coercive Idelogical Movements*. Cambridge, MA: MIT Press. 3-28.

Lasswell, H. D. (1927/1971). *Propaganda Technique in World War I*. Reprint Ed. Cambridge, MA: MIT Press.

Leach, D. K. (2005). The Iron Law of *What* Again? Conceptualizing Oligarchy Across Organizational Forms. *Sociological Theory* 23(3): 312-337.

Ledyard, J. O. (2008). Incentive Compatibility. In: S. N. Durlauf and L. E. Blume: *The New Palgrave Dictionary of Economics*. 2nd Ed. New York, NY: Palgrave Macmillan. 158-164.

Leiderer, S. (2012). *Fungibility and the Choice of Aid Modalities*. UNU-WIDER Working Paper 2012/68. Helsinki: United Nations University.

Leonard, D. K., J. N. Brass, M. Nelson, S. Ear, D. Fahey, T. Fairfield, M. J. Gning, M. Halderman, B. McSherry, D. C. Moehler, W. Prichard, R. Turner, T. Vu and J. Dijkman (2010). Does Patronage Still Drive Politics for the Rural Poor in the Developing World? A Comparative Perspective from the Livestock Sector. *Development and Change* 41(3): 475-494.

Lepenies, P. (2009). *Wirtschaftsnobelpreis 2009: Eine Absage an den ökonomischen Mainstream*. KFW-Development Research Paper. Frankfurt a. M.: KFW Entwicklungsbank.

Levine, R. (2009). Comment on: "The Other Invisible Hand: High Bandwidth Development Policy". In: J. Cohen and W. Easterly: *What Works in Development? Thinking Big and Thinking Small*. Washington, DC: Brookings Institution Press. 203-206.

Lewis, W. A. (1953). United Nations Primer for Development: Comment. *The Quarterly Journal of Economics* 67(2): 267-275.

Lewis, W. A. (1955). *The Theory of Economic Growth*. London, UK: George Allen & Unwin.

Lipset, S. M., M. A. Trow and J. S. Coleman (1956). Union Democracy: The Internal Politics of the International Typographical Union. Glencoe, IL: Free Press.

List, F. (1841). Das nationale System der politischen Oekonomie. Erster Band: Der internationale Handel, die Handelspolitik und der deutsche Zollverein. Stuttgart/Tübingen: J. G. Cotta'scher Verlag.

Machiavelli, N. (1532/1988). *The Prince [edited by Quentin Skinner and Russel Price]*. Cambridge, UK: Cambridge University Press.

Mallaby, S. (2010). The Politically Incorrect Guide to Ending Poverty. *The Atlantic* 306(1): 92-104.

Manor, J. (1999). The Political Economy of Democratic Decentralization. Washington, D.C.: World Bank.

Marć, Ł. (2015). *The impact of aid on total government expenditures: New evidence on fungibility*. WIDER Working Paper 2015/010. Helsinki: United Nations University.

March, J. G. and H. A. Simon (1958). *Organizations*. New York, NY: John Wiley & Sons.

Markussen, T. (2011). Inequality and Political Clientelism: Evidence from South India. *Journal of Development Studies* 47: 1721-1738.

Marriage, Z. (2006). The Comfort of Denial: External Assistance in Southern Sudan. *Development and Change* 37(3): 479-500.

Martens, B. (2002a). Introduction. In: B. Martens, U. Mummert, P. Murrell and P. Seabright: *The Institutional Economics Of Foreign Aid*. Cambridge, UK: Cambridge University Press. 1-33.

Martens, B. (2002b). The role of evaluation in foreign aid programmes. In: B. Martens, U. Mummert, P. Murrell and P. Seabright: *The Institutional Economics Of Foreign Aid*. Cambridge, UK: Cambridge University Press. 154-177.

Martens, B. (2005). Why Do Aid Agencies Exist? *Development Policy Review* 23: 643-663.

Martens, B., U. Mummert, P. Murrell and P. Seabright, Eds. (2002). *The Institutional Economics Of Foreign Aid*. Cambridge, UK: Cambridge University Press.

Marx, K. (1867). Das Kapital. Erster Band. Buch I: Kritik der Politischen Ökonomie. Hamburg: Otto Meissner.

Masaki, T. and N. van de Walle (2014). *The impact of democracy on economic growth in sub-Saharan Africa, 1982-2012*. UNU-WIDER Working Paper 2014/057. Helsinki: United Nations University.

Maslow, A. H. (1943). A Theory of Human Motivation. *Psychological Review* 50: 370-396.

Masud, N. and B. Yontcheva (2005). *Does Foreign Aid Reduce Poverty? Empirical Evidence from Nongovernmental and Bilateral Aid*. IMF Working Paper 05/100. Washington, D.C.: International Monetary Fund.

Mattsson, J. (2014). "Much has been done, but far from enough." Published 2014-03-31 on *Devex.com*. Available from https://www.devex.com/news/much-has-been-done-but-far-from-enough-83186

Mauro, P. (1995). Corruption and Growth. *The Quarterly Journal of Economics* 110(3): 681-712.

Mayring, P. (1983). Qualitative Inhaltsanalyse: Grundlagen und Techniken. Weinheim: Beltz.

Mayring, P. (2010). Qualitative Inhaltsanalyse: Grundlagen und Techniken. 11th Ed. Weinheim: Beltz.

McConnell, T. (2011). "'He started it' Museveni says, as he blames opposition leader for arrest." Published 2011-05-02 on *The Times*. Available from http://www.thetimes.co.uk/tto/news/world/africa/article3004557.ece

McConnell, W. J. and C. A. Kull (2014). Deforestation in Madagascar: debates over the island's forest cover and challenges measuring forest change. In: I. R. Scales: *Conservation and Environmental Management in Madagascar*. Abingdon: Routledge. 67-104.

McKay, J. (2012). Reassessing Development Theory. In: D. Kingsbury, J. McKay, M. McGillivray and M. Clarke: *International Development: Issues and Challenges*. Basingstoke: Palgrave Macmillan. 53-78.

McKenzie, D. (2011). "A rant on the external validity double double-standard." Published 2011-05-02 on *World Bank Blog*. Available from http://blogs.worldbank.org/impactevaluations/a-rant-on-the-external-validity-double-double-standard

McSweeney, B. (2002). Hofstede's model of national cultural differences and their consequences: A triumph of faith – a failure of analysis. *Human Relations* 55: 89-118.

Meckling, W. H. (1976). Values and the Choice of the Model of the Individual in the Social Sciences. *Schweizerische Zeitschrift für Volkswirtschaft und Statistik* 112: 545-560.

Médard, J.-F. (1979). L'État sous-développé au Cameroun. *Année africaine 1977*. Paris: Éditions A. Pedone. 35-84.

Médard, J.-F. (1991). L'État néo-patrimonial en Afrique noire. In: J.-F. Médard: *États d'Afrique noire: formation, mécanismes et crises*. Paris: Éditions Karthala. 323-353.

Meier, G. M. (2001). The Old Generation of Development Economists and the New. In: G. M. Meier and J. E. Stiglitz: *Frontiers of Development Economics: The Future in Perspective*. Oxford, UK: Oxford University Press. 13-50.

Meisel, J. H. (1958). *The Myth of the Ruling Class, Gaetano Mosca and the Elite*. Ann Arbor, MI: The University of Michigan Press.

Michels, R. (1911). Zur Soziologie des Parteiwesens in der modernen Demokratie: Untersuchungen über die oligarchischen Tendenzen des Gruppenlebens. Leipzig: Werner Klinkhardt.

Michels, R. (1912). La sociologia del partito politico nella democrazia moderna: studi sulle tendenze oligarchiche degli aggregati politici. Torino: Unione Tipografico-Editrice Torinese.

Michels, R. (1915). Political Parties: A Sociological Study of the Oligarchical Tendencies of Modern Democracy. New York, NY: Hearst's International Library.

Michels, R. (1925). Zur Soziologie des Parteiwesens in der modernen Demokratie: Untersuchungen über die oligarchischen Tendenzen des Gruppenlebens. 2nd Ed. Leipzig: Alfred Kröner.

Miguel, E. and M. Kremer (2004). Worms: Identifying Impacts on Education and Health in the Presence of Treatment Externalities. *Econometrica* 72: 159-217.

Mikkelsen, B. (2005). Methods for Development Work and Research: A Guide for Practitioners. 2nd Ed. London: Sage.

Mill, J. S. (1861/1977). Considerations on Representative Government. In: J. M. Robson: *Collected Works of John Stuart Mill. Vol. XIX.* Toronto: University of Toronto Press.

Mills, C. W. (1956). *The Power Elite*. New York, NY: Oxford University Press.

Miravete, E. J. (2008). Price Discrimination. In: S. N. Durlauf and L. E. Blume: *The New Palgrave Dictionary of Economics. Vol. 6.* 2nd Ed. New York, NY: Palgrave Macmillan. 626-629.

Mitroff, I. (1998). Smart Thinking for Crazy Times: The Art of Solving the Right Problems. San Francisco, CA: Berrett-Koehler.

Moore, M. (2008). Between coercion and contract. In: D. Bräutigam, O. H. Fjeldstad and M. Moore: *Taxation and State-building in Developing Countries*. New York, NY: Cambridge University Press. 34-63.

Moore, M. and G. Teskey (2006). *The CAR Framework: Capability, Accountability, Responsiveness*. DFID Discussion Note for Governance and Conflict Advisers. London: DFID.

Mosca, G. (1923). *Elementi di scienza politica*. 2nd Ed. Torino: Fratelli Bocca.

Mosca, G. (1939). *The Ruling Class*. New York, NY: McGraw-Hill.

Mosca, G. (1953). *Elementi di scienza politica. Vol. II.* 5th Ed. Bari: Gius. Laterza & Figli.

Mosley, P. (1986). Aid-effectiveness: The Micro-Macro Paradox. *Institute of Development Studies Bulletin* 17: 22-27.

Moss, T., G. Pettersson and N. van de Walle (2006). *An Aid-Institutions Paradox? A Review Essay on Aid Dependency and State Building in Sub-Saharan Africa*. CGD Working Paper 74. Washington, D.C.: Center for Global Development.

Moyo, D. (2009). Dead Aid: Why Aid Is Not Working and How There Is a Better Way for Africa. New York, NY: Farrar, Strauss and Giroux.

Mugerwa, Y. (2014). "Witch-hunt fear as Uganda lists 'top gays'." Published 2014-02-26 on *The Times*. Available from http://www.thetimes.co.uk/tto/news/world/africa/article4016241.ece

Munk, N. (2013). The Idealist: Jeffrey Sachs and the Quest to End Poverty. New York, NY: Doubleday.

Murray, M. P. (2006). Avoiding Invalid Instruments and Coping with Weak Instruments. *Journal of Economic Perspectives* 20(4): 111-132.

Murrell, P. (2002). The interactions of donors, contractors, and recipients in implementing aid for institutional reform. In: B. Martens, U. Mummert, P. Murrell and P. Seabright: *The Institutional Economics Of Foreign Aid*. Cambridge, UK: Cambridge University Press. 69-111.

Murshed, S. M. and L. A. Serino (2011). The pattern of specialization and economic growth: The resource curse hypothesis revisited. *Structural Change and Economic Dynamics* 22(2): 151-161.

Musgrave, A. (1981). "Unreal Assumptions" In Economic Theory: The F-Twist Untwisted. *Kyklos* 34(3): 377-387.

OLD [Oxford Latin Dictionary], Oxford, UK: Clarendon Press, 1982.

Nederveen Pieterse, J. (2010). *Development Theory*. 2nd Ed. London: Sage.

Nelson, F. and A. Agrawal (2008). Patronage or Participation? Community-based Natural Resource Management Reform in Sub-Saharan Africa. *Development and Change* 39(4): 557-585.

Neuendorf, K. A. (2002). *The Content Analysis Guidebook*. Thousand Oaks, CA: Sage.

Neuendorf, K. A. (2010). Content Analysis—A Methodological Primer for Gender Research. *Sex Roles* 64(3-4): 276-289.

North, D. C. (1981). *Structure and Change in Economic History*. New York: W. W. Norton & Co.

North, D. C. (1990). *Institutions, Institutional Change and Economic Performance*. Cambridge, UK: Cambridge University Press.

North, D. C., J. J. Wallis and B. R. Weingast (2009). *Violence and Social Orders: A Conceptual Framework for Interpreting Recorded Human History*. Cambridge, MA: Cambridge University Press.

North, D. C. and B. R. Weingast (1989). Constitutions and Commitment: The Evolution of Institutional Governing Public Choice in Seventeenth-Century England. *Journal of Economic History* 49(4): 803-832.

Nunn, N. (2009). The Importance of History for Economic Development. *Annual Review of Economics* 1(1): 65-92.

Nunn, N. and L. Wantchekon (2011). The Slave Trade and the Origins of Mistrust in Africa. *American Economic Review* 101(7): 3221-3252.

Nunnenkamp, P. and H. Öhler (2012). Funding, Competition and the Efficiency of NGOs: An Empirical Analysis of Non-charitable Expenditure of US NGOs Engaged in Foreign Aid. *Kyklos* 65(1): 81-110.

Nurske, R. (1953). Problems of Capital Formation in Underdeveloped Countries. Oxford, UK: Basil Blackwell.

OECD (1991). *Principles for Evaluation of Development Assistance*. Paris: Organisation for Economic Co-Operation and Development.

OECD (1993). *A History of the DAC Expert Group on Aid Evaluation* OCDE/GD(93)4. Paris: Organisation for Economic Co-Operation and Development.

OECD (2000). *Glossary of Evaluation and Results Based Management (RBM) Terms*. Paris: Organisation for Economic Co-Operation and Development.

OECD (2011). *Meeting the Challenge of Financing Water and Sanitation: Tools and Approaches*. Paris: Organisation for Economic Co-Operation and Development.

OECD (2012a). *Promoting Growth in All Regions*. Paris: Organisation for Economic Co-Operation and Development.

OECD (2012b). "Purpose Codes: sector classification." Available from http://www.oecd.org/dac/aidstatistics/purposecodessectorclassification.htm

OECD. (2014a). "Aid (ODA) disbursements to countries and regions [DAC2a], updated 15 December 2014." from http://stats.oecd.org.

OECD (2014b). *Development Co-operation Report 2014*. Paris: OECD Publishing.

OECD (2014c). *Official Development Assistance (ODA) Data for 2013*. Paris: Organisation for Economic Co-Operation and Development.

Oleinik, A. (2010). Mixing quantitative and qualitative content analysis: triangulation at work. *Quality & Quantity* 45(4): 859-873.

Olson, M. (1965). *The Logic of Collective Action*. Cambridge, MA: Harvard University Press.

Ostrom, E. (1990). Governing the Commons: The Evolution of Institutions for Collective Action. Cambridge, UK: Cambridge University Press.

Ostrom, E. (2007a). Challenges and growth: the development of the interdisciplinary field of institutional analysis. *Journal of Institutional Economics* 3(3): 239-264.

Ostrom, E. (2007b). Institutional Rational Choice: An Assessment of the Institutional Analysis and Development Framework. In: P. A. Sabatier: *Theories of the Policy Process*. 2nd Ed. Boulder, CO: Westview Press. 21-64.

Ostrom, E., C. Gibson, S. Shivakumar and K. Andersson (2001). Aid, Incentives, and Sustainability: An Institutional Analysis of Development Cooperation, Stockholm.

Ostrom, V. and E. Ostrom (1977). A Theory for Institutional Analysis of Common Pool Problems. In: G. Hardin and J. Baden: *Managing the Commons*. San Francisco: W.H. Freeman & Co. 157-172.

Panda, S. (2015). Political Connections and Elite Capture in a Poverty Alleviation Programme in India. *The Journal of Development Studies* 51(1): 50-65.

Pande, R. (2008). Understanding Political Corruption in Low Income Countries. In: T. P. Schultz and J. A. Strauss: *Handbook of Development Economics. Vol. 4*. Amsterdam: North Holland. 3155-3184.

Pande, R. and C. Udry (2006). Institutions and Development: A View From Below. In: R. Blundell, W. K. Newey and T. Persson: *Advances in Economics and Econometrics. Vol. 2*. New York, NY: Cambridge University Press. 349-412.

Pareto, V. (1916). *Trattato di sociologia generale*. Firenze: G. Barbéra.

Pareto, V. (1935). *The Mind and Society. Vol. 4*. New York, NY: Hartcourt Brace Jovanovich.

Parry, G. (1969). *Political Elites*. London, UK: George Allen and Unwin.

Pauly, C. (2014). Brücke ins Nichts. *Der Spiegel* (40/2014): 76-78.

Payne, J. W., J. R. Bettman and E. J. Johnson (1993). *The Adaptive Decision Maker*. Cambridge, UK: Cambridge University Press.

Pedersen, K. R. (2001). The Samaritan's Dilemma and the Effectiveness of Development Aid. *International Tax and Public Finance* 8: 693-703.

Peeler, J. (1992). Elite Settlements and Democratic Consolidation: Colombia, Costa Rica, Venezuela. In: J. Higley and R. Gunther: *Elites and Democratic Consolidation in Latin America and Southern Europe*. Cambridge, UK: Cambridge University Press. 81-112.

Persson, T. and G. Tabellini (2009). Democratic Capital: The Nexus of Political and Economic Change. *American Economic Journal: Macroeconomics* 1(2): 88-126.

Pigou, A. C. (1929). *The Economics of Welfare*. 3rd Ed. London, UK: Macmillan.

Pigou, A. C. (1920/1932). *The Economics of Welfare*. 4th Ed. London, UK: Macmillan.

Pinhanez, M. (2012). Rekindling Governments from Within: Getting Public Sector Elite Officials to Support Government Reform in Brazil. In: A. H. Amsden, A. DiCaprio and J. A. Robinson: *The Role of Elites in Economic Development*. Oxford, UK: Oxford University Press. 307-326.

Platteau, J.-P. (2004). Monitoring Elite Capture in Community-Driven Development. *Development and Change* 35: 223-246.

Platteau, J.-P. (2009). Institutional obstacles to African economic development: State, ethnicity, and custom. *Journal of Economic Behavior & Organization* 71(3): 669-689.

Platteau, J.-P. and A. Abraham (2002). Participatory Development in the Presence of Endogenous Community Imperfections. *Journal of Development Studies* 39: 104-136.

Platteau, J.-P., V. Somville and Z. Wahhaj (2014). Elite capture through information distortion: A theoretical essay. *Journal of Development Economics* 106: 250-263.

Poerksen, U. (1995). *Plastic Words: The Tyranny of a Modular Language*. University Park, PA: Pennsylvania University Press.

Potter, R. B. (2014). Theories, strategies and ideologies of development: An overview. In: V. Desai and R. B. Potter: *The Companion to Development Studies*. 3rd Ed. Abingdon: Routledge. 83-87.

Prahalad, C. K. (2001). *The Fortune at the Bottom of the Pyramid*. Upper Saddle River, NJ: Wharton School Publishing.

Preacher, K. J. (2015). Extreme Groups Designs. In: R. L. Cautin and S. O. Lilienfeld: *The Encyclopedia of Clinical Psychology. Vol. 2*. Hoboken, NJ: Wiley & Sons. 1189-1192.

Preacher, K. J., D. D. Rucker, R. C. MacCallum and W. A. Nicewander (2005). Use of the Extreme Groups Approach: A Critical Reexamination and New Recommendations. *Psychological Methods* 10(2): 178-192.

Pritchett, L. (2002). It Pays to be Ignorant: A Simple Political Economy of Rigorous Program Evaluation. *Journal of Policy Reform* 5(4): 251-269.

Pritchett, L. and M. Woolcock (2008). Solutions When the Solution Is the Problem: Arraying the Disarray in Development. In: W. Easterly: *Reinventing Foreign Aid*. Cambridge, MA: MIT Press. 147-177.

Pritchett, L., M. Woolcock and M. Andrews (2013). Looking Like a State: Techniques of Persistent Failure in State Capability for Implementation. *Journal of Development Studies* 49(1): 1-18.

Provost, C. (2012). "The rise and fall of microfinance." Published 2012-11-21 on *TheGuardian.com*. Available from http://www.theguardian.com/global-development/poverty-matters/2012/nov/21/rise-fall-microfinance

Provost, C. (2014). "Rwanda: a puzzling tale of growth and political repression – get the data." Published 2014-04-03 on *TheGuardian.com*. Available from http://www.theguardian.com/global-development/datablog/2014/apr/03/rwanda-genocide-growth-political-repression-data

Putnam, R. D. (1976). *The Comparative Study of Political Elites*. Englewood Cliffs, NJ: Prentice-Hall.

Rajan, R. and A. Subramanian (2007). Does Aid Affect Governance? *American Economic Review* 97(2): 322-327.

Rasmusen, E. (2007). *Games and Information: An Introduction to Game Theory*. 4th Ed. Malden, MA: Blackwell.

Ravallion, M. (2009). Comment on: "The New Development Economics: We Shall Experiment, but How Shall We Learn?". In: J. Cohen and W. Easterly: *What Works in Development? Thinking Big and Thinking Small*. Washington, DC: Brookings Institution Press. 51-54.

Read, C. (1898). *Logic: Deductive and Inductive*. London, UK: Grant Richards.

Reinert, E. S. (2007). How Rich Countries Got Rich and Why Poor Countries Stay Poor. London, UK: Constable & Robinson.

Reinikka, R. and J. Svensson (2004). Local Capture: Evidence from a Central Government Transfer Program in Uganda. *The Quarterly Journal of Economics* 119(2): 679-705.

Reis, E. P. (2012). Poverty in the Eyes of Brazilian Elites. In: A. H. Amsden, A. DiCaprio and J. A. Robinson: *The Role of Elites in Economic Development*. Oxford, UK: Oxford University Press. 179-199.

Reis, E. P. and M. Moore (2005). Elites, perceptions and poverties. In: E. P. Reis and M. Moore: *Elite perceptions of poverty and inequality*. Cape Town: David Philip. 1-25.

Remmer, K. L. (2004). Does Foreign Aid Promote the Expansion of Government? *American Journal of Political Science* 48: 77-92.

Reno, W. S. (1998). *Warlord Politics and African States*. London, UK: Lynne Rienner.

Reno, W. S. (2011). *Warfare in Independent Africa*. New York, NY: Cambridge University Press.

Renton, A. (2007). "Does food aid do more harm than good?" Published 2007-05-27 on *theguardian.com*. Available from http://www.theguardian.com/lifeandstyle/wordofmouth/2007/may/27/in1987iwasworking

Reuter, N. (1994). Institutionalismus, Neo-Institutionalismus, Neue Institutionelle Ökonomie und andere „Institutionalismen": Eine Differenzierung konträrer Konzepte. *Zeitschrift für Wirtschafts- und Sozialwissenschaften* 114(1): 5–23.

Reynolds, T. W. (2012). Institutional Determinants of Success Among Forestry-Based Carbon Sequestration Projects in Sub-Saharan Africa. *World Development* 40(3): 542-554.

Rhoades, R. E. (1992). The coming revolution in methods for rural development research. In: N. S. Scrimshaw and G. R. Gleason: *Rapid Assessment Procedures - Qualitative Methodologies for Planning and Evaluation of Health Related Programmes*. Boston, MA: International Nutrition Foundation for Developing Countries.

Rigon, A. (2014). Building Local Governance: Participation and Elite Capture in Slum-upgrading in Kenya. *Development and Change* 45(2): 257-283.

Rioja, F. K. (2003). Filling potholes: macroeconomic effects of maintenance versus new investments in public infrastructure. *Journal of Public Economics* 87(9-10): 2281-2304.

Rist, G. (2007). Development as a Buzzword. *Development in Practice* 17(4/5): 485-491.

Rist, G. (2014). *The History of Development*. 4th Ed. London: Zed Books.

Robinson, J. A. (2003). *Politician-Proof Policy*. Background Paper to the 2004 World Development Report. Washington, D.C.: World Bank.

Robinson, J. A. (2012). Elites and Institutional Persistence. In: A. H. Amsden, A. DiCaprio and J. A. Robinson: *The Role of Elites in Economic Development*. Oxford, UK: Oxford University Press. 29-49.

Robinson, J. A. and T. Verdier (2013). The Political Economy of Clientelism. *The Scandinavian Journal of Economics* 115(2): 260-291.

Rodrik, D. (2000). Participatory Politics, Social Cooperation, and Economic Stability. *The American Economic Review* 90(2): 140-144.

Rodrik, D. (2007). One Economics, Many Recipes: Globalization, Institutions, and Economic Growth. Princeton, NJ: Princeton University Press.

Rodrik, D. (2008). Second-Best Institutions. *The American Economic Review* 98(2): 100-104.

Rodrik, D. (2009). The New Development Economics: We Shall Experiment, but How Shall We Learn? In: J. Cohen and W. Easterly: *What Works in Development? Thinking Big and Thinking Small*. Washington, DC: Brookings Institution Press. 24-47.

Rodrik, D., A. Subramanian and F. Trebbi (2004). Institutions Rule: The Primacy of Institutions Over Geography and Integration in Economic Development. *Journal of Economic Growth* 9: 131-165.

Romer, P. M. (1990). Endogenous Technological Change. *Journal of Political Economy* 98(5): S71-S102.

Romer, P. M. (1994). New goods, old theory, and the welfare costs of trade restrictions. *Journal of Development Economics* 43(1): 5-38.

Romer, P. M. (2010). *Technologies, Rules, and Progress: The Case for Charter Cities.* CGD Working Paper. Washington, D.C.: Center for Global Development.

Rosenstein-Rodan, P. (1943). Problems of Industrialization of Eastern and South-Eastern Europe. *Economic Journal* 53(210/211): 202-211.

Ross, S. A. (1973). The Economic Theory of Agency: The Principal's Problem. *American Economic Review* 63: 134-139.

Rosser, A. (2006). *The Political Economy of the Resource Curse: A Literature Survey.* IDS Working Paper 268. Brighton: University of Sussex.

Rostow, W. W. (1960). *The Stages of Economic Growth: A Non-communist Manifesto.* Cambridge, UK: Cambridge University Press.

Rottenburg, R. (2009). *Far-fetched Facts: A Parable of Development Aid.* Cambridge, MA: MIT Press.

Rutherford, M. (2001). Institutional Economics: Then and Now. *Journal of Economic Perspectives* 15: 173-194.

Sachs, J. D. (2003). Institutions Matter, but Not for Everything. *Finance & Development* (June): 38-41.

Sachs, J. D. (2005). The End of Poverty: Economic Possiblities of Our Time. New York, NY: Penguin Press.

Sachs, J. D. (2012). Government, Geography, and Growth: The True Drivers of Economic Development. *Foreign Affairs* 91(5): 142-150.

Sachs, J. D. (2014). "The Case for Aid." Published 2014-01-21 on *Foreign Policy Online.* Available from http://foreignpolicy.com/2014/01/21/the-case-for-aid/

Sachs, J. D. and A. M. Warner (1995). *Natural Resource Abundance and Economic Growth.* NBER Working Paper 5398. Cambridge, MA: National Bureau of Economic Research.

Sah, R. K. (1991). Fallibility in Human Organizations and Political Systems. *Journal of Economic Perspectives* 5(2): 67-88.

Sala-i-Martin, X. (2002). *15 Years of New Growth Economics: What Have We Learnt?* Working Paper 172. Santiago: Central Bank of Chile.

Sala-i-Martin, X., G. Doppelhofer and R. I. Miller (2004). Determinants of Long-Term Growth: A Bayesian Averaging of Classical Estimates (BACE) Approach. *The American Economic Review* 94(4): 813-835.

Samuelson, P. A. (1954). The Pure Theory of Public Expenditure. *The Review of Economics and Statistics* 36: 387-389.

Samuelson, P. A. (1955). Diagrammatic Exposition of a Theory of Public Expenditure. *The Review of Economics and Statistics* 37(4): 350-356.

Sandbrook, R. (2000). Closing the Circle: Democratization and Development in Africa. London, UK: Zed Books.

Sappington, D. E. M. (1991). Incentives in Principal-Agent Relationships. *Journal of Economic Perspectives* 5: 45-66.

Schmidtchen, D. (2002). To Help or not to Help: The Samaritan's Dilemma Revisited. In: G. Brennan, H. Kliemt and R. D. Tollison: *Method and Morals in Constitutional Economics: Essays in Honor of James M. Buchanan*. Berlin: Springer. 470-484.

Schou, A. (2007). Demand-driven Poverty Programmes and Elite Capture in Malawi: Between Prebendalism and Benevolence. *The European Journal of Development Research* 19: 594-613.

Schreier, M. (2014). Qualitative Content Analysis. In: U. Flick: *The SAGE Handbook of Qualitative Data Analysis*. London, UK: Sage. 170-183.

Scoones, I. (2007). Sustainability. *Development in Practice* 17: 589-596.

Scott, W. R. (2014). *Institutions and Organizations*. 4th Ed. Thousand Oaks, CA: Sage.

Seabright, P. (2002). Conflicts of objectives and task allocation in aid agencies. In: B. Martens, U. Mummert, P. Murrell and P. Seabright: *The Institutional Economics Of Foreign Aid*. Cambridge, UK: Cambridge University Press. 34-68.

Seers, D. (1972). What are we Trying to Measure? *Journal of Development Studies* 8(3): 21-36.

Sen, A. (1980). Equality of What? In: S. McMurrin: *The Tanner Lectures on Human Values*. Cambridge, MA: Cambridge University Press. 195-220.

Sen, A. (1999). *Development as Freedom*. New York, NY: Norton.

Shapiro, C. (1983). Premiums for High Quality Products as Returns to Reputations. *Quarterly Journal of Economics* 97(4): 659-679.

Shleifer, A. (1985). A Theory of Yardstick Competition. *The RAND Journal of Economics* 16: 319-327.

Shleifer, A. and R. Vishny (1993). Corruption. *The Quarterly Journal of Economics* 108(August): 599-617.

Simon, D. (2013). Neoliberalism structural adjustment and poverty reduction strategies. In: V. Desai and R. B. Potter: *The Companion to Development Studies*. 2nd Ed. Abingdon: Routledge. 86-92.

Simon, H. A. (1945). *Administrative Behavior*. New York, NY: The Free Press.

Simon, H. A. (1947). Administrative Behavior: A Study of Decision-Making Processes in Administrative Organization. 1st Ed. New York: Macmillan.

Simon, H. A. (1957). *Models of Man: Social and Rational*. New York: John Wiley & Sons.

Simon, H. A. (1997). *Empirically Based Microeconomics*. Cambridge, UK: Cambridge University Press.

Smith, A. (1776). An Inquiry Into the Nature and Causes of the Wealth of Nations. London, UK: W. Strahan and T. Cadell.

Solimano, A. and D. Avanzini (2012). The International Circulation of Elites: Knowledge, Entrepreneurial and Political. In: A. H. Amsden, A. DiCaprio and J. A. Robinson. Oxford, UK: Oxford University Press. 53-86.

Spence, M. (1973). Job Market Signaling. *The Quarterly Journal of Economics* 87: 355-374.

Spence, M. (1974). Market signaling: informational transfer in hiring and related screening processes. Cambridge, MA: Harvard University Press.

Spilimbergo, A. (2007). *Democracy and Foreign Education*. IMF Working Paper 07/51. Washington, D.C.: International Monetary Fund.

Spilimbergo, A. (2009). Democracy and Foreign Education. *American Economic Review* 99(1): 528-543.

Stern, N. H. (1974). Professor Bauer on Development. *Journal of Development Economics* 1(3): 191-211.

Stigler, G. J. and G. S. Becker (1977). De Gustibus Non Est Disputandum. *The American Economic Review* 67: 76-90.

Stiglitz, J. E. (1975). The Theory of "Screening," Education, and the Distribution of Income. *The American Economic Review* 65: 283-300.

Stock, J. H. and F. Trebbi (2003). Who Invented Instrumental Variable Regression? *Journal of Economic Perspectives* 17(3): 177-194.

Straffin, P. D. (1983). Changing the Way We Think about the Social World. *The Two-Year College Mathematics Journal* 14(3): 229-230.

Straub, S. (2008). Infrastructure and Growth in Developing Countries: Recent Advances and Research Challenges. Policy Research Working Paper 4460. Washington, D.C.: World Bank.

Straubhaar, T., H. Vöpel and J. Zweynert (2012). Kein endgültiges Wahr oder Falsch: Die Wirtschaftslehre ist keine Naturwissenschaft mit exakten Gesetzen. *Financial Times Deutschland* (2012-04-03): 24.

Subramanian, A. (2011). "Nicholas Kristof and Aid." Published 2011-05-20 on *CGD Blog*. Available from http://www.cgdev.org/blog/nicholas-kristof-and-aid

Svensson, J. (2000). Foreign aid and rent-seeking. *Journal of International Economics* 51: 437-461.

Svensson, J. (2003). Why conditional aid does not work and what can be done about it? *Journal of Development Economics* 70: 381-402.

Svensson, J. (2006). The institutional economics of foreign aid. *Swedish Economic Policy Review* 13: 115-137.

Swaroop, V., S. Jha and A. S. Rajkumar (2000). Fiscal effects of foreign aid in a federal system of governance: The case of India. *Journal of Public Economics* 77(3): 307-330.

Tebaldi, E. and R. Mohan (2008). *Institutions-Augmented Solow Model And Club Convergence*. MPRA Working Paper 10386. Munich: University of Munich.

Tebaldi, E. and R. Mohan (2010). Institutions and poverty. *The Journal of Development Studies* 46: 1047-1066.

Temple, J. R. W. (2010). Aid and Conditionality. In: D. Rodrik and M. R. Rosenzweig: *Handbook of Development Economics. Vol. 5*. Kidlington: North Holland. 4415-4523.

Thorndike, E. L. (1920). A Constant Error in Psychological Ratings. *Journal of Applied Psychology* 4(1): 25-29.

Thornton, J. (2014). Does foreign aid reduce tax revenue? Further evidence. *Applied Economics* 46(4): 359-373.

Tiebout, C. M. (1956). A Pure Theory of Local Expenditures. *Journal of Political Economy* 64(5): 416-424.

Tirole, J. (1986). Hierarchies and bureaucracies: On the role of collusion in organizations. *Journal of Law, Economics, and Organization* 2: 181-214.

Toro, F. (2014). "Shouldn't 'anti-poverty' and 'pro-middle class' be synonyms?" Published 2014-08-21 on *Campaign for Boring Development.* Available from http://boringdevelopment.com/2014/08/21/shouldnt-anti-poverty-and-pro-middle-class-be-synonyms/

Transparency International (2011). "2011 Corruption Perception Index." Available from http://www.transparency.org/cpi2011/in_detail#myAnchor3

Tremmel, J. (2003). Nachhaltigkeit als politische und analytische Kategorie – Der deutsche Diskurs um nachhaltige Entwicklung im Spiegel der Interessen der Akteure. Munich: ökom.

Truman, H. S. (1949). "Inaugural Address, January 20, 1949." *The American Presidency Project.* Available from http://www.presidency.ucsb.edu/ws/?pid=13282

Tucker, A. W. (1950). A Two-Person Dilemma. *Reprinted in: The Two-Year College Mathematics Journal* 1983, 14(3): 228.

Tull, D. M. (2006). China's engagement in Africa: scope, significance and consequences. *The Journal of Modern African Studies* 44(3): 459-479.

Turner, J. F. C. and R. Fichter, Eds. (1972). *Freedom to Build.* New York, NY: Macmillan.

Tversky, A. and D. Kahneman (1981). The Framing of Decisions and the Psychology of Choice. *Science* 211(4481): 453-458.

UNDG (2011). *Results-Based Management Handbook.* New York, NY: United Nations Development Group.

UNDP (1990). *Human Development Report 1990.* New York, NY: Oxford University Press.

UNDP (2008). Creating Value For All: Strategies for Doing Business With The Poor. New York, NY: United Nations Development Programme.

United Nations (1951). Measures for the Economic Development of Under-developed Countries: Report by a Group of Experts appointed by the Secretary-General of the United Nations. New York, NY: United Nations.

United Nations (2010). *The Millennium Development Goals Report 2010.* New York, NY: United Nations.

United Nations (2014a). *The Millennium Development Goals Report 2014.* New York, NY: United Nations.

United Nations (2014b). The road to dignity by 2030: ending poverty, transforming all lives and protecting the planet. Synthesis report of the Secretary-General on the post-2015 sustainable development agenda A/69/700. New York, NY: United Nations General Assembly.

Usher, D. (1968). The Price Mechanism and the Meaning of National Income Statistics. Oxford, UK: Clarendon Press.

van de Walle, N. (2001). *African Economies and the Politics of Permanent Crisis, 1979-1999.* Cambridge, UK: Cambridge University Press.

van de Walle, N. (2012). The path from neopatrimonialism: democracy and clientelism in Africa today. In: D. C. Bach and M. Gazibo: *Neopatrimonialism in Africa and Beyond.* Abingdon, UK: Routledge. 111-123.

Varian, H. R. (1992). *Microeconomic Analysis.* New York, NY: W. W. Norton & Company.

Varian, H. R. (2010). *Intermediate Microeconomics: A Modern Approach.* 8th Ed. New York, NY: W. W. Norton & Company.

Vermillion, D. L. (2001). Property Rights and Collective Action in the Devolution of Irrigation System Management. In: R. Meinzen-Dick, A. Knox and M. D. Gregorio: *Collective Action, Property Rights and Devolution of Natural Resource Management: Exchange of Knowledge and Implications for Policy*. Feldafing: Deutsche Stiftung für Internationale Entwicklung/Zentralstelle für Ernährung und Landwirtschaft. 183-220.

Voigt, S. (2004). Dictators and Social Contracts. In: C. K. Rowley and F. Schneider: *The Encyclopedia of Public Choice*. Dordrecht: Kluwer. 146-153.

Voigt, S. (2009). *Institutionenökonomik*. 2nd Ed. Paderborn: Wilhelm Fink.

Voigt, S. (2012). How to Measure the Rule of Law. *Kyklos* 65(2): 262-284.

Voigt, S. (2013). How (Not) to measure institutions. *Journal of Institutional Economics* 9(1): 1-26.

von Soest, C., K. Bechle and N. Korte (2011). How Neopatrimonialism Affects Tax Administration: a comparative study of three world regions. *Third World Quarterly* 32(7): 1307-1329.

Wagner-Tsukamoto, S. (2003). Human Nature and Organization Theory: On the Economic Approach to Institutional Organization. Cheltenham, UK: Edward Elgar.

Wallis, J. J. (2011). Deconstructing the dominant discourse: Chang on institutions and development. *Journal of Institutional Economics* 7: 589-593.

Weber, M. (1920). Die protestantische Ethik und der Geist des Kapitalismus. Vol. 1. Tübingen: Mohr.

Weber, M. (1922). *Wirtschaft und Gesellschaft. Vol. 3.* Tübingen: Mohr.

Werker, E. and F. Z. Ahmed (2008). What Do Nongovernmental Organizations Do? *Journal of Economic Perspectives* 22(2): 73-92.

Werlin, H. (1999). The Slum Upgrading Myth. *Urban Studies* 36: 1523-1534.

Westmeyer, H. (2015). Explanation: Conceptions in the Social Sciences. In: J. D. Wright: *International Encyclopedia of the Social & Behavioral Sciences. Vol. 8.* 2nd Ed. Amsterdam: Elsevier. 593-597.

Whittle, D. (2013). *How Feedback Loops Can Improve Aid (and Maybe Governance)*. CGD Working Paper. Washington, D.C.: Center for Global Development.

Wiese, L. v. (1936). Vilfredo Pareto als Soziologe. *Zeitschrift für Nationalökonomie* 7(4): 433-446.

Williamson, C. R. (2010). Exploring the failure of foreign aid: The role of incentives and information. *The Review of Austrian Economics* 23(1): 17-33.

Williamson, O. E. (1963). Managerial discretion and business behavior. *The American Economic Review* 53: 1032-1057.

Williamson, O. E. (1975). Markets and Hierarchies: Analysis and Antitrust Implications. New York, NY: The Free Press.

Williamson, O. E. (1985). *The Economic Institutions of Capitalism*. New York, NY: The Free Press.

Williamson, O. E. (2000). New Institutional Economics: Taking Stock, Looking Ahead. *Journal of Economic Literature* 38: 595-613.

Willis, K. (2011). *Theories of Development*. 2nd Ed. Abingdon: Routledge.

Winters, J. A. (2011). *Oligarchy*. New York, NY: Cambridge University Press.

Winters, M. S. (2010). Accountability, Participation and Foreign Aid Effectiveness. *International Studies Review* 12(2): 218-243.

Wirtz, M. and F. Caspar (2002). *Beurteilerübereinstimmung und Beurteilerreliabilität.* Göttingen: Hogrefe.

Wong, S. (2012). Tackling Elite Capture by the 'Counter-Elite' and 'Co-Opt-Elite' Approaches in Bangladesh and Ghana. In: A. H. Amsden, A. DiCaprio and J. A. Robinson: *The Role of Elites in Economic Development*. Oxford, UK: Oxford University Press. 329-350.

World Bank (1988). Road Deterioration in Developing Countries: Causes and Remedies. Washington, D.C.: World Bank.

World Bank (1989). Sub-Saharan Africa: From Crisis to Sustainable Growth. Washington, D.C.: World Bank.

World Bank (1994). World Development Report 1994: Infrastructure for Development. New York, NY: Oxford University Press.

World Bank (1997a). Helping Countries Combat Corruption: The Role of the World Bank. Washington, D.C.: World Bank.

World Bank (1997b). *World Development Report 1997*. New York, NY: Oxford University Press.

World Bank (1998). *Assessing Aid: What Works, What Doesn't, and Why*. New York, NY: Oxford University Press.

World Bank (2003). *World Development Report 2004*. Washington, D.C.: World Bank.

World Bank (2007). Detailed Implementation Review: India Health Sector 2006-2007. Vol. II. Washington, D.C.: World Bank.

World Bank (2008a). *CDD and Elite Capture: Reframing the Conversation*. Social Development How To Series, Vol. 3. Washington, D.C.: World Bank.

World Bank (2008b). The Monitoring and Evaluation Handbook For Business Environment Reform. Washington, D.C.: World Bank.

World Bank (2014a). *Applying Results-based Financing in Water Investments*. Working Paper 89326. Washington, D.C.: World Bank.

World Bank. (2014b). "Concessions, Build-Operate-Transfer (BOT) and Design-Build-Operate (DBO) Projects." Retrieved 2015-02-28, from http://ppp.worldbank.org/public-private-partnership/agreements/concessions-bots-dbos.

Worrall, T. S. (1990). Labor Contract Theory. In: F. H. Hahn: *The Economics of Missing Markets, Information, and Games*. Oxford, UK: Clarendon. 336-348.

Wright, J. and M. Winters (2010). The Politics of Effective Foreign Aid. *Annual Review of Political Science* 13: 61-80.

Wright, P. G. (1928). *The Tariff on Animal and Vegetable Oils*. New York: Macmillan.

Zang, X. (2012). Why Are the Elite in China Motivated to Promote Growth? In: A. H. Amsden, A. DiCaprio and J. A. Robinson: *The Role of Elites in Economic Development*. Oxford: Oxford University Press. 231-247.

Zuckerman, A. (1977). The Concept "Political Elite": Lessons from Mosca and Pareto. *Journal of Politics* 39(2): 324-344.

Zweynert, J. (2009). Interests versus culture in the theory of institutional change? *Journal of Institutional Economics* 5(3): 339-360.

Appendices

Appendix A Sample vs. Subsample Comparison

Tests on contingency tables (Chi-square...)

Contingency table (SAMPLE / SECTOR):

	Agric	Comm	Edu	Energy	Health	Trans	UrbDev	WatSan
n=137	33	1	9	9	17	10	32	26
n=320	54	16	45	8	33	46	74	44

Test of independence between the rows and the columns (SAMPLE / SECTOR):

Chi-square (Observed value)	22.171
Chi-square (Critical value)	24.322
DF	7
p-value	0.002
alpha	0.001

Test interpretation:
H0: The rows and the columns of the table are independent.
Ha: There is a link between the rows and the columns of the table.
As the computed p-value is greater than the significance level alpha=0.001, one cannot reject the null hypothesis H0.
The risk to reject the null hypothesis H0 while it is true is 0.24%.

Fisher's exact test:

p-value (Two-tailed)	0.002
alpha	0.001

Test interpretation:
H0: The rows and the columns of the table are independent.
Ha: There is a link between the rows and the columns of the table.
As the computed p-value is greater than the significance level alpha=0.001, one cannot reject the null hypothesis H0.
The risk to reject the null hypothesis H0 while it is true is 0.19%.

t-test for two independent samples / Two-tailed test (PRIM BUDGET)

Hypothesized difference (D): 0

Significance level (%): 0,1

Population variances for the t-test: Assume equality

Summary statistics:

Variable	Obs.	Minimum	Maximum	Mean	Std. deviation
PRIM BUDGET I 320	320	92099.000	95242949.000	6628617.669	11021590.152
PRIM BUDGET I 137	137	430000.000	61000000.000	5565801.942	9172433.005

99.900% confidence interval on the difference between the means:

] -2488859.241 ; 4614490.695 [

Difference	1062815.727
t (Observed value)	0.991
ltl (Critical value)	3.312
DF	455
p-value (Two-tailed)	0.322
alpha	0.001

Test interpretation:
H0: The difference between the means is equal to 0.
Ha: The difference between the means is different from 0.
As the computed p-value is greater than the significance level alpha=0.001, one cannot reject the null hypothesis H0.
The risk to reject the null hypothesis H0 while it is true is 32.22%.

Two-sample comparison of variances (PRIM BUDGET)

Summary statistics:

Variable	Obs.	Minimum	Maximum	Mean	Std. deviation
PRIM BUDGET I 320	320	92099.000	95242949.000	6628617.669	11021590.152
PRIM BUDGET I 137	137	430000.000	61000000.000	5565801.942	9172433.005

Fisher's F-test / Two-tailed test:

99.900% confidence interval on the ratio of variances:
] 0.878; 2.291 [

Ratio	1.444
F (Observed value)	1.444
F (Critical value)	1.645
DF1	319
DF2	136
p-value (Two-tailed)	0.014
alpha	0.001

Test interpretation:
H0: The ratio between the variances is equal to 1.
Ha: The ratio between the variances is different from 1.
As the computed p-value is greater than the significance level alpha=0.001, one cannot reject the null hypothesis H0.
The risk to reject the null hypothesis H0 while it is true is 1.44%.

Appendix B Full List of BCS Questions & Weightings

The weightings for the overall category rating are indicated behind each sub-section.

Relevance

1.1 What was the level of relevance of the project during its lifetime and what is its relevance today? (30%)

- Were the project purpose and overall objectives consistent with and supportive of Partner Government policies? (If necessary, specify if they were focused on policy changes) Would it still be so today? (For NGO projects: Was the project coherent with NGO strategy in the area/sector?)
- Did it support EC development and cooperation strategies in the concerned field (special consideration given to Country Strategy Paper (CSP)/National Indicative Plan (NIP), Paris declaration, EU effectiveness agenda)? Would it still be so today?
- Did the project (and does it still) respond to the needs of the target groups?

1.2 Was the design of the project appropriate for reaching its objectives? (30%)

- What kind of project approach was conceived in the project design? Please, briefly comment on sector and level/s of intervention (community; institutional and/or policy level).
- Did a log-frame or similar tool exist? If yes, what was its quality? If not, why not?
- Were the overall objective (OO), project purpose (PP) and results clear and logical, and did they address clearly identified needs?
- Was the PP achievable in the project framework?
- Were the OVIs/ targets suitable and informative, e.g. were they Specific, Measurable, Achievable, Realistic and Time-bound (SMART)?
- Were the planned activities, outputs and outcomes appropriate to achieve the PP?

- Were the risks and assumptions adequate? Were risk management arrangements in place?
- Was sustainability an integral part of the design i.e. was there a phase out/hand over strategy?
- Were changes made to the project design? If yes, did they contribute to significant design improvements?
- Was the planned institutional set-up of the project appropriate (e.g. local partners, implementing stakeholders and modality)?
- Were (results-based) monitoring and evaluation tools/activities included in the design? Were other learning tools foreseen?

1.3 Was the design sufficiently supported by all stakeholders? (30%)

- Were key stakeholders involved in the design process?
- Were the OO and PP clearly understood by the project partners?
- Were the timescale and/or range of activities realistic with regard to the stakeholders' capacities?
- Were coordination, management and financing arrangements clearly defined and did they support institutional strengthening and local ownership?
- Was the sustainability strategy fully understood by the partners?
- If applicable: How well has the project design been adapted to make it more relevant?

1.4 Did the project design sufficiently take cross-cutting issues into account? (10%)

- Were the relevant cross-cutting issues (environment, gender, human rights and governance, donor coordination or others) adequately mainstreamed in the project design?

Efficiency

2.1 How well was the availability/usage of means/inputs managed? (20%)

- To what degree were inputs provided / available on time and at planned cost to implement activities from all parties involved? Point out and briefly comment on reasons for major delays and deviations (at project's end), if any.
- Were inputs monitored regularly to encourage cost-effective implementation of activities? By whom were they monitored?

- Were project resources managed in a transparent and accountable manner? Has a final audit been carried out? If yes, what were the conclusions?
- Were all contractual procedures clearly understood and did they facilitate the implementation of the project?

2.2 How well was the implementation of activities managed? (20%)

- At project's end, to what extent were activities implemented as scheduled and with the planned committed funds? If not, please briefly comment on reasons for major deviations.
- How well were activities monitored? Was the log-frame or similar tool used as a management tool? If not, why not?
- If an exit strategy was defined, how well was it implemented?
- Was any other monitoring tool used by the projects management and/or other relevant parties (e.g. activity or resource schedule, others)?
- If appropriate, how flexible was the project in adapting to changing needs?
- If appropriate how did the project co-ordinate with other similar interventions to encourage synergy and avoid overlaps?

2.3 How well were outputs achieved? (35%)

- Have all planned outputs been delivered?
- What was the quality of outputs?
- Did the outputs achieved contribute to the intended results (outcome and impact)?
- Were they correctly reflected through the Objectively Verifiable Indicators (OVIs)/targets?
- Was the achievement of outputs regularly monitored by the project? Did the project use any internal results-based monitoring system?

2.4 How well worked the Partner Contribution/Involvement? (25%)

- Did the inter-institutional structures e.g. steering committees, monitoring systems, allow efficient project implementation?
- Did all partners provide their financial and/or human resources contributions? If not, comment on the reasons for deviation.
- How did EC procedures, or their effective application, affect the implementation (positively or adversely)?
- Was the communication between the partner country responsible, the EC Delegation and the project management satisfactory?

Effectiveness

3.1 How well did the project achieve its planned results (as in outcomes)? (50%)

- Were the planned results achieved?
- Were the OVIs/targets for the PP appropriate and were they reported against?
- What was the quality of the results/services available?
- Did all planned target groups access/use project results available so far?
- Were there any factors which prevented/helped target groups access the results/services?

3.2 Was the PP achieved? (50%)

- To what extent was the project able to adapt to changing external conditions (risks and assumptions) in order to ensure benefits for the target groups?
- If any unplanned negative effects on target groups occurred, to what extent did the project management take appropriate measures?
- To what extent did unplanned positive effects contribute to results produced / services provided?

Impact

4.1 What is the direct impact of the project at overall objectives level? (60%)

- Has the project contributed to any direct impact?
- To what extent have the OVIs/targets been achieved?
- Have any factors contributed positively to the project's direct impact?
- Have any external factors jeopardised the project's direct impact? Are any external factors likely to jeopardise the project's direct impact?

4.2 To what extent does /will the project have any indirect positive and/or negative impacts? (i.e. social, cultural, gender and economic) (40%)

- Have there been/ will there be any unplanned positive impacts on the planned target groups or other non-targeted communities arising from the project? How has this affected the achievement of the Project Purpose?

- Did the project take timely measures for mitigating the unplanned negative impacts? What was the result? Are target groups in the position to mitigate unplanned negative impacts?
- Did/do donor coherence, complementarity and coordination exist and have they had/do they have any indirect impact on the project?

Sustainability

5.1 Financial / economic viability (30%)

- If the services/results had to be supported institutionally, are funds currently made available? If so, by whom?
- Are the services/results currently affordable for the target groups?
- Are the beneficiaries and/or relevant authorities/institutions able to afford maintenance or replacement of the technologies/services introduced by the project?
- Have the benefits continued even when economic factors have changed (e.g. commodity prices, exchange rate)?
- Was there a financial/economic phase-out strategy; if so, did its implementation hold true?

5.2 What is the level of ownership of the project by target groups today? (30%)

- How far was the project embedded in local and/or existing structures?
- To what extent were target groups and possibly other relevant interest groups / stakeholders involved in the planning / implementation process?
- Are target groups still making decisions on project's results/services?
- Are target groups making use of relevant results?
- Did the target groups plan and ensure to continue delivering the stream of benefits? If yes, how has it materialised?

5.3 What has been the level of policy support provided and the degree of interaction between project and policy level until now? (20%)

- What support has been/is being provided from the relevant national, sectoral and budgetary policies?

- Have changes in policies and priorities affected the project and how well has it adapted in terms of long-term needs for support? If further changes are likely, how will the project adapt in terms of long-term needs for support?
- Was any other public policy and/or private sector support provided to enable the continuation of project benefits?

5.4 How well has the project contributed to institutional and management capacity? (20%)

- How far is the project embedded in institutional structures that survive beyond the life of the project?
- Were project partners properly developed -technically, financially, and managerially- to continue to deliver the project's benefits/services? How this has contributed to institutional capacity?
- Are adequate levels of suitable qualified human resources available to continue to deliver the project's stream of benefits?
- Are there good relations with new or existing institutions? Do they continue with some or all of the project's activities?

Appendix C Screenshot of a BCS

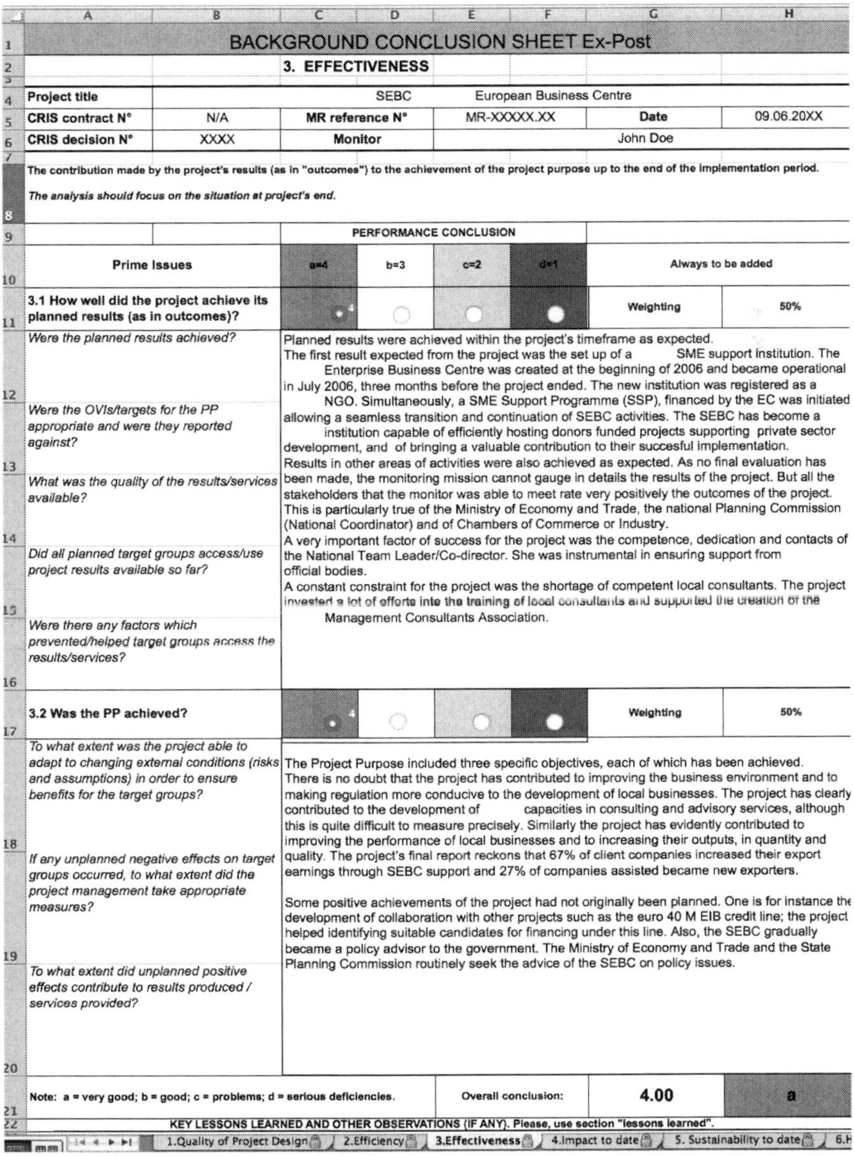

BACKGROUND CONCLUSION SHEET Ex-Post							
		3. EFFECTIVENESS					
Project title		SEBC		European Business Centre			
CRIS contract N°	N/A	MR reference N°		MR-XXXXX.XX		Date	09.06.20XX
CRIS decision N°	XXXX	Monitor		John Doe			

The contribution made by the project's results (as in "outcomes") to the achievement of the project purpose up to the end of the implementation period.

The analysis should focus on the situation at project's end.

Prime Issues	a=4	b=3	c=2	d=1	Always to be added	
	PERFORMANCE CONCLUSION					
3.1 How well did the project achieve its planned results (as in outcomes)?	4				Weighting	50%
Were the planned results achieved? *Were the OVIs/targets for the PP appropriate and were they reported against?* *What was the quality of the results/services available?* *Did all planned target groups access/use project results available so far?* *Were there any factors which prevented/helped target groups access the results/services?*	Planned results were achieved within the project's timeframe as expected. The first result expected from the project was the set up of a SME support institution. The Enterprise Business Centre was created at the beginning of 2006 and became operational in July 2006, three months before the project ended. The new institution was registered as a NGO. Simultaneously, a SME Support Programme (SSP), financed by the EC was initiated allowing a seamless transition and continuation of SEBC activities. The SEBC has become a institution capable of efficiently hosting donors funded projects supporting private sector development, and of bringing a valuable contribution to their succesful implementation. Results in other areas of activities were also achieved as expected. As no final evaluation has been made, the monitoring mission cannot gauge in details the results of the project. But all the stakeholders that the monitor was able to meet rate very positively the outcomes of the project. This is particularly true of the Ministry of Economy and Trade, the national Planning Commission (National Coordinator) and of Chambers of Commerce or Industry. A very important factor of success for the project was the competence, dedication and contacts of the National Team Leader/Co-director. She was instrumental in ensuring support from official bodies. A constant constraint for the project was the shortage of competent local consultants. The project invested a lot of efforts into the training of local consultants and supported the creation of the Management Consultants Association.					
3.2 Was the PP achieved?	4				Weighting	50%
To what extent was the project able to adapt to changing external conditions (risks and assumptions) in order to ensure benefits for the target groups? *If any unplanned negative effects on target groups occurred, to what extent did the project management take appropriate measures?* *To what extent did unplanned positive effects contribute to results produced / services provided?*	The Project Purpose included three specific objectives, each of which has been achieved. There is no doubt that the project has contributed to improving the business environment and to making regulation more conducive to the development of local businesses. The project has clearly contributed to the development of capacities in consulting and advisory services, although this is quite difficult to measure precisely. Similarly the project has evidently contributed to improving the performance of local businesses and to increasing their outputs, in quantity and quality. The project's final report reckons that 67% of client companies increased their export earnings through SEBC support and 27% of companies assisted became new exporters. Some positive achievements of the project had not originally been planned. One is for instance the development of collaboration with other projects such as the euro 40 M EIB credit line; the project helped identifying suitable candidates for financing under this line. Also, the SEBC gradually became a policy advisor to the government. The Ministry of Economy and Trade and the State Planning Commission routinely seek the advice of the SEBC on policy issues.					
Note: a = very good; b = good; c = problems; d = serious deficiencies.		Overall conclusion:		4.00	a	

KEY LESSONS LEARNED AND OTHER OBSERVATIONS (IF ANY). Please, use section "lessons learned".

The above screenshot shows the *effectiveness* sheet of an actual BCS (some data modified). The *effectiveness* sheet only contains 2 sub-sections.

Appendix D Principal Component Analyses (Ratings)

Principle Component Analysis (PCA) / Sample n=457

PCA type: Pearson (n-1)

Rotation: Varimax / Number of factors = 2

Summary statistics:

Variable	Obs.	missing	Minimum	Maximum	Mean	Std. deviation
RELV	457	0	1.000	4.000	2.786	0.594
EFCY	457	0	1.000	4.000	2.718	0.673
EFCT	457	0	1.000	4.000	2.733	0.691
IMPT	457	0	1.000	4.000	2.748	0.710
SUST	457	0	1.000	4.000	2.556	0.699

Correlation matrix (Pearson (n-1)):

Variables	RELV	EFCY	EFCT	IMPT	SUST
RELV	**1**	**0.435**	**0.432**	**0.376**	**0.351**
EFCY	**0.435**	**1**	**0.611**	**0.443**	**0.343**
EFCT	**0.432**	**0.611**	**1**	**0.623**	**0.449**
IMPT	**0.376**	**0.443**	**0.623**	**1**	**0.538**
SUST	**0.351**	**0.343**	**0.449**	**0.538**	**1**

Values in bold are different from 0 with a significance level alpha=0.001

Bartlett's sphericity test:

Chi-square (Observed value)	747.736
Chi-square (Critical value)	29.588
DF	10
p-value	< 0,0001
alpha	0.001

Test interpretation:
H0: There is no correlation significantly different from 0 between the variables.
Ha: At least one of the correlations between the variables is significantly different from 0.
As the computed p-value is lower than the significance level alpha=0.001,
one should reject the null hypothesis H0, and accept the alternative hypothesis Ha.
The risk to reject the null hypothesis H0 while it is true is lower than 0.01%.

Principle Component Analysis:

Eigenvalues:

	F1	F2	F3	F4	F5
Eigenvalue	2.857	0.739	0.635	0.453	0.317
Variability (%)	57.135	14.780	12.691	9.050	6.344
Cumulative %	57.135	71.915	84.606	93.656	100.000

Eigenvectors:

	F1	F2	F3	F4	F5
RELV	0.395	-0.500	0.745	0.198	0.005
EFCY	0.446	-0.458	-0.402	-0.524	-0.394
EFCT	0.498	-0.072	-0.374	0.212	0.750
IMPT	0.474	0.374	-0.152	0.585	-0.520
SUST	0.415	0.628	0.347	-0.547	0.113

Factor loadings:

	F1	F2	F3	F4	F5
RELV	0.667	-0.430	0.593	0.133	0.003
EFCY	0.754	-0.394	-0.320	-0.352	-0.222
EFCT	0.842	-0.062	-0.298	0.143	0.422
IMPT	0.801	0.322	-0.121	0.393	-0.293
SUST	0.701	0.540	0.277	-0.368	0.064

Correlations between variables and factors:

	F1	F2	F3	F4	F5
RELV	0.667	-0.430	0.593	0.133	0.003
EFCY	0.754	-0.394	-0.320	-0.352	-0.222
EFCT	0.842	-0.062	-0.298	0.143	0.422
IMPT	0.801	0.322	-0.121	0.393	-0.293
SUST	0.701	0.540	0.277	-0.368	0.064

Contribution of the variables (%):

	F1	F2	F3	F4	F5
RELV	15.591	25.026	55.445	3.935	0.002
EFCY	19.919	20.973	16.186	27.433	15.490
EFCT	24.812	0.525	13.993	4.492	56.178
IMPT	22.452	13.990	2.324	34.181	27.054
SUST	17.226	39.485	12.053	29.959	1.276

Squared cosines of the variables:

	F1	F2	F3	F4	F5
RELV	**0.445**	0.185	0.352	0.018	0.000
EFCY	**0.569**	0.155	0.103	0.124	0.049
EFCT	**0.709**	0.004	0.089	0.020	0.178
IMPT	**0.641**	0.103	0.015	0.155	0.086
SUST	**0.492**	0.292	0.076	0.136	0.004

Values in bold correspond for each variable to the factor for which the squared cosine is the largest

Principle Component Analysis (PCA) / Sample n=137

PCA type: Pearson (n-1)

Rotation: Varimax / Number of factors = 2

Summary statistics:

Variable	Obs.	missing	Minimum	Maximum	Mean	Std. deviation
RELV	137	0	1.000	4.000	2.810	0.588
EFCY	137	0	1.000	4.000	2.752	0.694
EFCT	137	0	1.000	4.000	2.708	0.759
IMPT	137	0	1.000	4.000	2.810	0.791
SUST	137	0	1.000	4.000	2.562	0.716

Correlation matrix (Pearson (n-1)):

Variables	RELV	EFCY	EFCT	IMPT	SUST
RELV	**1**	**0.460**	**0.386**	**0.365**	**0.430**
EFCY	**0.460**	**1**	**0.643**	**0.543**	**0.357**
EFCT	**0.386**	**0.643**	**1**	**0.728**	**0.534**
IMPT	**0.365**	**0.543**	**0.728**	**1**	**0.631**
SUST	**0.430**	**0.357**	**0.534**	**0.631**	**1**

Values in bold are different from 0 with a significance level alpha=0.001

Bartlett's sphericity test:

Chi-square (Observed value)	291.777
Chi-square (Critical value)	29.588
DF	10
p-value	<0,0001
alpha	0.001

Test interpretation:
H0: There is no correlation significantly different from 0 between the variables.
Ha: At least one of the correlations between the variables is significantly different from 0.
As the computed p-value is lower than the significance level alpha=0.001,
one should reject the null hypothesis H0, and accept the alternative hypothesis Ha.
The risk to reject the null hypothesis H0 while it is true is lower than 0.01%.

Kaiser-Meyer-Olkin measure of sampling adequacy:

RELV	0.794
EFCY	0.777
EFCT	0.773
IMPT	0.767
SUST	0.778
KMO	0.776

Principal Component Analysis:

Eigenvalues:

	F1	F2	F3	F4	F5
Eigenvalue	3.054	0.726	0.663	0.309	0.247
Variability (%)	61.089	14.516	13.268	6.177	4.949
Cumulative %	61.089	75.605	88.873	95.051	100.000

Eigenvectors:

	F1	F2	F3	F4	F5
RELV	0.369	0.846	0.237	-0.304	-0.019
EFCY	0.441	0.190	-0.636	0.580	-0.168
EFCT	0.493	-0.261	-0.263	-0.378	0.690
IMPT	0.489	-0.382	0.056	-0.383	-0.682
SUST	0.432	-0.185	0.684	0.531	0.172

Factor loadings:

	F1	F2	F3	F4	F5
RELV	0.644	0.721	0.193	-0.169	-0.010
EFCY	0.771	0.162	-0.518	0.322	-0.083
EFCT	0.862	-0.222	-0.214	-0.210	0.343
IMPT	0.855	-0.325	0.046	-0.213	-0.339
SUST	0.755	-0.158	0.557	0.295	0.086

Correlations between variables and factors:

	F1	F2	F3	F4	F5
RELV	0.644	0.721	0.193	-0.169	-0.010
EFCY	0.771	0.162	-0.518	0.322	-0.083
EFCT	0.862	-0.222	-0.214	-0.210	0.343
IMPT	0.855	-0.325	0.046	-0.213	-0.339
SUST	0.755	-0.158	0.557	0.295	0.086

Contribution of the variables (%):

	F1	F2	F3	F4	F5
RELV	13.582	71.566	5.602	9.213	0.037
EFCY	19.465	3.613	40.442	33.668	2.813
EFCT	24.310	6.818	6.916	14.290	47.667
IMPT	23.958	14.576	0.316	14.638	46.512
SUST	18.685	3.427	46.724	28.193	2.971

Squared cosines of the variables:

	F1	F2	F3	F4	F5
RELV	0.415	**0.519**	0.037	0.028	0.000
EFCY	**0.595**	0.026	0.268	0.104	0.007
EFCT	**0.743**	0.049	0.046	0.044	0.118
IMPT	**0.732**	0.106	0.002	0.045	0.115
SUST	**0.571**	0.025	0.310	0.087	0.007

Values in bold correspond for each variable to the factor for which the squared cosine is the largest

Appendix E Sample vs. Subsample Comparison

t-test for two independent samples / Two-tailed test: Rating AMEAN

99.900% confidence interval on the difference between the means:
] -0.201 ; 0.143 [

Difference	-0.029
t (Observed value)	-0.559
|t| (Critical value)	3.312
DF	455
p-value (Two-tailed)	0.576
alpha	0.001

Test interpretation:
H0: The difference between the means is equal to 0.
Ha: The difference between the means is different from 0.
As the computed p-value is greater than the significance level alpha=0.001, one cannot reject the null hypothesis H0.
The risk to reject the null hypothesis H0 while it is true is 57.63%.

Two-sample comparison of variances (RAMEAN)

Hypothesized ratio (R): 1

Significance level (%): 0,1

Summary statistics:

Variable	Obs.	missing	Minimum	Maximum	Mean	Std. deviation
RAMEAN | 320	320	0	1.200	4.000	2.699	0.488
RAMEAN | 137	137	0	1.000	4.000	2.728	0.557

Fisher's F-test / Two-tailed test:

99.900% confidence interval on the ratio of variances:
] 0.466; 1.216 [

Ratio	0.767
F (Observed value)	0.767
F (Critical value)	1.645
DF1	319
DF2	136
p-value (Two-tailed)	0.060
alpha	0.001

Test interpretation:
H0: The ratio between the variances is equal to 1.
Ha: The ratio between the variances is different from 1.
As the computed p-value is greater than the significance level alpha=0.001, one cannot reject the null hypothesis H0.
The risk to reject the null hypothesis H0 while it is true is 5.97%.

Tests on contingency tables (Chi-square...)

Contingency table (SAMPLE / RAMEAN):

	4-3,6	3,4	3,2	3	2,8	2,6	2,4	2,2	2	1,8-1
n=137	8	10	15	22	27	12	14	14	5	10
n=320	16	15	18	73	54	40	36	29	24	15

Test of independence between the rows and the columns (Chi-square):

Chi-square (Observed value)	12.477
Chi-square (Critical value)	27.877
DF	9
p-value	0.188
alpha	0.001

Test interpretation:
H0: The rows and the columns of the table are independent.
Ha: There is a link between the rows and the columns of the table.
As the computed p-value is greater than the significance level alpha=0.001, one cannot reject the null hypothesis H0.
The risk to reject the null hypothesis H0 while it is true is 18.78%.

Fisher's exact test:

p-value (Two-tailed)	0.186
alpha	0.001

Test interpretation:
H0: The rows and the columns of the table are independent.
Ha: There is a link between the rows and the columns of the table.
As the computed p-value is greater than the significance level alpha=0.001, one cannot reject the null hypothesis H0.
The risk to reject the null hypothesis H0 while it is true is 18.61%.

Appendix F Full List of the Coding Frame

Symptom ID	Political Elite	Agency Elite	Local Elite	Target Group /AP	Active	Extractive (P)	Extractive (O)	Passive	Observable phenomenon	Ref Theory	Ref Case Study	Underlying incentive situation	Incidence
Elite													
01	y	n	n	n	n	n	y	n	Politicians exert strong control over an agency in control of regulation, generation, transmission, and distribution of a public utility (i.e. power).		188	Control enables politicians to hand out electricity connections and subsidies to favored electoral clients (rich farmers, organized urban slum dwellers, etc.). "Cross subsidization" of winners (politically connected groups) at the expense of losers (masses).	Maharashtra state politicians and the Maharashtra State Electricity Board, HDVC Converter Terminal (India)
11	y	n	n	n	y	y	n	n	Politicians exert strong control over project implementation	51		Top-down control enables central actors to reward supporters and punish detractors. Aid funds enable inefficiency; weak accountability/lack of feedback mechanisms	Infrastructural projects *Pritchett & Woolcock* (2004: 199)
26	y	p	n	n	n	y	y	n	Tariffs not covering actual costs of production (resistance against change from consumers)	52		High costs and few immediate benefits for politicians to move to economically efficient policy: Resistance against change from consumers, decision makers fear the loss of substantial personal benefits (monetary or political).	
72	y	n	n	n	n	y	y	n	Tariffs not covering actual costs of production (resistance against change from politics)	52	205	Keeping respective company dependent on support from politics; indirect "design" to maintain control over distribution.	*World Bank* (2003: 162)
15	y	y	p	n	y	y	n	n	Failure of providing support to Initiatives for local development.	74		Strengthening local leadership capabilities may be threatening to those in central leadership positions. Protective resistance against change of access to elite positions.	
14	y	y	y	n	n	y	y	n	Low compliance with or formal fulfillment of conditionalities: Terms agreed to prior to the funding, promises to reform in the future are given and broken repeatedly	67, 75	175, 186	Mechanisms subject to reform generate rents for the agents, aid needed as a resource. Conditionalities do not exert a substantial power; recipients often receive assistance even after not performing on previous agreements.	*Pedersen* (1996, 1998) Forest Dept. in Orissa Capacity Building Project (India)

Symptom ID	Political Elite	Agency Elite	Local Elite	Target Group /AP	Active	Extractive (P)	Extractive (O)	Passive	Observable phenomenon	Ref Theory	Ref Case Study	Underlying incentive situation	Incidence
20	y	n	n	n	n	y	n	n	Government: No support of an agency part of a reform (e.g., regulation agency) despite acceptance of the reform -> agency dependent on donor support	113	204, 207	Donor conditions as the "price" of aid support: 1. Meeting the donor's demand for institutional change without wholesale changes to government structures (institutions can be designed to ensure influence) 2. Regulation authorities provide the government with a "buffer" from public criticism generated by rate hikes or privatization actions.	Energy Regulation Board, Zambia
16	y	n	n	n	n	y	n	n	Government: Promotion of a structural reform project (for a sector) by ministries despite no desire for actual change		179	Ministries' and departments' patron-client relationships are maintained through the particular monopoly power exerted by stewardship of the concerned portfolio (such as for forests).	
17	n	y	n	n	n	y	n	n	Agency: Cooperation for a structural reform project despite no desire for change (project will potentially cut its privileges)	59	180	The increase in staff and budget associated with aid projects increases its director's standing and career advancement to higher grades.	
21	y	n	n	n	y	n	y	n	Misdesign of institutions(1): creating counterproductive dependencies Institutional incoherence, e.g., agency or authority under responsibility of wrong ministry		205, 207	Superficial fulfillment of donor conditions, while details of institutional dependencies secure influence for politicians or respective actors	Energy Regulation Board, Zambia
61	y	n	n	n	n	n	y	n	Misdesign of institutions (2): Incentive structures of (regulation) agencies not compatible with public interest (i.e. incentives for approving price hikes)		206	Superficial fulfillment of donor conditions, while details of institutional dependencies secure influence for politicians or respective actors	Energy Regulation Board, Zambia
23	y	n	y	n	n	y	y	n	Failure of aid project to enhance capabilities of officials in governmental organizations	67	178	Highly dependent administration on aid is more susceptible to top-down decision making within its own governmental apparatus; aid dependency also reduces the accountability of its government to its own people, since it is not fiscally accountable to them.	Rigid hierarchical structure in Orissa Forest Department is geared towards executing orders, rather than encouraging initiative and problem solving.

Symptom ID	Political Elite	Agency Elite	Local Elite	Target Group /AP	Active	Extractive (P)	Extractive (O)	Passive	Observable phenomenon	Ref Theory	Ref Case Study	Underlying incentive situation	Incidence
28	y	y	y	n	y	n	y	n	Failure of measures towards more efficiency/capacity building interventions in governmental organizations.	52	179, 188, 190	Patron-client system is upheld by "winners" of the system (interest groups and politicians) and prevents a change towards a more efficient organization: Costs too high, immediate benefits low; institutions are seen as "cash cow" by politicians. Aid budget inflow supports creating a bigger pool of patronage.	Orissa government; Maharashtra State Energy Board, HDVC Converter Terminal Project (India)
24	y	p	p	n	n	y	n	n	Failure of aid project to reduce oversized overhead of administrative structures.		188	Aid funding expands the "pool of patronage" also for awarding supporters with jobs, potentially enlarging the overhead of already overstaffed administration.	In 2000, the MSEB counted about 125,000 personnel on its payroll.
25	y	y	y	n	n	y	n	n	Corruption and rent-seeking behavior is not cured by respective capacity building project.	55	216	Development project that do not take these rules-in-use into account make things worse when they inject resources into a rent-seeking bureaucracy. The increased availability of funds tends to fuel the rent-seeking process.	Orissa Forest Department (Orissa, India)
27	y	y	y	n	n	n	y	n	Low efforts in monitoring/enforcing rules and excluding free-riding; illegal taps into power lines, inadequate bill collection, nonpayment of power bills and bribery of utility workers.	91	189, 194	Patron-client-system including jobs leads to an HR overload and large hierarchies in public administration. Number of players in "layer" manner (hierarchy) reduces overall efficiency, low effort is better strategy for agent. Hierarchy and top-down architecture is enhanced by aid dependency through low accountability (23)	Maharashtra power station; MSEB/HDVC Converter Terminal
57	n	y	y	n	n	y	y	n	Low efforts in supervision and inspection: Government inspectors in infrastructure projects take bribes for looking the other way.	105		local contractors have an incentive to put forth low effort and reduce inputs. (P-A) In a rent-seeking environment, aid infusion fuels opportunities for bribery and low-quality work.	
32	y	n	n	n	n	y	n	n	Output-over-outcome: Assets (outputs) are set up independently of connection to actual outcome.		188	Capture by politicians and/or contractors; actors personally involved in final selections within a tendering process take a direct cut of projects (i.e. "success fee" by the winning contractor). Contracts are handed out as patronage for political support.	Maharashtra State Energy Board, HDVC Converter Terminal Project

Symptom ID	Political Elite	Agency Elite	Local Elite	Target Group /AP	Active	Extractive (P)	Extractive (O)	Passive	Observable phenomenon	Ref Theory	Ref Case Study	Underlying incentive situation	Incidence
34	n	y	y	y	n	n	y	y	Uncooperative behavior in CPR setups: sustainable resource management difficult to establish with local users.	40, 51		Project design distributes power unevenly: incentives do not promote collectively sustainable behavior. Ownership of resources is often with an agency that exerts the economical extraction. Since local resource users are not able to make a living through using the resource, their incentive to conserve diminishes.	Sustainable Forest Management Irrigation systems: head-enders vs. tail-enders
50	y	n	n	n	n	n	y	n	Maintenance of infrastructure is continuously underfunded (TA/equipment/construction projects)	39, 95	210	Missing incentives for maintenance through continuous donor bail-outs; leading large technical capital projects to generating aid dependence, need for major rehabilitations every 10-15 years.	Kafue Gorge Hydropower Station Rehabilitation project, Zambia
52	y	n	n	n	n	y	n	n	Political or economic reforms and measures to increase tax base are delayed or denied support	43, 52		External aid funding enables recipient governments to greatly expand their spending and sizes without the urge of creating more income; moral hazard of indiscriminate aid availability: Weak incentives to pursue policies to generate stronger base for tax revenues or find alternative revenue sources	Remmer 2004
53	y	y	y	y	n	y	n	n	Reforms attempted by the donor are not sustained after funding is terminated and donor exits.	66		Imposed conditionalities lead to both a lack of commitment and a lack of local credibility	Brunetti & Weder 1994; Johnson & Wasty 1993)
55	n	y	y	n	n	n	y	n	Employees of public administration entities are extracting side payments from citizens.	53	216	Jobs may be bought and sold, with problem that this system is rather sustainable: Public employees may need to find ways of gaining private returns to make their investment in obtaining a public position worthwhile.	described by Wade (1985, 1989) for India
70	n	n	y	n	n	n	y	n	Low quality of professional service provision	43, 105		Missing incentive structure to adopt to a professional code and a professional association; limited ability for principals to bring lawsuits for malpractice.	
60	n	y	y	n	n	n	n	n	Public employees devoting their working time to private activities such as running their own private businesses.	44	216	Product of patronage unit of jobs. Long-term employment but low pay: employees have to engage in extra job opportunities.	

Symptom ID	Political Elite	Agency Elite	Local Elite	Target Group /AP	Active	Extractive (P)	Extractive (O)	Passive	Observable phenomenon	Ref Theory	Ref Case Study	Underlying incentive situation	Incidence
71	n	n	y	n	n	n	n	y	Local Elite: Low interest in maintaining public goods and limit free riding / hampered sustainability	37		Donors fail to solve the underlying incentive problems of coll. action.; crowding-out of local engagement	Rural school construction: maintenance/repair of buildings
54	y	n	n	n	n	n	y	n	Repeated interventions from politicians for the sake of buying support from woo voters		215	Weak accountability mechanisms; existence of strong one-party or patronage systems weakened those between politicians, the bureaucracy, and the citizenry, despite the nominal multiparty democracy.	
05	y	n	y	n	n	y	y	n	Lack of qualified staff in public administration	67	215	Staff placement is part of patronage system and geared towards top-down orders.	Conservation Farming Unit, Zambia
08	y	y	y	n	n	y	y	n	Local communities are not accorded privileges of ownership – although they have the greatest stake in responsible management of their natural resources.	101	177, 181	Local governmental departments are provided legal monopoly in protecting (i.e., excluding) and raising revenue from local resources. Departments oppose devolving ownership and resist increased participation.	Participatory Forest Management (Orissa, India)
63	y	y	y	n	n	n	y	n	Elite actors who have authority to make their own collective choice rules do not invest in this effort.	54		Second-order public-good problem of devising new rules: All actors in the situation receive the benefit in future rounds regardless of whether they spent any time and effort trying to devise new rules	
06	y	y	n	n	n	y	n	n	Low effectiveness of gov't employees as field staff		216	The differences in salaries (and thus professional status and prestige) may inhibit the development of an environment for mutual learning: Extension workers who earn less than 5 per cent of the directors' salaries might be reluctant to be advised by their well paid colleagues.	
13	y	n	n	n	n	n	y	n	Crowding out of private investors from an infrastructure or utility market.		189, 194	Sustainability of *investment* in the energy sector (as opposed to the sustainability of the donor-financed *hardware)* is not very high Donor investments help in the *short run* to expand production, but creates a bigger pool of patronage.	Maharashtra State Energy Board, HDVC Converter Terminal Project (India)
31	y	n	n	n	n	y	n	n	Exaggeration of target groups in humanitarian emergency regions	125		Humanitarian emergencies are taken advantage of by recipient government leaders to generate income	

Symptom ID	Political Elite	Agency Elite	Local Elite	Target Group /AP	Active	Extractive (P)	Extractive (O)	Passive	Observable phenomenon	Ref Theory	Ref Case Study	Underlying incentive situation	Incidence
												through aid.	
48	y	p	n	n	n	y	n	n	Humanitarian ODA interventions lead to unwanted (perverse) outcomes	89, 125	174	Problem of aid fungibility: Donor's disbursed funds flow into budget of recipient and can be reallocated to other uses.	Food aid in Somalia prolonging the war
30	y	n	n	n	y	n	y	n	Governments create barriers to trade / resistance against removing those barriers.	55		Barriers confer considerable benefits to protected sectors and thus motivate to engage in rent-seeking behavior.	Bates 1988
Other: Historical (not EC-related)													
07	*n*	*n*	*n*	*n*	*n*	*n*	*n*	*n*	*Low **credibility** of gov't employees as field staff in promoting new techniques*		*219*	*The credibility of an extension officer is a crucial factor for the farmers' incentives to adopt new techniques. Official personnel who have long promoted different techniques may be concerned with losing face with their clients*	*Conservation Farming Unit: Expansion through the Ministry of Agriculture, Food and Fisheries, one way of sustaining the conservation farming idea, may actually undermine the usefulness of the CFU approach.*
02	*y*	*n*	*n*	*y*	*y*	*n*	*n*	*n*	***Resistance against price increases** from interest groups and the public.*		*203, 206*	*Patronage system is historical cause: Good (electricity etc.) had been heavily subsidized previously by politicians for the sake of buying support.*	*The Zambia National Farmers Union and the Zambian Chamber of Commerce and Industry argue that the Board has become another bureaucracy that is interested in generating more income for itself and the government.*

Symptom ID	Political Elite	Agency Elite	Local Elite	Target Group /AP	Active	Extractive (P)	Extractive (O)	Passive	Observable phenomenon	Ref Theory	Ref Case Study	Underlying incentive situation	Incidence
03	y	n	y	n	n	n	y	n	***Low payment morality*** *for the repayment of loans*		214	*Patronage system: Politicians' interventions in the agricultural sector (i.e. fertilizer donations) for the sake of buying support from woo voters. Farmers have grown accustomed to receiving goods (fertilizers and seeds) from government officials and politicians in the past. While these goods were delivered on loan terms, they were de facto donations.*	
04	y	n	n	n	n	n	y	n	***Inefficient agricultural practices***		214	*Heavy subsidies during the one-party era of the country are responsible for the extreme inefficiency of the whole sector.*	
56	y	y	y	n					***Bureaucratic structures dominate business sector****s, reluctance against moving towards i.e. privatization*		203	*The former or de-facto one-party systems distort(ed) market signals to a great extent. Operating within a market-like system is new for public employees.*	*Zambia Energy Sector*
49	y	y	n	n	y	n	n	n	***Tax avoidance:*** *Taxpayers seek ways to reduce their tax burden, as they see no benefits coming from their payments.*	56	193	***Low quality of service provision:*** *Given that the MSEB imposes its losses on the state's budget, the cost of power is also being borne by those who pay taxes and those who might otherwise benefit from state services and investments.*	*Maharashtra State Energy Board, HDVC Converter Terminal Project (India)*
Other: Donor Side (not EC-related)													
38	y	p	n	n					*Reform demand not taken seriously by government officials*		191, 192	*If aid is a result of donor industry lobbying, reform-urgency not taken seriously by government officials => weak incentives for recipient to reform*	*Signaling of financing of the HVDC project owes much of its existence to intervention from the Swedish Ministry of Foreign Affairs and its clear intent to promote development of the Swedish industry.*

Symptom ID	Political Elite	Agency Elite	Local Elite	Target Group /AP	Active	Extractive (P)	Extractive (O)	Passive	Observable phenomenon	Ref Theory	Ref Case Study	Underlying incentive situation	Incidence
39	*n*	*n*	*n*	*n*					*Specific local knowledge is missing in project (i.e. seasonal changes, topographical specifities etc.); Significant asymmetries of both time-and-place knowledge and scientific knowledge exist in context of development aid*	*42*	*180*	*Not put into practice because it is not in the interest of the remote executive team, nor the consultants, who exercise day-to-day ownership but have no stake in the communities themselves.*	*Farmers who have used a stream to irrigate are usually well aware where the stream crosses a long section of sandy and unstable soil. If the engineers designing a donor-funded irrigation project do not learn this information, the canal may wash out after only a few years of operation. (Hilton 2002)*
40	*n*	*n*	*n*	*n*					*Large infrastructure projects are preferred within donor agency*	*70*	*154 ?*	*Pressure to disburse makes large capital-intensive projects more attractive to management of donor agency; at the same time, staff time is lower than i.e. with institution-building projects*	
42	*n*	*n*	*n*	*n*					*Effectiveness of projects is secondary topic in mass media (GiveWell is one of the first organizations)*	*110*		*Process of giving is more important than actual success for donors/philanthropists Warm-glow effect: Aid's success is an attractive quality*	
43	*n*	*n*	*n*	*n*					*Preference for high-budget, low-personnel designs*	*114*		*Donor office career advancement is linked to the number of projects signed and funds disbursed, not maintaining restraint.*	
44	*n*	*n*	*n*	*n*					*Asymmetry and loss of information in the donor agency's hierarchy*	*136*		*Selection process: Each actor has an incentive to select and transmit primarily the information that will benefit him or her personally.*	

Symptom ID	Political Elite	Agency Elite	Local Elite	Target Group /AP	Active	Extractive (P)	Extractive (O)	Passive	Observable phenomenon	Ref Theory	Ref Case Study	Underlying incentive situation	Incidence
45	*n*	*n*	*n*	*n*					*Near-term priorities of the consultant regarding the completion of the contractual terms with donor agency are more strongly reflected in the project over the long-term interests of the beneficiary communities.*		*180*	*Consultants exercise day-to-day ownership but have no stake in the communities themselves. Supervision of consultant not possible by donor agency due to lack of manpower. Administrative and supervisory gaps are filled by consultant. Given that Sida normally faces a high rate of turnover in its staff assignments, the main source of project continuity is frequently the consultant.*	*Participatory Forest Management (Orissa, India)*
47	*n*	*n*	*n*	*n*					*Short-term solutions in institution building do not turn out sustainable.*		*207*	*Creating institutions in a very politically sensitive area obviates against a short-term strategy and will most likely require sustained efforts on the part of the donor to make a long-term impact.*	*Energy Regulation Board (Zambia)*
62									*Adverse selection of projects in the portfolio of a development agency*	*45*		*As donor agencies ratchet up the conditions to be met by recipients in exchange for aid, those in least need of aid will opt out. This leaves those less able to meet the conditions in the pool, and seeing this, creates incentives for the agency to increase the conditions. Eventually, the riskiest projects will remain.*	*This is actually even more present today with the competition of donors like China.*

Appendix G Symptom Types Top vs. Bottom Group

Test of independence between the rows and the columns (Chi-square with Yates' continuity correction): TOTAL Pos vs. TOTAL Neg

Chi-square (Observed value)	133.759
Chi-square (Critical value)	10.828
DF	1
p-value	< 0.0001
alpha	0.001

Test interpretation:
H0: The rows and the columns of the table are independent.
Ha: There is a link between the rows and the columns of the table.
As the computed p-value is lower than the significance level alpha=0.001,
one should reject the null hypothesis H0, and accept the alternative hypothesis Ha.
The risk to reject the null hypothesis H0 while it is true is lower than 0.01%.

Fisher's exact test:

p-value (Two-tailed)	< 0.0001
alpha	0.001

Test interpretation:
H0: The rows and the columns of the table are independent.
Ha: There is a link between the rows and the columns of the table.
As the computed p-value is lower than the significance level alpha=0.001,
one should reject the null hypothesis H0, and accept the alternative hypothesis Ha.
The risk to reject the null hypothesis H0 while it is true is lower than 0.01%.

Test of independence between the rows and the columns (Wilks' G^2):

Wilks' G^2 (Observed value)	145.080
Wilks' G^2 (Critical value)	10.828
DF	1
p-value	< 0.0001
alpha	0.001

Test interpretation:
H0: The rows and the columns of the table are independent.
Ha: There is a link between the rows and the columns of the table.
As the computed p-value is lower than the significance level alpha=0.001, one should reject the null hypothesis H0, and accept the alternative hypothesis Ha.
The risk to reject the null hypothesis H0 while it is true is lower than 0.01%.

Association coefficients (1):

Coefficient	Value
Pearson's Phi	0.564
Contingency coefficient	0.491
Cramer's V	0.564
Tschuprow's T	0.564
Goodman and Kruskal tau (R/C)	0.318
Goodman and Kruskal tau (C/R)	0.318
Cohen's kappa	0.551
Yule's Q	0.878
Yule's Y	0.593

Test of independence between the rows and the columns (Chi-square with Yates' continuity correction): PosYY vs. NegYY

Chi-square (Observed value)	91.937
Chi-square (Critical value)	10.828
DF	1
p-value	< 0.0001
alpha	0.001

Test interpretation:
H0: The rows and the columns of the table are independent.
Ha: There is a link between the rows and the columns of the table.
As the computed p-value is lower than the significance level alpha=0.001,
one should reject the null hypothesis H0, and accept the alternative hypothesis Ha.
The risk to reject the null hypothesis H0 while it is true is lower than 0.01%.

Fisher's exact test:

p-value (Two-tailed)	< 0.0001
alpha	0.001

Test interpretation:
H0: The rows and the columns of the table are independent.
Ha: There is a link between the rows and the columns of the table.
As the computed p-value is lower than the significance level alpha=0.001,
one should reject the null hypothesis H0, and accept the alternative hypothesis Ha.
The risk to reject the null hypothesis H0 while it is true is lower than 0.01%.

Test of independence between the rows and the columns (Wilks' G^2):

Wilks' G^2 (Observed value)	104.628
Wilks' G^2 (Critical value)	10.828
DF	1
p-value	< 0.0001
alpha	0.001

Test interpretation:
H0: The rows and the columns of the table are independent.
Ha: There is a link between the rows and the columns of the table.
As the computed p-value is lower than the significance level alpha=0.001,
one should reject the null hypothesis H0, and accept the alternative hypothesis Ha.
The risk to reject the null hypothesis H0 while it is true is lower than 0.01%.

Association coefficients (1):

Coefficient	Value
Pearson's Phi	0.695
Contingency coefficient	0.571
Cramer's V	0.695
Tschuprow's T	0.695
Goodman and Kruskal tau (R/C)	0.483
Goodman and Kruskal tau (C/R)	0.483
Cohen's kappa	0.693
Yule's Q	0.941
Yule's Y	0.702

Two-sample comparison of variances:
POS YY vs. NEG YY

Hypothesized ratio (R): 1

Significance level (%): 5

Summary statistics:

Variable	Obs.	missing	Minimum	Maximum	Mean	Std. deviation
PosYY I TOP	17	0	0.000	9.000	5.294	2.173
NegYY I BOT	17	0	0.000	11.000	4.471	4.064

Fisher's F-test / Two-tailed test:
95% confidence interval on the ratio of variances:
] 0.104; 0.789 [

Ratio	0.286
F (Observed value)	0.286
F (Critical value)	2.761
DF1	16
DF2	16
p-value (Two-tailed)	0.017
alpha	0.05

Test interpretation:
H0: The ratio between the variances is equal to 1.
Ha: The ratio between the variances is different from 1.
As the computed p-value is lower than the significance level alpha=0.05,
one should reject the null hypothesis H0, and accept the alternative hypothesis Ha.
The risk to reject the null hypothesis H0 while it is true is lower than 1.67%.

Test of Independence between the rows and the columns (Chi-square with Yates' continuity correction): PosNN vs. NegYN+NegNN

Chi-square (Observed value)	32.104
Chi-square (Critical value)	10.828
DF	1
p-value	< 0.0001
alpha	0.001

Test interpretation:
H0: The rows and the columns of the table are independent.
Ha: There is a link between the rows and the columns of the table.
As the computed p-value is lower than the significance level alpha=0.001,
one should reject the null hypothesis H0, and accept the alternative hypothesis Ha.
The risk to reject the null hypothesis H0 while it is true is lower than 0.01%.

Fisher's exact test:

p-value (Two-tailed)	< 0.0001
alpha	0.001

Test interpretation:
H0: The rows and the columns of the table are independent.
Ha: There is a link between the rows and the columns of the table.
As the computed p-value is lower than the significance level alpha=0.001, one should reject the null hypothesis H0, and accept the alternative hypothesis Ha.
The risk to reject the null hypothesis H0 while it is true is lower than 0.01%.

Test of independence between the rows and the columns (Wilks' G^2):

Wilks' G^2 (Observed value)	37.517
Wilks' G^2 (Critical value)	10.828
DF	1
p-value	< 0.0001
alpha	0.001

Test interpretation:
H0: The rows and the columns of the table are independent.
Ha: There is a link between the rows and the columns of the table.
As the computed p-value is lower than the significance level alpha=0.001, one should reject the null hypothesis H0, and accept the alternative hypothesis Ha.
The risk to reject the null hypothesis H0 while it is true is lower than 0.01%.

Association coefficients (1):

Coefficient	Value
Pearson's Phi	0.447
Contingency coefficient	0.408
Cramer's V	0.447
Tschuprow's T	0.447
Goodman and Kruskal tau (R/C)	0.200
Goodman and Kruskal tau (C/R)	0.200
Cohen's kappa	0.373
Yule's Q	0.901
Yule's Y	0.628

Test of independence between the rows and the columns (Chi-square): PosYY Top vs. NegYY Bottom

Chi-square (Observed value)	56.594
Chi-square (Critical value)	13.816
DF	2
p-value	< 0.0001
alpha	0.001

Test interpretation:
H0: The rows and the columns of the table are independent.
Ha: There is a link between the rows and the columns of the table.
As the computed p-value is lower than the significance level alpha=0.001, one should reject the null hypothesis H0, and accept the alternative hypothesis Ha.
The risk to reject the null hypothesis H0 while it is true is lower than 0.01%.

Fisher's exact test:

p-value (Two-tailed)	< 0.0001
alpha	0.001

Test interpretation:
H0: The rows and the columns of the table are independent.
Ha: There is a link between the rows and the columns of the table.
As the computed p-value is lower than the significance level alpha=0.001, one should reject the null hypothesis H0, and accept the alternative hypothesis Ha.
The risk to reject the null hypothesis H0 while it is true is lower than 0.01%.

Test of independence between the rows and the columns (Wilks' G^2):

Wilks' G^2 (Observed value)	60.314
Wilks' G^2 (Critical value)	13.816
DF	2
p-value	< 0.0001
alpha	0.001

Test interpretation:
H0: The rows and the columns of the table are independent.
Ha: There is a link between the rows and the columns of the table.
As the computed p-value is lower than the significance level alpha=0.001,
one should reject the null hypothesis H0, and accept the alternative hypothesis Ha.
The risk to reject the null hypothesis H0 while it is true is lower than 0.01%.

Association coefficients (1):

Coefficient	Value
Pearson's Phi	0.525
Contingency coefficient	0.465
Cramer's V	0.525
Tschuprow's T	0.442
Goodman and Kruskal tau (R/C)	0.276
Goodman and Kruskal tau (C/R)	0.163

Appendix H Implementing Partner Top vs. Bottom

Test of independence between the rows and the columns (Chi-square with Yates' continuity correction): Type of Implementing Partner / NGO vs. PUBLADM

Test of independence between the rows and the columns (Chi-square with Yates' continuity correction):

Chi-square (Observed value)	12.404
Chi-square (Critical value)	6.635
DF	1
p-value	0.000
alpha	0.001

Test interpretation:
H0: The rows and the columns of the table are independent.
Ha: There is a link between the rows and the columns of the table.
As the computed p-value is lower than the significance level alpha=0.001, one should reject the null hypothesis H0, and accept the alternative hypothesis Ha.
The risk to reject the null hypothesis H0 while it is true is lower than 0.04%.

Fisher's exact test:

p-value (Two-tailed)	0.000
alpha	0.001

Test interpretation:
H0: The rows and the columns of the table are independent.
Ha: There is a link between the rows and the columns of the table.
As the computed p-value is lower than the significance level alpha=0.001,
one should reject the null hypothesis H0, and accept the alternative hypothesis Ha.
The risk to reject the null hypothesis H0 while it is true is lower than 0.02%.

Test of independence between the rows and the columns (Wilks' G^2):

Wilks' G^2 (Observed value)	17.407
Wilks' G^2 (Critical value)	6.635
DF	1
p-value	< 0.0001
alpha	0.001

Test interpretation:
H0: The rows and the columns of the table are independent.
Ha: There is a link between the rows and the columns of the table.
As the computed p-value is lower than the significance level alpha=0.001,
one should reject the null hypothesis H0, and accept the alternative hypothesis Ha.
The risk to reject the null hypothesis H0 while it is true is lower than 0.01%.

Association coefficients (1):

Coefficient	Value
Pearson's Phi	0.769
Contingency coefficient	0.609
Cramer's V	0.769
Goodman and Kruskal tau (R/C)	0.591
Goodman and Kruskal tau (C/R)	0.591
Yule's Q	0.970
Yule's Y	0.779

Two-sample t-test / Two-tailed test:

ROM Workbook Sample: Rating AMEAN / NGO vs. PUBLADM

Hypothesized difference (D): 0
Significance level (%): 0.1
Population variances for the t-test: Use an F-test

Summary statistics:

Variable	Obs.	missing	Minimum	Maximum	Mean	Std. deviation
RAMEAN I 6	184	0	1.200	4.000	2.664	0.505
RAMEAN I NGO	273	0	1.200	4.000	2.821	0.444

Fisher's F-test / Two-tailed test:
99.900% confidence interval on the ratio of variances:
] 0.833; 2.037 [

Ratio	1.292
F (Observed value)	1.292
F (Critical value)	1.552
DF1	183
DF2	272
p-value (Two-tailed)	0.055
alpha	0.001

Test interpretation:
H0: The ratio between the variances is equal to 1.
Ha: The ratio between the variances is different from 1.
As the computed p-value is greater than the significance level alpha=0.001, one cannot reject the null hypothesis H0.
The risk to reject the null hypothesis H0 while it is true is 5.53%.

t-test for two independent samples / Two-tailed test:
99.900% confidence interval on the difference between the means:
] -0.305 ; -0.008 [

Difference	-0.156
t (Observed value)	-3.492
ltl (Critical value)	3.312
DF	455
p-value (Two-tailed)	0.001
alpha	0.001

Test interpretation:
H0: The difference between the means is equal to 0.
Ha: The difference between the means is different from 0.
As the computed p-value is lower than the significance level alpha=0.001,
one should reject the null hypothesis H0, and accept the alternative hypothesis Ha.
The risk to reject the null hypothesis H0 while it is true is lower than 0.05%.

Association Coefficients (1)

Coefficient	Value
Hedges' g	0.333

Appendix I Budget Variable

Comparison of two samples (Wilcoxon, Mann-Whitney, ...):

PRIM BUDGET Top vs. Bottom Group

Hypothesized difference (D): 0
Significance level (%): 1
p-value: Exact p-value

Summary statistics:

Variable	Obs.	Minimum	Maximum	Mean	Std. deviation
PRIM BUDGET I TOP	17	430000	14100000	2262615.235	3240820.820
PRIM BUDGET I BOT	17	750000	61000000	14024335.882	19308546.796

Mann-Whitney test / Two-tailed test:

U	70.000
Expected value	144.500
Variance (U)	842.917
z	-2.566
p-value (Two-tailed)	0.009
alpha	0.01

The p-value is computed using an exact method. Time elapsed: 0s.
Test interpretation:
H0: The difference of location between the samples is equal to 0.
Ha: The difference of location between the samples is different from 0.
As the computed p-value is lower than the significance level alpha=0.01,
one should reject the null hypothesis H0, and accept the alternative hypothesis Ha.
The risk to reject the null hypothesis H0 while it is true is lower than 0.95%.

Distribution fitting: PRIM BUDGET / n=457

Significance level (%): 5
Distribution: Normal
Estimation method: Moments

Summary statistics:

Variable	Obs	Min	Max	Mean	1st Quartile	Median	3rd Quartile	Std. deviation
PRIM BUDGET	457	92099	95242949	6310005.514	1000000	1900000	7500000	10502838.840

Statistics estimated on the input data and computed using the estimated parameters of the Normal distribution:

Statistic	Data	Parameters
Mean	6310005.514	6310005.514
Variance	110309623708346.000	110309623708346.000
Skewness (Pearson)	3.622	0.000
Kurtosis (Pearson)	17.946	0.000

Kolmogorov-Smirnov test:

D	0.279
p-value	<0.0001
alpha	0.05

Test interpretation:
H0: The sample follows a Normal distribution
Ha: The sample does not follow a Normal distribution
As the computed p-value is lower than the significance level alpha=0.05,
one should reject the null hypothesis H0, and accept the alternative hypothesis Ha.
The risk to reject the null hypothesis H0 while it is true is lower than 0.01%.

Chi-square test:

Chi-square (Observed value)	180820291723.317
Chi-square (Critical value)	14.067
DF	7
p-value	< 0.0001
alpha	0.05

Test interpretation:
H0: The sample follows a Normal distribution
Ha: The sample does not follow a Normal distribution
As the computed p-value is lower than the significance level alpha=0.05,
one should reject the null hypothesis H0, and accept the alternative hypothesis Ha.
The risk to reject the null hypothesis H0 while it is true is lower than 0.01%.

Comparison between the observed and theoretical frequencies:

Class	Lower bound [	Upper bound [	Frequency (Data)	Frequency (Distribution)	Chi-square
1	0.000	9600000.000	363	159.477	259.736
2	9600000.000	19200000.000	52	122.105	40.250
3	19200000.000	28800000.000	23	42.836	9.186
4	28800000.000	38400000.000	10	6.855	1.443
5	38400000.000	48000000.000	2	0.497	4.543
6	48000000.000	57600000.000	3	0.016	548.684
7	57600000.000	67200000.000	3	0.000	38021.032
8	67200000.000	76800000.000	0	0.000	0.000
9	76800000.000	86400000.000	0	0.000	0.000
10	86400000.000	96000000.000	1	0.000	180820252838.443

Tests on contingency tables (Chi-square...)

Correlation PRIM BUDGET vs. Rating AMEAN (n=457)

Contingency table (Median PRIM BUDGET / Median RAMEAN):

	RAMEAN < Median	RAMEAN > Median
PRIM BUDG < Median	112	119
PRIM BUDG > Median	125	101

Test of independence between the rows and the columns (Chi-square with Yates' continuity correction):

Chi-square (Observed value)	1.867
Chi-square (Critical value)	3.841
DF	1
p-value	0.172
alpha	0.05

Test interpretation:
H0: The rows and the columns of the table are independent.
Ha: There is a link between the rows and the columns of the table.
As the computed p-value is greater than the significance level alpha=0.05,
one cannot reject the null hypothesis H0.
The risk to reject the null hypothesis H0 while it is true is 17.18%.

Fisher's exact test:

p-value (Two-tailed)	0.160
alpha	0.05

Test interpretation:
H0: The rows and the columns of the table are independent.
Ha: There is a link between the rows and the columns of the table.
As the computed p-value is greater than the significance level alpha=0.05, one cannot reject the null hypothesis H0.
The risk to reject the null hypothesis H0 while it is true is 16.04%.

Association coefficients (1):

Coefficient	Value
Pearson's Phi	-0.068
Contingency coefficient	0.068
Cramer's V	-0.068
Tschuprow's T	0.068
Goodman and Kruskal tau (R/C)	0.005
Goodman and Kruskal tau (C/R)	0.005
Cohen's kappa	-0.068
Yule's Q	-0.136
Yule's Y	-0.068

Tests on contingency tables (Chi-square...)

Bottom Group: PRIM BUDGET vs. NegYY

Contingency table (NegYY / PRIM BUDGET):

	PB > 2m	PB ≤ 2m
NegYY > 1	8	2
Neg YY ≤ 1	1	6

Test of independence between the rows and the columns (Chi-square with Yates' continuity correction):

Chi-square (Observed value)	4.743
Chi-square (Critical value)	3.841
DF	1
p-value	0.029
alpha	0.05

Test interpretation:
H0: The rows and the columns of the table are independent.
Ha: There is a link between the rows and the columns of the table.
As the computed p-value is lower than the significance level alpha=0.05,
one should reject the null hypothesis H0, and accept the alternative hypothesis Ha.
The risk to reject the null hypothesis H0 while it is true is lower than 2.94%.

Fisher's exact test:

p-value (Two-tailed)	0.015
alpha	0.05

Test interpretation:
H0: The rows and the columns of the table are independent.
Ha: There is a link between the rows and the columns of the table.
As the computed p-value is lower than the significance level alpha=0.05,
one should reject the null hypothesis H0, and accept the alternative hypothesis Ha.
The risk to reject the null hypothesis H0 while it is true is lower than 1.52%.

Test of independence between the rows and the columns (Wilks' G²):

Wilks' G² (Observed value)	7.758
Wilks' G² (Critical value)	3.841
DF	1
p-value	0.005
alpha	0.05

Test interpretation:
H0: The rows and the columns of the table are independent.
Ha: There is a link between the rows and the columns of the table.
As the computed p-value is lower than the significance level alpha=0.05, one should reject the null hypothesis H0, and accept the alternative hypothesis Ha.
The risk to reject the null hypothesis H0 while it is true is lower than 0.53%.

Association coefficients (1):

Coefficient	Value
Pearson's Phi	0.648
Contingency coefficient	0.544
Cramer's V	0.648
Tschuprow's T	0.648
Goodman and Kruskal tau (R/C)	0.420
Goodman and Kruskal tau (C/R)	0.420
Cohen's kappa	0.643
Yule's Q	0.920
Yule's Y	0.661

Appendix J Qualitative Variables

LQ – Logframe Quality

Test of independence between the rows and the columns (Chi-square with Yates' continuity correction):

Chi-square (Observed value)	3.889
Chi-square (Critical value)	10.828
DF	1
p-value	0.049
alpha	0.05

Test interpretation:
H0: The rows and the columns of the table are independent.
Ha: There is a link between the rows and the columns of the table.
As the computed p-value is lower than the significance level alpha=0.05,
one should reject the null hypothesis H0, and accept the alternative hypothesis Ha.
The risk to reject the null hypothesis H0 while it is true is 4.86%.

Fisher's exact test:

p-value (Two-tailed)	0.046
alpha	0.05

Test interpretation:
H0: The rows and the columns of the table are independent.
Ha: There is a link between the rows and the columns of the table.
As the computed p-value is lower than the significance level alpha=0.05, one should reject the null hypothesis H0, and accept the alternative hypothesis Ha.
The risk to reject the null hypothesis H0 while it is true is 4.61%.

Test of independence between the rows and the columns (Wilks' G^2):

Wilks' G^2 (Observed value)	5.894
Wilks' G^2 (Critical value)	10.828
DF	1
p-value	0.015
alpha	0.05

Test interpretation:
H0: The rows and the columns of the table are independent.
Ha: There is a link between the rows and the columns of the table.
As the computed p-value is lower than the significance level alpha=0.05,
one should reject the null hypothesis H0, and accept the alternative hypothesis Ha.
The risk to reject the null hypothesis H0 while it is true is 1.52%.

Association coefficients (1):

Coefficient	Value
Pearson's Phi	-0.447
Contingency coefficient	0.408
Cramer's V	-0.447
Tschuprow's T	0.447
Goodman and Kruskal tau (R/C)	0.200
Goodman and Kruskal tau (C/R)	0.200
Cohen's kappa	-0.429
Yule's Q	-0.778
Yule's Y	-0.478

AG - Ambitious Project Goals

Test of independence between the rows and the columns (Chi-square with Yates' continuity correction):

Chi-square (Observed value)	3.447
Chi-square (Critical value)	10.828
DF	1
p-value	0.063
alpha	0.001

Test interpretation:
H0: The rows and the columns of the table are independent.
Ha: There is a link between the rows and the columns of the table.
As the computed p-value is greater than the significance level alpha=0.001, one cannot reject the null hypothesis H0.
The risk to reject the null hypothesis H0 while it is true is 6.34%.

Fisher's exact test:

p-value (Two-tailed)	0.051
alpha	0.001

Test interpretation:
H0: The rows and the columns of the table are independent.
Ha: There is a link between the rows and the columns of the table.
As the computed p-value is greater than the significance level alpha=0.001, one cannot reject the null hypothesis H0.
The risk to reject the null hypothesis H0 while it is true is 5.10%.

Test of independence between the rows and the columns (Wilks' G^2):

Wilks' G^2 (Observed value)	5.185
Wilks' G^2 (Critical value)	10.828
DF	1
p-value	0.023
alpha	0.001

Test interpretation:
H0: The rows and the columns of the table are independent.
Ha: There is a link between the rows and the columns of the table.
As the computed p-value is greater than the significance level alpha=0.001, one cannot reject the null hypothesis H0.
The risk to reject the null hypothesis H0 while it is true is 2.28%.

Association coefficients (1):

Coefficient	Value
Pearson's Phi	0.424
Contingency coefficient	0.390
Cramer's V	0.424
Tschuprow's T	0.424
Goodman and Kruskal tau (R/C)	0.180
Goodman and Kruskal tau (C/R)	0.180
Cohen's kappa	0.420
Yule's Q	0.730
Yule's Y	0.433

FD – Flexible Design

Test of independence between the rows and the columns (Chi-square with Yates' continuity correction):

Chi-square (Observed value)	9.410
Chi-square (Critical value)	10.828
DF	1
p-value	0.002
alpha	0.01

Test interpretation:
H0: The rows and the columns of the table are independent.
Ha: There is a link between the rows and the columns of the table.
As the computed p-value is lower than the significance level alpha=0.01,
one should reject the null hypothesis H0, and accept the alternative hypothesis Ha.
The risk to reject the null hypothesis H0 while it is true is 0.22%.

Fisher's exact test:

p-value (Two-tailed)	0.001
alpha	0.01

Test interpretation:
H0: The rows and the columns of the table are independent.
Ha: There is a link between the rows and the columns of the table.
As the computed p-value is lower than the significance level alpha=0.01,
one should reject the null hypothesis H0, and accept the alternative hypothesis Ha.
The risk to reject the null hypothesis H0 while it is true is lower than 0.06%.

Test of independence between the rows and the columns (Wilks' G^2):

Wilks' G^2 (Observed value)	15.707
Wilks' G^2 (Critical value)	10.828
DF	1
p-value	< 0.0001
alpha	0.01

Test interpretation:
H0: The rows and the columns of the table are independent.
Ha: There is a link between the rows and the columns of the table.
As the computed p-value is lower than the significance level alpha=0.01,
one should reject the null hypothesis H0, and accept the alternative hypothesis Ha.
The risk to reject the null hypothesis H0 while it is true is lower than 0.01%.

Association coefficients (1):

Coefficient	Value
Pearson's Phi	-0.713
Contingency coefficient	0.580
Cramer's V	-0.713
Tschuprow's T	0.713
Goodman and Kruskal tau (R/C)	0.508
Goodman and Kruskal tau (C/R)	0.508
Cohen's kappa	-0.702
Yule's Q	-1.000
Yule's Y	-1.000

MQ – Internal Monitoring Quality

Test of independence between the rows and the columns (Chi-square with Yates' continuity correction):

Chi-square (Observed value)	8.873
Chi-square (Critical value)	10.828
DF	1
p-value	0.003
alpha	0.01

Test interpretation:
H0: The rows and the columns of the table are independent.
Ha: There is a link between the rows and the columns of the table.
As the computed p-value is lower than the significance level alpha=0.01,
one should reject the null hypothesis H0, and accept the alternative hypothesis Ha.
The risk to reject the null hypothesis H0 while it is true is 0.29%.
Fisher's exact test:

p-value (Two-tailed)	0.001
alpha	0.01

Test interpretation:
H0: The rows and the columns of the table are independent.
Ha: There is a link between the rows and the columns of the table.
As the computed p-value is greater than the significance level alpha=0.01,
one cannot reject the null hypothesis H0.
The risk to reject the null hypothesis H0 while it is true is 0.12%.
Test of independence between the rows and the columns (Wilks' G^2):

Wilks' G^2 (Observed value)	12.407
Wilks' G^2 (Critical value)	10.828
DF	1
p-value	0.000
alpha	0.01

Test interpretation:
H0: The rows and the columns of the table are independent.
Ha: There is a link between the rows and the columns of the table.
As the computed p-value is lower than the significance level alpha=0.01,
one should reject the null hypothesis H0, and accept the alternative hypothesis Ha.
The risk to reject the null hypothesis H0 while it is true is lower than 0.04%.
Association coefficients (1):

Coefficient	Value
Pearson's Phi	-0.640
Contingency coefficient	0.539
Cramer's V	-0.640
Tschuprow's T	0.640
Goodman and Kruskal tau (R/C)	0.410
Goodman and Kruskal tau (C/R)	0.410
Cohen's kappa	-0.563
Yule's Q	-0.935
Yule's Y	-0.691

PD – Participatory Design

Test of independence between the rows and the columns (Chi-square with Yates' continuity correction):

Chi-square (Observed value)	11.462
Chi-square (Critical value)	10.828
DF	1
p-value	0.001
alpha	0.001

Test interpretation:
H0: The rows and the columns of the table are independent.
Ha: There is a link between the rows and the columns of the table.
As the computed p-value is lower than the significance level alpha=0.001,
one should reject the null hypothesis H0, and accept the alternative hypothesis Ha.
The risk to reject the null hypothesis H0 while it is true is lower than 0.07%.

Fisher's exact test:

p-value (Two-tailed)	0.000
alpha	0.001

Test interpretation:
H0: The rows and the columns of the table are independent.
Ha: There is a link between the rows and the columns of the table.
As the computed p-value is lower than the significance level alpha=0.001,
one should reject the null hypothesis H0, and accept the alternative hypothesis Ha.
The risk to reject the null hypothesis H0 while it is true is lower than 0.03%.

Test of independence between the rows and the columns (Wilks' G^2):

Wilks' G^2 (Observed value)	15.302
Wilks' G^2 (Critical value)	10.828
DF	1
p-value	< 0.0001
alpha	0.001

Test interpretation:
H0: The rows and the columns of the table are independent.
Ha: There is a link between the rows and the columns of the table.
As the computed p-value is lower than the significance level alpha=0.001,
one should reject the null hypothesis H0, and accept the alternative hypothesis Ha.
The risk to reject the null hypothesis H0 while it is true is lower than 0.01%.

Association coefficients (1):

Coefficient	Value
Pearson's Phi	-0.674
Contingency coefficient	0.559
Cramer's V	-0.674
Tschuprow's T	0.674
Goodman and Kruskal tau (R/C)	0.454
Goodman and Kruskal tau (C/R)	0.454
Cohen's kappa	-0.652
Yule's Q	-0.930
Yule's Y	-0.680

RM – Resource Management

Test of independence between the rows and the columns (Chi-square with Yates' continuity correction):

Chi-square (Observed value)	9.293
Chi-square (Critical value)	10.828
DF	1
p-value	0.002
alpha	0.01

Test interpretation:
H0: The rows and the columns of the table are independent.
Ha: There is a link between the rows and the columns of the table.
As the computed p-value is lower than the significance level alpha=0.01, one should reject the null hypothesis H0, and accept the alternative hypothesis Ha.
The risk to reject the null hypothesis H0 while it is true is 0.23%.

Fisher's exact test:

p-value (Two-tailed)	0.001
alpha	0.01

Test interpretation:
H0: The rows and the columns of the table are independent.
Ha: There is a link between the rows and the columns of the table.
As the computed p-value is lower than the significance level alpha=0.01, one should reject the null hypothesis H0, and accept the alternative hypothesis Ha.
The risk to reject the null hypothesis H0 while it is true is lower than 0.10%.

Test of independence between the rows and the columns (Wilks' G^2):

Wilks' G^2 (Observed value)	13.367
Wilks' G^2 (Critical value)	10.828
DF	1
p-value	0.000
alpha	0.01

Test interpretation:
H0: The rows and the columns of the table are independent.
Ha: There is a link between the rows and the columns of the table.
As the computed p-value is lower than the significance level alpha=0.01,
one should reject the null hypothesis H0, and accept the alternative hypothesis Ha.
The risk to reject the null hypothesis H0 while it is true is lower than 0.03%.

Association coefficients (1):

Coefficient	Value
Pearson's Phi	-0.690
Contingency coefficient	0.568
Cramer's V	-0.690
Tschuprow's T	0.690
Goodman and Kruskal tau (R/C)	0.477
Goodman and Kruskal tau (C/R)	0.477
Cohen's kappa	-0.688
Yule's Q	-0.947
Yule's Y	-0.717

Appendix K EC Symptom Contingencies

Symptom ID#	1	8	11	14	15	16	17	19	20	21	23	24	25	26	27	28	31	32	34	35	50	52	53	54	57	61	70
TOP																											
PosYY	3	3	9	3	14	7	5	1		1	11		1		1			8	2	4	2		1	1	2		1
NegYY		1	1		2						1							2		1				1			
BOTTOM																											
Pos YY	1		2	1	1	1	4		1	1	2				1	1		1				1					
NegYY	6	1	8	3	2	6			2	3	9	2		1	12		1	11			6	1			3	1	

Index